T0168152

SOUTHERN SEEN

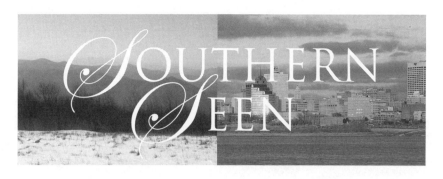

SOUTHERN SEEN

MEDITATIONS ON PAST AND PRESENT

LARRY T. McGEHEE

EDITED BY
B. J. HUTTO

FOREWORD BY
JOHN EGERTON

The University of Tennessee Press
Knoxville

Copyright © 2005 by The University of Tennessee Press / Knoxville.
All Rights Reserved. Manufactured in the United States of America.
First Edition.

The press and the author gratefully acknowlege the Watson-Brown Foundation, Inc., for its generous support of this publication.

This book is printed on acid-free paper.

Library of Congress Cataloging-in-Publication Data

McGehee, Larry T., 1936-
Southern seen: meditations on past and present/ LarryT. McGehee; edited by B.J. Hutto; foreword by John Egerton.—1st ed.
    p. cm.
ISBN 1-57233-359-6 (pbk.: acid-free paper)

1. Southern States—Civilization. I. Hutto, B.J. II. Title
F209.5.M324 2005
975—dc22   2004012099

CONTENTS

Three ▪ EDUCATION: "IN PATHS OF RIGHTEOUSNESS"

Four ▪ PEOPLE: "FOR HIS NAME'S SAKE"

Five ■ CONFLICT: "THROUGH THE VALLEY OF THE SHADOW"

Six ■ FOOD: "THOU PREPAREST A TABLE FOR ME"

Seven ■ PLAY: "MY CUP RUNNETH OVER"

Seven ■ RELIGION: "IN THE HOUSE OF THE LORD"

FOREWORD

Sometime during the latter half of 1982, as he was in the midst of a mid-career job change, Larry McGehee decided to submit himself, on a weekly basis, to the discipline of writing an essay. Just as preachers go about preparing their weekly sermons, or professors their principal lectures, McGehee took up a self-imposed ritual familiar to all serial writers: rain or shine, ready or not, with or without inspiration, you roll a blank sheet of paper into the old Royal manual (or modern upgrade) and start typing—and if it takes you half an hour or half the day, you grind out about 750 words that sing, or at least hum. Sometimes they may be a little out of tune—or worse, barely serviceable—but on the best days they soar, and even bid to become memorable, worthy of Sinatra or Elvis or Willie Nelson. Or, as McGehee might prefer for comparison, W. J. Cash or Harry Golden or Ralph McGill. As it is for athletes, surgeons, high-wire artists, and all risk-taking performers, so it is for columnists: no excuses, no slack, no fear—just show up on time and get the job done. The goal is deceptively simple—to do your best, be effective, have an impact—but the execution is often fraught with perils. That's why they call it a practice.

McGehee was finishing an eleven-year stint as an administrator at the University of Tennessee (the first eight as chancellor of its campus at Martin, in west Tennessee, and the last three as a special assistant to the president of the UT system, on the main campus in Knoxville). In the next academic year, 1982–83, he would begin a new challenge as vice president and professor of religion at Wofford College, a United Methodist Church-related liberal arts institution in Spartanburg, South Carolina. As an academician with a Ph.D. in religious studies from Yale, he knew firsthand the weekly disciplines of scholars and preachers, but those of newspaper editors and writers were more of an observation or an aspiration than a mastered skill.

"I guess I have always been a journalist at heart," he explained to me years later. "When I was majoring in English at Transylvania College, my fantasy was to become a sage country editor who had gone away to the city and returned to wax eloquent on the virtues and limitations of both worlds." Born and raised in a great little country town—Paris, Tennessee—McGehee had grown up reading the prose of just such an editor, Bryant Williams (second in four generations of publisher-editors of the *Paris Post-Intelligencer*). Then, after college in Kentucky, he had gone as a Danforth Fellow to spend six years completing three degrees at Yale, after which he joined the administration and faculty of the University of Alabama in Tuscaloosa. Journalism still appealed to him, but there was no time then to indulge the fantasy.

Sixteen years later, on the eve of his move to Wofford, McGehee found himself thinking again about journalism. The weekly column idea seemed to emerge from nowhere, gently tapping him on the shoulder and then tugging at his sleeve until he finally took notice. There were things he felt a need to say in print, and here was a medium that would allow him that privilege. McGehee decided to begin writing short essays on a variety of subjects, just whatever struck his fancy, and offer them free of charge to editors of small daily papers and a few weeklies in three or four southern states. He made up a list, typed and copied a few columns, folded and stuffed the envelopes, stamped and mailed them. And that's how "Southern Seen," a not-for-profit cottage industry, was born.

Time flies when you're having fun. As he paused in 2002 to take a measure of his production on the twentieth anniversary of that first effort, even McGehee was a bit surprised to discover that he had written and distributed more than a thousand weekly columns and another six hundred or so book-review essays. At various times over the period, about 140 papers in eight states have carried his work; at present, just over a hundred of these, with a combined circulation in excess of one million, feature it regularly in their pages. At least three dozen papers in Alabama, Tennessee, Kentucky, and South Carolina have published the column almost every week since the beginning. And all the while, the price has never changed—it's still free. Wofford even pays the postage, and gladly; after all, the good will generated by "Southern Seen" is beyond measure.

Little wonder that the readership has climbed to such a high level. Anyone who grew up within hailing distance of the postwar South (by which I mean World War II, rather than the one old-timers used to call "The War") can recognize the landscape through McGehee's eyes—and not by sight alone, but through all the senses. He gives you vivid word pictures of the rural and urban geography, and a whiff of the barbecue and the peach cobbler; you can almost feel the tug of a fish on a fly fisher's rod, and hear the home run *crack!* of a Louisville Slugger, and taste the richness of his Aunt Dorothy's blackberry jam cake with caramel icing.

You can tell a lot about what matters most to Larry McGehee by noting the themes he uses to divide the two-hundred-plus columns in this collection into eight sections: Outdoors, Place, Education, People, Conflict, Food, Play, Religion. He and his editor, B. J. Hutto, read through all the columns and picked the ones they liked best; then they made another cut to arrive at the final choices, which represent less than 20 percent of his total output. (Hutto, incidentally, is a former student of McGehee's, one of many who thrived on his teaching and came to appreciate the columns as an effective instructional tool.)

The pieces chosen for this collection create a profile of the author that was not quite what McGehee had expected to find when he went back over the material.

"There's more conflict in here than I would have guessed," he said, "more contemplation of the Civil War and its continuing hold on us. I come across as more serious than I expected, more conservative—and less funny, less provocative. I seem to have a nostalgic and sentimental attachment to the years of my boyhood and youth. And I don't think I'm as good a writer as that romantic figure in my youthful fantasy."

McGehee is too harsh a critic of his own considerable skills. If these essays are evocative of a simpler time, when he was a carefree teenager, they also capture the bittersweet qualities of that time, more bitter than sweet for many, such as the black minority fettered by segregation. If he returns again and again to the Civil War, it is not to lament the "Lost Cause" or to glorify the conflict but to ponder the costs of disunion. And as for the quality of his writing, I need cite only one passage to refute his own overly negative assertion. This is from an essay on birds:

> Once I held a hummingbird on the palm of my hand. . . . I thought
> it was dead, but it lay warm in my hand, and I thought I felt the beat
> of its oh-so-tiny heart. It had knocked itself unconscious against the
> plate glass window of our sun porch. It suddenly awoke and arose,
> straight up like a helicopter, then hovered and switched from vertical
> to horizontal warp-speed in a ninety-degree angle—and was gone.

But not really gone.
No one who has held a hummingbird is ever the same.
I held onto it forever by releasing it. It hovers in my memory . . .
the moment eternity lay in my hand.

I rest my case. No one who can capture such a rare and stirring image as that should be allowed to get away with claiming a serious lack of writing skills. And he's funnier than he lets on, too. Truth be told, this is a writer who has demonstrated amazing discipline and consistency over the past two decades—and loved every minute of it, apparently, even in the days of acute suffering when words wouldn't come from a keyboard turned to stone, and the only wish was for a quick and painless death. Writing is a hazardous craft, and mere survival is a significant measure of success.

McGehee, in paraphrase of the great William Faulkner, has not merely survived but prevailed. He is still confronting the terror of the blank page every week, still stuffing and stamping envelopes (although more and more of his dispatches travel electronically, and "Southern Seen" is now universally available through the Wofford College Web site).

Southern Seen, the selected columns, saves in book form nearly one-fifth of the pieces McGehee has written thus far—and he's not finished yet. If this volume becomes a standard reference work in southern studies and American studies classes from the Chesapeake to the Pedernales, as it should, I can imagine another collection following upon it, drawing both from the columns not included here and from the ones he has yet to write.

There's so much unused material for him to draw from. The South may be less chaotic and unpredictable than it used to be, but it still has more than its share of eccentric characters, exotic places, distinctive music, and colorful language—not to mention religious mysticism, political craziness, and great food. McGehee may seem to be lamenting the faded glories of a simpler time, but underneath all that I think he's thanking his lucky stars that he has the South to write about and not some other less turbulent, less hospitable, less intriguing, more orderly, more postmodern, and colder corner of the United States.

I'm pretty happy about that myself. You'll be too, when you read these essays.

John Egerton

PREFACE

Throughout his freshman year at Harvard in 1909–10, William Faulkner's Quentin Compson, appearing in *The Sound and the Fury* and *Absalom, Absalom!*, spent long hours with his Canadian roommate, Shreve McCannon, trying to explain the South. On June 2, 1910, he jumped off the Charles River Bridge. A plaque marks the spot, fictional though the suicide was. At the end, Shreve asks, "Now I want you to tell me just one thing more. Why do you hate the South?" And Quentin answers: "'I don't hate it,' Quentin said, quickly, at once, immediately. 'I don't hate it,' he said. *I don't hate it* he thought, panting in the cold air, the iron New England dark; *I don't. I don't! I don't hate it! I don't hate it.*"

In my fantasies, I sometimes think of myself as Quentin Compson grown up, as who he would have become had he not elected death at age nineteen. I know with pristine clarity what love-hate sentiments wracked Quentin's heart. The inner play between poles of hate and love for the South have been the joy and the curse of my life, now nearly a half century longer than Quentin's was. For me, love for the region has always triumphed over hates, but both are there nonetheless, like the tattoos L.O.V.E. and H.A.T.E. on the knuckles of the clinched hands of the obsessed preacher in the movie *Night of the Hunter.*

I have made my career out of studying, critiquing, and loving the South. At my ministerial ordination in 1963, the charge specified that I would minister to the South through higher education service, rather than as a church pastor. Since 1982, I have written this weekly newspaper column, "Southern Seen," as a ministerial service, explorations of liberal arts subjects for small southern newspapers unlikely to have many paid syndicated columnists.

By now, some seventeen hundred "Southern Seen" weekly columns have covered topics such as southern personalities, places, idiosyncrasies, foodways, sports, outdoor life, literature, art and architecture, politics, race, religion, war, and weather. Collectively, the essays represent a field known in higher education as southern studies. This interdisciplinary field is a subdiscipline in my teaching field, American studies. American studies and southern studies programs typically combine study in history, sociology, religion, art, government, philosophy, and economics, and sometimes add natural sciences, languages, ethnic studies, and gender studies. A lingering hope for Wofford College as I near retirement is that it will combine faculty and curricular resources it already possesses and find a sponsor for its own American studies program and major.

We live in an unfamiliar age of conglomerate businesses and consolidated schools characterized more by congestion than by congregation. Ours is a statistical age driven by numbers, especially those of "markets," but people matter more than numbers.

The popularity of antique shops and of genealogy searching tells us there is widespread reaction to the present and fear of the future. I am among many Americans looking backward to the known more often than looking forward to the unknown. A whiff of wisteria will set me off wishing wistfully for simpler and happier days; perhaps I am as old and reactionary as I am gray and balding.

Yet, there is more to this fascination and fear than just emotionalism and feeling. The human mind is more than just a picture album of memories or a horror house of projections. The mind is an organizer of lives, exploring the meaning of living and selecting paths to take among a million forks in our roads. Unless we are willing to admit that we human beings are nothing more than accidents in the history of this planet and universe, brought here by chance and driven while here by forces beyond our control, we have to assume some responsibility for our personal actions and for the shape of our society.

We can't do much about today and tomorrow without understanding yesterday. That's why I preach fervently that young people ought to spend a lot of time in humanities and social science courses, among library shelves, in historical places outside classroom and library, and in gleaning the stories of their elders.

One sunken treasure that we find by immersing ourselves in our regional culture is very good company. People, stories, ideas, events, and times don't really die. They are always there, resting on the bottom under the whirlpools and waves of today, waiting for us to rediscover them and share them. Out of our immersion into our submerged past comes insight into those patterns and purposes that make the most sense, that survive time and currents of change and surface over and over again to help us invent our future.

No writer lives or writes in a vacuum, and my indebtedness to others is enormous. Among those to whom I express appreciation are professors and administrators, colleagues and students, at Transylvania University, Yale University, the University of Alabama, the University of Tennessee at Martin, the University of Tennessee at Knoxville, the Center for the Study of Southern Culture at the University of Mississippi, and Wofford College. I also extend thanks to the Kettering Foundation, the Society for Values in Higher Education, the American Council of Education, and the Association of American Colleges and Universities. Having entered higher education in 1954 and never having left it, I have been blessed with friendships and collaborations too varied and numerous to single out and thank appropriately. Among them, however, I must mention by name my mentors, the late Raymond F. McLain, Frank A. Rose, Irvin E. Lunger, and Jeff Bennett; my most supportive professors, Hal Douglas and the late Liston Pope, Sid Ahlstrom, and Ed Dirks; and my most supportive colleagues, David Mathews, Ed Boling, Joe Johnson, Jack Reese, Joe Lesesne, Bernie Dunlap, Joe Sutton, Billie Ann Pace, and Jim Wilder, as well as close friends David and Betty Lollis, Guy and Nell Waldrop, and Jim and Mason Barrett. The former students I should thank would fill a class roll book if I tried to list them, so I must just assume they know who they are.

The institutions of education I have known and loved are also too numerous to list and do justice, but special gratitude singles out four of them. This book is a personal celebration of Wofford College upon the occasion of its 150th anniversary in 2004, of Transylvania University upon its 225th anniversary in 2005, of E. W. Grove High School upon its 100th anniversary in 2006, and of the University of Tennessee at Martin's recent (2000) centennial observance. Because so many of the fields of study in those places are represented in my weekly columns, this celebration of their anniversaries includes some of the "Southern Seen" essays in which they occasionally are mentioned.

Gratitude is also owed the editor of this book, William Joseph "B. J." Hutto of Orangeburg, South Carolina, a Phi Beta Kappa graduate in English and religion in Wofford's Class of 2002, now enrolled in Duke University Divinity School. His interest in southern studies subject matter, viewed critically and objectively as a member of a much younger generation (for whom this book is intended as much as it is for AARP members such as I), significantly influenced the choice of essays, and his eye for grammar and style provided indispensable and enviable editorial honing. B. J. aspires to pastor a Baptist Church, but until then he is content to spend his days as the original disciples did in their pre-ministry years, on a fishing boat.

Appreciation is also expressed to John Egerton. Having known a few published southern authors and having read and admired from a distance several hundred others, I am elated that the one whose writings I have most admired is gracing this publication. A native of Cadiz, Kentucky, and now a resident of Nashville, John is the author and editor of numerous books, including *Speak Now Against the Day: The Generation Before the Civil Rights Movement in the South,* which won the Robert Fitzgerald Kennedy Award. Among his other publications are *Southern Food: At Home, on the Road, and in History,* considered the definitive work on the subject, and *Generations,* winner of the Lillian Smith Award and the Weatherford Award. If you don't read my essays, reading John's foreword alone will be worth the price of admission to the book.

Most of all, of course, I express love and thanks to my family, to those no longer living or barely hanging on who pushed me ever onward and upward in interests and aspirations.

Especially do I thank and revere my wife, Elizabeth Boden (Betsy) McGehee, a history major and former teacher and accomplished promoter of domestic tranquility, and our daughters, Elizabeth (Liz), a copy editor at the *Washington Post,* and Margaret (Molly), a Ph.D. candidate in American studies at Emory University. Betsy, Elizabeth, and Molly have always shared my curiosity in and explorations of things southern and are extraordinarily well read and conversant in that field. I just happen to be the one recording what we have read, observed, and discussed during our happy years together. It has not always been easy for them, living as they have with a moody and eclectic and somewhat eccentric Quentin Compson.

Spartanburg, South Carolina
April 2004

Chapter 1

OUTDOORS
"IN GREEN PASTURES"

BACKROADS

For people close to the land, tourist season doesn't come in summer when the crops need tending nor in the fall when harvest is at hand. People of the land are winter's tourists. Thanksgiving signals that time to get out and around, even if it's only to a neighbor's or out into the fields to hunt.

Seen from a plane, a county's roads form a lace doily tatted by forgotten grandmothers. Or they make a spider's web, pulling us in our cars to a central town that sits like a spider waiting for lunch.

The fortunate few stay on back roads, off the asphalt and away from the hungry city. They ride dirt and gravel county trails that link one small high school gym to another in a circle around the town. Get out among them while you still can. Plunk yourself into the polygons formed by crossed-roads, and on road-enclosed farms plunge yourself into anachronisms of tobacco, sorghum, cotton, and hay. Visit smokehouses and outhouses while they still stand, and grin back at the jack-o'-lantern faces old weather-beaten barns make with their window lofts and doors.

These are the county's battlefields, these fenced-off, reddened farms where winsome women aged so quickly from working while their leather-faced men straddled tractors that sent plows and discs deep into the dragon earth and came home covered with the dragon's powdered red blood. And these same idled knights, on days too wet or cold to fight the earth, squatted by one another at one-pump stores, hunkering to trade knives and finely honed tales and a chew—brothers to their bird dogs.

Take yourself out into the fields and enjoy game that gets harder to find each year. Look for its tracks in manure-mush leaves beneath the oaks and down dry creek bottoms and along crinkled perimeters of receding ponds and cattail swamps and in eroded gullies that fences span like suspended tennis nets. Listen when quail flush how the air explodes, the flurried fury of a flushed covey flapping like loose tin sheets crackling in a high wind on top of an abandoned and bleached barn. Watch the winged coffee cans rise, group, and swoop away. Feel foxes' eyes as they watch you from where they stand frozen into ceramic stateliness up at the receding shadow line of the woods. Spot them, before they thaw and flow back into the woods' darkness.

Wade across a golden pond of sage, its wind-waved surface rippling against islands of green cedar treetops. Then sit where the foxes stood at the edge of forest and field and whiff the chloroforming odor of musty mildew where melting November frosts have made mattresses of dead leaves. Lean back against a hickory tree, and nod off awhile in peace under the cathedral God made long before man built a Chartres or Notre Dame. Then waken quickly when shells start popping from the vaulted bough-ceiling as the sanctuary stillness is broken by the squirrels above dropping hickory hulls.

Sit silently until sundown and watch as the west streaks red with all the color and glory of the Second Coming captured by the picture on a funeral-home fan.

Early December is a strange time for tourists, and for resurrections. When the grass has withered and the leaves fallen, one somehow doesn't think of the miracles of Easter and of Lazarus. When the last lazy squirrel wraps its tail about him and snuggles into a tree-trunk home-hole, one doesn't think of new life and new birth and hope in bloom. When the last lingering leaf clings to the out-stretched fingertip of an emaciated and bare tree limb, making one last plea before the snows mercifully cover its nakedness, why would one think of peace, or beauty, or healing? Only butchered meat is cured this time of year—and one seldom thinks of other curings. But the land is at work in its sleep, repairing itself for spring. The old and tired reach now for renewal. Those who love the land know this is their season of restoration. They know to get out while they can, out on to the back roads. Impose Now and New upon Old and Yet-To-Be. Picture the land in stereopticon splashes of color, imposed upon your soul, poured through the pores of your skin, splashed through the windshields of your mind.

Uninspired by the spider-city and undivided by its subdivisions, find wholeness and hope again, out on the land.

November 29, 1982

POISON IVY

I've been itching, literally, to talk about my case of poison ivy.

I went out to clear a big patch of decaying, honeysuckle-covered pine straw and limbs down by the fence in our backyard. I had visions of plowing up that section and planting azaleas and mountain laurels in that shady grove. After all, I figured, every direct male ancestor of mine for the last three centuries has lived on a farm, first in Virginia and, after 1833, in west Tennessee. I assumed all that agricultural breeding must have been passed on to me naturally. I was a man of the land.

Now that I think about it, those ancestors always seemed to get hired hands or live-in bachelor relatives to do their farming for them, but it does seem that I would have picked up some skill at clearing and planting somewhere over the years.

So, in late June, I stripped down to sneakers and cut-off jeans and plunged into that briar patch out back, thinking of the suntans I used to get, thirty years and thirty pounds ago. Both my body and my yard were going to become marvels to behold, all in one day's work.

My green-thumb wife came out back a couple of times to tell me that, considering the 95-degree weather, the humidity, and the size of my stomach hanging over my shorts, my project seemed a bit rash.

Of course, that kind of advice only makes a husband cut, root and dig harder. By day's end, I had a third of the area cleared, and a pile of debris stacked higher than the whole patch I was clearing; the work was neither fun nor funny. And I don't think it funny at all for her to keep saying it was all "a little rash."

It was "a big rash." All over me.

After two weeks of Benadryl and cortisone tablets, it is going away. My allergist was very profound when he examined me, "You must be allergic to poison ivy and poison oak." For that kind of diagnosis he went to med school?

Last time I had the itch was four years before, from clearing out a little stump hole. That time I consulted my pharmacist. We settled on a dark bottle of something that came with an "applicator" that wasn't anything but a Popsicle stick. I had to scrape all the rash spots and then pour the stuff out of the bottle on the raw spots. It must have been two hundred proof alcohol, but it worked. That year I had ivy burn instead of a suntan.

But the FDA or someone took that patent medicine off the market, and I had to go to the doctor this time. And that brought back happy memories from college years of my first encounter with poison plants and skin doctors. I somehow got picked to be the one-man decorating committee for our fraternity Fall Tea Dance. (A tea dance was an afternoon dance, slow music, in pre-rock-and-roll days.) With a stroke of genius, I recruited a young lady to help me decorate, promising to take her to the dance in return.

My sainted mother had told me repeatedly, from the time I was six years old, that nice boys never take girls to the woods. But off we went to gather leaves of autumn red and gold, the fraternity's colors, to decorate the tea dance trellises. How was I to know that those red leaves that everyone complimented were sumac?

We both wound up at the dermatologist's office, in an age when radiation was the treatment. Every week for two months we had to be radiated, lead shields covering what few uninfected areas we had. Even worst, he told me to take a daily hot bath with some sort of white powder dissolved in it. Trouble was, the only bathtub in our dormitory belonged to our house parents, who used it for themselves and their three children.

I'll always be grateful for the use of their tub everyday during the lunch hour. And I didn't miss the cafeteria lunches much anyway. I did miss the girl, however. She never spoke to me again.

Once the poison gets in the bloodstream, it never goes away, I'm told. After this third and latest bout with the stuff, I believe that. I also now believe my wife. Pulling up poison ivy is a rash act. I even believe my mother. Don't take nice girls to the woods.

The rashness of youth will hound you in middle age. That pile of vines and the uncleared two-thirds area out back will sit there until I can afford a hired hand.

July 25, 1983

After the long drought of July, enough quick thunderstorms have hit our area to wash the dust off the leaves. The kudzu across the southland is green again.

The late poet James Dickey once wrote a poem entitled, simply, "Kudzu," which begins: "Japan invades. Far Eastern vines / Run from the clay banks they are // Supposed to keep from eroding. / Up telephone poles, / Which rear, half out of leafage / As though they would shriek, / Like things smothered by their own / Green, mindless, unkillable ghosts. / In Georgia, the legend says / That you must close your windows // At night to keep it out of the house." A lesser-known poet, Bill Horne, wrote, "After a rain . . . / he hacked his way to a corn row / through a tangle of kudzu, / planted for pretty, regretted since / and soon encompassing all."

A *Saturday Review* writer once said New York City was planting kudzu in vacant lots when buildings were torn down, to create "instant mini-parks of green." The writer was southern-born and predicted the total evacuation of New York City within a year once kudzu took root there. In a recent southern novel that is a parable for the South's love-hate relationship with kudzu, a clump of kudzu shaped like a praying Jesus is turned into a religious shrine and visited by thousands of people until someone douses it with gasoline and sets it afire, sending salvation seekers off to other soul-soils such as football fields and Elvis's homeplace. One comic wag on the Mindspring Web site suggests that kudzu grows well in anything, including cement, and that it should be planted only at night (lest your neighbors spot you). The best fertilizer is 40W nondetergent motor oil, which should be added every thousand feet or every two weeks, whichever comes first. A good mulch for kudzu is concrete blocks. Kudzu growers are advised that the best time to sell their houses is during the fall and winter off-season, while the houses can still be seen.

Green kudzu has a ferocious look. When it is parched and brown in winter, the wayfarer feels safe. But when it is green it coils everywhere, like an endless python, ready to spring out and squeeze us into unconsciousness before slithering off into the gullies it hides to digest us. That's why the best place to dump your unwanted cat or burned-out refrigerator is in a kudzu patch: instant invisibility.

Kudzu is a weedy vine (*Pueraria lobata*) and a member of the bean family (*Fabaceae*). It grows an average of a foot a day, and it can reach fifty feet in height. It is rich in protein and can be used to feed livestock if it doesn't strangle or devour pigs and cattle in the process. In Asia, kudzu roots are used as foods (probably because eating it was the only way to keep it from taking over). The vines die each fall, but the roots survive.

Kudzu in America is popularly thought to have been introduced from Japan in the Dust Bowl days of the 1930s by agricultural researchers at Auburn or Clemson. Actually, it first arrived in 1876, America's Centennial Year. The same year the French sent us the Statue of Liberty, Japan sent us kudzu. Kudzu is the South's defining product, replacing cotton and tobacco sometime in the 1930s (encouraged by the U.S. Department of Agriculture's paying eight dollars an acre to plant it) after arriving in America at the Centennial Exposition in 1876 and at the Japanese Pavilion of the New Orleans Exposition of 1884–86. I don't want to look a gift horse in the mouth, but sometimes I suspect the Japanese sent us kudzu to soften us up for World War II. It was a little like the old lady who poisoned five husbands, one at a time over many years, with daily drops of arsenic in their coffee.

The agricultural advantages of kudzu are well known. It prevents soil erosion, and it feeds nitrogen bacteria into the soil to restore the growing ability for crops. It does that without having to be sprayed, sprigged, or watered. However, kudzu is also known for spreading everywhere rapidly until whole green mountains appear on flatlands where pine trees, telephone poles, barns, and cattle herds have been gobbled up. Southerners pronounce it like a sneeze, "KUD-zoo," and other regions call it "KOOD-zoo." It was grown in China before it went to Japan, at least two thousand years ago.

Until 1910, it was mostly used here for decorating yards. From 1910 to 1935, farmers planted it to provide pastures and food for livestock. Its biggest promoter was C. E. Pleas, in the Florida panhandle, who even wrote a book in 1925 called *Kudzu—Coming Forage of the South*. A historical marker to kudzu now stands at Pleas's farm on U.S. 90. Its use for soil conservation came after 1935. R. Y. "Kudzu" Bailey, of Spartanburg, South Carolina, wrote a very popular pamphlet in 1939. The best popularizer, however, was Channing Cope of Atlanta, who wrote for the *Constitution* and had a front-porch radio show. He formed the Kudzu Club of America in 1943, and earned his title of "Father of Kudzu," especially after his 1949 book, *Front Porch Farmer*, sold like the plant he extolled.

By 1945, there were half a million acres (and other things) in the South under kudzu, and Cope set a goal of eight million acres by 1950. The reaction set in about 1955. Headlines in 1976 celebrated kudzu's one hundredth year in America by declaring it the South's second great invader (the Yankees were the first, and the boll weevil was ignored). The stories reported that the South was losing this new war, too. This year there are two million kudzu acres in the South.

Chattanooga no longer holds its annual Kudzu Ball (which used to be held at the same time as its Cotton Ball). Greensboro, Alabama, no longer crowns a Kudzu Queen. There are still computer companies, advertising companies, a hockey league, a singing group, a number of newsletters and magazines, several festivals and cookbooks, all of which bear the kudzu name.

The name lingers, but the weed itself may actually be receding. It could be that southerners are fighting to take their land back from an invader more insidious and recent than the Yankees of the last century (who came in armies of soldiers followed by armies of capitalists).

On the other hand, maybe kudzu, which does seem to have a mind of its own, has just moved inland, away from the highways and out of sight. That would explain why farmers, who were 70 percent of the population around 1900 but only 2.5 percent of it today, have disappeared—either evacuated from kudzu's path or covered by it—and why much of our food seems to be imported from abroad. It would also explain what it is back there in the woods that is driving deer out onto the highways.

Its real damage is in forests rather than fields. In the woods, it spreads unchecked and strangles the trees. Kudzu festivals celebrate its better qualities, and if its hold on trees and telephone poles could be contained, it might regain public favor. I know of at least two regional kudzu festivals, one in east Tennessee and the other in upper South Carolina. There one finds a wide variety of kudzu foods, kudzu baskets and beds, and kudzu medicines.

Kudzu: a mixed blessing, a strangler that also makes a good green salad.

August 15, 1983, and June 22, 1998

BIRDDOGS

Our family made a trek to the local animal rescue shelter to adopt a new cat, a successor to deceased and lamented Tommy and Friday. To get to the cat wing of the shelter, we had to go through the dog room; some of the dogs were hounds. The trip brought to mind a couple of years immediately after World War II when old Camp Tyson, the army post near my home-town, was the site for the national foxhound field trials. The thousands of acres that once teemed with soldiers were the gathering place for hundreds of foxhounds. Each had a number painted on its side for judging purposes. When they were in their pens, all howling at once, they could have drowned out an air-raid siren.

Foxhounds were very special status symbols for southerners. They were once associated with the leisurely life of southern plantation owners and their sons, but after the Civil War, when plantations were gone, foxhounds stayed on. Every dirt farmer had at least one. Foxhounds were reminders of a way of life that was gone and for which a war had been fought. Fox-hounds were also signs of social and economic ambitions, the faith that the South would rise again. Even when Herbert Hoover was promising "a chicken in every pot," the southerner was more interested in land for his hound.

Sometime after World War II, however, southerners became a little more realistic about their aspirations. They didn't give up on having hounds and on wanting to own the places on which to keep them, but they shifted to birddogs instead of foxhounds. You can't eat foxes. Or, if you can, you don't. But you can eat quail. And you don't need to ride a horse to hunt them. Birddogs are more practical than foxhounds. That gathering of hun-dreds of hounds at Camp Tyson in the late 1940s was like a gathering of Confederate veterans in 1900: the passing of an era, the last link to the English gentry tradition of foxhunting that the South had copied for so long. It was a sign that a New South was rising, of two-car garages and pickup trucks instead of ten-horse stables.

Quail smothered in gravy is great for breakfast. In fact, now there are even quail farms where quail are raised in captivity like chickens for sale to restaurants. It sort of goes against the grain; they don't even need birddogs to catch them.

Without birddogs, there would be no birddog stories. It's a little like fishing. The tales are more important then the actual hunting or fishing, which is really taxing and tedious work. We'd rather talk about it than do it. Some of the South's best stories, really superb replacements for the Uncle Remus tales, are birddog stories. William Faulkner's best works are his hunt-ing stories, better even than his novels. He was a great hunter who enjoyed the campfire tales of other hunters more than he enjoyed pulling a trigger himself.

A typical birddog story will make one's dog out to be better than anyone else's. They run something like this one, about Zeke: one bragging bird hunter mercilessly bored everyone in the coffee shop crowd, talking about his bird dog. Finally one listener told him his dog couldn't hold a candle to one he knew of out in the country and took the braggart to see for himself. Out at a farm, they met an old farmer with a body gnarled with age and a chin stained with tobacco juice. The old man showed them his hounds, a dozen feisty yappers scampering around the dirt yard. The braggart asked to see the best one. "That'd be Zeke, that one over under the porch," the farmer said. He pointed to a dog that looked as old and crippled as himself. Then he called the dog, who shuffled over slowly, and they headed for the fields. Half way across the field, the old dog lazily pointed at a bush, and a covey of quail flew up; the braggart wasn't much impressed. Farther on, they came to two bushes. The dog pointed to one with his paw and the other with his head. The braggart laughed at the dog's confusion, until a covey flew out of both bushes. A little farther on, the dog rolled over on its back, its feet in the air. The younger hunter laughed again, until a covey flew out of the tree overhead. Next the dog stuck its nose down a groundhog hole. The young hunter laughed. The dog barked once, took out its nose, and a covey flew out of the hole.

By now, the bragging hunter was beginning to concede defeat. Just then the dog pointed at another bush. Nothing flew out. The hunter laughed again. "See, there's nothing there at all," he said. "It's all been just luck." The farmer spit a long squirt of tobacco. "Just wait a second," he said. Just then a covey of quail flew into the bush. "Ole Zeke was just telling you where the birds were going to be." "I've got to have that dog," the convinced young hunter yelled. "Name your price." "Ain't for sale," said the farmer. "Besides, why would you want an old dog that's blind in both eyes?"

And that's why the South needs birddogs. We need to keep our tales from dragging.

Some folks are just natural hound collectors. I've never been that lucky. We went through a long line of beagles, cocker spaniels, and mutts when I was younger. They all ran away or died before we could get attached to them. I blame that—and a lot of other things—on my brother, who was bitten by a dog when he was about four and had to have rabies shots. They killed the dog. I always figured the dogs we got afterward knew that and wanted no part of us.

Closest I ever came to feeling kin to a hound was with Jip, my grand-parents' sad-looking birddog that seemed to like to go BB-gun hunting with me out near their place. There was a great sand gully there that had grown up with pines and shrubs in the middle of old oaks and hickories. Jip and I would roam the place all day long. I think he was with me one October when I set it on fire by shooting some Halloween firecrackers in the sage field part.

I loved the trips to that old farm. You could tell it was old-style living; the hallway Jip slept in most days used to be a dogtrot connecting the two main rooms that had functioning fireplaces and featherbeds where company gathered day or night. Between the great food and the featherbed luxury were long, long hours that any boy could find ways to fill.

Jip seemed to wake up when I visited, as if he spent most of his time sleeping in that hallway or under the wooden front porch waiting for me to arrive. He was already old when I came along, and those trips into the gully across the gravel road in front of the house must have stirred some memories and habits of his from his own pup days.

I remember when I came to stay once and found Jip had died. The bachelor uncle who lived on the place took me across to the gully and showed me where Jip was buried. I went back that afternoon and collected sandstones from the gully and used them to outline Jip's grave, and I wrote his name with them in the center of the red rock rectangle.

I believe I still could find his grave today.

March 19, 1984, and September 15, 1986

NIGHT

Our backyard lights were burned out, but when I looked out the yard was so bright I thought someone had replaced them. It was the night of April's full moon on Palm Sunday. We take for granted our "night lights." Inside we have ceiling lights, porch lights, bathroom mirror lights, table lamps, and chandeliers, and outside we have streetlights, auto headlights, floodlights, and spotlights. Factories run three shifts with artificial lighting. Traffic churns along the turnpikes all night long with taillights, headlights, and inter-change lights. All-night service stations and one-stop grocery shops are lit up twenty-four hours a day, seven days a week.

But sometimes there are moments when there are only moonlight, star-light, and lightning bugs. And sometimes there are nights when we lack even those. Nights—real nights of deepest darkness—are almost lost to us.

I try to remember what darkness must have been, and it defies the imagination. The closest I can come to it in my own experience is a faint memory of getting into featherbeds at my grandparents' farm right after supper, but even there my memory is of coal-oil lamps and flickering fires in the fireplace.

Betsy and I missed our best chance for total darkness when we were in New Haven during the great eastern blackout in the early 1960s. The lights went out all over New England except, for some unknown reason, in New Haven. People who were trapped in elevators, tunnels, and subways still talk about their experiences in complete darkness.

Remembering absolute, total darkness is hard to do for our generation. Even when all is dark outside, one sees the blue glow of late night television sets from the windows of neighbors' homes. And in times of power failures one thinks of candles and flashlights, not of total darkness.

Then again, I suppose there were a few dark moments in my own past. I remember crawling through a narrow tunnel at the back of Ruskin Cave in Tennessee. I remember World War II blackouts when we banked the fire, turned out all lights, and lowered the shades until the siren sounded "all clear."

All this light and loss of night is very recent, almost within our own life-times. Our parents had their nights, and their parents had even longer ones. And without air-conditioning to keep them inside and lights by which to see, they had far greater appreciation for darkness and night than do we or our children.

Strangely enough, they remember nights as being quieter and safer. They recall names of comets they saw, constellations of stars they memorized, and moonlight serenades and torchlight parades.

What does it mean for a world to become, "overnight," if you'll pardon the expression, an "open-all-night" world? What does it do to communities and conversations and chirping tree frogs for night to vanish and for day to be unending?

Where there were rhythms to the night to which our minds and bodies were accustomed, now there is only an unchanging progression. Is that a loss or an advancement for civilization? I think of how progressive it seemed to light the henhouses all night, so the chickens would be fooled into thinking it was daytime and would lay more eggs. Did those hens enjoy life any more after they got their lights?

Children are no longer afraid of the dark, but they are ignorant of its existence. Is that enlightening? Perhaps it is progress, but it seems to me that life in a city without darkness is like life in a house without trees, or like meals of frozen dinners all year long. The contrasts and changes of the natural world are blotted out, and both the body and soul lose something in the process and processing.

May 7, 1984

FISHING

Up on beautiful Keowee-Toxaway Lake, we sat on a dock watching fiberglass boats powered by multihorsepower motors skim the surface in crisscross patterns. It brought to mind changes of our times—harnessing rivers to create electric and nuclear power, fertilizer plants, industries, and recreation areas and state parks. Holding that thought of change, I flipped open the tackle box of our host.

Suddenly the past crashed in upon me. There in the metal compartments were a part of my lost past—fishing lures we used in our youth— River Runt, Hula Popper, Jitterbug, Silver Spoon, and Hawaiian Dancer, each in its proper cubicle, next to plastic worms and plastic skirts. There they all lay, as if only last week we untangled the old Shakespeare reel and flipped the metal clasp of the family tackle box and put them away. There, almost within sight of Caesar's Head and Table Rock mountains, I had a mountaintop experience; it was as if all rivers I have known and all lakes upon which I have loafed flowed together, and that somehow time was standing still at this particular lake while all the time already lived could catch up with it. Visions of father, brother, cousins, uncles, grandfather, and school friends flew out of those old baits as if from Pandora's box. Time doesn't flow backward to make us children again; it moves forward to catch up with us. Opening a dusty box in an attic or flipping through a yellowing photo album pulls time forward—as the creaking top of a tackle box did for me.

Some student of southern fiction recently asserted that the acid test of a true southern novel is whether or not a dead mule shows up somewhere along the way in telling the story. I was checking my memory of novels to see if he was spoofing me, and I came up with my own theory. Almost every southern novel somewhere or another will have fishing in it. We've lived all other the South now—Tennessee, Alabama, Kentucky, South Carolina—and had kinfolk in the rest—Florida, Virginia, Georgia, Mississippi, Louisiana, Texas, and Arkansas. Nobody and nothing in the South are ever far away from fishing. When cotton started playing out as the mainstay crop, and folks started moving to factory towns, fishing became the great southern escape, rivaled only by television and football.

That may be fading away now, although water is still important. Boating and water skiing have replaced riverbank poling and casting and trolling and trotlines as recreation. But there was a Golden Age of fishing in the South, somewhere from the end of World War II (when army surplus boats and pontoons were so available) up until the recent time when returning veterans who made it so popular have gotten too old to keep wetting their hooks.

There was a time when a whole race of men got together over coffee every morning and debated rods and reels, outboard motors, boat shapes, artificial lures, and the other high-tech equipage of fishing as avidly and as knowledgeably as their sons and grandsons talk about computers and cellular phones today. There were men in those days who fished with old crank phones, stunning the fish into submission, and others who dropped dynamite and even hand grenades in the river. They took their technology very seriously.

I had an uncle in Louisiana, back from the army, who spent every free moment he could steal designing artificial lures. He carved models of minnows and frogs and variations of the Heddon River Runt, painted them or covered them with frog skin, and tried to get major companies to buy them. I don't recall him making much money from them, but he pursued the perfect casting lure with all the fervor of Hemingway's Old Man chasing the giant marlin and Captain Ahab chasing Moby-Dick.

One old-timer back home who had lost a leg in World War I never seemed to miss a clear day at the river. I was pumping gas at my dad's store one day when Mr. Cravens screeched to a stop in his handicap-equipped Buick and yelled for help. His wooden leg had come unscrewed, and he wanted me to screw it back on before the fish stopped biting.

Everyone seemed to have the fishing fever in those days. Lots of us learned to unsnarl backlashes and to flick our wrists just so, trying to get under submerged limbs without getting caught in them. A couple of times Arthur Shemwell let us stay in his houseboat, moored in the cove where the Paris Landing State Park Marina is today, and the buffalo fish were so big and numerous they would climb on top of each other to get breadcrumbs we threw them, and we could catch them in nets. Other times, we could stand below Springville Dike and catch fish by hand from the dozens in the spillway.

But the older I get, the less the complicated fishing technology appeals to me. The best fishing is Huck Finn fashion, with very little separating the fish from the fisherman. My best memories are of a cane pole, a home-made lead weight and homemade cork float, with an old can full of dirt and fat earthworms dug personally from under a wet log or out of some-body's rose garden or picked up after a heavy rain, and sitting on a river-bank down Rattlesnake Hill (atop which the state park hotel is now, where a mule-drawn sorghum mill and cane field used to stand) in the shade of giant oak trees but near some bank-side willows, crappie fishing but catch-ing mostly perch and brim and sunfish.

Ours was a lazy boy's fishing: fisher and fish united even as they opposed one another. We threw back what we caught, looked around for arrow-heads and terrapins, talked about how to get girls to pay attention to us, poured a package of salty peanuts into an RC and swigged it down, sniffed at ourselves to smell the fish and worm smells, swatted mosquitoes—and relished the Good Life.

Having had it once, without realizing it until too late, do we have to die to get Heaven back? Sometimes I look up and see big white clouds shaped every bit like riverbanks, and wonder where angels tuck their wings so they can lie flat on their backs while fishing in that big blue sky-sea.

A large part of being southern is the link between man and land, the roots that almost all southerners have planted deep before they leave home. No matter how far away we get, the roots are still there, covered by the flowing lakes of time and distance and forgetfulness and ambitions, but still there.

Those kinds of roots are what those old lures snagged.

Clarence Cason was a tormented Alabama journalist/educator who could not reconcile the Old South with the New and, at age 37, committed suicide in 1935 just before his book, *90 Degrees in the Shade,* appeared. Before he dove into the murky mud of poverty, hookworms, racism, carpetbaggers, and demagogues that was the gist of his book, Cason seemed to draw a deep breath—to write a paragraph about southern fishing: "Although I know that it is heresy to suggest such an idea in the midst of an age of progress," Cason wrote, "it may be that ultimate truth lies in the spiritual attitude of the southerners who are always going fishing. A person who has achieved an immunity from the everlasting inner demand that he improve upon his earthly position must possess an unusual degree of cosmic equilibrium. He must have learned in some way that composure of the human spirit is all that actually matters. He has attained, without conscious effort, the serenity for which all men strive."

Southerners find peace on creek banks and lakes where fishing lines connect us to the mysteries of the deep. Cason made the mistake of not following his own advice. Once he finished his book, he should have gone fishing.

Fish are slippery, elusive things, but they can be caught. Perhaps the secret attraction to fishing is that fish are a metaphor for life. Life, as you know, has its own ways of being hard to hook and reel in. Life can get out of hand, but fishing reassures us that it doesn't always have to. Jesus made time to go fishing. One wonders what he would have been without it. Would he have seen things as poetically or expressed inner thoughts so articulately or lived so meaningfully without fishing? Good fishing is the same thing as patience, a rare commodity in a whirl-away world. "Pacific" is a wonderful word for it—peacefulness, attunement, alignment, and serenity. The tranquility of the fisherman is a marked contrast to the frenetic amateur, thrashing about the riverbank to cut loose the lures caught in bushes behind him or deliriously unraveling the bird's nest of a fouled reel or casting faster and faster, and fruitlessly, where nothing bites.

Fish are survivors of rocks and torrents, of eddies and whirlpools, of storms and quicksand, of predators and channels. To look for them is to look for oneself. To catch them is to have mastered self-control. It has often seemed to me that there is something eastern and religious about true fishing. It comes very nigh to being the occidental version of oriental Zen Buddhism, and I have my own name for it: Fin Buddhism.

The South and its universe—and each of us—change each day, but there are special spots of silence where change can be put in perspective.

There are tackle boxes of the soul that we should bring out and unlatch.

July 23, 1984, February 22, 1993, and July 21, 1997

Where does everyone go in January?

I'll bet it was in a January that those wandering Hebrews made their golden calf, and the earth swallowed a passel of them. Our Januarys are like that. The people are gone, swallowed up. Were they ever really there?

Last month, in December, you couldn't stir them with a stick. People were everywhere. Even Christmas couldn't keep them home. For the week after, they stayed on out, exchanging things and hitting the after-Christmas sales. Now they are gone. Bowl games are about over, and the regular shows are showing reruns, so they aren't watching television.

Where do they go? Are we hibernating mammals that pull into our dens for January and February? Outside, it is crisp, breathtakingly nippy, gray—and deserted. This is the real time, not December, when "not a creature is stirring, not even a mouse." Except for the weather, January would be an ideal time for all those highway men who turn double-lanes into one-lanes. They wouldn't have us to get in their way, and vice versa. But the road repair crews are gone, too. Gone wherever people go in January. We'll not see them again until asphalt season, after Easter.

Where do people go? Deer and duck blinds and ski lodges don't account for more than a fraction of them. They can't all be in Florida or on the Caribbean; the highways, airports, and bus stations aren't teeming. Logically, there are no fewer people in the world in January than there were in July or December, but there seems to be so many fewer. January must be an optical illusion.

The illusion has something to do with weather, shopping seasons, holidays, fiscal years, and fatigue. The converging and merging of all these factors coincide with winter. In man's race to set his own calendar rather than use nature's old one, January remains man's last link to the natural cycle of things. Central heating has not yet conquered January in the way that air-conditioning has done away with July.

Nature conspires in January, as it has for centuries, to force upon the world a time of rest and a time for family. It is a time for recovery and planning, for recounting and patching, a time when interiors—of homes, and bodies, and minds—are more important than exteriors.

January gets its name from the Roman god Janus, who had two faces. Often Roman homes had a mask of the two-faced god over the door, to watch goings out and comings in. January is an ideal Janus month, a time for looking both ways at once, studying the past year while entering a new one.

January is inventory time for people as well as for business. One sits by the fireside and counts gains and losses. They are far more numerous than the cancelled checks the IRS box shows. Inventories in January include measuring gains and losses in self-esteem, family affection, friendships, work satisfaction, health, world affairs, and human relations. January is humanity's self-assessment time.

Maybe the tradition of starting January with black-eyed peas, collard greens, and hog jowls is only southern; the meal is to bring good luck for the year. The thing that appeals most about that January 1 menu, however, is that it is soul food. There is something about January, when half of us seems to have vanished and the other half seems less harried and frenetic, that is soul feeding.

Military convoys have halted and gone into winter camps; snow supplies that will become spring streams for summer lakes are building up. Last year's bestsellers are finally getting read, and jigsaw puzzles on card tables are taking shape. Even the birds, scratching the ice under the birdfeeder for a few spilled grains, seem more at ease and less anxious to be on the wing. The quiet is deafening, and our souls are deepening. Both faces of Janus are smiling. Last fall's popcorn snaps. Last summer's peach preserves taste sweeter. Time is January's gift.

January 7, 1985

SNOW AND PECANS

"Where are the snows of yesteryear?" We waited in vain for Christmas snow, and finally one came.

The snow outside is now boot-top deep. Beneath it the mud is axle deep. Car rutted in the earth, I am indoors awaiting the melting, the return of electric power, the arrival of spring, and the tow truck. The snow came at my call, even though I had nothing to do with its coming. I wished, then waited, and then welcomed it. It came in splendor, white sheets of ghosts of winters past drifting in and out of the years in silent echo of times past when snows came twice or thrice or not at all each season. The first hours of snow are its best. After that, lush turns to slush. This snow came at midnight, and by dawn every branch and twig of the trees bore a feather pile of puff. The white ribbons etched the black boughs into pen-and-India-ink artworks begging for a painter, a photographer, or a jigsaw puzzle maker to capture for me to keep forever. The scene was seductive and deceptive, for soon the boughs broke under the weight of what seemed so light and unlikely a load.

Our credibility with our daughters about the beauties of southern snows was almost shot. They have never seen deep snows such as we claim to have fought to trudge to schoolhouses miles away. They doubted, with reason, such snows ever existed. We had even begun to have our own doubts. A little doubt is a healthy thing, but if too many years pass without deliverance on promises of dismissed school, snowballs, ice castles, and snow cream, one is justified in suspecting snow is a figment of the flaky imaginations of aging elders.

Descriptions of being snowbound for weeks in 1951 had become tiresome to our youngsters. They put those stories in a category with tales we read them at bedtime—stories of gingerbread houses, hens laying golden eggs, and troll bridges. They listened to us, and the weathermen, with the ears of skeptics, as if predictions of snow are like the magical expectations of tooth fairies, Santa Claus, the Easter Bunny, or Godot. The sleds we bought them years ago have hung on dusty basement pegs, red runners rusting like Little Boy Blue's toy soldier. Reading Emerson's "The Snowstorm" or Frost's "Stopping by Woods on a Snowy Evening" made no more sense to them than singing about "those old cotton fields back home." They don't miss the snows because, like hotdog roasts and neighborhood kick-the-can evenings, they never knew them. "Camping out" for them is a night in a Holiday Inn or in sleeping bags on the den floor. Seeing is believing, and they have led sheltered lives. Nature doesn't impinge upon and inspire today's young as it did our generation and earlier ones. We swaddle our young in cellophane and wrap them in air-conditioning and central heating, shuffling them quickly between house door and car door and school door, insuring them against termites and mice, and letting their view of nature come from Jacques Cousteau, *National Geographic,* and the *World Book.*

Pecans teach the same lesson as snow. Last September, I got greenish-yellow stains on my thumbs showing our youngest daughter how the green ovals falling from our pecan trees contain brown pecan shells like those she sees in cellophane bags around our place at Christmas. Inside the shells I showed her the whole pecan halves like the ones she eats on pecan pies. She was impressed by my knowledge. The stains also remind me that among the hundred catalogs we got in the mail was one for Alabama pecans, already shelled, roasted, and salted. (We are on every mailing list in the world, I think. Take away catalogs and ninety percent of the mail carriers of the nation would be unemployed.) It suddenly struck me again, as had the lack of snow, that I have sadly neglected her education. We have seen to it that she is exposed to good teachers and good books and cultural events and violas. But it never occurred to me that she would think, at age eleven, that the natural state of pecans is in a bag or box or on a grocery shelf. I assumed that she would learn better by watching the chipmunks on the Disney Channel, I guess. Or perhaps I assumed, since she has been a Brownie and a Girl Scout for several years now, that Scouts would teach her about pecans and nature in some form other than the pecan crunchy cookies she peddles each year.

The fate of each generation is to marvel at the generation that follows it. I sit in awe of the young who worry about acne as we did but who sit unblinkingly at a computer terminal or who fine-tune a stereo cassette player and understand the words that rock singers spew forth. It is both comforting and disconcerting to find something that I know that our youngster doesn't. If she doesn't know where pecans come from, what else have I neglected in her education? Does she know what a tack hammer is? Unless she has to crack open pecans, maybe she'll never need to know that. Has she ever seen a nutpick? Do we even have one around so that I can show her how to use it? And while looking for the nutpick, where are the other learning machines of my own youth? Where is the old orange juicer, with the crank on the side? Will our daughter ever have the chance—or need—to squeeze an orange?

Outside, two tall pines out back have uprooted and fallen down, happily missing the car and the power lines. Out front, the top of the giant magnolia has broken and hangs down like a six-year-old's front tooth just before it gets one final yank. All across the city, roads are blocked and landscapes wrecked by the trees that have fallen under the assault of a snowfall. Worst of all, large limbs have snapped from our three pecan trees. We asked only for something simple and scenic, some spiceful import to cover for but a little while the browned kudzu (itself an import) that covers the red sands. But simplicity is deceptive. The spiceful is spiteful. The cheap fix is not cheap, and simple solutions to monotony dissolve in costly chaos. The white blanket soon grays. The trees that have stood beside us day after day fall before the sudden snows we wished upon them.

What else should we have expected of a bad-weather friend? How much hidden cost is in this snow we welcomed with open arms and now wish on its way? My warm welcome of the snow is beginning to chill. Two things I love, a good snow and my trees, are at war with each other. The invited winter visitor from the North has become an invader, carpetbag in hand. Hospitality is turning into hostility. Like an Arab sheik in flowing white robes, the snow has made me a hewer of firewood, a shoveler of drives, a foot-trudger of immobilized roads to distant food markets, a slave of the snow.

The blessing behind the curse is that our children have now at last seen snow. City-reared young'uns see things with different eyes, and my eyes are being opened by what they see—and miss seeing. It's unnatural. How can they learn the universal language of youth, of "doing what comes naturally," guarded as they are from the natural?

Our children need to know personally some horse other than Mr. Ed, some bird other than Big Bird. They need their absentee mother, Mother Nature, in order to find out why it isn't nice to fool her.

They need to know snow doesn't come from an aerosol can or pecans from a mail-order house, and we need to see what an unnatural world we are building around them.

March 6 and October 6, 1986, and February 21, 1987

BIRDS

In my time, I have seen roosters chasing dogs and geese chasing humans, flapping and squawking across a yard like noisy hovercraft. Last week, I saw a blue jay chase a squirrel, and I found doves on my car top.

Few people looking down a gun barrel will pull the trigger if they pause to look a dove in the eye. There is a vacantness there that bespeaks innocence.

Other birds have their own winsome attributes: the red head atop the black and white speckles of the woodpecker, the crest and color of the cardinal, the green head of the mallard, and even the cheerleader blue-and-white uniform of the jay. The more we watch the birds who have adopted us the more we understand the temptation to transfer family feelings to creatures of nature. They have the virtues of innocents, and their songs and antics are sales pitches for simplicity and naturalness. They are messengers from a world we see too little of and recall fondly. They are umbilical cords to an unasphalted past and prophecies of what an Edenic life beyond may be like.

I was cleaning out the birdfeeder this week, getting it ready for another fast-food winter for our little flock. Out in the yard the doves and quail have already begun coting and coveying, and we covet their visits. We even have a "See Rock City" birdhouse for some of them.

I was thinking of the biblical line about "not a sparrow falleth." Was that meant as an analogy, in which each human being is considered precious? Or was it meant literally, without any reference to humans, simply "for the birds?"

Alfred Hitchcock showed us another side of birds in that old movie where hordes of them descend upon the people of a town. Every time I see it, it reminds me of an older movie about Brigham Young in which clouds of locusts cover the Mormon settlement in Utah until seagulls arrive and save the day. Sometimes flocks are a curse; sometimes they are blessings.

A country preacher in Tennessee recently reminded me of the year the starlings came to Tennessee. They came by the thousands and stripped the trees and land, driving out the other birds from the cornfields and the feeders. Experts tried to drive them away with shotguns, then music and noise, and finally with chemical sprays that would take away their flight and expose them to freezing weather.

He was making a point—an analogy—about human beings. His point was that we appreciate other people if we know them one by one, like the visiting cardinal and the small cote of doves, but that our view of people changes when they come in masses and have no names or differences. That's when people start saying "they all look alike" and figuring ways to avoid them or to get rid of them. The real point of my preacher friend's parable, I think, was that we have not yet faced up to the hardships modern living presses upon us. There are more people than ever in the world, and in America more of us than ever have to live in flocks in cities and towns.

Underneath a teeming mall today is an old country store. Underneath the mass of starlings is the single sparrow and the little birdfeeder. The human dilemma is how to live in both worlds—the personable world of the first part of this century and the mass and mobile world of the latter quarter of the same century.

The solution to the dilemma has not yet appeared. I suspect, until it does, we had best be about doing our old business of looking after each other one on one.

One of my favorite tearjerker movie scenes is from *Mary Poppins.* In the middle of the movie, an elderly charwoman, played by the veteran actress

Jane Darwell in her old age (she played the stoic mother in *Grapes of Wrath*), sits alone on the steps in the midst of a public square, scattering bread crumbs while Julie Andrews's voice is heard singing, "Feed the Birds." In her poverty, Miss Darwell collects pennies from the sale of the crumbs. As the song ends and the camera moves up and away from her, she becomes a dot in the midst of marble banks and offices and government buildings.

The effect of that scene is as strong as hearing Mahalia Jackson sing "His Eye Is on the Sparrow." It warns us that the institutions we build in order to tend to the work of the public square very often evolve and expand into layered bureaucracies which misplace their statements of original purpose. If we forget the birds, soon we will forget each other. We may feed only the faceless economy or our egos instead.

We need our institutions, of course. They are our own birdhouses and feeders, our networks to one another and our systems of communication. We cannot do without them, so we create them. The trick is in keeping them from becoming ends unto themselves, cut off from their original purposes.

We have had in our yard for several years now a pair of cardinals, a pair of redheaded woodpeckers, a family of wrens, several doves, a pair of jays, some mockingbirds, and a pair of thrushes—not to mention the pair of rabbits, the dozen squirrels, and the half-dozen chipmunks. It is impossible for these to be the same creatures year after year, and so they must be the children and grandchildren of those here before.

We notice that the birds never nest in last year's nests. Sometimes they use twigs and debris from the old nests, but they use them to make new ones. Even the wrens in the wrenhouse remove last year's bedding and build anew. So here, in microcosm and in the city, our birds teach us about the annual cycles of nature's renewal. Theirs is a lesson we and our institutions need to copy and to learn: the importance of being clear about the purposes of our institutions and of our selves, and the need we have for renewal of them and of our selves.

Once I held a hummingbird on the palm of my hand. To hold a hummingbird! I knew then what poet William Blake meant two hundred years ago: "To see a World in a Grain of Sand / And Heaven in a Wild Flower, / Hold Infinity in the palm of your hand / And Eternity in an hour." I thought it was dead; but it lay warm in my hand and I thought I felt a beat from its oh-so-tiny heart. It had knocked itself unconscious against the plate-glass window of our sun porch.

It suddenly awoke and arose, straight up like a helicopter, then hovered and switched from vertical to horizontal warp-speed in a ninety-degree angle—and was gone.

But not really gone.

No one who has held a hummingbird is ever the same. I held on to it forever by releasing it. It hovers in my memory. The blue jay squawking after the squirrel jogs that memory of the moment eternity lay in my hand. In turn, that memory calls me to a revival of purpose and renewal of form for myself, for my family, and for the institutions we help build and sustain.

In the Septembers of our lives and of each year, what more could we ask than this privilege of rediscovering purpose and recommitting to renewal?

Keep your birdfeed dry and your birdhouses dry. Don't let the starlings startle you away.

October 20, 1986, and August 27, 1990

FLOODS

In Augusta, Georgia, March flooding left a woman homeless for the second time in two years. In Elba, Alabama, a man lost his home for the fourth time. Having learned a lesson, he has decided not to rebuild there. In California, multimillion-dollar mansions slipped off the bluff overlooking the ocean, and hundreds of other homes were condemned; El Niño ate away their safety-net back yards. Some of the evacuated residents vow to rebuild there.

The ground on our own South Carolina hillside is so soaked from March rains that each new rain just runs on off to the creek at the foot of the hill. Heavy manhole lids in streets are pushed up and over by geysers of rushing water.

Growing up in west Tennessee, we heard stories of floods but never saw one. FDR and TVA protected us with series of river locks and dams. But we know how the Mississippi running backward in the great New Madrid earthquake created Reelfoot Lake in 1812, and we knew personally many veterans and refugees of the great floods of 1927 and 1937.

Water is strange. Our lives depend on it. Shortages of water drive people insane, or disease them, or cause wars, or kill them through dehydration. The greatest argument for the theory that we came from the sea millions of years ago is that, while we are land-living, we are water-requiring.

But there is, as the cracker-barrel philosophers would say, "such a thing as too much of a good thing." John M. Barry didn't know how many floods there would be in the year he published a best-selling book, *Rising Tide* (Simon and Schuster). It's a long and intriguing account of the flooding of the Mississippi in 1927, and in it Barry makes a convincing case that that flood changed history.

The Mississippi River is the great aorta of North America. What water doesn't drain east from Appalachia into the Atlantic or west from the Rockies into the Pacific, drains inwardly to the Mississippi, creating a river "valley 20 percent larger than that of China's Yellow River, double that of Africa's Nile and India's Ganges, fifteen times that of Europe's Rhine." And 41 percent of the continental United States, with all or parts of 31 of 48 states, lies in the valley. It is the longest river in the world, and only the Amazon and the Congo have larger drainage basins.

Five years ago, despite the dams and levees, the Mississippi flooded. At its peak, below St. Louis, the 1993 flood carried one million cubic feet of water per second. In 1927, the flood peaked at *three million* cubic feet a second. It spread across the riverbank farms and towns thirty feet deep. For months, the Red Cross housed and fed seven hundred thousand evacuees of the 1927 disaster.

In the wake of the Great Mississippi Flood of 1927 came transformations to our nation. This is a great cause-and-effects saga.

It accelerated the exodus of black people (857,000 in the 1920s alone) from the South to the northern industrial centers. With millions of lives affected, New Orleans' banks failed, contributing to the Depression the nation was about to enter. New Orleans decayed as one of the nation's major cities. The 1927 flood changed the old-line aristocracy of the Delta in Mississippi and New Orleans. It marshaled science and engineering resources in ways that would set the pattern for the atomic energy and space exploration teams later in the century. It created lakes and tourist centers far from the Mississippi banks. It affected the outcome of presidential elections, causing first Herbert Hoover and then Franklin Roosevelt to win the highest office. It created the New Deal and TVA. It enshrined Huey Long as governor of Louisiana. It stimulated blues music, virtually synonymous with the roll of the river.

But if the 1927 flood was the worst, there have been some others not far behind it.

Sifting through my mother-in-law's photos and folders and feeling like intruders in the dust of a dead person's personal memories, among the frozen glimpses of her own childhood and those of her children and grand-children, we found a picture of downtown Louisville during the Flood of '37. It had been taken a half-century earlier when Grandmother, widowed and struggling to keep herself and three young children afloat in the Depression, was working for the *Louisville Courier-Journal*. We heard her describe the '37 flood often, usually at family gatherings where other older kinfolk from western Kentucky and southern Indiana added their own eyewitness accounts to hers. My own side of the family down in west Tennessee had their own stories of this biggest event in their lives. I was eight months old when it happened, but heard it described so often that it now seems to be the first thing in my memory.

In the years that followed, the '37 flood assumed larger-than-life pro-portions for me as I crossed the bridges and dams of TVA and traced the lines from the river's power plants that crisscross the South like the netting of the minnow seines we once used in creeks that fed that same river.

The '37 flood, like the '27 flood before it, was a watershed event for the South, a moment when the South changed and began the long process of urbanizing and industrializing that has made it something quite dis-tinctly different from what it was a half century ago. And having been there, in its beginning, this event has marked my own life's course uncon-sciously and comprehensively. The uncovered photo uncovered a great deal.

The facts of the '37 flood are a matter of record. On January 1, the Tennessee and Cumberland Rivers were already flooding, causing the Ohio and Mississippi to reach their bank tops. Then the real rains came for twelve days beginning January 13, and soon 165 billion tons of water were dumped in two hundred thousand square miles across 196 counties in twelve states. When it was over, seventy-four thousand homes and build-ings were destroyed or damaged, and nine hundred lives were lost.

I have sometimes wondered if this '37 flood didn't somehow prepare the nation for Pearl Harbor and World War II at a time when Depression and isolationism were pulling the country apart. From Louisiana back up to West Virginia, national guardsmen, the army, the engineers, the navy, the coast guard, civilian boat owners, government officials, power crews, and media people rushed into action, creating order and organizations overnight. In the vanguard was the Red Cross, with its fifty-five thousand workers and volunteers. Most of these people would see similar catastrophies and respond just as selflessly and actively when war came a few years later. Churches and schoolchildren that later would be collecting food and scraps for armed forces rehearsed their roles in this '37 flood. Hundreds of homeowners took in and fed the outcasts.

Great need and great forces drive common people into greatness. Ambivalence and ambiguities get lost in big causes, but causes, like floods, rise only to ebb, and normalcy returns. The sociologists and observers of the modern era claim we live in disjointed, unique, and chaotic times, but the truth is that for decades ours has been a nation of normalcy. Few events since World War II have mobilized the spirit and the energy of the people. Not even the shattering effects of the economy have pulled us together, and the civil rights cause and Vietnam polarized as much as they galvanized.

What the '37 flood washed up and what World War II kept visible was man's vulnerability. There are few places mankind can hide from reality. The waters of nature and the winds of war exempt no one, even those far removed from the floodplains and war fields. Our noblest moments come, as the scriptures affirm, when we momentarily put ourselves last and others first. But these are unnatural moments for us all, and the great unanswered question of civilization is how to make natural and sustained what is abnormal and fleeting—caring for and feeding strangers materially and spiritually in times of "business as usual."

The Floods of 1927 and 1937 and 1993 send us the same message: a warning to humans not to think too highly of their skills. Man-made levees do not hold forever. New river channels and dams do not either. Hidden from the landscape in our cities and automobiles, without a tin roof above us tattooing Nature's coded message to us, we may think that human nature is more powerful that Nature itself. But that is self-deception. Nature's invisibility does not give us human invincibility. And now, the waters of 1998 descend. Raindrops are messages from heaven. Listen to the raindrops.

February 14, 1987, and March 16, 1998

HEAT

This summer has been so hot that the popcorn in the fields has been popping off its ears into its shucks. Week after week the temperature has remained above 95 degrees, and the sunny South has turned into a micro-wave oven. In summer heat, we notice few changes between youngsters today and those of our own era. Boys are wearing crew cuts, and some have peroxided their hair or have gotten Mohawks or even shaved their heads entirely, just as did their fathers before them. Girls seem less pudgy and their swim costumes more scanty than in our day, but perhaps that's just an illusion.

One big difference is that none of the youngsters at the local pool seem to have that awful purple dye dabbed all over them that our mothers used to protect our mosquito and chigger bites from infection. It was something called "gentian violet," and we were convinced that they bought it from Doc Bomar, the local veterinarian. Another difference is that these modern pools have concrete block walls between the dressing rooms where ours had knothole pine.

Somewhere in this town of fifty thousand souls where we now live, there must be an icehouse—but who knows where? Back in our young days, the icehouse was as packed with customers and loafers as the August tent revival was with sinners. In galvanized washtubs filled with hunks of ice, we picked apart fifty-pound cubes, we iced down twelve-ounce, five-cent "knee-highs," iced down legitimately purchased twenty-five-cent watermelons (the stolen ones couldn't be brought home), iced down candy bars, and even iced down our feet, while we sucked greedily on ice slivers and icicles.

We loaded ice into hand-cranked wooden ice-cream freezers and fought to sit on the damp burlap on the cold metal across the top of the bucket, the best seat in the house. These "cool kids" today don't know what cool is. We were born with antennae for breezes and relief from the heat— damp concrete basements, air-conditioned movie theaters, dogtrots out in the country farmhouses. And after the First Baptist Church installed central air, we all converted—every summer. How could we resist that BYPU's one-two punch—central air on Sundays and the best hayrides in the fall?

In our more youthful days, we would have welcomed this heat. We would have piled into cars and headed for the Tennessee River to bask like hippopotamuses (or hippopotami?) in the flowing waters. Probably the waters are too low and slow to do that now, in the midst of this drought that has stopped Mississippi River boat traffic.

And, besides, the old gang is really old now and scattered too far from the river to take advantage of it. In that aging group somewhere are a Methodist minister who at age forty was arrested by the Coast Guard for returning to his youth by skinny-dipping in weather such as this, and a Baptist minister who at age twelve lost his trunks and had to make his way pantless over a mile from the river to the cabin a half dozen of us had for a hot Monday. There are also a few notorious watermelon thieves, probably unreformed criminals, wishing they could take the same risks now.

It's less taxing to let our memories stir instead of our bodies in such humidity as these last months have brought; the heat warms up some good ones. In hot times like this we easily understand and appreciate why Mark Twain's thoughts drifted back so often to his own river—and his own youth.

David Brinkley blames the nation's problems on air-conditioning. If you are over forty, you know what he means. He thinks air-conditioning has enabled Congress to stay in session year-round and that the more government there is, the more troubles we have.

Air-conditioning has other consequences as well. For one thing, it has changed the clothing business. Summer suits and dresses used to be very light and absorbent. Now, the only heat we feel is in the gauntlet we run between a cool car and a cool house or a cool office. You can now wear the same clothes year-round.

Air-conditioning also affects food. Summer was once a good time for salads, cottage cheese, ice cream, and other light snacks. Now our menus are less seasonal, and if you can't stand the heat in the kitchen, you air-condition it. This shows in the nation's waistlines. Bears lost weight in the winter, but we used to shed ours in the summer. Now, year-round eating leaves rings around the stomach.

Two things in particular that air-conditioning has frozen out, to our loss, are ice-cream suppers and picnics. Recently I went shopping for an old-fashioned wooden ice-cream freezer, complete with hand crank. They don't seem to exist anywhere except in antique shops, next to the lost washboards and wooden croquet sets of yesteryear. People may be eating more ice cream than ever before, but they are eating it year-round instead of in the heat of summer. Moreover, ice cream is being eaten in isolation. It was intended as a social food, to be shared at marble-top tables in soda-fountain parlors (now extinct) or in back-yard conclaves of kin and friends.

There is something sacrilegious, almost hedonistic, about anyone eating ice cream alone.

Picnics are going, too. Air-conditioning is only partly to blame. It did eliminate flies, ants, and stickiness but, to do so, it had to kill the picnic itself. You see more picnics in the fall now than in the summer. Tailgate picnics at football games are popular, mainly because fall weather resembles summer air-conditioning so much; I wonder if watermelons know there is no such thing anymore as being "out of season."

Fast food restaurants are another reason picnics are dying. One can stay in the air-conditioned car, go through the drive-in window to get the food, and have a small family picnic while the car is still rolling: a movable feast. The faceless voice from the drive-through menu that asks for your order has replaced all those aunts and grandmothers bearing covered dishes.

I can recall the criticisms leveled at a Lexington, Kentucky, church thirty years ago that had a neon sign out front reading "Air-Conditioned." Those who blasted the church for being "too worldly" then know now that it was really being prophetic. It saw a New Jerusalem ahead and moved on before its competitors did. Of course, the sermons lost their fire and brimstone in the process, and religion may have become a little too comfortable.

Maybe we don't need backyard mixing, or dinner on the grounds, or some old finger-pointing sermons anymore. Maybe life somehow is better when the temperature is always the same. Maybe we don't need seasoning at all, or one another either, in the way seasons once brought us together.

On the other hand, it might be fun to cut off all the air conditioners for one designated Sunday every summer month, just to see if we are missing something that our parents had and that we lost somewhere in our youth.

One thing is for sure. Air-conditioning makes it hard to understand Ecclesiastes, where it says, "For everything, there is a season." Not when we stay cool year-round.

June 24, 1985, and September 5, 1988

THREE A.M.

An old song begins, "It's three o'clock in the morning." Another song, "One More for the Road," has Sinatra singing, "It's a quarter to three." The tunes came to mind recently when I went through a spell of waking up just before three every morning, no matter what time I went to bed. My friends assured me it is not an uncommon phenomenon for people my age. The songs about being awake at three in the morning seem to confirm their diagnosis.

Further confirmation came in running across an F. Scott Fitzgerald quote from "The Crack-Up," probably written in the early 1930s. Fitzgerald wrote, "In a real dark night of the soul it is always three o'clock in the morning."

Fitzgerald may have stolen his three o'clock line from Henry David Thoreau's *Walden,* published in 1854 and based on Thoreau's life in the woods from 1845 to 1847. Thoreau wrote, "I am less affected by their heroism who stood up for half an hour at Buena Vista [in the Mexican War], than by the steady and cheerful valor of the men, who inhabit the snowplow for their winter quarters; who have not merely the three-o'clock-in-the-morning courage, which Bonaparte thought was the rarest, but whose courage does not go to rest so early, who go to sleep only when the storm sleeps or the sinews of their iron steed are frozen." Thoreau took his three o'clock phrase from Napoleon and gave him credit for it, something which Fitzgerald didn't. The other part of the Fitzgerald quote—about the "dark night of the soul"—appears in "The Ascent of Mount Carmel," written about 1578–80 by St. John of the Cross.

If we keep tracing this thing back far enough, we may find that people were waking up or lying awake at three in the morning even before there were clocks. Maybe there is some biological hourglass in us that causes it. My friends dismiss it by saying, "The older we get, the less sleep we need." Or perhaps it is the unfamiliar "sound of silence" which wakes us. That's what we notice most at that hour. With the street traffic gone and the television set turned off, the two noises left are the chirping of the tree frogs outside and the exaggerated creaks of the house inside. Another explanation is anticipation. The previous day has ended and an agenda needs to be prepared for the new one soon arriving, and the mind responds accordingly.

The mind has a mind of its own. Mine wakes me automatically at six in any time zone regardless of whether it is standard or daylight saving time. Maybe the more recent three o'clock wake-up call is just a preliminary preparation for six o'clock, like the music that plays on a clock radio for fifteen minutes before the alarm sounds. Or perhaps, as Fitzgerald and Bonaparte hint, three o'clock is soul and courage time. Maybe it is nature's way of reminding us that we get so busy with details during the day that we put off the really big things that require us just to sit, think, and see. When we drop back a bit, we can see where all the miscellaneous parts fit.

That seems to be the best explanation. One morning awakened at three, I took apart a 1930 Ford Model A and then reassembled it piece by piece— all in my head and in my bed. It was something I could actually have done forty years ago. Nowadays, though, I do well to know how to open the hood of my car, and I understand almost nothing about all that stuff packed together under it.

What appear to be logs and logjams in the daylight are parts of a forest at three in the morning. The parts fit into a whole that makes more sense then. And because the whole appears at three, only a few hours before the real awakening and arising, each morning starts out with a clearer perspective that daylight takes all day to burn away. We can "keep our cool" if we have a time to get it—"In the cool, cool, cool of the evening."

We need, for our bodily renewal, our nightly sleep. But we also need, for our mental and spiritual renewal, those three o'clock awakenings.

September 24, 1990

SWEPT YARDS

Recently riding down a once-familiar country road, formerly red gravel but now asphalt, I noticed that the farmhouses that remain are red-bricked. Electricity and phone lines run from the road to them, and they now have bathrooms and running water inside as well. Only about a fourth of the houses of forty years ago still stand. Of all the improvements, the most striking are the lawns. These front yards once were but dirt and dust. One swept them or raked them, but one did not mow them; they had no grass to keep or cut.

Once their owners' grandfathers followed plows and mules down the furrows of surrounding fields, and once their fathers sat astride red or green tractors over the same fields and furrows. Today those heirs who have stuck it out on the family farms sit atop rider mowers, making circles in the lush, thick grass of their front yards. Most of them work in town or are retired, and their fields lie unused or leased to others.

They wear jumpsuits or khakis and caps with cute sayings on them instead of overalls and broad-brimmed straw hats. They still buy seed, but the annual crops they sow now are fescue, rye, Bermuda, or zoysia. Forty acres have shrunk to forty yards, and irrigation systems have been replaced by sprinklers on hoses from house faucets. Here and there a few keep white boxes of bees in rows along the edge of fields which once knew sorghum cane and molasses mills. In the midst of such changes hailed as Progress, the littlest things are missed the most.

When those grass-carpeted lawns were dirt, they were trod by flocks of chickens, clucking and pecking their way endlessly toward becoming centerpieces for daily noonday feasts and Sunday visits from the preacher. The yards swarmed, too, with green flies, buzzing and biting. An ambitious soul could sit on the plank porch, tilted back in a cane-bottomed chair against a porch post or the board siding of the house, and spray the flies closest at hand, pretending to be an anti-aircraft artillerist defending an island from squads of Japanese Zeros. Sometimes cousins, each armed with his own Gulf spray gun, would keep score of how many they felled. No matter what the body count, they kept on coming.

The same saga was repeated inside with the mosquitoes. They, too, are gone now. When last did we see more than one green fly or hear the buzz of more than one "skeeter?"

When the men came in from the fields or the children in from play, their overalls were festooned with "beggar's lice," rows of them that matched the rows of "granny-beads" of dirt in the rolls around their necks. Where are the beggar's lice and granny-beads of yesteryear?

Those were the days when one knew the blackberries were ripe because the chiggers were biting. Little red bugs bit deep, embedding themselves under the skin. In chigger season, one washed with coal oil, normally kept for the lanterns and lamps of the house. Some sophisticates tried to suffocate them by painting them with fingernail polish. Chiggers and scratches were the price one paid for picking blackberries. They were that day's retelling of the price Adam and Eve paid for the apple in their Garden. Where have all the chiggers gone?

Wasps were another feature of those farmhouses. One marveled at their industriousness and architectural skills, wondering as they built nests that a chambered nautilus would envy, what function they performed for the world. The only one that came to mind was that they kept many people from spending too much time in the outdoor privy. No outhouse was complete without a wasps' nest—and a catalog.

Those residual farmhouses still have porches, but no one sits on them except retired couples watching the workers from town driving past at day's end. The farmhouses still have yards, but they are covered with green carpets of grass that remind one of what undertakers roll out for graveside services. The food in the few farmhouses left is still good, but the families are smaller and the feasts less frequent, and usually the food comes from the electric freezer instead of from the fields.

Others look back to "days of wine and roses," but what can compare with days of beggar's lice and granny-beads, chiggers and wasps? Where have all the green flies flown?

The farmhouse yards have been swept clean—but not as in yore.

October 15, 1990

MACHINERY

A button on the dashboard of my car switches the speedometer gauge from miles-per-hour to kilometers-per-hour. I might use it to fool my heavy-footed wife into thinking she is doing sixty when we are actually going a safer forty, but the odds are minimal that I will ever use it for anything except as a toy. The only place it might be useful would be if I drove the car around Europe. In the struggle to regain lost customers, new-model cars are offering extra, added attractions such as this. Nor are they alone in gadgetry seducing. This "kph" button is a symbol of how we define most progress and success in technological terms. Almost daily we get something in the mail from computer-program companies, offering some new disk we, allegedly, "simply can't do without." One company offers us an annual contract for someone to come by and check our computers for viruses.

Just for fun this year, while sorting through my cardboard box of 1990s receipts for our IRS return, I stacked receipts for machines next to that for medical bills. We spent more last year buying, servicing, warranting, insuring, and repairing our machines than we did for doctors, dentists, optometrists, prescriptions, and other personal family health care combined. One reason the average family size has spiraled down from eight at the end of the nineteenth century to six at the end of World War II to four today is that we have so many machines to tend to. What an average American household spends on its machines each year is equivalent to the cost of rearing two children or to hiring a full-time live-in handyman and maid.

From A to W, from air conditioners to water heaters, machines are replacements for sons and daughters, even for dogs and cats. They even replace husbands and wives, judging from the census figures on unwed single-person families.

Like children and pets, our machines have to be cared for and fed, require enormous personal attention, and are temperamental. They can balk, and they can talk back. Even as we speak (or squeak), there are revolutions ignited by gadget envy ablaze in many of the nations of the world. America is admired for its technological abundance and hated for it at the same time. The rest of the world wants what we have. Some nations are so desperate that they are even willing to forego our sophisticated missiles and planes if they can only get our televisions and our boom boxes.

Oh, friends! Do not be so eager in envy to rush headlong toward that cliff's precipice! Pause and reflect! Our machines are not always the servants to us they are touted to be. They have an invidious way of becoming our families. In exchange for their promises and flattery, we become responsible for their maintenance more than they for ours. They lull us into the elitism of thinking that any problem can be solved with newer technology and into the democracy of thinking that anyone can afford such technology. We awaken to find ourselves the servants of our mechanized servants, living in debtors' prisons made of our plastic credit cards.

What option do we have? How could we do or be otherwise? We buy because we are bombarded into buying from all sides with artistry in multimedia advertising, with the pressure of peers and family, and with our own self-imposed appetites and awe. If we do not buy, the national economy nosedives. The unemployed from manufacturers we failed to support fill the streets, welfare costs rise and taxes rise to pay them, and we spend in taxes for others what we could have spent for machines for ourselves. What power we hold as consumers! We are the nail the horseshoe needs to fit the horse, which bears the king, who saves the kingdom! What frightening power is ours as consumers! The best way to help the poor is to buy more things for ourselves. Austerity is an Abominable Snowman.

And what frightening responsibility such frightening power places upon us! Fail to buy, and guilt tramples us into the dust of despair. We will have let our families and nation down. We will be called selfish. We will have neglected our public duty and tarnished our citizenship. The system depends on our consuming, not on our savings.

March 25, 1991

MIGRATIONS

Our hummingbirds have left for the winter, headed south for their annual flight across the Gulf of Mexico. They arrive in late May and stay until early September, and we are sad to find them gone. They have feasted from the feeders off our back porch all summer. Their daily aerial antics and air shows have made the jet fighters of *Top Gun* and Desert Storm look primitive.

Hummingbirds are slightly over three inches long. Their muscles comprise 25 to 30 percent of their weight. They flap their wings at a rate of 2,000 to 3,000 times a minute, completely turning them over in a figure-eight pattern that allows them to both hover and make sharp angular turns and move vertically or horizontally with ease. Their lungs expand 250 times a minute when resting, and their hearts beat 1,260 times a minute when active; they use ten times the energy of a human running nine miles an hour.

If you weighed 170 pounds and were a hummingbird, you would burn 155,000 calories a day and evaporate 100 pounds of perspiration an hour. If you ran out of body water, your skin would reach the melting point for lead. You would spontaneously combust. (A well-known grocery-store tabloid has a monthly story about some humans spontaneously igniting and exploding without known cause.)

It will take our hummingbirds 2.1 grams of food to cross the 600 miles of the Gulf, nonstop.

Their aerial agility, daintiness, and energy are great mysteries to us, but even more mysterious are their migrations. How do they know when to leave and when to return? How do they know where they are going and where to return? Experts think the length of the days has something to do with the built-in calendars of hummingbirds, but they aren't sure. They speculate that temperature changes and food supply cycles also affect them. Experts also explain that hummingbirds, like ducks and geese, get their directions to and from by following the four great "flyways" of North America. But what are these flyways? Who or what put them there? Who can see or feel or smell them? How are they marked? One can better understand the annual treks of the caribou, along long-worn paths through familiar landmarks, than explain the inexplicable travel patterns of the swallows of Capistrano and the hummingbirds of the Southeast.

The flights of butterflies from here to South America are just as awesome as those of hummingbirds. The winter and spring Vs of waterfowl are also majestic, especially when silhouetted against a full moon, each convoy honking at us at it passes. The lazy bears of the mountains, of course, migrate no further than their hibernation caves, and the squirrels curl up for the winter in hollow trees in hill hollows.

Here on the Carolina edge of the Smoky Mountains we see migrants of all sorts; not all are birds and animals. Each spring through fall, the mountains teem with human migrants. The number of residents of Florida who have dual citizenship in the Carolina hills is astonishing. These human migrants are almost as interesting to watch as hummingbirds or geese. They move with almost the same meticulous allegiance to calendars as do salmon or moose. Is there some hidden genetic link between migrant birds, animals, fish, and humans about which we know little or nothing?

Lemmings make a one-way migration; they run to the sea and drown. Some fish throw themselves from the sea up onto the shores and asphyxiate themselves. A few aged or ailing Eskimos still park themselves on breaking ice and float southward as it melts. Those one-way migrations are amazing mysteries of mobility in themselves, but they cannot compare for suspense and awe with the entertaining round-trip treks of hummingbirds and mountain Floridians, boundless in energy but predictable in timing, always knowing when they are coming and going and where they want to be.

We watch for them as much as we do the spring jonquils, fall's falling leaves, and snow on Christmas Day. In the certainty of their moving, they reassure us. Our humanity can sense, but has yet to be able to explain, the Prime Mover behind, beneath, and before us all.

October 14, 1991

ANIMAL LANGUAGE

Legend has it that on Christmas Eve the animals can talk. It is a sweet idea but one which demonstrates quite a bit of human chauvinism. The implication of the legend is that humans are superior to their fellow animals because they have the power of speech. Thus, the miracle of Christmas Eve is that our inferiors are temporarily granted some approximation of our exalted status.

The truth is that our talk about being superior to other animals masks our own insecurity, our fear that we may actually be the inferiors. Wealth and position—and token acts of kindness they make possible—are edges we invent to try to set us apart from and above others who may actually be our peers or our betters. Consider the birds of the air and the beasts of the fields. In their own patterns of evolution, they have endless grace and abilities, instincts and beauty that we lack and cannot help but envy.

Animals hear and make sounds we cannot; they survive in places and on foods we cannot; they fly and run with speeds we cannot; they do without the health care and machines we cannot; they have an orderliness and energy we cannot; and they adapt to nature's "cultural diversity" by sharing space and resources we cannot.

Perhaps, as William Faulkner said in his Nobel acceptance speech, the purpose of man's puny voice is to reassure himself that he exists. Perhaps other animals are so superior to us that they have no need of our language. Perhaps instead of our condescending on Christmas Eve to let them elevate themselves to our level by speaking, it is they who are condescending by lowering themselves to our primitive and inferior levels to speak in our language. Perhaps they feel we say little worth hearing and discussing.

Their patterned predictability probably misleads us into thinking other animals are peons to man. Their mating, nesting, feeding, and migration habits are so routinized that they are like factory and office workers punching time clocks. But what that really says is that we also categorize blue-collar workers and unemployed fellow humans as lower-life forms of other animals and, hence, as "inferiors."

This condescension of superior humans toward inferiors can be found elsewhere at Christmas than in the legend of the animals talking. It was at the heart of the crass Scrooge's resentment of clerk Bob Cratchit for having Christmas Day off. In pre–Civil War times, it was implicit in the tradition of giving the slaves Christmas Day off from work. It still permeates our philanthropy, for we are more solicitous, usually only temporarily so, of children, the hungry, the homeless, and employees at Christmastime. Christmas is too often a time when human animals speak to their inferiors. For the rest of the year it is considered natural *not* to do so and unbecoming *to* do so.

Does being poor or "beneath" someone in an organization chart or in social status really have to mean being inferior? (If the animals do talk on Christmas Eve, then that would be a good topic to chew one's cud over or to bleat about.) Is mankind all that it is quacked up to be?

Jesus, whose birthday Christmas celebrates, spoke to us through animals: through the lost one hundredth lamb, through the tiniest fallen sparrow, through fishes of the sea, through the camel in the needle's eye, and through the donkeys that carried him to Bethlehem to be born and to Jerusalem to die. The idea of animals talking together in the same language on Christmas Eve has in it echoes of Pentecost, when the wind rushed in and people of many languages suddenly spoke and understood as one. Maybe what the animals talk about amongst themselves in their Christmas Eve forums is we humans—about how, like lost sheep, we have gone astray, wandering, with time and distance taking us farther and farther from the Bethlehem manger and its livestock. We have fled from them into Egypt and seem unable to find our way out.

And in their pity for us, their nomadic inferiors, perhaps the animals annually resolve to continue giving us their songs, the beauty of their feathers and furs, their aerobatic and submarine shows, their meat, eggs, honey, butter, cheese, and milk for our tables, and the fossil fuels of their ancestors' bones for energy. Perhaps they find some hope for us in that so few of us now depend upon them for transportation, although they still condescend to carry us in other ways.

The gift of Christmas is the animals' infinite patience with us. Maybe patience is a high form of animal love.

December 23, 1991

THE MISSISSIPPI

It had been several years since I had seen "The River," but last week I returned to it. "The River," of course, is the Mississippi. I grew up near it, although closer to the Tennessee and Cumberland Rivers, which are but primitive country lanes compared with the wide thoroughfare of the Mississippi. With grandparents in Memphis, I saw the Mississippi often enough to respect it. Having seen it, once I learned to read, I could appreciate Mark Twain in ways others could not.

It is still as muddy, sweeping, and shifty as it always was. For something that is never the same from minute to minute or from year to year, it gives the appearance of never changing. Heraclitus built a philosophy on such a river as this: "You can't step in the same river twice." Life along its banks has changed even as the river seems constant. There are new industries, new churches, new families with nonsouthern names, new skyscrapers, and even a basketball arena under a gigantic life-sized pyramid.

Back behind the banks, there are larger but fewer farm fields and more paved arteries, but there still remains plenty of empty space and open sky and plain folks. Alex Haley, another author who has bought attention to that region—as Twain did up on the Missouri side and Walker Percy did down nearer New Orleans—was laid to rest recently back behind the Mississippi banks in the little town of Henning, whose name the world now knows because of *Roots*.

Our daughter, during her vacation days in June looking for her mother's ancestors out in Montana, went rafting on a river at Jackson Hole. I envy her the experience. My own unfulfilled dream is to ride the Mississippi; I've crossed it and sat on its banks many times but have never gotten to ride it. Years ago while in New Orleans, my wife and I got to board the *Delta Queen,* an old-fashioned classical riverboat. It was docked near the French Market and was giving a free calliope concert. Ever since, I've wanted to cruise on it—either upriver or down, I'm not particular.

Now the *Delta Queen* has a new (and bigger) sister, the *American Queen*. Recently christened (with a bottle of Tabasco), it offers a variety of cruises, ranging from three to sixteen days, mostly on the Mississippi, but some on the Ohio and Tennessee Rivers as well. To ride leisurely down from Cincinnati past Louisville, St. Louis, Memphis, and Vicksburg, with chandeliers blazing and calliope blasting, to cap off this century's end with a salute to the one before, the one which gave it birth, would be an experience.

Steaming on the Mississippi may not seem as dangerous as rafting on western whitewaters, but don't be deceived. On its inaugural trip the *American Queen* ran aground on a sandbar. The bottom of that river is floored with wrecks from last century's boats that suffered worst fates. The worst maritime disaster in America history was the sinking of the *Sultana* on April 27, 1865, a northern charter boat returning freed Yankee prisoners to their homes. Conservative estimates counted about eighteen hundred dead. Others believe that over two thousand men died on the Arkansas side of the river just above Memphis. The river teems with stories of tragedy or near tragedy.

In May of 1825, the famous French general Lafayette was nearing the end of his year-long, glorious return tour of the country he helped found fifty years earlier. A grateful nation greeted him everywhere he went. He came up the Mississippi to St. Louis, turned up the Ohio, then went down the Cumberland to Nashville to visit Andrew Jackson, came back up to the Ohio, and was headed toward Louisville on the steamboat *Mechanic*. With him were his son, his secretary, and a manservant. Tennessee's governor Carroll was along for that leg of the journey. About ten o'clock that evening, Lafayette went to bed. Just after midnight, the boat shook violently and then stopped. At first it was assumed the boat had hit a sandbar, but then it turned out it had struck a snag and was sinking rapidly. Lafayette was awakened and hurried to a lifeboat but refused to leave without a snuffbox given him personally years before by George Washington. The secretary retrieved it, and Lafayette was finally placed in the lifeboat. He and its occupants were rowed to a wooded shore where he discovered his son was missing. The French servant was found clinging to the cabin roof, and the son turned up later, after first checking to see that everyone else was safely off of the steamboat. Governor Carroll waded out into the river to grab a mattress floating by and persuaded Lafayette to rest on it. Other survivors salvaged food. Concerned about the location, Lafayette was rowed across the river, but as the lifeboat crossed, lights from two rescue ships, the *Paragon* and the *Highland Laddie,* appeared, coming from Louisville. The fifty marooned passengers boarded the *Paragon* and continued to Louisville. Lafayette lost his carriage, his luggage, and a pile of correspondence, but he retained his dignity, courage, and good manners. The story of his adventure endeared him even more in the hearts of those many Americans who already revered him.

Cruising the Mississippi is every bit as hazardous as rafting the whitewaters. However, I have been prepared for some time to run the risk. No lack of courage has prevented me from making the pilgrimage. Only a lack of wherewithal stands in my way. Riding the waves on the *American Queen* does cost a wee bit more than rafting in Wyoming. Prices range from $141 to $646 a night, tips not included. A full sixteen-day trip could cost a couple somewhere between $5,000 and $21,000. I wonder what they would charge to tow me if I just rented a rowboat and tied up to one of the railings? Maybe by hitchhiking that way, I could save enough for that cross-country train trip I'm also saving up for.

There is a naval base at Millington, north of Memphis, hundreds of miles from oceans. It used to strike us as strange to see sailors in whites and naval officers in blues in Memphis, so far from carriers and battleships. To easterners unfamiliar with what lies west of it, the Mississippi is an ocean. America has always been two nations, separated by the Mississippi Ocean. East and west separations came more naturally, and have lasted longer than the artificial north and south ones. Yankees and southerners have had to work hard to be different from each other; with easterners and westerners it has been a native instinct. It is easier for easterners to cross the Canadian border than to cross the Mississippi. Most easterners get as far as the eastern Mississippi River shore, see its analogy with Jordan's swelling tide, and then turn back like Hebrews reluctant to cross. They had to give away free land and gold mines to get folks to go across in settlement days. The Mississippi was more of a barrier westward than it was a gateway.

But flowing southward, the river was another matter all together. America almost went to war several times over it. Even when America had no navy at all and an army of only about seven thousand soldiers, it was ready to take on Spain or England or France for the rights to the river. The Mississippi dragged the rich topsoil and produce of the north southward. It became a symbol of southern power and aspirations. In the Civil War, northern victory as far back east as Virginia came only after capturing and controlling it.

In the quiet surface constancy of its exterior, masking its roiling and relentless underbelly, it was also a symbol of the modern dynamo, a God-made machine of such energy and power that mortal men seeking immortality had no choice but to try and copy it. Manmade technology has succeeded in copying it, but always in miniature; we mortals have a long way to flow before we match the power of the Mississippi.

Often damned but never dammed and never doomed—it treats and greets us as the irrelevant twigs we are, paralyzing us with its panorama of majesty and might while carrying us in fantasy or reality on its racing currents.

April 27, 1992, and August 6, 1995

GARDENING

In this election year, it occurs to me that in the unlikely event that I ever run for a public office, it behooves me to confess my sins now so the voters will have plenty of time to forgive and forget them.

The major shortcoming on my record is that I have broken one of the Ten Commandments. I hasten to add that it was broken unintentionally, in all innocence. The particular commandment in question is the tenth one. My recollection of it over the years has been that it says, "You shall not covet your neighbor's house . . . , your neighbor's wife, or his manservant, or his maidservant, or his ox, or his ass." The tenth doesn't mention anything at all about it being wrong to covet your neighbor's yard or garden.

I have never tried to hide the fact that I am envious of my next-door neighbor's yard work. All the while he was running two businesses he was spending evenings and weekends working in his yard. For a while, when we first moved in a decade ago, I had aspirations of trying to compete with him. That hope lasted a couple of weeks: I lacked the energy, funds, knowledge, and green thumb needed to be a serious contender. It seemed to me that my most neighborly act would be to keep our yard as scrawny and shoddy as possible, so that his would appear even more lovely.

Despite this unselfish sacrifice on my part, I have not been able to rid myself of green-eyed envy. For years now I have watched him fertilize and mulch, transplant and trim, sow and reap. His grass is of a brilliant green year-round, uniform in height, thick as fur, with nary an onion or a dandelion or a clump of crabgrass. He blow-dries it in the fall, and I suspect he vacuums it after each weekly mowing. If he ever expanded his house to cover his front yard, he wouldn't even need to lay carpet.

His yard itself is relatively small and confined to the immediate front of his house. The two sides and back contain flower gardens, and the immediate front, between his arc of driveway and the street, is a small woods of pines and dogwoods. At first, I thought this design was labor-efficient. With such a little patch of grass to tend, it seemed to me, the flowers in the gardens and the trees would take care of themselves.

How wrong I was. He has planted every conceivable type of shrub and flower and cares for them as if they were children. As I watch him toiling amongst them, I swear he is talking to them. When the thermometer dips in winter, he is out in the dark covering them with gauze; when rain is scarce in summer, he is out watering them; and every day year-round he seems to be feeding them something from sacks or from his old green pickup truck. His plants are children, and he is their daycare center director.

I was wise to choose not to compete. First of all, it was unnecessary. The view of his works from our place is so open that we can pretend his place is ours. Our service, my wife's and mine, is to be Adam and Eve, enjoying a Garden of Eden without having to work in it. But second, it was a competition I could never have won. His stewardship of his grounds escalated slowly but perceptibly over the years. Three or four years ago, he sold his businesses. One can hardly call it "taking early retirement," for he merely shifted his focus to full-time yard work. I don't know how hard Trojans worked, but if it was as hard as reputed, he must be of Trojan descent. The only difference is, he has no wooden horse except a couple of sawhorses in his carport, although he does put wooden reindeer out in front of the house at Christmas.

Psychologists and sociologists tell us that the human brain contains both male and female inclinations. When men were hunters and farmers and breadwinners and women were housekeepers and cooks, the two genders within each of us were separated. Man has come out of the fields and forests into the city, but the love of land remains with him. What seems to be happening in workplace, home, politics, and everywhere else in our society, is a blurring of the gender lines. Men display the same artistry, skills, and hard labor on the immediate exterior of their homes that women have always shown in the interior.

As I started out to say, I have broken the Tenth Commandment by envying my neighbor's yard. The commandment covers his house, wife, manservant, maidservant, ox, and ass. But now, rereading Exodus 20, verse 17, I discover a catch-all clause, which reads, "or anything that is your neighbor's."

I confess my sin. I am green with envy, but let he who is without sin among us cast the first beer can on my neighbor's yard.

August 31, 1992

GULLIES

A friend in my age bracket and I recently expounded the virtues of soil erosion to some thirty-something youngsters who have grown up in the South without ever seeing a sand gully. We recalled how we spent Saturday afternoons after the mandatory ten-cent cowboy movies playing cowboys-and-Indians, or G.I.s and Japanese, up and down the ravines. We replayed days when scout troops or neighborhood gangs organized Capture the Flag teams which crept around labyrinthine washes toward enemy flags mounted on residual ridges. We remembered, too, wire fences stretched like tennis nets across eroded chasms so deep a John Deere tractor could drive under a fence without the driver having to bend his sun-burned neck. We spoke of flash floods racing down these dry desert valleys during fall rain.

My friend was reminded of the envy his gang had for one of their number who owned a "toot-de-doot," a trumpet for cavalry charges up the gullies, made from the empty toilet paper roll from the local service-station restroom. The rules of that day forbade anyone from taking the roll before it was empty. We had rules just as honorable and rigid for all the games we invented, such as Keep Away, sort of a broken-field football game. Protocol making, consensus reaching, and rules following were natural art forms in those days.

Neither of us would ever have thought the day would come when we would miss soil erosion. We were reared in an age when gullies were symbols of southern sin. The scars on the soil were linked to scars on the southern soul. The South then was a single organism to us, possessing a single soul. We had not yet learned to discriminate between races, between classes, between sexes, or between town and farm homes. The South's scars, we were assured, were temporary, something to be proudly endured but patiently erased. They were somehow tied to the Lost Cause; the South had sand gullies because it had lost The War, not the one America was in at the time, in the early 1940s, but The War. However, the setback to the region from having lost The War, we were assured, was only temporary (maybe as much as a hundred years, but we had ancestors older than that, some of them still living). A New South was on its way. Southern soil erosion and southern soul erosion would disappear together.

So we volunteered for 4-H and FFA and FHA clubs and planted pines in the gullies. Sure enough, the gullies disappeared (except where they are camouflaged with kudzu, which doesn't fool any of us), and a New South emerged. Shoe sales escalated, grits sales went down, asphalt covered roads, brick or aluminum siding covered dog-trot houses, graduation rates skyrocketed in consolidated high schools, factories took in farmers, people paid taxes, Dairy Queen cones replaced molasses and biscuits, car washes sprang up, and golden arches made southern towns look like the rest of the nation.

Why, then, are my friend and I uneasy and nostalgic? What did we lose in outlasting the Lost Cause? Why do we lament for the erosion of yesteryear? Probably the answer has something to do with the difference between living by rules we made for ourselves and living by new rules that seem to come invisibly from somewhere else as a price for progress. We can't decide if age somehow has made us feel more controlled than in control, or if regional progress is so dizzying that we have no time or means left for inventing protocols and rules for new conditions.

Ashley Wilkes never got over the death of his civilization; Scarlett O'Hara and Rhett Butler did, and quickly. Scarlett and Rhett learned new rules rapidly and even added some of their own, but they were unattractive people. Ashley lived with ghosts, and Scarlett and Rhett lived with graspers. Ashley held on to his gullies while Scarlett and Rhett filled them, planted them, and turned them into profits.

An old civilization is gone; a new one still is not yet fully birthed. Perhaps what the ironic memories of bygone gullies are telling us is to pause a moment just to consider what plans and protocols would make this region better than its nonsouthern models. Perhaps by critiquing and controlling Progress we can make up our own new rules for broken-field-running and capturing the flag. Perhaps we can turn empty toilet rolls into New Year's toot-de-doots, trumpeting quality in our lives. We may not know much about creating visions, but we can make something up. It's worth a try. After all, tomorrow is another year.

December 28, 1992

TURKEYS

We were somewhere on the high plateau just north of the Newport, Tennessee, exit on I-40, only a mile or two from a bustling town, and my wife, riding in the passenger seat, was shocked to see a wild turkey. It was standing at the edge of a field, tail folded in, looking out at the passing traffic. I was driving and only caught a glimpse of it, enough to think it was only a billboard for Wild Turkey bourbon, but my wife saw it fully. It was truly alive and not a sight easily forgotten. We have driven slowly along that stretch of interstate several times since then, hoping to find it and to have again what so far is truly a "once-in-a-lifetime experience."

Don't be deceived by the stacks of Butterball turkeys in your supermarket this Thanksgiving or the pounds of sliced turkey at your favorite delicatessen. A wild turkey is indeed a *rara avis* (i.e., a "rare bird"). Wild turkeys are the blood kin of buffalo and Native Americans; they are scarce, rarely seen, and vanishing before our eyes. Also like these, they are symbols of America, especially around Thanksgiving. Once their abundance made them emblematic. Nowadays, however, it is their rarity that does so.

An old truism, bordering on being something Yogi Berra would have said, holds that "you don't miss them until they're gone." Well, of course not. How can something be missed if it's not missing? The importance of the turkey at Thanksgiving time 1994 A.D. is that it is missing and ought to be missed. Birds of a feather flock together only where there are enough of them to congregate. The wild turkey's modern symbolism is not in its flocking, but in its solitariness. It is a lonely old bird.

As symbol, it stands as reminder of what once was. The bird we were fortunate enough to see stood beside an interstate highway. Pavement is far more a national symbol for our times than is the anachronistic wild turkey. In William Faulkner's wonderful hunting stories, which I think are his best writings, he describes how the bear and the wilderness have disappeared together, eaten up first by clearing the forests for farms, and then by the coming of developers of towns and factories and shopping centers. For Faulkner, the old symbol of America was the bear, and the new was the bulldozer.

Science and technology and the manmade things science and technology provide are the real symbols. We have moved in less than a century's time, quite understandably but nonetheless sadly, from the natural world into the manmade one. Everything is so new, we are ill-prepared for how to live on what amounts to a radically new planet. We are feeling our way along in this new world of progress and material things.

The memory of the missing turkey may be of some help in making an easier adjustment. We can learn from the turkey how to don camouflage and to fade into our environment; we can learn from the turkey how to preen ourselves with pride and when to spread our tail feathers; we can learn how to forage and how to roost. Most of all, we can learn that staying linked to the land and flocking together are good things a new society ought not to give up too quickly.

Benjamin Franklin was a scientist, perhaps the best America had in his day, but isn't it strange that Franklin wanted the turkey to be the national symbol rather than his kite or bifocals or stove? Franklin lost that argument. The eagle, another scarce bird these days, was elected national symbol. Maybe it's just as well. Otherwise, we might be following the fortunes of the Philadelphia Turkeys this NFL season.

November 21, 1994

HOT PATCHES

What's needed in this brave new world we have created are hot patches. For the young who have never seen them, let me describe them. Automobile and bicycle tires used to have separate inner linings called inner tubes, as did the lace-up leather footballs and basketballs of those days. Inner tubes would develop punctures. Rather than leaving one's car abandoned on the side of the road or postponing a game to replace a ball, a patch was a quick expedient. One simply removed the inner tube from the tire or ball and glued on a patch taken from a band-aid-style box (with a rough lid to rub on the hole to take the glue better). Then one put the deflated inner tube back into the tire or ball and, using a manual pump (with needle in the case of the balls), one pumped in air.

In those days, one never made a trip without expecting at least one flat tire, and one seldom got through a whole sandlot game of football or basketball without a blowout. (There was never more than one ball available in any neighborhood. The most important and envied kid on any team was the one who brought the ball.) Some tires and balls had more patches than an Eagle Scout has merit badges.

All that has changed, of course. Tires and game balls today are as sophisticated as the complicated automobiles and professional teams they serve; often, they are even self-healing.

Nothing stays the same anymore. We aren't surprised that our young don't know what a coal yard or icehouse was. But who would have dreamed that someday basketball players would wear shoes that could be pumped up or that a whole generation of kids would live in a world without ever seeing, much less riding, a passenger train?

A teacher barely gets used to a textbook before it is replaced with another. A dictionary hardly gets printed before ten thousand new words need to be added to it. The fall phone book arrives and within a month 5 percent of the numbers in it are wrong. An upgrade replacement for your new computer is being built in factories even as you sign the credit papers to buy it. If you buy a Rand McNally road atlas, be ready to replace it within the year. If you buy a globe, get one that you can write new names and draw new lines on.

We surf upon Internet seas and submerge in 999-channel television sets. Roll over, Beethoven. A "classical music" album these days is one that lasts more than one week at the top of the charts. As for medical advances and space explorations, we can't even begin to count the changes. Once a visit to a doctor's "office" was actually to an office, usually on a second-story overlooking a court square, and we thought space travel had reached its zenith when jet planes appeared at the end of World War II.

But, then, we also thought civilization had peaked when the ballpoint pen and the shockproof wristwatch came out at about that same time. Both in sheer numbers and in the ability to astonish us, the marvels that have fluttered out amongst us in the last half of the twentieth century make Pandora look like a reactionary piker. Change is our way of life. The globe has become a giant mobile home. We learn to live with momentum and in movement, or we die. The trouble with change is that it has taken over. It's not small change anymore. It's just plain flabbergasting. If nothing is constant, to what do we moor ourselves?

November 12, 1995

FARMS

This is the season of the year when the full October moon looks like a floating pumpkin. The leaves are turning into glory, and the night air is nippy as it plays across the dew. Harvest season is at hand, but a whole generation of American youngsters is growing up without ever seeing a harvest, except in some history-text picture of Pilgrims celebrating Thanksgiving.

Where did America's farms go? Why have they gone? Are they, like the commuter on the subway, "trapped forever 'neath the streets of Boston," never to return? Will our children or grandchildren grow old without ever being on a farm, believing food grows in supermarkets?

After a decade of Farm Aid concerts by Willie Nelson and John Mellencamp, performer Neil Young expressed some disappointment to a crowd of forty thousand who heard twelve hours of music in Columbia, South Carolina, on October 12. Young said that, despite Farm Aid and other alarm systems, farms are still fading and failing at a depressing rate of five hundred a week. Agricultural advocate-poet Wendell Berry, writing from his self-sufficient farm in Henry County, Kentucky, puts an even worse statistical spin on the matter. In a book of his passionate essays, *Another Turn of the Crank* (Counterpoint Press), Berry says that as of October 1993 the Census Bureau no longer recognized farming at all. Farming is a "non-thing" now. Between 1950 and 1991, says Berry, we averaged losing half a million people a year from our farm population.

Apparently the Census Bureau believes that there are so few American farmers left that there is no need to count them any longer. There are probably more white owls, gray wolves, black grizzly bears, and snail darters nowadays than there are farmers. I know for a fact there are more deer and mosquitoes. By 1991, there were only 4.6 million farmers left (2 percent of the population), and many of those (32 percent of the managers and 86 percent of the farmhands) lived elsewhere than on the farms they tended.

These statistics defy all kinds of economic logic. One would think that if there are more and more people in our nation (and there are) and that if they eat more than ever (and they do), that the demand for farm products would have escalated (and it has), creating in turn a demand for more farms and more and more farmers, but just the opposite is true. Somehow, through mechanization and fertilizers, the food demands of the nation have been met and in abundance so great as to make food production by farming unprofitable. Ergo, farmers are an endangered species.

I share the convictions of both the Farm Aid singers and of Wendell Berry in feeling that our American quality of life is enormously poorer because of the vanishing farms and farmers. Farm Aid seeks to arouse millions of us to insist that government stop this erosion of the farm resource; Berry believes that farmers must help themselves survive by returning to small organic farms and solar power.

My own feeling is that there is, very literally, a hungering for farm produce—especially for fresh fruits and vegetables, not to mention molasses and real country ham—that makes the problem one of marketing. My modest proposal is that farmers revive farms by establishing local co-op markets in the vacated stores around the court squares of small towns in counties that once were agricultural in their economic base. Deserted stores everywhere are being converted into law offices and antique malls, and people are beginning to return to the public squares. The return of the public to the public square, the return of farmers to farming, and the return of the vanishing agrarian and rural philosophy that builds great communities and enhances good art and letters and lifestyles all would be greatly facilitated by simply having more fresh-food local produce shops on the court squares.

It has not been many years since such homegrown markets could be found in basements of courthouses or in wagons and pickup trucks around the court squares or nearby at hitch yards. I believe that since multitudes of people are hungering for such high quality food, such shops could easily rival the designer-jean and quality-label shops so popular among our nation's consumers. A town or county with several quality food specialties could quickly make a national name for itself, as Cadiz, Kentucky, did with its Kentucky hams or Benton County, Tennessee, did with sorghum molasses or as Murray, Kentucky, did with popcorn.

Appreciative consumers fed by accessible markets might prove to be the salvation of farming and of the agrarian way of life. Chew on that idea.

October 21, 1996

GINGKO TREES

Although mid-November has come, the leaves of the gingko trees outside my window are still green. Usually by now, they have turned their brilliant yellow and fallen in a single day, forming perfect-circle golden skirts around their trunks.

Gingkos are my most-favorite trees. The stunning flames of fall's maple leaves and the seductive pastels of spring's apple, peach, and pear trees take a distant second place to the mysterious oriental presence of a gingko.

Its proper name is *Ginkgo biloba,* but it has nicknames. Some call it "the Maidenhair tree," because its leaves resemble those of maidenhair fern. The leaves are fan-shaped, and the leaf veins are unique. They are not "palmate" like maples with main veins diverging from a stem base, nor "parallel" like grasses with main veins beside each other, nor "pinnate" like rhododendrons with a main mid-vein with sub-veins radiating from it. Gingko leaves fan out from the stem to make a fan-shaped leaf with diverging veins, none of which is a main vein, dividing over and over into pairs. (Technically, this is called "dichotomous venation.")

Native to eastern China, the gingko trees are prehistoric, the oldest existing tree. Scientists say that 200 or 150 or 50 million years ago, gingko trees had spread around the globe, into temperate climate zones. Somehow one species survived time and the Ice Age, but only in the region of China from which it originally sprang. They were plant-dinosaurs that lived, although fossils of their ancestors are still found and treasured by serious rock gatherers everywhere. Ironic as it may seem, the same Orient that sent kudzu that threatens to strangle us sent gingkos to make our lives golden.

Legend has it that Buddhist monks in eastern Chinese mountains, either transplanting cuttings of male gingkos or planting the foul-smelling seeds of female gingkos, grew them inside monastery walls a thousand years ago, until English botanists took the seeds back to England and from there spread the nearly extinct tree around the globe. In homage to those Buddhist monks, the gingko leaves are sometimes called "the fingernails of Buddha," and those carpets they form upon falling remind us of the yellow Buddhist robes we used to see in National Geographic or in James Fitzpatrick movie travelogues.

Gingkos are the stuff of Japanese legend, old and new, as well. In the 1600s, tea-master Sen Sotan planted a ginkgo outside his teahouse in Konnichian. When fire raged through Kyoto many years later, Konnichian was not burned. Supposedly, snow atop the gingko, melted by the flames, wet the roof and saved the teahouse. Each late November, tea ceremony students gather at Konnichian and eat sweets made of powdered fruits from the tree that saved the house. The teacup bears the gingko leaf symbol in tribute. In more recent times, it is said that one of the very few surviving plant forms at Hiroshima after the atomic blast was the gingko.

There are old gingkos lining New York's Fifth Avenue. They are resistant to urban smog and diseases. Being old, they are of the rare female fruit-bearing type, the cones of which smell awful upon falling and decaying. In China, this fruit is roasted and eaten like nuts or made into powders, pastes, and medicines. In America, gingko products are a health-food fad.

Most American ornamental gingkos are males, grown from winter-transplanted cuttings, well-watered, and often getting a hundred feet tall, but without fruit.

If you gaze long enough at a gingko tree, you can feel yourself in touch with both creation and infinity. It takes us back to the very beginning of life, and it points us forward to unending horizons. Its magic November carpet beckons us to ride both back and forward, a long airborne current from history to hope.

November 17, 1997

DEER

Dawn fog was barely lifting as my mother and I drove eastward in mid-December from west Tennessee toward Christmas in South Carolina. Suddenly we spotted three tiny deer worming their way from the roadside into the thicket of trees on the north side of the highway.

On this trek the previous Christmas, we had stopped by a field within the city limits of her small town and counted twenty-seven deer grazing peacefully like cattle. This year, she reported, deer have been sighted a block from her house, near the heart of the town. Live ones are expected next year on the courthouse lawn.

Back in the early 1960s, driving home for Christmas from graduate study in Connecticut, we took a wrong turn and wound up on the estate of *Reader's Digest* in Pleasantville, New York. A deer scampered across the road in front of us, and we were transfixed by such a rare sight. I thought of that when reading a Scripps Howard report by John Lang about deer having grown into America's greatest wild hazard. He estimated that 150 people would die in 1998 from automobile encounters with deer.

Lang also reported that the white-tailed deer population had grown from 300,000 in 1900 to between 18 and 28 million deer almost a century later, that 267,000 auto crashes (4 percent of all crashes) are caused by them yearly, that between 9,000 and 16,000 injuries to humans are caused by them annually, and that dead deer on the highway numbered 17,000 in West Virginia, 25,000 in Ohio, 45,000 in Pennsylvania, 68,000 in Michigan, 40,000 in Wisconsin, and 50,000 in Georgia.

In my native Tennessee, there are 180,000 licensed hunters chasing 800,000 deer. The deer are winning the race.

The repairman working on our home announced to us that he is "unavailable during deer season." He looks on killing deer as his civic duty.

My seventh birthday was celebrated with a movie party at the Capitol Theater, watching Disney's *Bambi*. I moped around so much afterwards that my mother gave me twelve cents to go back and see the movie again. I was more appalled by the sound of gunfire from unseen hunters in that movie than by the carnage of World War II in the *Movietone* newsreel.

For generations who have grown up thinking of Bambi and Bambi's mother as sacred cows (to mix animal metaphors) and who are proud to name all eight of St. Nicholas's sleigh deer, the idea of deer as pests doesn't sit well.

Why did Franklin Roosevelt yearn for "a home where the buffalo roam, where the deer and the antelope play?" He got his wish, but he didn't go west to find deer; they have come east to him—by the millions. America, ready to enter a new millennium, has become a home where deer play. Unfortunately for them, there is frequently "heard a discouraging word" about their prospects for survival.

Recent sighters of Santa's sleigh swear that it was being drawn this Christmas by only five reindeer, and that Santa now wears a bulletproof vest.

Next thing you know, someone will think to give deer licenses and guns to the homeless and unemployed of the nation and tell them to "go get 'em."

December 29, 1997

'POSSUMS

The 'possum's real name is opossum. The scientific name for the opossum is *Didelphis marsupialis,* but the opossum got its vernacular name from Captain John Smith (of Pocahontas fame), who in 1608 used the Algonquin name, "apasum," which over time was variously spelled opassom, opussom, ouassom, apossume, ospason, opuson, pooassum, apossum, until opossum was settled on in 1787 (about the time of the U.S. Constitution). Smith wrote, "An Opasson hath an head like a Swine, and a taile like a Rat, and is of the bignes of a Cat. Under her belly she hath a bagge, wherein she lodgeth, carrieth, and sucketh her young."

There are seventy-seven varieties of opossums in the western hemisphere, and in the continental United States most are found in the eastern states but also on the Pacific coast. Because the armadillo of the western United States looks like an eastern opossum wearing an armor shell and also likes to cross highways, I once though they were of the same family, but I was in error.

Like the kangaroo, opossums have pouches. The opossum is the only pouched mammal (marsupial) on the North America continent. They range from seven to forty-one inches long (including tails) and have front feet with five toes and back feet with four toes and a fifth shaped like a thumb. They eat anything, being omnivorous, but prefer carrion and insects. They sleep in burrows (not hanging by their tails from trees, as commonly thought) in daylight and hunt at night. The female opossum produces, after thirteen days gestation, anywhere from four to twenty-four babies in each litter sometimes twice a year; usually only eight or nine survive.

With urbanization, the opossum has moved into cities, attracted by food supplies, and has become a common urban pest. The 'possum's natural enemies are owls, dogs, winter weather, and hunters. Its more recent major enemy is the automobile. The average life span of a 'possum is just a little more than one year (although some live three years in captivity). To protect themselves, they pretend to be dead, from which we get the common phrase "playing 'possum."

Back in my hunting days, I picked them up by their tails. Loving Walt Kelly's Pogo, who was such a cute and intelligent ("we have met the enemy, and he is us") cartoon character, I assumed they were gentle. Considering now their fifty sharp, dirty teeth, I shiver at the risks I ran.

Cherokee legend explains that the 'possum's tail is long and hairless because Rabbit, which used to have a lovely bushy tail until Bear took it away, out of envy sent Cricket to dress the 'possum's splendid tail for a dance. When vain Possum danced and showed off his tail, Cricket's hair ribbons came off and left the bare tail showing. The other animals' laughter so mortified the 'possum that he fell down speechless and pretended to be dead.

I ate 'possum once. It wasn't bad, but it was very greasy. Gourmets debate how best to cook 'possum. Here's a recipe with sweet potatoes: "Skin and clean opossum, removing small sacs from small of back and under forelegs. Place opossum in 4 cups of water in a saucepan; add salt and black pepper to taste along with 6 chopped red peppers; and simmer until pan liquid is halved. Pare and slice 4 large sweet potatoes, and put the opossum in a baking pan with the pan liquid and potatoes. Bake at 350 degrees an hour, or until tender, basting some."

Another recipe uses apples: "Parboil a young, cleaned opossum in salted water until tender, stuff with choice of dressing, place on rack in a roaster and cover with strips of bacon. Mix a tablespoon of sugar and a tablespoon of lemon juice in 3 cups of water and put it in the pan. Bake at 350 degrees for 2 hours, then drain out the liquid except for 1 cup, and surround the opossum with pared apple quarters and bake for another hour. One opossum serves 3 to 4 people."

The famous African American poet Paul Lawrence Dunbar contested these recipes back around 1891 in his poem "Possum," taking white cooks to task for skinning opossums before cooking them. To Dunbar, cracklin' 'possum skins were the best part of a feast.

You can't find 'possum in the groceries (except out back in the dumpsters, maybe).

July 21, 1998

Because the land was, we were; because the land is, we are. When this land wears the black upon brown upon bronze colors of fall, it sometimes seems as if this space has melted and run together in milk chocolate ecumenicity, except that in the melting, the spirit of something thought long gone with the deer and the bear hovers over this flat land.

Sage fields dominate our memories of that county, fields we hunted as soon as we were old enough to carry popguns. Over the years the hunting fields shrank, cultivated and sold and developed until only a few hilltop groves and moats of fallow sage fields remained. The hum of wild bees harvesting honey was replaced by the hum of combines and then by the hum of highways and then by the hum of factories, with something lost in translation each time.

The sage grew shorter as we grew taller. Over our heads when we first entered it, it was only shoulder high by the time we had slingshots and Red Ryder BB guns. The day came, sage now waist high and we a foot taller and teen-aged, when we carried shotguns, parking in graveled church lots, pouring brass-bottomed shells of assorted Crayola colors into our pockets, following cedar rows into the field.

A few feet in, silent and empty space exploded with the flurried flapping of a flushed covey of quail sounding like a loose sheet of tin rattling on a deserted barn roof and looking like a gross of winged coffee cans. They rose, grouped and swooped off as we relished sight and sound, our guns unlifted.

Feeling eyes from the top of the field, we spied a pair of maned red foxes, frozen in majestic statuesque stateliness like African lions at the shadow line of trees meeting the sun-bathed field. We stared transfixed by their stares until they lost interest in us and thawed and flowed into the darkness behind them.

We worked our way toward where they had stood. At the field's upper edge a double-strand barbed-wire fence, rusted and weaving where some of its cedar posts have fallen, was down and overrun with honeysuckle matting. We walked across it to the shadows and sat against a hardwood looking west down the hill across the field. Tall broomstraw rippled in the sunlight, transforming the field into a golden pond, its wind-waved surface broken only by occasional dark green islands of young cedar tops, some destined to become Christmas trees.

The overlays of the forest carpet were hushed, their damp leaves matted together with melted fall frost and their crackling muted by the renewing processes of decay that fill the woods with musty mildew odors, not strong enough to hide our scent from a brown rabbit ambling easily in stop-start skips along the fallen fence, catching our smell where we crossed it and then hiding.

The stillness of the sanctuary was broken by hickory shells thrown from the vaulted ceiling of the trees above; the squirrels' barrage of nuts drew us out of reveries and naps to discover that the far sky was now lavender and pink around the setting sun's orange sphere that seemed to rest like a basketball on top of the old gatepost below the field. It streaked and smeared the sky and clouds with colors, a Second Coming scene. It was a sign of resurrections and of prodigals welcomed home.

We did not fire a shot all day.

November 9, 1998

SKUNKS

Just as darkness set in at the Rough River State Park Lodge in central Kentucky, we finished a walk, ending up at the swimming pool from which it had started.

From woods at the end of the lodge ambled an animal. Silhouetted against the brightly lit pool, it looked like an anteater or like a furry long-snouted dachshund dog with a very furry long tail taped to it. Low to the ground, it glided gracefully and rather rapidly down between the pool fence bars and into the wading pool area to the left. A couple of us wandered down toward the pool for a closer inspection. As we did, the creature emerged from the pool and continued its amble northward. We drew closer, close enough to see that the animal was black with white stripes and had a big black tail with a white stripe where the side body stripes converged.

It was a stunningly handsome skunk.

Hearing us behind it, it turned and raised its tail. At that point, we turned, too, and high-tailed it out of there. I have seen dead skunks along the highways all my life, have smelled the passing of skunks all my life as well, and have seen several documentary films and read illustrated articles about skunks, but I had never seen a live one so "up close and personal."

The sighting brought to mind long-forgotten words to a Gene Paul–Johnny Mercer song: "I'm a lonesome polecat / Lonesome sad and blue / 'Cause I ain't got no feminine polecat / Vowing to be true."

This skunk was so handsome that I wanted to find reasons to like it. My pleasure is shared seriously by others; there are associations of skunk pet owners, and the American Domestic Skunk Association in Cleveland, Georgia, provides medical, rescue, adoption, foster care, and skunk training advice on "the care and well being of the pen-raised domestic skunk."

But our Kentucky skunk was definitely not pen-raised and domesticated. The three major categories of wild skunks are striped skunks (*Mephitis mephitis*), spotted skunks (*Spilogale putorius*), and hog-nosed skunks (*Conepatus mesoleucus*). The musks of all three have been analyzed carefully by chemists and consist of combinations of ingredients. Skunks are members of the weasel family. Skunks benefit the ecology and us by eating home and farm pests such as mice, rats, moles, aphids, grubs, beetles, yellow jackets, grasshoppers, and cutworms.

The most frequent problem skunks present is living under houses. The best solution to this problem is prevention: fencing buried around under-house openings helps, as does keeping food (such as dog and cat food) away from porches and houses. Once a skunk does come to visit, the best solution is to be sure there are plenty of openings by which it can leave. In almost all cases it will stay briefly and peaceably and leave at night to seek food, probably not returning at all. Skunks don't travel in daylight because their eyes are very weak and can't stand bright light. At night, they are able to see for two feet—but cast their spray fifteen feet!

Like raccoons, skunks are susceptible to rabies. It is a myth that they carry rabies by nature. They get rabies, as do we, from being bitten by a rabid carrier.

Their mating season is in late February and early March, and judging from their relatively high population, lonesome polecats find some way to put up with one another for those few days. Skunks are born about sixty-three days later, in late April and early May, and are weaned by summer (mid-May to late July). From August through November seems to be the period of most frequent skunk sightings.

One skunk legend holds that a skunk can't spray you if you lift it by its tail.

Any adventurous soul willing to try this is welcome to do so.

September 12, 1999

Chapter 2

PLACE
"BESIDE STILL WATERS"

MISS ROSALIE

This is a story about a fictional person, Miss Rosalie Winston, with only a kernel of truth about what she did. Miss Rosalie's past eighty. She was a MacAfee whose parents died of yellow fever and left her young and alone with a big house and no money. The parents have had fresh flowers on their graves every afternoon for sixty years now.

A couple of years after they died, the flowers stopped for a while. Miss Rosalie's credit at the florist, and elsewhere, had run out. Then, the flowers started again. And every Sunday, in the MacAfee pew at church, Miss Rosalie sat in a new dress with an orchid pinned on it. And at every local christening, wedding, graduation, funeral, or church supper, there would be flowers from Miss Rosalie.

Late in life, she married Horace Winston, an L&N bachelor-conductor who was usually on the road, but who came to church with Miss Rosalie regularly once he retired, wearing new buttons on his old blue conductor's suit where brass ones had been, and with the gold chain of his railroad watch going through his vest button as if hooked to his navel. He used the watch to signal the preacher to get services started and ended.

Everyone figured that Mr. Horace knew what the whole town had known about Miss Rosalie for forty years, which was that late each afternoon

Miss Rosalie went to the cemetery to steal flowers. Not all the flowers, of course: a basket or spray a day for her parents and an orchid for herself along toward Sunday and then enough more for any special event anywhere in town.

She'd rearrange the remaining flowers much better than the funeral home van driver had left them. So it wasn't a few unmissed flowers that interested folks. It was Miss Rosalie's taking everything that held the flowers—vases, pots, baskets, easels, moss-packed wreath backs—and selling them to the florist. She'd hit the cemetery in late evening, and first thing next morning the florist's truck would back down to her garage and load up. And each Monday morning the mailman would deliver a check in a plain envelope to her from the florist.

The town made itself a cheerful part of this conspiracy by making up explanations for Miss Rosalie's income: first a nonexistent MacAfee inheritance, then an inflated estimate of Mr. Horace's salary and later of his retirement pension, and finally, when he died, some insurance policies he was reputed to have left.

While the town shared the fun and profits, Miss Rosalie became Big Business personified, literally as well as figuratively, since she loved to eat and expanded as her income did. The town reaped dividends in no-cost castoffs because she gave generously to church and charity, sent flowers to be auctioned at bazaars, supported an army of grocers and farmers with her appetite and entertainments, kept widowed Lucy Washburn (the seamstress) and her five children alive with weekly dress orders, and held the florist's prices down because he passed on some of the savings from recycling the receptacles to his customers and kept them silent.

There is an artistic as well as an economic appreciation for Miss Rosalie. The cemetery is kept free of litter by her, the cleanest in the county actually, with none of that gloomy funeral aftermath strewn about. And everyone expecting to die, which is everyone, knows there will be at least one mourner and one bunch of flowers at their funeral. As long as her sizable legs hold her up, there's going to be life in that cemetery.

Part of the town's conspiracy is that folks avoid driving by the cemetery when Miss Rosalie is there. If a car comes by, she makes a beeline for her parents' tombstone and hides there. As she has grown older and stouter, she has slowed down considerably but makes the run to hide anyway, looking like a dirigible with her chiffon dresses and bonnet ribbons fluttering behind her.

Mr. Horace is buried near her parents now, and his death was the test of the town's consent to keep silent about Miss Rosalie. Almost everyone ever receiving flowers from Miss Rosalie sent flowers to Mr. Horace's funeral, and the people filled the church and later covered an acre of the cemetery. Most of them stood at the funeral of this little man they hardly knew, and most kept their eyes open to count the flowers.

Next Sunday Miss Rosalie showed up in church in a new black dress wearing a corsage of three orchids pinned to it atop her ample breast and, as if to say "thank you," another orchid as a wrist corsage.

November 22, 1982

LEADERSHIP

In the two-chair barbershop I used to visit, the front chair was the young owner's, a Baptist lay preacher with a full head of blond, blow-dried hair. But the back chair was the former owner's, old Mr. Layton (not his real name), who had cut hair at the same chair for sixty-two years. It had a rut around it as deep as mule tracks around a sorghum mill. Each morning at 7:00 and each evening at 6:00, Mr. Layton could be seen walking the six blocks between his home and work, black umbrella in hand. On Sunday mornings, he walked with his wife to and from the church behind his shop.

Local legend had it that Mr. Layton not only had never owned an automobile, he had never even ridden in one. Legend also had it that not only had he never been out of the county, he had never even been out of the town. In fact, in a town that was Methodist on the north side of the railroad track that split the town in even halves, he had never even been out of the south-side Baptist half. All that was only legend, of course. He told me personally that once when he was seventeen he had gone to a countywide Baptist picnic in a hayride wagon.

Well, Mr. Layton died. After more than eighty years, he finally went somewhere. Mrs. Layton took sick one night, and the doctor told Mr. Layton to get her to a specialist in Memphis. Mr. Layton called the blond Baptist barber, and they loaded Mrs. Layton in the backseat and took off down the U.S. two lane southwest of town. At the first pair of headlights they met, Mr. Layton screamed and threw his arms around his face, shouting, "Pull over! Pull over and let them pass!" He must have been remembering that wagon ride of his youth, when roads were one lane.

Legend has it Mr. Layton died of a heart attack on that road to Memphis, but that his widow recovered quickly, sent for the life savings they had never gone anywhere to spend, and never returned to the house south of the tracks in the little town. Change strikes people in funny ways. We talk a lot about people being so "set in their ways" that "you can never change them." Mr. Layton came to mind as I was reading one of the few political-science books I ever enjoyed. By Aaron Wildavsky, its title is *The Nursing Father: Moses as a Political Leader* (University of Alabama Press).

Wildavsky takes an age-old debate, about whether the leadership style of a political leader can ever change, and shows how it can change not once but several times, as it did with Moses. I like the way Wildovsky takes biblical materials familiar to almost everyone to make lessons for social science.

He sees Moses as a leader growing in abilities through four different "regimes" (or contexts). In Egypt, he is a leader under a "slavery" regime. Passing out of Egypt and over the Reed Sea (that is, the Red Sea), he is a leader in an "anarchy." He forces the wandering people into a third stage, that of an "equity" regime. Finally, the nation of Israel begins to emerge as a "hierarchy." In its best moments, Israel is a hierarchy (rules, civil service, law and order) with features of equity (equality, participation of all the people, freedom of expression).

The book gets its "nursing father" title from Numbers 11:12. Moses, always the reluctant and argumentative leader of an exasperating collection of fugitives, complains that after getting them safely out of Egypt he is made to stay with them and to care for them all through the rest of the journey. And even then he is not allowed to enter the Promised Land himself. Like the good parent and strong leader he was, Moses had his greatest success in getting Israel to a place organized well enough to survive without him. This is a book with clear ramifications for leadership flexibility in home, job, and nation: a complicated science made clear and commonsensical.

The leopard can change its spots. Even Coca-Cola can change its secret formula. We can change our ways. Mr. Layton would have been a different man if he had read it.

May 20, 1985

HISTORIC SITES

Here is what our two daughters tell us they learned from our August vacation:

"Flash in the pan" comes from the gunpowder that flashes on a flintlock muzzleloader gun. When the trigger is pulled, the spark caused by the flint striking steel ignites the gunpowder on the "pan," and that causes the gunpowder in the barrel to ignite and push the bullet out. Today, "flash in the pan" means something that happens quickly and noisily and then is over with (lesson learned at the armory at Colonial Williamsburg).

"Three sheets to the wind." Windmills have four sails, or arms. Colonial windmills, like European ones, were used for grinding grain. The sails turning, windblown, caused a center post to grind the corn or wheat. When the windmill was in operation, the miller would cover the arms with sheets, or sails, to catch the wind. Some millers were bored by the grinding routine and took to drink, and if they forgot to put the sail on one of the four arms, the mill would vibrate and rock unevenly. The reeling windmill and the reeling miller matched each other, "three sheets in the wind" (learned at the mill at Williamsburg).

"Hickory dickory dock." Grandfather clocks often had wooden mechanisms inside. To make the gears and pulleys work, grease had to be applied often. Animal fat and lard were the most available lubricants, but they attracted mice. Hence, "the mouse ran up the clock" and was struck with misfortune (and the chime arm) if its run happened to "be on time" (learned at President James Monroe's restored home, Ash Lawn).

"Pop goes the weasel." Homemade cloth was common, especially from the Revolutionary days onward; spinning wheels were found in every house. They made monotonous, rhythmic sounds as their parts churned about. Two central parts hitting each other with a popping sound were called the monkey and the weasel, atop the three- or four-legged stool that looks like a shoemaker's bench. The sound of the monkey and weasel in rhythm led to the jingle everyone still sings (learned at Michie Tavern near Monticello, Thomas Jefferson's home).

Among the other things learned this vacation were how to take shortcuts past guided tours to get to the drink machines, gift shops, and restrooms more quickly, how to find out if souvenirs were made in Taiwan or Pennsylvania, what outlet malls and amusement parks are nearest historic landmarks, what hours motel pools are least crowded, and how to stand in lines.

In the process, despite ourselves, we were implanted in the midst of history. To get to the bookstores that sell the T-shirts and pennants at the College of William and Mary (1693), Hampden-Sydney (1776), University of Virginia (1819), and Washington and Lee (1749), one has to see history everywhere, in the Wren building at William and Mary, the Lee tomb and chapel at W&L, or the rotunda and quadrangle at UVa.

To locate the graveyard of our ancestors outside Farmville, Virginia, we had to get to dusty courthouse ledgers filled with ornate handwriting in brown ink script and then drive narrow county roads through barren but beautiful countryside to the top of Leigh's Mountain. We couldn't avoid, and are happy we didn't, some hundred historic markers and half-dozen parkways, including the Blue Ridge, and the Shenandoah Valley. We discovered Jamestown and linked the doe and fawn we found in the swampy woods around the settlement to the beginnings of the nation. On one back road, an eagle suddenly soared from the brush and raced our car, another symbolic tie. We stumbled gladly, from misreading a road map, upon Appomattox.

The only bad part of vacation tours is the tourists. The happiest ones we met were those who were deaf or in wheelchairs, protected from noise and from being bumped by inevitable bigmouthed and big-bottomed fellow citizens who show up on every tour. Back road spaces, unguided late evening walks, and solitary cemetery side trips, like ghosts from the American past, are necessary antidotes for annoying moments of too much exposure to togetherness in the sheep pens of public places. Vacation over, we returned to get the rest it had not provided.

September 2, 1985

BB GUNS

Cable television last month had a Christmas movie about the schemes of a boy in the 1940s to get a Daisy Red Ryder BB gun. In the end, he got his wish. My own Red Ryder BB gun memories start where that boy's left off. I don't recall getting the gun as much as what I did with it afterward, also in the 1940s.

It was a beautiful gun, with its blued metal barrel and polished wood stock and barrel grip. A knotted rawhide thong dangled from a steel ring on the side, and the wooden stock had Red Ryder's autograph branded boldly upon it. The BBs were poured through a funnel made by one's left hand, rolling like small ball bearings out of a heavy cardboard tube that had cost a nickel.

I practiced on the little paper targets that came with it until they gave out a day or two after I got it. The only advantage of those stationary targets was that the BBs could be picked up and used again. The practice really wasn't necessary. We had started out many years earlier, aiming sticks and then cap pistols and popguns and escalating to slingshots, and had been using borrowed Red Ryders from the older boys up the street for a year before getting our own. By that time, all the imaginary Indians and Japanese in the wooded and sandy gullies nearby had been wiped out, and we were ready for other game.

The six or seven of us who had grown up together in those gullies and on the sandlot baseball field next to them organized a hunting party. When it was over, I had learned the most important lesson about hunting I would ever know: it's no fun to kill for the fun of it. Five birds fell that unforgotten day—a couple of sparrows, a thrush, a blue jay, and a red-headed woodpecker. Laid side by side at day's end, they have never left my memory. The notch carved on the gunstock that day never got any companions.

But, if we couldn't shoot birds without guilt-filled nightmares, we could shoot each other. We divided into teams and laid out careful rules. The teams had to be balanced in age spreads and in firepower. Everyone had to wear heavy blue jeans, and there could be no shooting above the waist. No one could shoot from less than fifty feet away. Usually that meant a hit would sting like a bee for about five seconds. Occasionally, of course, someone slipped up. Bailey Abernathy caught one just above the belt once, and it broke the skin.

The games broke up as we grew up. The older boys got more power-ful Daisy pump guns before moving on to CO_2 gas-propelled weapons, then real .22 rifles and .410 shotguns. Some of them are still out there, forty years later, in duck blinds with shotguns that sound and kick like cannons and in deer stands with scoped rifles that are the modern age's descendents of our limited firepower's parents.

The global arms race has been with us all along, and one wonders sometimes if the Defense Department general testing a new modern won-der ever dreams at night of a Red Ryder BB gun with lever action, a hundred-shot magazine, and a little metal V-sight.

What if the Geneva Summit had limited weapons to Red Ryders? Would there have been a rush on for heavy denim jeans, and agreements to shoot only below the belt?

January 13, 1986

HAZING

In the haze of memory, hazing and hunting seasons are knotted together. School hazings and squirrel hunting had in common the great theme of Initiation, the ritual of the young being introduced into worlds from which they hitherto had been prohibited. Hazings nowadays are rare. Probably they depended upon the hazer being a close enough acquaintance for his authority to go unquestioned by the hazee. Certainly they were more common when schools and towns were smaller; hazing of strangers by strangers just doesn't sit right. Among youngsters who had grown up together, a year apart, it was awkward enough.

The forms ranged from the mischievous to the malignant. At one end of the spectrum was the silly and public hazing: wearing beanies, having to wear costumes to school, or dyeing one's hair with food coloring. At the other end was the dangerous and private hazing: paddlings, road trips with one's clothes off, swallowing oysters tied by a string, or drinking raw eggs.

The point supposedly was to welcome a newcomer into the freshman class or the club. Some hazers seemed to forget that point and concentrate on making another one: that human beings can be fiends. I can't recall the name of the redheaded basketball player who delighted in wielding the paddle he had made in shop class. A handful of fellow freshmen and I who had the misfortune to share sixth-period gym with the football and basketball teams are unlikely to forget the boy's face. My own memories of it are upside down, seen from bending over and looking back up between my legs in the locker room. We skipped a lot of showers that year in order to escape.

That was about the same time in our lives we were graduating from BB guns and .22-rifle target shooting to hunting real game. The memory of entering the woods for the first time is very much the same as entering high school. Both had been visible but forbidden spaces, reserved for the initiated. It was the duty of the initiated to issue the invitations and to act as guides into the mysteries of growing up; one earned one's invitation. Initiation was a sign of acceptance into a closed circle. What seemed like cruelty back then now seems, years later, as more cruel to those who were bypassed and excluded, never invited on a road trip or a hunting trip.

We know that hunting is a dying art and that hazing has been phased out most places, or so they say. But cliques still abound, selectivity and exclusion still go on, although perhaps more private than public now. One wonders what new shapes it has taken. We hope the cruelties it can inflict are gone, but that the rites of passage into accepting responsibility for one-self and those younger still survive.

September 1, 1986

SOUTHERN SYMBOLS

The Fourth of July is full of symbols—flags and flutes, hot dogs and hot weather, politics and picnics, baseball and apple pie. Symbols are shorthand for things of significance. The star atop the Christmas tree has a long story and deep meanings encapsulated in a symbol, the rainbow-colored peacock on television is a symbol of a major network, a trademark on a soft drink is a symbol of an old and important cola company, and the auto company symbol on the hood of a car takes us past highway department symbols for speed, turns, and crossings.

Recently there has been a revival of some old debates about the rebel flag. The problem with the Confederate battle flag as a symbol is that it symbolizes different things to different people. Each party has to explain in detail to others what the symbol means. If a symbol means different things to different people, it is not a symbol. It if has to be explained, it isn't a shorthand that most folks recognize and share.

A flag's about as conspicuous and democratic a symbol as we can imag-ine. It's a good symbol of a shared cause and/or a shared memory. Every school has its flag, every marching band depends upon its flags as much as upon its trombones and drums, and no war can be fought without one. We can't carry symbols like Mt. Rushmore or the Statue of Liberty around with us easily, but we can sure wave a flag. One of the fun things our children do in school, Sunday school, or summer camp is to design flags. They trans-late what they have learned into symbols they can display and share with others. The more easily the symbols selected are understood, the better the flag design is.

The South has always been strong on symbols. If new flags for the South were being designed today, what would they bear?

Once a white flag would have been appropriate—symbolizing the dom-inance of King Cotton and the planters. Peanuts, pigs, peaches, and the Democratic Party donkey would have been popular nominees, too. Perhaps a belt made of green fabric, coiled like the serpents on the old colonial flags, would be appropriate, since the South is now called the Green Belt. Or loop the belt around a big blazing sun for the Sun Belt. You could weave the green belt out of kudzu for those who link the South with that unfortunate symbol; it does have the virtue of attaching itself to all southerners.

A Saturday night television show is promoting red necks and arms as their symbol for the South. Some diehard fans would be happy if the flag carried a face of Elvis, with Graceland in the background. Jim and Tammy Bakker, Disney World, the boll weevil, and pink flamingoes also get votes. All of these are much more creative than the tigers, lions, and bulldogs chosen by the region's athletic teams.

One good ol' boy, perhaps with a tad of cynicism, suggests sewing together small flags from all the other countries that have bought land or built factories in the South—to demonstrate the region's internationalism.

Southerners may not have much money, but they do have a surplus of imagination. One new southern flag designer says he doesn't care what symbol is used on the flag as long as the fabric itself is black velvet with the symbol painted in fluorescent hues. Similar ideas from others include flying a patchwork quilt or a chenille bedspread.

One fellow wants a country ham on the flag; another wants sorghum; another wants biscuits. One suggests flying a flag made of oilcloth with breakfast stains left on it. Grits get several nominations, but no one has found a way to picture them. There are also some expected suggestions: things like corn, cornbread, and corn liquor, or horses and hound dogs. Two fried chicken legs, crossed, is an interesting entry. A similar design, using catfish, also has possibilities.

One gets the impression, however, that the flag makers are flying their ideas at half-mast—or half-jest. This is serious business and ought to have a lot more thought, research, and rationale. Too many of the ideas show the South as outsiders parody it, people indoctrinated by the stereotypes of *The Beverly Hillbillies* or *The Dukes of Hazard*.

The flag symbol that is beginning to get my personal support is the possum. Whether we read library books (*Collected Pogo Works of Walt Kelly*) or bumper stickers ("Eat More Possum"), no one has to explain to a southerner what a possum is. Nor does it take much explanation for us to see how appropriately symbolic of our region and people the possum is.

The most intellectual and serious treatment of the possum as the ultimate southern symbol is from a legitimate scholar, Marion Montgomery, an

English professor at Georgia, and author of *Possum and Other Receipts for the Recovery of "Southern" Being* (University of Georgia Press). Normally one could read so short a book (134 pages) in an evening, but this book is so complex, so rich, and so deep that it has taken me three readings and three weeks just to begin to understand it. Only now am I beginning to withdraw my initial judgment ("Totally Incomprehensible!") of Montgomery's *Possum*. I have paid it my highest compliment by not making a single yellow highlighter mark in it; it's too powerful a book to be touched. Every sentence is loaded, and a paraphrase or précis is pretty near impossible.

"Possum," Montgomery reminds us, has at least two definitions. It is, most familiarly, a southern animal of an unendangered species that looks to have been assembled by a committee, dates back to prehistoric times with the gingko trees, can live off the refuse of cities as easily as in the countryside, and usually dies only when flattened by a car. An unflattened possum may only be feigning death (i.e., "possuming"). The key point is that the possum lives very close to the land and is mired in the world of harsh realities, not aloft in fanciful dreams.

But "possum" is also Latin, translated "I am able," which, since the days of Adam, is man's boast that he can pull himself up by his own bootstraps (or even barefooted).

Possums teach us that "being southern" is something quite apart from mere geography. Montgomery thinks Thomas Aquinas, Augustine, and even Solzhenitsyn are southern in spirit—and that it is the spirit that ultimately counts. Being southern means that past cannot be divorced from present, that head cannot be severed from heart, that body cannot be subtracted from spirit, that man's boastful independence cannot be deprived of a strong sense of dependencies wholly outside of man's powers.

I'll read Montgomery again, but tentatively I will say that I'm almost persuaded that "the possum rampant" ought to be prominent upon any new southern flag.

June 29 and July 6, 1987

GALOSHES

In the middle of the recent wet and cold spell we bumped into a gray-haired man wearing knickers and galoshes. Either item would have caught any bypassing eye, but to see them together in one costume calls for a double take. We didn't know you could buy knickers or galoshes anywhere anymore, and we thought the only place to see them was in the historical dress section of the Smithsonian. We were sorely tempted to follow him to see if the knickers swished and the galoshes sloshed as those of our own youth did.

My brother and I wore knickers to school through the fourth grade. Outside of school we got to wear blue jeans or short pants. Our knee socks we could wear year-round with anything. We held the socks and the knickers legs up with rubber bands because garters seemed sissy. We couldn't figure where the knickers came from. We never saw them on the counters at Penney's or in the Sears catalogs. We suspected there was some little crossroads country store out in the county that had overstocked them in the nineteenth century and that our parents were its only customers. If anyone else in the school—or the universe—wore them, we were unaware of it. Some of them even had buttons instead of zippers and suspender hooks instead of belt loops.

We alternated shoes, too. For Sundays, we had brown dress slippers half the year and saddle oxfords from Easter on through the summer, with taps on the toes and heels to make them last. We polished our go-to-meeting shoes every Saturday night, right after taking our baths. For the rest of the week, we had brown high-tops for school and high-top tennis shoes for play.

The galoshes were high-topped, too, black rubber with metal buckles. They always seemed two sizes smaller than our shoes, hard as the dickens to pull on and impossible to remove without taking the shoes off at the same time. That was no problem with the Sunday slippers, but next to impossible with the week-day high-topped lace-up shoes or tennis shoes. We prayed the rains and snows would fall on Sundays.

The galoshes had lives of their own. During the World War II rubber shortages, we'd try to sneak them onto the rubber drive piles of tires and inner tubes, but they somehow always walked back home. If we had buried them, they would have wiggled free. If we could have found any instrument sharp enough to cut them, we could have used them for patches for our football and bikes. Galoshes were indestructible, which is probably why the mothers and aunts of that time were sure that they would protect us.

Galoshes sat out dry spells on the back door steps much as do Dutch wooden shoes (which are comparable in comfort), but no one filled them at Christmas time; yet they were not empty of gifts. Those of us who wore galoshes and knickers remember them long after today's expensive designer ski boots and designer clothes have come and gone. To think of knickers and galoshes is to hold hands again, in memory, with those who pushed us in and tugged us out of our yesteryears.

January 18, 1988

MOVIE HOUSES

The last time I paid to go to a movie was a year ago. By the time we bought three tickets, a tub of popcorn, three soft drinks, and three candy bars, the tab was over twenty dollars. For the cost of a family movie expedition, I figure we can wait to watch movies on the movie channel or buy them on VCR tape and have them forever—or even buy a book.

Our old hometown was without a movie theater until recently. Now there's a twin-screen out near the shopping centers at the edge of town. Its immediate forebearers were two drive-ins from the 1950s, both now long vacated. Its grandparents were two downtown theaters from the Depression and World War II days, later converted into a dollar store and a discount shoe shop.

The ambiance of those old movie houses is hard to recapture. Trying to describe them is important because young folks need to understand how movies shaped early America—and because we old folks who are turning into TV couch potatoes need to remember. My first brush with the law came when I was seized by the owner-operator, Mrs. Hal Lawrence, for being in the ladies' room of the Capitol Theatre. I was three years old, and it was the only restroom to which my mother had introduced me. After several hundred movies, I came to love—and miss—Mrs. Lawrence as much as a grandparent.

Back then, movies changed three or four times a week, usually Sunday-Monday, Tuesday-Wednesday, Thursday-Friday, and Saturday. Saturday was cowboy day, normally a rotation of Roy Rogers and Gene Autry with occasional Sunset Carsons, Johnny Mack Browns, Lash Larues, and Durango Kids thrown in, along with another chapter of a Saturday serial, many of which seemed to feature Buster Crabbe. Saturday showings began at 10:30 A.M. instead of the usual weekday 1:30 P.M., and most youngsters sat through twice. On Sundays, only one evening showing was allowed, beginning around 8:30 after evening church services.

During the week, we could see Bette Davis, James Cagney, Humphrey Bogart, Cary Grant, Gary Cooper, Barbara Stanwyck, Robert Taylor, and a host of other hundreds from Hollywood stables. Most shows were black-and-white. In our town in those days, a Technicolored movie was a major event, although not quite as major as getting to see *Gone with the Wind* or *Snow White* when released every five years. About the closest thing to an X-rated movie was *Forever Amber.* Some folks didn't miss a movie, three nights out every week.

Tickets were twenty-five cents for adults and ten cents for under-twelves. Major murmurings of mutiny arose when prices went to thirty-five and twelve cents. (About the same time, haircuts were going from fifty up to sixty cents, and gasoline was under twenty cents a gallon even when rationed.) "P.K.s" (Preachers' Kids) didn't have to pay at all, and it was smart to be best friends of a P.K. willing to share his or her tickets because they couldn't go to movies on Sundays.

In their final years, our two downtown theaters offered no food except popcorn—a nickel a bag. There had been a time, much earlier, when a sweet shop operated off the lobby, a shadow of the huge candy counters one found at the majestic movie cathedrals in Memphis or Nashville. (If one ran rapidly enough, one could also get to our sweet shop between Sunday school and church each Sunday morning.)

For small towns with little evening entertainment beyond Sunday and Wednesday evening prayer meetings, radio, the telephone party line, and occasional Rook games, movie houses were community centers. Their stages hosted live "stars" as well as movies. Hypnotists, mind readers, and war-bond salesmen shared footlights with dish drawings, talent shows, beauty contests, Chautauqua lecturers, and "follow-the-bouncing-ball" sing-alongs. Smiley Burnette dropped in occasionally, and the local paper once reported he had bought a retirement farm out in the county.

With their live and on-film celebrities, their *Movietone* newsreels, and their huge air-conditioning machines—the first and only ones in town—movie houses showed us the future. Between the movies and the war news we grew up aware that a wider world awaited us outside.

July 4, 1988

One place I find myself missing back home is Joe's Poolroom. It was in the same building as the police station, firehouse, public library, and city recorder's office but got left out when they built a new library and new city hall and razed the old court square building.

It's funny that I miss Joe's. For the life of me, I can't remember ever going in it. It was off-limits to me and to several hundred other youngsters. If warnings from mothers weren't enough to keep us out of Joe's, the very fact that its windows were painted dark green half-way up signaled we weren't even to look into the place, and with the police station next door, we knew instant incarceration faced any of us who dared to place toe across threshold.

Yet somehow, without ever entering one, all southern boys knew intimately how a poolroom looked, sounded, and smelled. We knew it had oiled and sawdusted, splintered and cracked, wooden floors. We knew it smelled of stale beer from scattered long-necked, brown glass returnable bottles and of smoke curling up into inverted funnels of green lampshades from unfiltered cigarettes burning close to the noses of squinty-eyed men hunched over green felt tabletops, their white shirtsleeves rolled up and elbowed with blue chalk dust.

We knew a brass rail ran along the base of the bar and could guess how it felt against the arch of a foot, and we pictured how scattered cuspidors matched the brass of the rail. We knew the single restroom in the back would be small, barely room for one person, and always dirty, perhaps with a single eye-hook for a lock and a metal "MEN" on the door. We knew the alley behind would be stacked with brown cardboard return cases full of empty beer bottles.

We even knew who would be "in there": single men from the volunteer fire squad, veterans of the war, a retired railroad man or two, former football heroes, an assistant coach, a couple of salesmen on their lunch break from stores along the square, traveling men from the boardinghouse a block away, some old-timers spinning tales to some youngsters listening spellbound and slack-jawed—plus a few mysterious "regulars" whose only livelihood seemed to be being there whenever the poolroom was open.

For all of its being a "forbidden" place, a poolroom somehow never struck anyone as an "evil" place. Joe and his wife were good folks, highly regarded throughout the town, and their children regularly won the school popularity awards. The threshold we were being forbidden to cross wasn't really the poolroom; it was adulthood. A "billiards hall" was only a symbol mutually agreed upon by the whole community of the line between growing up and being grown. Like the invisible but crystal clear line between squirrel hunting and deer hunting, a poolroom was there to tell us not to rush into wasting our childhood, not to hurry to grow up too fast.

Half a block away there's a vacant lot where another building once housed "Deacon" Jones's doughnut shop. Deacon had a fancy sign behind the register: two medieval jesters holding up a calligraphy quote that read, "As you travel along through life, brother / Whatever be your goal / Keep your eye upon the doughnut / And not upon the hole."

We all feel the holes inside us left by pool halls and fire halls, milk trucks and ice trucks of our pasts—and by long-gone loving people, town kin if not blood kin. Praise God for the inner eye of the soul that lets us see through memory the doughnuts of the past, fresh despite the holes of time. For which is truly more real—the vacant lot of today or the memory of what was on it yesterday?

July 18, 1988

IRON FENCES

As forests and fields have receded like male hairlines to make way for homes and highways and larger populations of people, another passing has been going on almost unnoticed.

Wrought-iron yard fences are disappearing.

Evidence of their passage is everywhere. Contrast pictures of homes from family albums, newspaper archives, pictorial history books, and your memories from fifty years back with a drive around town today. Iron fences are scarce. Some even have historical markers affixed to them, signifying they are things of the past. Iron fences are still used around institutions such as colleges, industrial office areas, and prisons, and even some very large estates of the rich and famous. But these are tall protective works for which ornamentation is secondary. Their primary purpose is to keep people out or in, and they just happen secondarily to look better than regular fencing, chain-link fencing, or barbed wire.

Residential wrought-iron fences of the kind so popular in the late nineteenth and early twentieth centuries, on the other hand, are primarily ornamental. They are only three or four feet high, and they function mostly as adornment. Erected in an age when a home, no matter how humble, was a castle, the statement they made was about the importance of property. They were proclamations of ownership and demarcations of property lines.

Iron fences were also expressions of aspirations for the future. Architectural historians can quickly demonstrate how southern mansions evolved from log cabins. A similar demonstration could be made of how iron fences evolved from prewire fortress wooden stakes and posts through a period of boards and planks on to shorter picket fences and then into substituting iron for wood in the pickets. The evolution was evidence of upward mobility, "moving up."

No doubt iron fences had functions other than looking good and making statements about a family's status and longevity in a community. Judging from their chest-high height, they served to keep horses and cows out of yards, not to mention pigs and dogs and peddlers. Leash laws for pets and city-limits prohibitions for livestock are actually very recent additions to civilization's codes. Some towns still resist enacting them. Many an iron fence still has an iron horsehead hitching post in front of it at curbside. (Some of us can recall wagon teams and riding horses being hitched to parking meters as recently as the late 1940s.)

That the fences came to be ornaments more than impediments, however, is proven by the absence of locks in their gate latches and by the vines and flowers growing on the fences. The best proof of their ornamental function, of course, is their ornamentation. Iron fences are not just uniform lengths of iron rods strung together. They were the work of craftsmen, laced with filigrees, ranging from simple to baroque. Arrowheads, fleur-de-lis, grape leaves, family crests, and scrolls are signs that ironwork was as highly prized as an art form as was statuary or painting. Indeed, since the word "pale" (or "pole") means both a fence post and a piece of the artwork on heraldry's crests, "beyond the pale" can mean "out past the family's fancy fence."

How the public saw a home's exterior, including its fence, was more important to the homeowner than what was inside the house—with the possible exception of the parlor, the sacrosanct public domain reserved for callers. If privacy was a homeowner's aim, why build a house near a street and make it face the street? Being seen approvingly was more important than privacy. Fences not only made good neighbors; they made admiring neighbors as well.

New homes make feeble nods to iron fences. Some suburban houses have a little wrought iron on a porch—a banister, a railing, or a bench, perhaps. Mostly, however, iron fences are relics of the past, passing away like gothic arches in churches or the railway rails. Iron artisans are as rare as icemen, blacksmiths, and tailors. America's Iron Age is rusting away; our gateways to the past are coming unhinged. Unite and "Picket for Fences!"

May 29, 1989

NEIGHBORHOODS

This is the time of year when I most miss Lee Street. Actually, there are several streets tied together in that memory lane, but Lee Street was a center artery for the Lee Street gang, our version of the Little Rascals and Our Gang back in the 1940s. Susie, Harriet, Billy, Buzzy, John, Joan, Ronnie, and I were at the core, but occasionally we let in the younger ones like Cindy and Mary Ann, or the older ones like Alan and Jim, or the ones from three or more blocks away like Joe, Andy, Bailey, Ralph, and Paul—especially when we needed baseball teams in the summer, sleds for Peden Hill in the winter, or Indians for us cowboys to shoot and hog-tie in spring.

October was the best of months. Vacations were over, so absenteeism from the gang was rare. There was still enough dusk to play kick-the-can, when we could spare one from the scrap metal drives we dutifully conducted in wartime. Homework was light, and there was plenty of time for games. Toys were scarce, and everyone pooled what they had. Susie had the Parcheesi set, and we played in her kitchen, sneaking out to steal grapes from the only arbor around. We avoided her side yard, because legend had it that an old well there had once collapsed and gobbled up a man. Harriet had the Old Maid cards and the Monopoly set, the only croquet set, and also the yellow bike we all used. Her mother was our best saver of newspapers, which we collected in our red wagon every month and sold for a penny a pound to the National Toilet Company to use for packing (not toilets, but cosmetics). We called the shredded paper "selzer" (short for "excelsior"), but you can't find it in the dictionary at all; it's gone, I suppose, like the fall of '44. Ronnie had the poker chips and play money and usually kept John's as well, since he was a Methodist preacher's kid and not supposed to be playing cards.

Someone always had a leather football or basketball, its inner tube patched like the tires of the prewar cars. We knew every car in town because there were so few. Baseballs were usually taped to keep the string in. Harriet and Susie had pianos, as did Ann Powers on the next block, and piano benches were filled with sheet music. Sing-alongs were spontaneous and frequent. Buzzy's house was next to the elementary school landfill where the street ended. Her daddy taught us to shoot a .22, leaning out a bedroom window and aiming at cans and rats in the gully. We were already pretty good shots, for the wooded gully and sand field and cattail swamp beyond it were our BB-gun range. Occasionally we had real skirmishes with counterpart gangs from Porter Street or from across the L&N tracks.

Everyone had a few real books and comic books, and when they had all been lent and read dog-eared, we borrowed from the third-grade teacher, who roomed with the Fitzsimmonses. Some afternoons we would spend with the Herdons, lapping up the color pictures in their tall stacks of *National Geographic,* best remembered as an early version of slow-moving color television and for pictures of topless natives.

All the mothers always had food. We invented the buffet long before restaurants commercialized it. The whole neighborhood got into that act, not just those families with children still at home. The Bradshers, the Satterwhites, the Pattersons, the Crutchfields, the Peeples, the Claxtons, and the Dumases all took us in.

We had no parks, no recreation director, and no lighted courts. We had no buses and only a few bikes. Most of the time we just walked everywhere—to church, to the movies, to the city park across town, to night games at the baseball field out near the high school, to the dairy or the court square drugstores, or to the funny-smelling city library kept by Miss Rose above the fire station at City Hall.

Sometimes we took skates apart and nailed the pieces on two-by-fours and mounted orange crates on the front and had soapbox derbies down Crawford Avenue until the police would come to say we were keeping the night-shift railroad men awake.

Someone among us was always wearing Band-Aids and mercurochrome. We fought each other often, regardless of sex, mainly for something to do. The girls always wore dresses, never shorts or slacks. The boys wore short pants and went shirtless and barefoot in the summer, blue jeans and tennis shoes in the gully and in the fall, and knickers in the winter.

Occasionally some older boy from outside would wander through and pretend great worldly wisdom by telling us a dirty joke back behind the school hedges. We'd laugh and then run home to ask our parents to explain what it meant.

Ah, innocence! Ah, neighborhood! What could Eden have had that Lee Street didn't? In the photo albums of our minds, the survivors, it is still there: good as it ever was and better.

October 16, 1989

BRIDGES

The old bridge over the Tennessee River near my hometown is being replaced. Because my peers and I grew up swimming in its shadow, the two old pools in town at City Park and Shady Nook having been closed and filled, this is not an event without sentiment. For us the bridge has always been there, and yet it is not that old at all. Our parents could speak of times "before the bridge went in" or "before the lake." I suspect my own age group will soon be telling our own progeny about the days "when the old bridge was still there."

I have a large black-and-white photo of it, some four by six feet in size and a bit yellowed with age. I am looking at it as I write. Fortunately it is not in color, because I don't remember the past in color. I came from the Kodak box camera and *Citizen Kane* movie times, and I reminisce in sepia blacks-and-whites. (Somehow that also explains to me why youngsters today don't buy saddle oxfords, but that is beside the point here.)

It certainly doesn't matter that much longer and bigger bridges can be ridden in Louisiana, Maryland, or Michigan. With its steel girders, ours looked a bit like a fallen and bent Eiffel Tower, and for semirural youngsters from Paris, Tennessee, who had never seen the real Paree, it served us just as well. Those were the days before Lego Blocks, back when youngsters made their own lead soldiers and owned their own Erector Sets and could link in their minds their home models with the real thing, the bridge and tiny figures atop it.

It hung in acrophobic suspension over space, swaying in sensitized synchronization with the wind's rhythms, its countervailing metal stitching west-east across the south-north bound waves, sometimes white-caps, sometimes ripples, sometimes glass. Tall-mast sailboats passed easily under it.

River traffic barged under it, while old Model A's and pickups and tractors chugged over it with only fragile metal lattices and short concrete curbs barring them from flying off into eternity in the adventure of meeting at the apex and, with an inch to spare, passing a van coming from the other direction. The center stripe of the highway here was an invisible wall more confining than Berlin's, and crossing it was just as risky. Tops of its pyramidesque bases rose from their submerged Nile-like hiding places, and long and level boulder-sided limestone levees led to it from both ends.

Arrowheads and beads from the Indian tribes still occasionally wash up on the shores the bridge unites, and trotlines with bottle floats still snare an occasional monster grandfather-catfish. Sometimes the water is low enough to see the old highway that ran south of the bridge before it was built; and just south of it, on the old hill that was a sorghum field and mill, is the state park inn, and even further south of that the water changes color where the old sulfur well still flows into the river. North from the bridge one can guess where Confederate Forts Heiman and Henry were.

Where once buggies hitched and later cars idled in old courting days, campers and marinas have taken over the best parking places of all four-corner lots of the bridge. Moonlight skinny-dipping has been eclipsed. At the high school minstrel picnic Regina Timmons jumped from the bridge and, fearful of being called chicken and ashamed that a girl went first, some of the football boys followed her. A couple of those of that vintage are now building the new bridge, and I find that appropriate—and symmetrical.

April 16, 1990

WAVING

I have an old habit, from a small town and rural upbringing, of waving at oncoming cars, cyclists, joggers, and folks working in their yards. My "wave" consists of raising my right forefinger from the steering wheel and wiggling it. I've done it for so many years that it is almost a reflex action now. Our girls laugh at me because it is such a tiny gesture, something like a tic.

After one too many episodes of being ridiculed by my offspring, I made them count the number of people who waved back. They were amazed. Almost 90 percent of the strangers we greeted responded either with a wave or a smile or a nod of the head. Our girls had no idea that strangers passing at such speeds notice one another, and they were astounded that complete strangers can communicate through a wiggling finger.

Friendliness toward casual acquaintances and complete strangers is a dying art form. We're not talking about the sidewalks of New York, where silence and averted eyes are protection against solicitors, cranks, and sheer overpowering numbers of people. Sometimes acknowledging strangers is impossible because there are too many of them. But that shouldn't mean we have to shut out everyone we pass or that we ought to cease all habits of civility.

Silence between strangers is a far worse Cold War than the one we waged for years against the USSR. Strangers will forever seem strange if we lack the courage and courtesy of speaking. Failing to acknowledge the presence of others with a word or gesture of greeting sends a message nonetheless—one of "intentional exclusion." Intentional exclusion is our way of declaring we don't think others are important enough to notice. To acknowledge the existence of others is to accept some responsibility for them and for conditions that they may represent. Intentional exclusion keeps us from the duties of intentional inclusiveness. An impersonal world is easier to live in than a personalized one.

If we nod to the homeless and hungry on the streets of any city, we have to face them. To face them in person means we have also to face the fact that we personally neglect them. Waving to an old person in a wheelchair on the porch of a nursing home, a convict picking up highway litter, or a migrant worker picking peaches turns a trip into a guilt trip—so we pass by on the other side, pretending they are not there. The easiest way to avoid guilt is to avoid people who make us feel guilty. We tint our windows so strangers can't see us, turn up the stereo so we don't hear them, stick to the interstates and stay off of the streets, move to the suburbs and stay out of the slums, send our kids to private academies, install answering machines on our phones—and avoid speaking or waving to strangers.

Lifting a finger to greet is dangerous because it may make us feel guilty about not lifting a finger to help. And, yet, a simple act of greeting is in itself a form of help. The truly amazing thing about our little family poll of responsive finger-raisers was not the high number of returned greetings, but the fact that these people—all of them, high and low, rich and poor—already had their eyes on us and could quickly return our greeting in the first place. That universal watchfulness can mean only one thing. An enormous hunger in human beings gnaws for evidences of humanity. We ache for our existence to be confirmed by some little sign from others that we are really here. A wiggled finger says to the stranger, "Yes! Believe me, you are alive! You count for something!"

Prove the difference a greeting can make. This week, deliberately wave at as many other drivers and as many wayside walkers as possible and visit with every check-out girl in every supermarket, drugstore, and gas station we patronize. Let's tell them this week without having to say the words—just by nodding, just by smiling, just by waving—that we know they are there.

This week, lift just one little forefinger. It's a novel way to light one little candle.

September 10, 1990

RUGBY

We celebrated our wedding anniversary, our youngest daughter's birthday, and an Alabama friend's retirement with an August weekend on a by-passed mountain plateau at Historic Rugby, northwest of Knoxville.

Founded in 1880, Rugby has survived for 110 years. It is not now the utopian community for second sons of English gentry that Thomas Hughes, famous author of *Tom Brown's School Days,* meant for it to be, although two of the friendly staff members with whom we spoke had definite English accents. The English and other settlers, who numbered as many as 450 at the peak of the colony's heydays, would be pleased with the survival. Many of the gingerbread Victorian board and batten homes still stand, most of them privately owned, but several are now the property of the preservation association. We stayed in Newbury House, the colony's first boardinghouse, which has five bedrooms available for guests at reasonable rates. Its grounds slope down to a wonderful pond.

We walked around many of the old homes and toured Kingstone Lisle, a home owned by Hughes in which his ninety-year-old mother lived the last decade of her life. We visited her grave and those of many other original settlers at the cemetery down the lane past the site of two large Tabard Inns, now burned, which leads down to a gentlemen's swimming hole. The variety of wildflowers and trees is extraordinary, and we want to return in the fall and spring seasons.

A brief downpour left the grounds cool and the trees dripping, and the next morning a wonderful fog covered all, a sight that must have made the original settlers homesick for England. We also visited a beautiful one-room church, complete with original pews, buttermilk artwork, and an organ, which is an active Episcopal mission that still holds Sunday morning services. Across the highway, we visited a large old schoolhouse, now the visitors' center, and a single-room library with a floor-to-ceiling collection of seven thousand rare volumes, most of them from the nineteenth century.

A new Harrow Row Cafe offered splendid foods, with options of English and American cooking. "Bubble and squeak," a dish of mashed potatoes and cabbage was interesting, and the oatmeal pecan pie was delectable. The fried toast on the English breakfast, when covered with local honey, was especially appealing, served with sausages called "bangers."

Other reproduction buildings or originals include a commissary, which is a craft and gift shop, and a bookstore replica of the old Board of Aid to Land Ownership building. The bookstore offers pieces printed by hand at the restored print shop. Printing, including a newspaper, played an important role in the early colony's life, but farming was to have been the colony's main industry. A cannery failed early because not enough tomatoes were planted and because the can labels had prices printed in shillings rather than cents. The original land covered seventy thousand acres, much of it now privately owned. Government projects surround the thousand acres remaining in the settlement.

In a way, its isolation is part of its attractiveness. Part of its mystique is in being a place offering a hundred stories to hear and a thousand variegated sights to see without feeling hurried or trampled. A Spring Music and Crafts Festival is held in May and a Rugby Pilgrimage in August, as well as a special "Christmas at Rugby" event. The restoration depends largely upon contributions, often made through Historic Rugby, Inc. Barbara Stagg has been executive director of the colony for many years; it has been especially active since 1976.

One can reach Rugby from I-40 west of Knoxville by way of Jamestown or Oak Ridge exits or from I-75 north of Knoxville by way of the Huntsville exit. Nearby Oak Ridge, with its atomic research, is an exciting contrast—both were communities carved out of wilderness.

Rugby is one of Tennessee's best-held secrets. We commend it highly, but in whispers, lest sudden success spoil it.

October 8, 1990

It's hard to get excited about Valentine's Day; it comes too soon after Christmas. Besides, how many people can tell you anything at all about St. Valentine? What kind of saint runs around nearly naked shooting people with arrows? Furthermore, the day holds no happy memories for me at all. The only Valentine's Day I remember at all was back in '49. I had saved up a dollar and went shopping at Fry's Drug Store for a present for the girl seated in front of me in eighth-grade study hall.

I thought Fate must have made her so beautiful and must have thrown us together by giving her a last name just ahead of mine alphabetically. We didn't date; junior high students weren't allowed to do that back in those days. We "ran around together," which was the same as dating, just like "folk dancing" was what we called dancing in gym class.

A simple Valentine card wasn't good enough for this Venus of a girl. Not even the expensive ones with padded red satin hearts and real lace edging would do. I ruled out a bottle of "Evening in Paris" as too suggestive a gift. So was a compact. (Girls today think a compact is a car.) I.D. bracelets were too expensive, and, besides, it was the afternoon of February 13, too late to get one engraved anyway.

I considered some pencils and a Big Chief tablet but ruled them out because we were in junior high now and had graduated to using two-ring notebook paper. With all that thinking about Love and looking for the perfect way to capture and express it, I worked up an appetite. So I spent half of my dollar for a banana split while I thought through the problem.

I was sitting on a stool at the marble-top counter, so I asked the soda jerk for advice just as I had seen despondent cowboys asking bartenders for advice in the Saturday westerns at the Capitol Theatre. Roy Rogers and Gene Autry and the Durango Kid never asked for drinks, just for directions: "Which way did they go?" or "Where's the sheriff?"

The soda jerk—he had to have been M. F. Hurdle, or Wade Jackson, or Pudgy Frazier—suggested "Sweets for the Sweet." So, as soon as I had spooned out the last of the chocolate fruit syrup in the banana split boat, I headed for the candy display, tables of pyramided Whitman Samplers and Russell Stover boxes. The choice wasn't hard to make. I only had fifty cents left, so I had to settle for a forty-nine-cent box of chocolate-covered cherries. Luckily it was a red heart-shaped box. I put it on the girl's desk the next morning.

She dropped me like a cold potato.

A few years later she added insult to injury by marrying a football hero and lifeguard four years her senior. So I don't care much for Valentine's Day. Those greeting card, candy, and flower displays that go up as soon as the Christmas sale items are taken away each year only remind me of when I gave away my hard-earned heart. Except for one thing: those hearts on display aren't broken.

But I did learn something from the experience. I learned why that little tubby guy carries a bow and feels like shooting people.

He, too, wants revenge.

February 11, 1991

VICKS SALVE

About everyone we know has had a head cold or flu this winter. We've played Ping-Pong with one in our household since Christmas Eve. Even the wise ones in our family who got flu shots last fall have had it. We keep waiting for one of us to break down and go to the doctor so the rest of us can use her or his prescription, but so far we have stuck to home remedies and self-pitying. We could have paid a doctor thrice with what we have "saved" by buying tablets, capsules, cold powders, and cherry- , orange- , and grape-flavored syrups off discount-store racks. I have the extravagant claims on the decongestant packages of the pharmacy memorized by now.

After two months of this, we are beginning to get desperate. I'm afraid we are going to have to call in the heavy artillery: Vicks Salve.

It's been around exactly a century now; they don't even call it that anymore. Now it's VapoRub. But it's still around, a million gallons a year are made, and it still comes in a blue bottle like the one our mothers and their mothers before them used. They'd open the flannel pajamas we had to wear when we were ailing, rub Vicks on our chests, and then pin pieces of white flannel around our necks like bibs. If we were really bad off, they'd stick a glob in a 'vaporizer' next to the bed, or rig up a steam kettle and Vicks under a tent and make us keep our heads in it.

Vicks was invented by a Greensboro, North Carolina, pharmacist named Lunsford Richardson. He called it "Magic Croupe Salve." His son, Smith Richardson, got his daddy to change the name and to drop the twenty other products he was peddling. Then salesmen in Model Ts took to the road, selling box loads to every country crossroads store and tacking up Vicks signs on every barn they could find with space left over from the "GARRETT'S SNUFF" and "SEE ROCK CITY" signs. Sales have gone down some in recent years because of all the pills and capsules on the market and because of the success of the company's other product, Nyquil—and maybe because white flannel is hard to find nowadays.

But up in New York City, there is a Smith Richardson Foundation which as of the end of 1989 had assets of $295 million and which gave away $17,611,395 to a multitude of good causes that year. And down in Greensboro are the H. Smith Richardson Charitable Trust, the Grace Richardson Fund, the Mary Lynn Richardson Fund, and the Grace Jones Richardson Trust, with combined assets of nearly $68 million and annual gift awards of over $2.5 million.

There has to be a whole lot of chest rubbing still going on for that kind of money just to be given away; that's rubbing things the right way. I also rejoice that, even though milk in bottles and ice from an ice wagon are gone, some things from the distant past are still around. There is a lot of motherly love and memory stored in those blue bottles of Vicks.

February 18, 1991

WOOLWORTH'S

The familiar red sign with its large golden capital letters has come down. Our local Woolworth's just closed. The one in my hometown closed many years ago. Long before Holiday Inn "invented" look-alike motels, catering to American mobility that craved familiarity even when (especially when) away from home, Woolworth's stores bound us together and to hometown roots. Now only a few are left, as rare as old green six-ounce Coca Cola bottles.

In search of my youth and in salute to its remaining symbols, I made a last pilgrimage to this local "dime store." Most of the counters and shelves were already emptied, but the unmistakable odor of blanched nuts lingered, mixing past and present. The oiled wooden floors and glass counter dividers have been gone for years, but until now the stores have hung on hauntingly, as much a part of every southern court square as its Confederate monument.

I recall the women clerks in their World War II hairstyles and the dresses they all wore: each was beautiful, and the prettiest ones seemed to work in ladies wear, attracting adolescents in that clean-sex era before *Playboy* ruined things by making things explicit. To reach them, or any other department, one had to risk being followed by an omniscient and omnipresent suited manager watching clerks and customers alike. One man reading of closings sent them a sizable sum of money, payment with accrued interest for an X-Acto knife he snatched fifty years ago. How that guilt-ridden alumnus who took the knife escaped escapes me. The toy section in those days would not have filled a corner in today's Toys-R-Us warehouse stores. It was only a portion of a countertop, filled with yo-yos, kite string, jacks, checkers, dominoes, balloons, and such. Plastic was new, and no one wanted it anyway. With a war on, metal toys disappeared, too. We knew the war was over when metal toys—cap pistols, cars, and trucks—came back.

At the front door, piles of citrus or chocolate-covered candy sold by the piece or pound met us, filling bins behind slanted glass. In the stationery section we met the world of commerce through rubber bands, paperclips, Big Chief tablets, pencils, and erasers from faraway and exotic places. In the book section, we found Nancy Drew nestled with the Hardy Boys near Jack London and Albert Payson Terhune, the hardbacks deliberatively separated as serious literature from the temporality and frivolity of Archie and Action comic books. The kitchen section was filled with nonelectric gadgetry, dazzling and affordable Christmas gift ideas for the mothers of the world: hand-operated can openers, eggbeaters, bottle-cap removers, potato peelers, and apple corers. Sears could only show us pictures of what we could lust after, but Woolworth's showed us the real things. We could see and smell and touch as often as we wished, and the more we saw, the more we wanted. Our imaginations expanded as our eyes widened.

And when we grew up, we were never intimidated by visiting New York City. No glass tower could awe us; we had seen large plate glass windows before. No machine could frighten us; we had seen cash registers work. We were no bumpkin strangers to the universe. We were at home in the world, for we had been weaned on Woolworth's. Probably change is as inevitable as it is reputed to be, but while Woolworth's stores were open, one could believe that wasn't entirely true. We shall miss them, as we do the tent revivals and gas-pump attendants who preceded them into the mists of days gone by. Like all old friends, we abused them even as we appreciated them. We seldom visited them. We just took them for granted. For many years now they have comforted us by being architectural postcards in the scrapbooks of our minds. They grew old, content to be out of the heavy traffic they no longer recognized. The death of a close and dear friend deserves a eulogy, and Woolworth's was that kind of friend.

Go in peace, red-faced old friend. Whatever facade replaces your familiar one, and whatever shop or office replaces your space, rest easy knowing some of us will remember you had been there first and had educated us well. Your golden letters were your crown, and you were a small-town royal palace.

February 17, 1992

MEN'S TIES

Not far from my old hometown, in the rear of a stately old home which is now a funeral parlor, is a beauty salon. With a wry sense of humor its owner named it "The Final Touch." One thing about the South, even in the most destitute times and places, is that southerners care about "keeping up appearances" and "making a good impression." One notices it most on Sunday mornings, when the women parade (since hats are no longer mandatory for church attendance) the fruits of their weekly visits to their beauticians. Ringlets and permanents rest atop bodies draped in colorful clothing. Even their eyeglass frames are chosen to show them at their best.

But southern men are as fastidious about fashion as women. Vanity knows no gender. Saturday night is still a ritual night for most southern men. Cars are washed, baths are taken, clothes selected and laid out for the coming morning, pants' creases checked, suit lint removed, socks darned, fingernails scrubbed and trimmed, hair shampooed and conditioned and blow-dried, and (almost the most important of all) the best pair of dress shoes spit-shined. Public appearances—whether for weddings, graduations, church, anniversaries, holidays, or funerals—are as important to southern men as to southern women. I have male friends who have decided what they want worn at their own funerals and have written down instructions to that effect. Going out in style, whether out into public or out of this world, is serious business for southern men.

Even if a southern male takes some shortcuts in the Saturday night fashion ritual, he never neglects its single most important part: his choice of ties. The tie is the focus of the whole enterprise. Its selection is to the male what the choice of a dress is to the female. Men have a rather limited choice of suits and sports coat ensembles. Most are dark blue or gray. (Brown used to rank equally with blue and gray, but notice sometime how seldom brown suits are seen in clothing stores these days.)

Tie styles have changed radically in the past years. They are wider and more colorful. Economists say this is a certain sign we are in an economic depression. Psychologists say it is a sign we are in a mental depression. Both are probably right. The real story may be that, with men buying fewer suits, clothiers rely on tie sales to get them through the slump. Making very radical changes in men's tie styles is comparable to lowering or raising women's hemlines: it gets your attention and bestirs a dormant fashion economy.

Many of us fool the merchants. We have preserved our old wide ties from the 1960s and 1970s, knowing their day would come around again. Today's tie flowers are not new; like century plants, their time to blossom has come around again. Some women can't be caught wearing the same thing twice. Men, on the other hand, never throw clothes away. I have one friend who boasts that he is still wearing shoes he wore in college over thirty years ago. He is on a first-name basis with the local shoe repairman. Although it seems to have shrunk in the shoulders and waist, I still wear my baseball jacket from almost forty years ago, and somewhere in our attic is a pair of white bucks from high school waiting the resurrection of Pat Boone styles.

Dressing up is part of being a southern man. It is a symbol of respect for the opinions of others and of self-respect as well. It is also a witness to the importance of habits and memories, for each repetition of the ritual revives memories and pays tribute to special occasions of the past. It also looks to the future, as an optimist's symbol of aspiration and of better times ahead. Further, dressing up binds men together; it is a membership badge into the fraternity; it is a uniform for the home guard troops; it is a hallmark of a democracy that erases income differentiations and ancestry. And, finally, it has something to do with sex as well. Peacock blood flows in us all. If "clothes make the man," the common southern male has faith that clothes (and the right cologne) will attract women to those who are single and will hold wives for those of us who are married.

March 30, 1992

SOUTHERN TIME CAPSULE

The approaching five hundredth anniversary of Columbus's discovery of new lands and Native Americans has set me to thinking about an appropriate commemorative ceremony. Any observance probably should include the burying of a time capsule to be opened in the year 2492 A.D. People a thousand years after Columbus could then see what people halfway through that millennium had treasured most.

That idea of a time capsule set me to thinking about making my last will and testament. What would I want to leave to posterity?

Here's the start of a list, just in case. With luck, I'll be amending it annually for some years to come:

- a Louisville Slugger wooden baseball bat with a Mickey Vernon autograph;
- a Daisy Red Ryder BB rifle with lever-action, leather side-thong, and wooden stock;
- a King James Bible with Concordance, maps, and illustrations;
- a Book of Common Prayer, the old version;
- a paperback revival hymnal;
- an old formula Coca-Cola in an original green 6 ½ ounces bottle with bottling city embossed on the bottom;
- a pre-Interstates roadmap atlas of the United States;
- an Indian-head penny;
- a buffalo nickel;
- a freshman college beanie;
- a girl's "no-break" dance program with tiny pencil attached to a gold string to be worn on her wrist;
- a box of Crayolas, original colors only;
- a blackboard eraser and chalk;
- a first-grade reader, the one with the exciting lives and times of Dick, Jane, and Spot;
- a heavy glass restaurant water tumbler;
- an ashtray;
- a pack of Juicy Fruit;
- a recipe book for old southern cooking;

- a Lionel electric train;
- a menu from the L&N dining car;
- a line-up from Sportsman's Park, St. Louis, for a Cardinals-Dodgers game in 1950;
- a photo of the 1949 Grove High School Blue Devils undefeated football team;
- an Indian Chief lined tablet;
- a package of Beechnut chewing tobacco;
- a set of cardboard silhouettes of friendly and enemy ships and of colored paintings of friendly and enemy planes from World War II;
- bubblegum baseball cards;
- a cap pistol;
- videotapes of Saturday Westerns, with an emphasis on pre–Dale Evans / Roy Rogers films;
- a pair of knickers;
- a .410 shotgun shell;
- a squirrel's tail;
- a 1930 Ford carburetor;
- a draft card;
- a curl of a girl's golden hair, owner's name forgotten;
- a beaded bracelet from Cherokee, North Carolina;
- a carved coconut shell from Gatlinburg;
- a World War II German helmet;
- early issues of Action Comics;
- a fifty years' collection of presidential campaign buttons and bumper stickers;
- a Congressional Record, rolled for easy burning;
- one pair each of saddle oxfords, white bucks, blue suede shoes, black high-top tennis shoes, and baseball cleats;
- a copy of One Hundred Best-Loved Poems;
- a set of photos from a six-for-a-quarter photo booth at the Memphis Fairgrounds;

- a homemade kite with flour-and-water glue;
- a pack of Authors cards;
- a Monopoly set;
- assorted marbles;
- cufflinks;
- a pocket watch;
- a washboard;
- a bar of Ivory Soap;
- a patched inner tube, either bicycle or auto;
- road gravel;
- a cylindrical glass milk bottle with milk separated from the cream on top;
- a pair of sole-saving metal toe taps;
- a package of watermelon seeds; and
- an old Sears catalog.

The list goes on, but the space available for this essay doesn't. Besides, you get the idea and probably have your own list to jot down now.

June 1, 1992

CEMETERIES

The movies do cemeteries a great disservice by exploiting them. In order to make terror profitable, the "Friday the Thirteenth" genre of graveyard horror destroys the aesthetic and educational virtues of resting places. In the real world off the screen, the nation's cemeteries are alive with history, art, literature, and landscaping. They are fun places to visit.

Among our favorites are the Lexington, Kentucky, city cemetery and Pisgah Cemetery ten miles away; Cave Hill in Louisville; the Bruton Church cemetery in Williamsburg; a cemetery in the historic section of Charleston; federal military cemeteries of Shiloh and Fort Donelson; old cemeteries in Memphis and Nashville; the Jefferson cemetery at Monticello; one in Bardstown, Kentucky, with a marker reading "Weep no more, my lady"; a North Carolina cemetery with an angel tombstone reading "Look Homeward,

Angel"; one with a whole family remembered through individual statues in Mayfield, Kentucky; a Moravian one (with the sexes separated) next to Salem College in Winston-Salem; some unnamed ones overgrown with vines that we stumbled across when rabbit hunting; and, of course, Arlington National Cemetery.

Each has its own personality. Some offer an outdoor museum of sculpture variations. Among the attractions are varieties of stone materials and shapes, of lettering, and of epitaphs and range of dates. Ready-made geneology is apparent in large family plots. Some have landscaping of which Frederick Olmstead himself would be proud.

The most personal cemeteries of all are those in which we recall the people. I use the present tense, for to walk among them and to remember them is, in a real sense, to resurrect them. Some of the most pleasant moments I have had with my mother have come from hiking through local cemeteries in our county. Names I recognize get faces and facts when she is along as tour guide. Like most people her age who have always lived in the same town, she is not only a family historian, but a community historian as well. She has taught me, without intending to do so, that one major advantage to people living so much longer these days is that people who have died get remembered longer.

In the oldest city cemetery we visit at home are a former congressman who was the son of Davy Crockett, a former governor who was also president of a large railroad and a famous college, and the founder of Grove Park Inn and of some famous patent medicines. But the less famous gravesites are just as interesting. We have kinfolk and dozens of old friends and acquaintances in each of the four larger cemeteries within a four-mile radius. Visits to hometown cemeteries inevitably bring surprises. We always find someone whose passing had eluded us, and we always find someone we otherwise probably would have forgotten altogether.

The sad moments come at the graves of infants. Although they have been spared a lot of hardships and heartaches that living inflicts upon us, their deaths can only be described as "untimely." But collectively, like a chorus of little angel voices, they seem to send a message that cuts through the pain of finding them. If it hurts so much to think of their dying too young, they seem to say, let the hurt remind us that life must be on balance a pretty nice thing after all. As a matter of fact, that is what all of the graves, both of those who lived a full threescore and ten and those who died before their time, do say when we walk among them. One thing that makes living worthwhile is the stored-up memories collected over the decades from associating with those we rediscover in cemeteries. In a single afternoon there one can relive a Saturday walk around the court square, or a Sunday morning in church, or a Thanksgiving family dinner.

In Shakespeare's *Henry IV*, Part I, Glendower boasts, "I can call spirits from the vasty deep," to which Hotspur retorts, "But will they come when you do call for them?" Indeed they do, for friendly shades of the past remain friendly in memory.

August 17, 1992

PARLORS

A transplanted Nordic friend of mine is trying to persuade his southern wife to move to Minnesota to help care for timber wolves allegedly threatened with extinction. Even now his family keeps dogs and allows them the freedom of the entire house. That led him to ponder why southern homes have so many "reserved spaces": living rooms, dining rooms, parlors, and libraries that are shut off and seldom used. Most southerners, he observed, seem to dwell in dens, kitchens, toolrooms, and bathrooms, and to make museums of the rest of their space.

His observations are essentially correct. Southerners do have a tendency to isolate certain rooms and their contents, such as silverware, the "good" china, antiques, or books. One explanation is that of evolution. The practice of reserving certain rooms for limited or no use goes back to days when Victorian homes and farmhouses had parlors used to seat the local minister when he called or young (supervised) couples when they were courting. Sometimes houses also had music rooms with pianos, played only when special company came or when some child was forced to forego baseball or buggy rides to practice. Modern homes evolved from those models.

Another explanation for isolated rooms is a practical one. In most southern households, both husband and wife now work. The number of children has declined radically from agricultural days when family units numbered an average of a dozen bodies sharing housekeeping chores to about four. The old tradition of having a grandmother living in the home, handling cooking and housekeeping, has also changed. The biggest change of all is in household labor. In the post–Civil War era, after slave labor disappeared, there was an enormous supply of paid domestic help willing to work for keep or very minimal wages. As the labor market has changed, especially in the last half of this century, domestic help has diminished strikingly.

There's no one around to take care of possessions, so they are in effect stored in houses rather than in sheds and barns. Yet northerners have possessions, too, and so there has to be some other explanation than the purely practical one for the southern peculiarity. It probably has something to do with the southern fascination with history. Family roots are terribly important in the South. "Forget, Hell!" on a bumper sticker is only a redneck rendering of the wider southern tendency to worship ancestors. One way we worship southern ancestors is to make home-shrines to them. Here we see grandmother's lace doily; over there is the ornate shaving cup grandfather used; next to it is the pressed-glass pickle dish that belonged to Aunt Daphne—all resting within an arc of brass-framed fading photos on the refinished washstand that belonged to great-grandfather, in the center of which is a large family Bible with pages of births, deaths, marriages, and family trees bearing assorted handwritings. Such shrines can't be placed in a kitchen or den. They belong in quieter rooms of their own, rooms kept closed off and entered infrequently and with reverence.

If one has no family heirlooms because some selfish cousin hauled off everything of Grandma's when she died, one has only to visit some of the antique shops that outnumber Stuckey's shops and Burger Kings in the South. History is purchasable; family roots are for sale. I know of two large restaurant chains that got started because their founders had stockpiled warehouses full of old southern furniture, signs, and implements and needed something to do with it all. They built restaurants decorated with selections of the stuff and trained their waiters to act surprised each time a customer remarks, "We had one just like that when I was growing up."

Closed-off rooms of our houses keep our pasts from being closed off. Peeking into them, we dream of rewards awaiting us when we reach retirement age. We shall not be shuttled off to nursing homes, but shall enter the forbidden rooms of our houses, light their candles, lounge on Victorian loveseats and horsehair couches, leave fingerprints on polished wood and footprints on immaculate carpets, and leaf through photo albums and molding books.

It sure beats moving to Minnesota to take care of timber wolves.

February 27, 1995

Gasoline prices here just leapt up by nineteen cents; gas now costs six times what it did when I got my driver's license in 1952. Candy bars are now ten times what they were (the year Ike was elected president), and soft drinks are twelve to fifteen times what they were in 1952.

We recall a time when politicians lamented that "what the country needs is a good five-cent cigar." Maybe what it needs is a good nickel candy bar and five-cent big bottle of Nehi soda. Newspaper prices are ten times what they were back then. Automobiles are also about ten times what they were then. Movies (excluding popcorn) cost about fifteen times what they did forty years ago. Paperback books cost more than hardbacks used to cost. I have shelves of $2.95 hardbacks from the '50s next to $6.95 paperbacks from recent times. Groceries, prescriptions, electricity, and phone service probably have had comparable increases.

What triggered this trip down memory lane for me was my monthly visit to the barbershop. Prices slip up a dollar there every year or two, and the going rate last week was fifteen dollars. Even at that the barber has to supplement his income by operating rental houses and selling customized golf clubs. The price of the haircut is one inflationary figure I don't regret. There is something distinctive about the smell of a barbershop that sticks with you lifelong, just as do the odors of a public library, a doughnut shop, a dry cleaners, or a courthouse. Once a month I pay the price for the pleasure of the reminiscence. I don't have to be in that revolving chair and under the sheet more than a minute before my eyes are drooping. As if I were an actor in *Star Trek*, I am transported back 485 miles and fifty years. Like something out of *It's a Wonderful Life*, I get to revisit the old Caldwell Barber Shop, long gone along with the hotel in which it was located a block off court square.

I still remember a Saturday after World War II when I was in for my regular "G.I. burr," and Gordon Council, the owner, told us the price was going up from fifty cents to sixty cents. It was my first clue that things were changing. Mr. Council had the fourth chair, at the back near the shine stand operated by a jovial man called Cricket. (My mother says he had the second chair, and that Loman "Shorty" Harris had the fourth, but I recall just the reverse.) Harlan Johnson, father of a good athlete a year ahead of me, had the first chair. I recall the third chair's face but can't remember his name. Some years later in life, I switched to the K&W shop on the other side of the square. Carl Willoughby, a member of our church, was co-owner and third chair with his partner, J. D. Kimball, up front and Des Floyd, another church member, in the middle; the shine boy usually opened the shop on Sunday mornings.

What impressed me most about those old barbershops was the wisdom. The seats along the wall facing the mirrors and barbers were usually filled with men just there for the talking: semiretired railroaders and farmers, faces turned to leather by time, all with haircuts cut short above the ears and oiled and parted carefully, wearing starched white shirts without ties. They never told dirty jokes, at least not while boys my age were around. They had opinions on everything from weather to politics to religion and shared them freely but with civility. Years later, when I saw *Spartacus* with Charles Laughton, Lawrence Olivier, and others as Roman senators gathered in a marbled bath deliberating the course of the empire, I recognized them instantly as barbershop pundits.

Barbershops almost died out in the late 1960s, when hair grew long and style salons sprang up. But no matter where I was or how old I became, I always found one that smelled and operated like the Caldwell or K&W. In New Haven, it was a Polish shop in a transitional neighborhood. In Kentucky, it was in the basement of another old hotel, also now razed. My favorite, in a very small west Tennessee town, had three chairs, big beveled mirrors, wooden floors, comb jars with blue antiseptic liquid, hand clippers, a big manual metal cash register, revolving ceiling fans, and an eighty-eight-year-old barber who knew everything.

April 15, 1996

CONFEDERATE MONUMENTS

My favorite reading this year was Howard Bahr's Civil War novel, *The Black Flower* (Nautical and Aviation Publishing Company), a love story set in the two days of the Battle of Franklin late in 1864, when General Hood sent the Confederate army on a last futile charge and six Confederate generals died.

The two days of the novel are separated by a short center chapter in which the heroine leaps decades ahead and visits the Franklin cemetery. The chapter comes close to being the most perfectly written passage I have ever read. Let me quote a piece of it:

> So the women could not forgive. Their passion remained intact, carefully guarded and nurtured by the bitter knowledge

of all they had lost, of all that had been stolen from them. For generations they vilified the Yankee race so that the thief would have a face, a name, a mysterious country into which he had withdrawn and from which he might venture again. They banded together into a militant freemasonry of remembering, and from that citadel held out against any suggestion that what they had suffered and lost might have been in vain. They created the Lost Cause, and consecrated that proud fiction with the blood of real men. To the Lost Cause they dedicated their own blood, their own lives, and to it they offered books, monographs, songs, acres and acres of bad poetry. . . .

But their greatest, their supreme and most poignant accomplishment, was the Confederate Soldier. Out of the smoke they plucked him, and set him atop a stone pedestal in the courthouse yard where he stood free at last of hunger and fear and raggedness and madness and violence; where he would never desert nor write home for a substitute, never run, never complain of short rations, never question the sacred Cause of which he was protector, and for which he had marched forth to willing sacrifice. But his musket was always at rest, and not for nothing was he always young, his eyes always soft as he looked backward over the long years. For he was really no soldier at all, but an image created by women, and he was born not of war but of sorrow and of fierce desire.

In earlier days, at mid-century before interstates took us away from the many court squares of the small county seats of the South, we saw granite statues of Confederate soldiers everywhere we went. Gaines M. Foster, a Wofford College alumnus, lists in his book *Ghosts of the Confederacy* (Oxford University Press) 544 Confederate monuments (excluding boulders and plaques). Of these 330 are in towns, and the others are mostly in cemeteries. Of the 544, only 94 were erected in the twenty years after the war (1865–1885) and only 100 in the fifteen years after that (1886–1899). With the turn of the century, the Confederate soldier came into his own. There were 306 statues erected from 1900 to 1912, and 241 of them were in towns rather than cemeteries, usually on public squares.

Many of the statues were mass-produced, and they seem peculiar for what they are supposedly saluting. The soldiers stand at rest, most of them look alike, and there is not much militancy or dash to them; they seem tired and without passions. In most towns, they have eroded, some with their rifles gone now, worn smooth by the elements and by the pigeons who have roosted there, and by armies of small boys who have climbed upon them for years, touching their ancestry without even realizing it.

A schoolmaster in Richmond said they were history books for people who couldn't read. A former general said they were "great interrogation marks to the soul of each beholder" calling us to pause to reflect in the rat-race hustling "in this great industrial age."

Howard Bahr teaches English at Tennessee's Motlow State Community College, but he is a native of Oxford, Mississippi, and was for many years the curator of Rowan Oak, William Faulkner's home. His sensitive novel makes stone men move. Somehow Bahr's recollection rescues us, at least for a while, from commonplace routines and callous daily living.

October 6, 1997

AMERICANIZED SOUTH

When Peter Applebome wrote *Dixie Rising,* its theme was that the South has risen again and that southern folkways have spread to the rest of the nation in such things as style of dress (denim), food (southern fried chicken), speech patterns (taken north in earlier job hunts), leisure-time interests (wrestling and NASCAR), entertainment (from Elvis to Garth Brooks), and race (black-white work and education patterns).

Mississippian Noel Polk in *Outside the Southern Myth* makes the reverse of that "Southernization of America" position. John Egerton made a similar case years ago in his book, *The Americanization of Dixie.*

Citing his little hometown of Picayune, Mississippi, as more representative of the South than are the scattered courthouse towns and Confederate monuments, Polk claims that the South has moved irrevocably past its "good ol' boy," "moonlight and magnolias," and "pickup trucks" stereotypes. In fact, Polk wonders if maybe most of the South was never really southern, at least after 1865. Lots of towns have no distinctly southern authors, no distinctly southern Civil War memories, and no distinctly southern motels or restaurants or factories or pharmacies. And most southern towns are as greedy for dollars and industry and "progress" as are most northern towns. In fact, by comparison, southern towns are far more Yankee-ized than towns in declining New England or the Great Lakes region, if the measure of

Yankee life-styles is aggressiveness in trying to make a dollar or being short on civility in human relations with clerks or making do with factory incomes. At the other end of the northern stereotypes, some older northern communities where things haven't changed at all for two centuries look suspiciously more like the fabled South than do most southern communities.

One suspects that Polk writes with tongue at least half in cheek. His own experiences in revivals, band trips, choice of reading matter, and kinship closeness reveal that he found something typically southern in his growing up, All-American as his experiences may seem to him. Still, Polk makes a strong argument that rock-and-roll music and ethnic diversity were universal and not distinctly southern. Arts committees and state councils can be found anywhere, as can gambling halls and lotteries, he says.

I probably agree with the Polk portrait of southern life as essentially American life. I would argue that there once was a distinct South and that what Polk sees is what has evolved as interstate highways, international corporate ownership of industry, eastern- and California-based television, job mobility, chain stores, and standardized health-care delivery have changed our region. Polk, being younger, lacks my perspective of having something else to remember.

Polk is an outstanding Faulkner scholar, and his book plays with a favorite Faulkner theme: southern-bred Americanization of the South, with native-son developers cranking up their bulldozers and knocking down the old ways of life, led by greedy southern men such as Flem Snopes or Quentin Compson who adapt the northern way of life to southern soil. But Polk underplays the roles of General Compson, Gavin Stevens, or the Benbows, Faulkner's representatives of a distinct culture that has been overrun by northern modernity.

There was a distinct South, remnants of which are still visible. It has lost a second Civil War, yielding its rural folkways to economic necessities and modern conveniences. The America-looking South was not, as Polk seems to suggest, essentially always here, but he is right in making us aware that what we now have is not too different from other regions of the country.

What we have, for those of us with romantic memories, is in some ways a step down instead of upward. The major change, however, was a necessary and welcomed one: we set ourselves to surrender the chains of race that weighed heavily on the South. Unfortunately, quite apart from the race change, we have forged, like Marley, new chains of dependencies and "development" and depersonalized living in the transition.

February 16, 1998

Back in the 1950s, New Circle Road in Lexington, Kentucky, was the city perimeter. Horse farms, an amusement park, and an occasional factory lay on its outer side. Driving along its northern side one could easily see a water tower still there today.

What made that Lexington water tower so memorable was that it is shaped like a giant white Dixie Cup. Old-timers remember Dixie Cups—the way we bought our ice cream, prepackaged, out of service-station and grocery-store freezers once soda fountains had begun to disappear and when Dairy Queens had closed for the day. They were also the most popular brand of paper cup for picnics and parties. Before Styrofoam and no-name competitors came along, to say Dixie Cup was to say paper cup, in the same way back then that Kleenex meant paper tissues, Scotch Tape meant clear tape, and Xerox meant copier. To many of us, the Dixie Cup Water Tower was as uniquely Lexington as Adolph Rupp or Man o'War.

Then we saw the Gaffney Peach. This giant peach-shaped water tower dominates the landscape on I-85 just south of the North Carolina state line, on the road from Charlotte to Atlanta. It is huge. It holds a million gallons of water and rests on a bed of ten million pounds of concrete. Built around 1980, its steel webbing took one and one half miles of welds to hold its peach skin and its twelve-foot brown stem and its sixty-foot, seven-ton green leaf. Tourists stopping to photograph it created such a traffic hazard that a special access road had to be built. If there was no Disney World to visit, the Gaffney Peach (financed in part by the Appalachian Regional Commission) would do in a pinch. (But there is a Disney World, where one can see the giant M-G-M Water Tower, a traditional shaped tower except for a black Mickey Mouse cap with ears atop it.)

On I-26 from Spartanburg to Columbia, Newberry, South Carolina, boasts a water tower shaped like a giant egg. One assumes that the poultry business is big in Newberry, but who cares? One can get the biggest dip of ice cream in South Carolina at the Ice Cream Churn there and gaze upon the Newberry egg while trying to lick the cone before it drips.

The Dole Pineapple water tower has dominated Honolulu since about the time FDR became president in 1933. Miniscule by comparison with the Gaffney Peach, the Dole Pineapple only held one hundred thousand gallons. No longer used, it is preserved by a state historical association. The Brooks Catsup Bottle water tower in Collinsville, Illinois, dates back to

1907. The catsup (not "ketchup," a Heinz word) plant is closed, but the bottle has been restored. It wins the prize for creativity and commercial gaudiness. One of the most spectacular water towers is one shaped like a metal teapot, very Swedish in look, in Lindstrom, Minnesota. The most beautiful American tower is in Scituate, Massachusetts, given by Thomas Lawson in 1920 and copied from a fifteenth-century Roman tower. Almost as spectacular, the Chicago water tower built in 1869 during the Chicago Centennial looks like a French cathedral topped by an English prison tower. The attractive Old Fresno Water Tower built in 1894 was to have housed a two-story library but never did. In Sunset Beach, California, three doctors bought the city water tower and turned it into a three-story home with an elevator. The University of Washington water tower was built in 1904, but in 1914 a Seattle publisher donated twelve bells, and the tower became the campus chimes, played from 1917 to 1949 by a blind music student–alumnus named George Bailey. Its water didn't save it from burning.

During Soup and Sandwich Month, a sign that read "& Soup" was added below the name of the water tower in Sandwich, Illinois. Wasaga Beach, Ontario, painted its round tower like a beach ball, a symbol of the vacation industry there. Several towns made golf balls or hot-air-balloons out of their towers. Here in Spartanburg, two canister-shaped towers try to hide in the landscape by wearing green paint like distant tree lines or moun-tain ridges.

Unusual water towers make Andy Warhol–like art and humor out of necessities, as the "See Rock City" artist did for hundreds of barns. We like most of them, but next thing you known, politicians will be wanting them shaped and painted in their images and honor.

July 28, 1998

BALTIMORE

Baltimore, Maryland, is a haunting place. Our eldest gave us a grand tour. Baltimore was "Nevermore" fine. We visited Fort McHenry, the oversized Stars and Stripes of which Francis Scott Key made famous. We walked on Federal Hill, overlooking the Inner Harbor. We passed the H. L. Mencken house several times, a Confederate museum, a flag museum, and the silo-shaped Shot Tower that held cannon balls years ago.

We located Edgar Allen Poe's tiny townhouse home, tucked inconspicuously in the low-income sector of town. Frequently we spied ravens, the birds that Poe made famous; they have not joined the urban flight. They were in the cemetery, at Federal Hill and on the wharf of the Inner Harbor, talking away and totally unintimidated by tourists. Professor Bernd Heinrich's *Mind of the Raven* shows that ravens are intelligent creatures capable of independent thinking that mimic radio static or motorcycles and human speech, follow wolves and bears to find food, and form teams to kill hawks. Heinrich's research explains why Poe's raven liked to perch in libraries and could speak, if only to say "Nevermore."

We ate Baltimore's famed crab cakes near the harbor and had Italian food in an exciting section of town called Little Italy, choosing it over an array of Thai, Japanese, Chinese, Indian, and African restaurants not far away. We lamented the passing of a noted German restaurant, seventy-three-year-old Haussner's, which had a collection of great art that Sotheby's will auction off.

We strolled the arc of the impressively large new home of the Baltimore Ravens NHL franchise, Psinet Stadium, next to Camden Yards, which it dwarfs and makes feel even more homelike in the process. Local folks miss the Colts. We sat in left-field bleachers in cathedral-like Camden Yards ballpark and watched the New York Yankees erase a Baltimore Orioles' 4-0 lead to win 9-5. When people bemoan baseball's demise, let them come to Camden Yards where baseball looks, sounds, and feels like it should (despite four-dollar soft drinks and five-dollar hot dogs).

We drove all over the city, awed by impressive arrays of architecture, dozens of religious buildings from Gothic cathedrals and baroque synagogues to neighborhood churches a century or more old scattered strategically among skyscrapers with some of the most significant innovations in design imaginable. Rows and rows of Georgetown-like townhouses line many Baltimore streets, some in need of renovation and others models of pristine inner-city living. Baltimore, like most major cities, is suffering from urban flight, with some twelve thousand taxpayers relocating outside the city each year leaving a tell-tale blight of vacant stores and unrepaired streets, but the spirit of the place is still lively. There are several museums, theaters, and good bookstores, plentiful hotels and restaurants and office buildings, and a good public transportation system. One can even ride by rail the fifty miles from Washington's Union Station to Baltimore's Camden Yards.

John Wilkes Booth, Lincoln's assassin, is alleged to lie in historic Green Mount Cemetery, established in 1839. A gatekeeper furnished a map of the graves with famous ones marked. We found graves of patriarch Junius Booth and some of his family, but no marker for John Wilkes. Looking for Booth turned up other surprises. We found the grave of Harriet Lane, White House hostess for the bachelor president James Buchanan. Not far from her is the grave of General Joseph E. Johnston, the Confederate general who, wounded and replaced by Robert E. Lee, served out west, led the retreat to Atlanta, and surrendered the last large army to Sherman in North Carolina after Lee surrendered in Virginia. Johnston was a Virginian but was buried with his wife in Baltimore. He died of pneumonia contracted from standing bareheaded in the rain at Union general Sherman's funeral. A less-famous but important Confederate general also in Green Mount is Isaac Trimble. Poet Sidney Lanier and CIA head Allen Dulles are there, too.

October 3, 1999

SENIOR PROM

For safety's sake, we seek something secured: some constancy, some consistency, and some certitude. Docks on our expanding sea of change are fewer and farther between than ever. The world around us changes with accelerating speed before our eyes. We live longer, but we also live much, much faster. We see in a decade more seismic shifts in the way we live than our parents saw in a lifetime. We dwell more and more in the fog of the coming world of our progeny and less and less on the solid ground of the familiar world of our progenitors. The no-man's-land between past and present, between verities and questionings, between energizing innocence and paralyzing sophistication, belongs to Everyman—and Everywoman. Once, like Icarus, we flew freely toward the heavenly sun; now we are happy for a less-dizzying earthly crag to which to cling or at which to aim.

Be at peace. Verily, such a thing does yet exist: Senior Prom.

The Senior Prom lives on. It is one of the few dinosaurs that has survived the post–World War and postindustrial Ice Age. Other entrenched Truths have fallen by the wayside, buried by the avalanche of Modernity and entombed in the glacier of Our Times: among them, nightly family dinnertime, Sunday night church services, circus tents, calling cards, front porch swings, Nash and Packard cars, passenger trains, Army football, and *Classics Illustrated* comic books.

The Senior Prom lives on. The trauma of getting the right date (or a date at all) is still there. So is the quest for the perfect dress and the most current tux (pastels out-rent black). The florists still mass-produce corsages. Parents still teach their sons how to pin them on, and daughters still prefer dresses with as little to which to pin a corsage as possible. The theme (usually something about "Reaching for the Stars" or "Over the Rainbow") is still stretched in cut-out letters over the stage. The balloons are the same shapes and colors they always have been. The hall still smells like Noxzema. The band still plays (though less frequently) a dance slow enough for any waltzer to catch the lyrics. The dances of preference are still outrageous and still have names; Electric Slide and Achy-Breaky Heart line dances are great-grandchildren of the Bunny Hop. The Twist, the Shag, and the waltz are still "in." The girls' high heels still wobble, and their feet (once the shoes come off early in the evening) are still tinted with fresh shoe dye.

The boys still huddle on one side and the girls on the other, eyeing each other with fear and lust across wooden floors. Sideline critiques still focus on breasts and buns. Old girlfriends still snipe with catty comments at new ones, and old boyfriends still call new ones out for parking-lot brawls. The chaperones still glower in little corner bunches, better at guarding the punchbowl against augmenters than at keeping dancers at arm's length from each other. The punch tastes the same as it did forty years ago, and the white cakes and the cookies look and taste the same as well; there are still breakfasts afterwards. "Fantastic" is still the favorite word.

A few changes are noticeable. Parents used to drive boys and their dates to the prom; now they arrive in new graduation-gift cars or rented limousines. Prices have gone up: tux rentals cost now what buying a tuxedo used to cost; dresses are the price of monthly mortgage payments, and you could paint your house for what a girl shells out for cosmetics. Hoop skirts are rare, and used flashbulbs don't litter the floor. The music is louder. No one has heard of no-break cards.

But little else has changed. Proms provide us with the permanence our lives need. They are as reassuring as the changing of the guard at Buckingham Palace. Parents still take snapshots and give last-minute advice at the front door as their fledglings leave their nests.

I never have really enjoyed dancing, although I wasn't bad at it in my college years.

"Why can't I dance?" I ponder to myself as I watch the very young piling into rented limousines or my own peers plodding around a country club floor. It may have been something traumatic in my own youth that kept me off the dance floors all these years.

My first dance was our graduation prom in the eighth grade. We were leaving junior high and moving on to high school, and our class held a graduation dance at the old City Auditorium. That was in 1950. I don't recall having a date. In fact, I don't recall anyone having a date.

The boys, most of whom weren't shaving yet, were wearing sport coats and ties—but not the white sport coats, pink shirts, black ties, and white bucks shoes we wore at high school dances in later years. The girls, who may have begun shaving by then, were in taffeta, flared-skirt, knee-length dresses. The boys tended to clump on one side of the floor, and the girls on the other. The chaperones, whom I recall as all being women teachers, wore more formal attire: ankle-length dresses with white corsages on their left bosoms.

Too shy to ask a girl to dance, I felt it my duty to ask a chaperone to dance. I chose the one I liked the most, our English teacher and girls' basketball coach, whom I loved madly. She wore a light green or blue satin dress. Miss Roberts was a great coach. She helped me count: one-two, one, one-two, one. Then she showed me how to make a square: one-glide, 90-degree angle right, one-glide, 90-degree angle right. I was on a cloud. I don't know if we were in step with the music at all. I just remember the joy of not tripping and the pleasure of seeming to know what I was doing.

Miss Roberts is still alive, and when I hugged her last summer while back in my hometown, I noticed that I am now taller than she. But back then in 1950, she was a head taller than I, and I kept my head turned sideways to keep from appearing to stare where I should not.

Then, the dance about half over, disaster struck. She quietly and very politely said, "Why don't you move your hand?" Puzzled by what she meant, I asked her to repeat what she said.

And Miss Roberts did: "Your hand. Move it up."

Because of my shortness, my right hand was resting quite comfortably and naturally—and totally without my consciousness of it—on her rear end.

Thank goodness it was a darkened dance floor. I blushed as red as the rose corsages the girls were wearing, thanked Miss Roberts politely, and then walked as hastily without drawing attention as I could to the men's room (which that night was the boys' room) to stop the nosebleed that my error had caused.

I don't know why that misplaced hand fifty years ago has haunted me ever since. I think I had just seen a horror movie, *The Beast with Five Fingers,* about an unattached hand kept in a box in Europe that crawled out and strangled women and then played a piano. Maybe I connected the two. Whatever the childhood terrors nestled inside me since that eighth grade-prom, dancing has since been an obligation, seldom a pleasure.

But even more hidden than that, perhaps, is a long-kept secret buried so deeply that I have even kept it from myself—until now. As I write this reminiscence, it suddenly dawns upon me that, guilty as I have felt for over a half-century about having my hand on Miss Roberts's derriere, my real guilt is this:

I enjoyed it.

May 4, 1993, and April 23, 2000

KEYS

Spring-cleaning doesn't phase us one bit. Throwing away things is foreign to our nature—much to my eternally forgiving wife's chagrin.

We have rubber bands from daily newspapers, assorted coins, a drawer of political campaign buttons and bumper stickers, stacks and stacks of books, years of monthly magazines, stacks of partial reams of paper, addressed unused envelopes from former residences, and every birthday and Father's Day card ever received from our daughters—not to mention a collection of Christmas cards judged "best of the season," and horseshoe nails from old barns and battle sites.

One steadily growing collection consists of several hundred keys: keys to homes and to offices we long ago left in Connecticut, Kentucky, Alabama, and Tennessee; keys left by a grandfather who died in 1954 and a grandmother who died in 1956; keys to file cabinets long forgotten; keys to Samsonite suitcases no longer owned; keys to Smith-Corona portable typewriters no longer used; big old-fashioned keys to farmhouse doors and padlocks no longer around; keys to whole generations of automobiles no longer owned; an honorary key to the city of Louisville; plus assorted club "keys" (Key Club, Rotary Club, Phi Beta Kappa, Omicron Delta Kappa, Phi Kappa Phi).

I remember no keys from my childhood. Surely the many homes in which we lived when I was growing up, moving about once every two years, had locks and keys, but my memory of childhood is of houses and neighborhoods with doors never locked.

Even when in college and home on vacations we had no house keys. One night I stayed out to 2:00 A.M. with other home-for-the-holidays friends and found the house door locked when we finally finished partying. I slept in a porch swing. It was a first vivid taste of reality, of being grown and gone and unable to go home again.

The first key I recall carrying was a key to a men's dormitory room in Kentucky. I was eighteen years old. The second key I had was a loaner, a car key to a 1948 Dodge that belonged to a fellow college student, an army veteran who was kind enough to let me use it for emergencies like dating or midnight doughnut runs. My third key was to an English department office where I graded freshman English papers for three years. My fourth was my own car key—to a 1950 black Studebaker given me at age twenty-one for Christmas of my senior college year. (That key also opened the car trunk in which I kept a case of the oil that the car burned faster than gasoline.)

The first and fourth keys were the important ones, the dormitory key symbolizing leaving home and the car key symbolizing moving onward and upward in the world, independently.

But even at age twenty-one, I was relatively unencumbered by keys, and the several hundred scattered in desk and bureau drawers and on key hooks in closets and on key rings in my pocket today have all come in my adulthood over the last forty-four years.

Giving up a key to an old apartment or an old car or an old suitcase is an act of closure we hesitate to commit. As long as we have the keys to our past, we feel we can return there, even though we know better. We refuse to face up to the fact we can't go home again or can't go back in time. Keys are part of that psychological self-delusion. They are what remind us of the kingdoms through which we have passed and the royalty—which is to say, the family and friends—embraced in passing.

We keep old keys around because we don't want to lock the doors of our past.

May 13, 2001

Chapter 3

EDUCATION
"IN PATHS OF RIGHTEOUSNESS"

A FEW WORDS

RAGE

Age and education give you the authority, citizenship the responsibility, to rage against mediocrity and injustice in your society, more especially in yourself.

Lest you leave your life on an altar of ethical neutrality or find your soul eroded by gentle raindrops of moral detachment, heed Dylan Thomas:

> *Do not go gentle into that good night;*
>
> *Rage, rage against the dying of the light*

REASON

More things are wrought by reason than this world dreams of; wherefore, make reason the nuclear weapon of your arsenal of rage, and by its use convince others of your integrity, if not your rightness. The hand that cradles the rock, the heart that heeds not the head, must not rule this world.

READ
> Bury yourself in good books and read them often;
> too soon the minister will bury you and read for you.
> Develop a thirst for printer's ink and quench it by reading,
> for from books flows the fountain of youth found by few.

LAUGH
> He who cannot laugh at himself always appears ridiculous.

LINGER
> Everything has its season;
> time will wait for what's worthwhile.
> Heed the South Alabama philosopher:
> *Pause to pick some flowers along your way.*

LOVE
> Love is the most unnatural human emotion.
> Although we have learned to transplant the human heart,
> we have not learned to transform it.
> Commit an unnatural act: *love one another.*

Commencement, the University of Alabama, May 14, 1972

ENGLISH LANGUAGE

A fund-appeal flier in my mail this week asked for a donation to help make English the official national language. I thought it already was.

Quite a debate has been raging in government and education circles in recent years over teaching English. Some parties feel that racial and national origins are so important that teachers and textbooks should use the primary language of the majority of their students. There is a rather legitimate concern that the students may lose the sense of their heritage or that they may be handicapped by having to learn and to compete in the English-language mode that is unnatural for them.

Opponents of that view make the case that an American heritage shared by all can only develop if we all speak and read the same language. They counter the handicap argument by pointing out that the handicap is only deferred by sticking to a non-English native language because once school days are over and the students enter the competition for jobs, the workman's language is English.

If both sides are right, and to a degree, they are, then the real question is not whether an American citizen will ever learn English, but at what point it should it be learned. There is no easy time for a non-English speaking American to learn English. It's a hard language. If English-speaking Americans who try to learn a foreign language are any guide in answering that question, most would agree that a second language is learned more easily in the early years, from age three through high school, than in the college and adult years.

A little controversy going on in Atlanta these days may shed some light on this subject. Atlanta has become a center of national and regional offices for major national and multinational corporations. Some of those headquarters have been hiring speech teachers to train their employees how *not* to speak in a southern accent or drawl. English, apparently is a "second language"; "Southern" is a primary one.

Perhaps we could have a little more sympathy for our Hispanic- or Asian-speaking fellow citizens who have fears of losing their tongues if forced to learn English. If the price for the South entering the mainstream of American economy is that we have to learn better English—instead of southern English—as our second language, surely we can understand how hard it is for others. Then together, perhaps, we can focus more on what we—government, educators, parents, citizens—can all do to make the teaching of English more natural and the learning less loathsome.

November 18, 1985

ENGLISH TEACHER

The changes at New Year's 1986 pale beside those of 1954. About then a generation gap opened up. Not between our parents and us, but between us and our younger brothers and sisters. My age group walked everywhere it went, wore khakis and ironed shirts, parted our hair, and liked Pat Boone. But two years behind us came aliens from another planet who bought and drove old cars, wore green suede jackets over white T-shirts tucked into belt-less blue jeans, peroxided their Mohawked or onion-peeled or flat-topped hair, and wailed with Elvis.

I think what brought the change was Miss Word leaving. She had taught eleventh-grade English since my mother's day. If her leaving for Missouri didn't cause the changes, it was surely a symptom of them. I know an English teacher named Miss Word sounds made-up by someone from *Sesame Street* or *Mr. Rogers' Neighborhood* but, believe me, she was very real. Cleanth Brooks, world-renowned literature scholar, has known a host of Miss Words. Brooks, the son of a west Tennessee Methodist minister, in his marvelous little book about how we southerners came to speak as we do, gives the Miss Words credit for drumming southern accents out of our system (somewhat). His book is *The Language of the American South* (University of Georgia Press).

When Miss Word left, the poetry went out of our lives. "Gone with the wind" (like Cynara's lover) were the agony of memorizing Milton's "Sonnet on His Blindness" and the ecstasy of Poe's "Annabelle Lee." She had made us gallop through Longfellow's "Paul Revere's Ride" and wade through Lanier's marshes and Bryant's "Thanatopsis." Without a Word standing guard over us, our language would be buried like Gray's "Elegy in a Country Courtyard" and empty as Goldsmith's "Deserted Village." When she folded her tents "like the A-rabs" and silently stole away, something that "walks in beauty like the night" went with her.

Of course, I exaggerate. Memory work and diagramming sentences went on after Miss Word was gone, my brother claims. What really was changing was the way we saw the world. For ages, down through my own, learning was the printed word. Now there came radio and recordings, video and movies, and wheels to take us away from libraries. We moved, in an Age of Progress, into a Word-less world.

Makers of trivia table games have not rediscovered us yet. They peddle questions on the Beatles, the Baby Boom, sports, and entertainment. There is a market of fifty-and-over citizens packed with memory work— and memories—of our Miss Words.

"Why, man," she did "bestride the narrow world like a colossus" (*Julius Caesar*). And in Word words that were probably Wordsworth's, she flashes still "upon that inner eye which is the bliss of solitude."

December 30, 1985

COLLEGE DAYS

Dear Eldest Daughter,

Is it possible that nearly four years have passed since we bundled you up and sent you off to college? Now you are graduating again. We hope college was what you expected it to be. More selfishly, we hope it was what we wanted it to be for you. We're never sure that the dreams of parents and those of their offspring are on the same wavelength.

We've kept up with you by reading report cards, phone bills, and canceled checks. From those long-distance peeks, we're satisfied with the college and proud of you.

We hope you'll take a minute to look back while you're getting dressed up to step out on graduation day. What were those four college years for? What we wanted them to be for you was "in-between time," with the right mix of just enough independence and yet just enough security to ease your way from high school into the real world. We wanted you to have the luxury of enough time to fall in love with learning and to make it habit-forming at the same time you were learning some marketable skills for making a living to support your learning habits. And we wanted you to have some fun and to find new friendships, too. If you had gotten too old for us to keep to ourselves, you were still too young for us to throw to the world, and your college has served you and us well as a halfway house.

Maybe you'll look back on college as "bright college years." You'll rarely meet alumni who dislike their college memories. Maybe that's why they call colleges "alma maters," meaning "our mothers." Colleges are maternal surrogates.

But the analogy for the college experience we like better than alma mater is Oz. Think about that story for a minute, while you are struggling with the unfamiliar button eye at the back of your unfamiliar white dress. (We're sorry the petition to wear designer jeans to commencement wasn't approved!)

Like Dorothy, you lived in the black-and-white world of the Midwest until a whirlwind of college recruiters came after you, swept you away in a tornado of promises, and set you down in a Technicolored campus. Lots of other students were around, too, called Munchkins. During orientation, they explained that the way out was to follow the yellow-brick road, which you recognize as curriculum requirements—course after course, brick after brick. They also warned to watch out for witches and goblins, which you would call flunking or getting booted. Fortunately, she had some good help from a cowardly lion, rusty tin woodsman, and mindless scarecrow, such as you had from some kindly professors and administrators.

And now you've come to the end of the road, and pretty soon you'll be seeing that Wizard, the president who tries to keep the college running, and he'll be handing you a diploma just like what happened to Dorothy's friends. If he's humble as we think he is, he'll probably admit that you could have left Oz on your own anytime you chose—that you could have made it on your own without the college.

Probably so. Half your high school classmates did. But you would have missed the flowers along the road. You would have missed the yellow in the bricks. You would have missed that eccentric love from bumbling but bright scarecrows. You would have missed the Munchkins and the witches, the Wizard and the castles.

Most of all, you would have missed the Technicolor, which now you can spend—and are duty bound to spend—the rest of your life applying to any corner of the black and white—and gray—world you are entering.

We congratulate you, and we thank you for walking the road so well.

Love, Mom and Dad

April 27, 1987

MATH LESSONS

Our seventh grader's math grade for this six weeks was hovering just below the line between a B and an A.

"Maybe the teacher will drop everyone's lowest grade," she hoped aloud after averaging her grades for the sixth time. "Don't they do that in the Olympics?"

I reminded her that in the Olympics they throw out the highest grade as well as the lowest. If she did that, her average would drop another point, not gain one. Then I threw her my real zinger. "Your Aunt Bess would turn over in her grave at the idea of changing a grade."

Daughter Molly was unimpressed. "Who is my Aunt Bess?" she asked.

I became indignant. "Who is Aunt Bess?" I shouted. "You mean you're kin to probably the world's greatest junior high school math teacher and don't even know who she was?" It seems completely irrelevant to me that Aunt Bess died years and years before our daughter was even born. Even if she had never known her, she had some obligation to act as if she had.

Aunt Bess was a fine teacher, married to John Q. Adams (not the president) but childless, who adopted all of her students and painstakingly initiated them into the extraterrestrial universes of Pythagoras and Euclid. She was in every aspect of appearance and manner the picture of how a real lady was supposed to look. By the time I entered her class her coal-black hair, piled faultlessly atop the back of her head, was graying, not randomly but in careful geometric patterns (acute triangles) swept back from her temples. Her Victorian long-sleeved, frilled, white blouses were pinned at the neck ("my Adams Apple," our Mrs. Adams said) by an oval cameo with a raised circular face upon it, perpetually reminding us of the contrasts between the enigmas of the ellipse and the simplicity of the circle. Behind her back, we called her Queen Bess; she was regal.

Perched above the cameo oval and between her triangular temples was Aunt Bess's only fault, rimless glasses with two circles of glass so thick that her eyes were also invisible behind them. Without the glasses, she was practically blind, which was why we were so delighted to have her umpire our recess baseball games—Victorian dress, frosted glasses, coiffured hair, cameo, and all.

The geometry of the infield square and of the outfield arc, the pentagon of the batter's plate, and the rectangle of the pitcher's mound, all seemed part and parcel of her. Playground time with "Miss Bess" was her classroom extended, and we hated rained-out days. She loved math, she loved baseball, and we found that she loved us, too. She taught us math by using baseball statistics. She knew them all by heart. She could have made a fortune writing them down for the bubblegum company's baseball cards. Her grading was like her umpire calls—clear, certain, unarguable. We fought to make home runs on her tests, to improve our performance "stats," to set records for RBI's and at-bats in her drills. Her own ambition was to get all of us to where none of us would "strike out."

Mathematics is supposed to be the most basic and most universal language known to man. By mathematics, we supposedly can communicate with strangers in other vocations than our own, with people in other countries than our own, and with generations long gone and yet to come. You would think anything that fundamental would be duck soup. Two plus two equals four everywhere and for all times, right?

Wrong. This most elementary language is complex, a maze of laws and rules and processes and connections that makes learning to speak or write English look like child's play (which it is).

Blessed indeed, therefore, is the struggling math student who slides into a Queen Bess's home plate.

May 23, 1988

Our daughter has discovered the wonderful world of allusions.

An allusion is a word, a phrase, or an image, which can be used as a capsule for a wide range of ideas.

For example, we can allude to Shakespeare's famous line, "all the world's a stage," and get instant communication of the world as a theater stage upon which we act our parts, or get the notion of role-playing to remind us that we all play many differing parts during the course of a lifetime or even of a day, or get the sense that life comes in stages, evolving and changing our appearances and identities from infancy to old age.

Among the allusions in which our daughter is taking special delight in her English themes these days are those that involve Greek and Roman gods and myths.

Recently this daughter had a difficult poem to analyze. When she decided that its main character was really Pan, the half-animal, half-human field and forest creature who delighted in playing a flute and chasing nymphs, she broke the code and scored a hit in class.

Antaeus is a good allusion for southerners. This character drew his strength from the soil. As long as he kept his feet on the ground, he was unconquerable. Hercules defeated him by lifting him off the ground until his strength was drained away. Antaeus is a great allusion to throw into a history paper on why Lee lost the battle of Gettysburg. Proteus is a bit more obscure.

Proteus could change shapes but also had to tell the truth when shackled: this allusion is useful for describing how persistence pays off; things are seldom what they seem on the surface—or even several layers beneath the surface. But if one sticks to the subject and digs deep enough, one will finally get to the truth.

Prometheus is the story of the Titan (half-man/half-god) whose curiosity and ambition to be godlike drove him to steal fire, one of the first symbols of man's power, from the gods. To call some character in a story Promethean is a great way to impress a teacher.

The current favorite in our household is Procrustes. It has reference to the human tendency to force equality onto a situation. A "Procrustean bed" was a torture rack that would stretch short people or cut off the legs of tall people to make everyone the same size. When the Queen in *Alice's Adventures in Wonderland* runs around shouting, "Off with her head," she is saying that someone is "too big for his britches" and needs to be "cut down to size." There are similarities between Prometheus and Procrustes who both had to pay penalties for their presumptuousness.

I had the good luck during my first six years of schooling to have an aunt as my grade school principal. She let me pick out a book each Christmas from the school book fair. One I recall with pleasure and still own was a little yellow-back book called *Chariots of the Gods*. I have discovered better and more complete mythology books since then, but I know that I would never have developed an appetite for them if that aunt—actually a great-aunt (truly a great one)—hadn't made me taste the stuff first. By the time another teacher, probably Mrs. Montgomery in the sixth grade, uncovered the history of Greece and Rome for us, I was ready and willing to dive in.

The same importance can be attached to other sources of allusions. All of us, without knowing it, quote the Bible, Shakespeare, and probably Thoreau and Emerson. Maybe a good prescription for making sure "the twig is bent" (where does that allusion come from?) in a person's youth is to give them a few good books, *101 Best Loved Poems* and *Bartlett's Quotations* among them. They make following plots or answering quiz questions more fun.

Someone has said that the purpose of education is to destroy our illusions. I don't share that philosophy. But if that is what education is about, then let it at least leave us with our allusions.

March 26, 1990

CONFORMITY

Surely some psychologist can explain why most of us are so fascinated by crayons. You know the type I mean. I'll avoid using their brand name. They're the ones in the yellow-orange and green boxes with matching yellow-orange and green paper wrappers around them, each carefully labeled with the color it is.

Not many of us really use them to color with, but they are nice to have around. You can rearrange them in color groups, either by contrasts or in sets by degrees of shading, with blue-green or red-orange for transitions between sets. Beyond stormy black and gray is a silver lining, and beyond it an infinite rainbow of color, with gold at the end. You can learn spelling and vocabulary from them. What poetry there is in "magenta" or "turquoise" or "burnt sienna" or "puce!" You can count them, or learn to count by using them for number 1's, the shape they bear. You can line them up on end in triangles at the end of a hardwood hallway and make a bowling alley, using marbles for bowling balls. Or you can melt a couple and mold them into a homemade bowling ball.

They come in boxes of six, eight, twelve, twenty-four, and sixty-four. Once I even had a box of seventy-two, which I held on to for years. I wouldn't even let our daughters have it because it was such a rarity. Breaking one is enough to make you cry. Wearing down and rounding out their sharp points and having to tear their wrapping to use them are the next greatest tragedies in using them.

My earliest memories of crayons are from the third grade. I don't recall having them around earlier during World War II, although surely we did. I can't imagine them being rationed and used as bullets, even though they are shaped like them.

One memory is of someone in class occasionally eating a crayon or chewing it for gum. I don't recall who it was, although it was probably Billy Oliver or one or more of the King twins, Horace and Morris, who loved to shock us any way they could.

The second third-grade crayon memory is more vivid. One day our regular teacher, Miss Rebecca Bayer, was absent. Her substitute passed out pages of outlined Thanksgiving turkeys and told us to color them. What I recall is this lady walking up and down the aisles and looking over our shoulders as we colored and telling us over and over, "Don't color outside the lines. Make your strokes in the same direction."

It was my first introduction to fascism, which I though we had just fought a war to defeat.

Our world consisted of lines. We lined up outside the front door each morning, waiting for the opening bell. We lined up to go to the rest room or to recess, to lunch and from one classroom to another, and to file out in the afternoon. We sat in assigned lined desks, rows of them bolted to the floor. (Remember the kind? With slanted tops that lifted and inkwell holes in the right hand upper corners? And generations of initials carved in the tops and generations of chewing gum stuck underneath?)

Kindly Miss Rebecca with her beautiful silver hair heaped up atop her head, except for stray strands she never seemed able to control, and bearing the worldly experience of what I assumed to be at least ninety-seven years, had never forced us to stay in the lines or to make our strokes in the same direction.

In those days of regimentation, when our lives were organized by math drill numbers and by the alphabet and by writing rules and by Palmer Method penmanship practice, Miss Rebecca was the symbol of promised freedom. She occasionally stopped class to play games at some time other than recess. And even at recess, she played sandlot ball with us. She kept books of her own in her rented room a block away and encouraged us to come by and borrow them.

And she let us color outside the lines—and in any color we wanted. My turkey the day she was absent was a respectable brown. But in my memory, I picture it as it would have been if Miss Rebecca had been there that November day.

Purple.

Purple for royalty, for this king or queen of the birds.

And purple, too, for regal Miss Rebecca, with whom the color purple is indelibly entwined in our hearts and minds. Twenty years later, when hippies and flower children appeared, the shocking children whom Billy Oliver and the King twins would have loved, we recognized them instantly.

They were pale imitations of Miss Rebecca Bayer, who let us color outside the lines.

July 16, 1990

TEACHER LOVE

Billy Oliver, my grade school classmate whom I haven't seen in years, wrote to correct my story a few weeks back about his eating crayons. He ate only the short green ones, he claims. Bill then changed the subject, recalling that we shared a fanatical love for our beautiful, red-headed, fourth-grade teacher, who left in mid-year to join her military husband.

Beyond being irrationally in love with the teacher, I remember very little else about the fourth grade. It was the last year I had to wear knickers, it was the year that Eugene Maddox practically beat me into accepting his insistent information that there was no Santa Claus, it was the year our class had two sets of twins—the redheaded King boys and the pigtailed Meals girls, and it was the year I served as class health inspector, making weekly cootie inspections of all scalps and sending helpful health notes home to my classmates' parents.

That was not exactly my "Summer of '42," but it was close enough, that "Fall of '45." And did I ever fall! According to Bill's letter, so did he. It comes as something of a shock at this late date to find he was as smitten with the teacher as was I. I had always thought that, with her husband away in the war, I had her all to myself. She was red-haired, green-eyed, and petite, a Maureen O'Hara look-alike but not as tall. And I, just inching my way into manhood at age nine, felt duty bound to be her Knight Protector. By some twist of my psyche I associated her with Bambi's mother—the vulnerable teacher of her young whose high purposes and virtuous life were threatened by dark forces surrounding us with guns out on the fields of war.

On the pretext of playing with classmates a mile from home, I daily patrolled the street in front of her house. As fall turned to winter, she began to invite me in out of the cold. In her living room, before an open fire, we played with metal mechanical toy cars her absent husband had shipped from occupied Germany, toys such as we had not seen in America because of metal rationing. And finally it ended, just as Bill recalls, with her resignation and departure in mid-year and with my inconsolable sadness at losing her.

It was to be three long years before I recovered enough to fall in love again, this time with our seventh-grade English teacher, who was also coach of the junior high women's basketball team. This time the risk of heartbreak seemed reduced because she was unmarried. But, alas, she too was whisked away, to teach and coach at the high school. And though I found her there when I arrived two years later, it was not quite the same. In the time lapse in between I had discovered other women of my own age, and she could never reclaim the sole possession over me she held when I was twelve or that my first love had when I was nine.

I think of them both at odd moments: when I walk through the metal cars lining Wal-Mart toy aisles, or when trying on tennis sneakers, or when breaking a sentence into its component parts and diagramming it in my mind. In moments of memory such as those, teaching and learning do not seem lost causes, though the first-love glow of great teachers has faded. In fact, looking back to that fixation with the redheaded figure from our fourth grade, I wonder how much of what I have done, having been in school for forty-eight years now, has been from fear of leaving her behind and thereby losing her forever.

Love and learning are too entwined to be separated. Looking back over all those years as a student, I can't recall having any poor teachers. Each one, young or old, female or male, luckily loved teaching, and consequently implied that they loved those students it was their lot to teach.

Now that I know how little they were paid and how seldom they were praised, I am more convinced than ever that what they did had to have been done out of love. Great teaching is more than techniques and testing, and the root of the educational crisis in our country today is that so little room has been left for love. We are right to dread that the great ones will be taken away by dark forces.

September 17, 1990

FOUNTAIN PENS

Habits are a long time in forming, but it takes even longer to break them once they are in place: take writing with a fountain pen for example. Every grown-up I knew in my youth wrote with a fountain pen. Changing from using pencils to writing with a fountain pen was a mark of adulthood, like changing from short pants and knickers to long pants.

In my case, my pencil-writing days coincided with the end of the Depression and with World War II. Pencils were appropriate then, both because of my age and because there wasn't much other choice. The big deal was to get a Bulova or Elgin watch or a Sheaffer, Parker, or Waterman fountain pen for high school graduation.

I was in the class of 1954. About the time we graduated, the whole universe was shaken by scientific revolutions. The atomic bomb is the major discovery of that era that most people would recall if asked, but for me it was but a minnow compared to the whales of (1) the ballpoint pen and (2) the shock-resistant waterproof watch.

The arrival of ballpoint pens and of unstoppable watches on the market was a major community event. Jewelry stores had mass demonstrations of ballpoint pens writing under water and on butter. Watches were dropped out of airplanes onto fields at fall football games to demonstrate their amazing resilience. We ogled these new mechanical marvels with the same awe we had shown a few years earlier for halftime demonstrations of flamethrowers and parachutists.

The arrival of the ballpoint pen set our generation apart forever from that of our parents. Terribly difficult choices had to be made about what kind of adults we wanted to become. Would we go with the new ballpoints and be liberated modernists or stick with the fountain pen and be traditionalists?

Similar sorts of decisions confronted us everywhere.

Would we stay at home or go away to college or to work? Would we marry the hometown girl or postpone marriage and select someone alien to our town? Would we have the traditional 4 or 5 children or settle for the new average of 2.3? Would we continue to walk or have more cars than we did children and ride everywhere we could? Would we live in a world of unlocked front doors and opened windows or nestle in air-conditioned vaults? Would we swim in dirty public creeks or dig our own private back-yard pools? Would we grow our own vegetables and meats or buy freezers? Would we crank our own ice cream or drive to the Dairy Queen instead? Would we play Rook or watch television? Would we read books or settle for *Newsweek* and *Playboy* instead?

Well, we know what choices we made. Ours was the transitional generation between small-town and mass America, between homemade and machine-made America, between production and consumption America. We did the only thing we could do.

We straddled the fence.

We are the lucky generation. We could pick and choose, a bit of something old-fashioned here and a bit of something new and innovative there. We have been blessed by being able to live in both worlds at the same time. And though the changes bombarding us are oft-times dizzying, we have muddled through pretty well as a generation.

These memories are being written on a personal computer. (There's little "personal" about it, since almost everyone around me has one just like it.) However, just before I switched it on and started typing, I wrote three thank-you notes by hand in permanent jet-black ink from my tortoise-shelled Waterman with its 14K-gold point.

I wouldn't have it any other way than this—that is, having it both ways.

May 13, 1991

SCHOOL BELLS

My mother couldn't wait until December to give me my present, a Christmas bell.

This is no ordinary bell, but a brass handbell that belonged to my late Aunt Charlie, principal from 1922 to 1955 of the Robert E. Lee Elementary School that my mother, her brother and sisters, my cousins, and my brother and I all attended, and across the street from which our family lived for the six or so best years of my life.

Aunt Charlie, or "Miss Charlie" as generations of schoolchildren remember her, had joined the school faculty there in 1909. When she was forced by age laws to retire forty-six years later, she went back to college to upgrade her teaching certificate by taking some physical education courses, lied about her age, and was hired to teach in Florida, where she taught another five or so years before returning to our family center in Paris, Tennessee.

Her students recall her mostly for her discipline. She used the big brass bell to start and end the school day and to call each class in from recess, but she didn't need it. More often she simply clapped her hands. Her former students liken that sound to a crack of thunder. She commanded instant attention and respect from every student she supervised. In her retirement, in her eighties, she attended a dinner across town, to which she walked. She had never learned to drive, and she preferred not to waste scant teachers' retirement money on a taxi. It was dark when the dinner was over, and a middle-aged former student, recalling the manners she drilled into him, offered to walk her home. She refused his offer, saying she was unafraid to go alone because "I can lick any man in this town—and have."

Her middle name was Irene, but no one ever used that. The Charlie allegedly came from a relative who died young. Through her career, she left behind more children she called her own than any spinster I have ever heard of.

She was actually my great-aunt, one of my grandfather's four sisters, all of whom were schoolteachers. They were all well-educated and well-read. Granddaddy himself had not gone to school, although he was as good at reading and figuring as anyone I've ever known. After thirty years delivering rural mail, he devoted the thirty-three years of his own retirement to politics, served on school boards, got a high school built in his district, got roads connecting the county schools built, and pushed hard for an education agenda all his life.

So Aunt Charlie's school bell has within it a lot of family tradition in the good cause of education. I have always lusted after the bell for what it symbolizes and have tried to lead my own life in continuity with the service to education those great-aunts and their brother bequeathed to me. Next year will mark my own half-century of being in schoolhouses. I know

I am here in faithfulness to the family fixation with education, but I've never had the slightest temptation to leave; there's too much left to do and to learn to ever think of not being an educator.

Aunt Charlie used to say she never had a bad student, and I've claimed to have never had a bad teacher. We probably have both been naive and utopian about how important education is and about the prospects for making and keeping education's institutions good, but in a world where good causes go begging, she chose one of the best ones to champion. By giving me her great cause to fight, she gave me the greatest gift of all. She was truly a very great great-aunt.

Getting her bell is icing on the cake. It passed upon her death to her youngest sister, and from her to her son, and thence to the son's widow, whose own children unselfishly agreed that I should have it. After several unbroken decades of getting pajamas and shirts from Mother for Christmas, she has at last located a perfect gift. It more than makes up for not getting an electric train years ago.

The bell will rest conspicuously in a glass dome on a walnut base with a brass plaque as long as I am still around. To my absolute delight, our daughters have already begun to lay claims for who will get it after that. It pleases me that they have developed such keen eyes for things of true value. I suspect they got some of that from a great, great Aunt Charlie they never knew.

August 12, 1991

TYPEWRITERS

Our daughter was filling out another scholarship application form last week and ran into a stumbling block. All these forms ask for short essays but usually indicate they can be written in black ink or typed. This one didn't give that option. It insisted on the essay being typed, double-spaced, in the space allocated for it on the form. The problem was we don't have a typewriter anymore. Neither do our friends. When we took the form to my office to type, we found five typewriters, but all of such advanced models that we couldn't figure out how to use them. Many people now have computers (word processors) instead of typewriters, but many models will not print on questionnaire-spaced forms or envelopes.

Isn't that amazing? A commonplace typewriter has become a thing of the past. It was a significant invention that had a lifetime of over a century.

You can see one in a museum like William Faulkner's home in Oxford, Mississippi, or Carl Sandburg's home in East Flat Rock, North Carolina, or in an occasional hard-liner newspaper editor's office in a small town. The technology of our youth is now an antique.

The same week we discovered the typewriter is becoming extinct we wandered into an office supply store. It had a couple of seductive glass cases filled with pens—expensive pens with famous brand names such as Parker, Cross, and Sheaffer. Not one of them was a fountain pen. Fountain pens can still be bought but usually on special order. In the ink section of the store, there were rows of ballpoint pen refill packages, but only one short row of liquid ink cartridge refills and only three bottles of ink, kept for old-timers like me, I suppose.

I work with a versatile young man whose most shining distinction is his beautiful handwriting. He says the best advice his father ever gave him was "that good handwriting will get you anywhere in this world." (My own father said the same thing about Saturday night shoe shining, while my mother felt a smile was the more important asset.) But good handwriting is disappearing. Letters preserved from previous generations are genuine works of art because the handwriting was so beautiful. Now it is a lost art.

I have noticed a parallel decline in recitation and oratory over the years. People don't memorize and spout poems the way they once did, nor do they compose poems themselves as other generations did. There's a conspicuous decline in political and pulpit oratory, and a rise in the "five-second sound bite" for media use.

And the same is the true for music. In our neighborhood, when we were growing up, a dozen of us would gather around upright pianos and, from sheet music taken from piano benches, sing over the shoulders of pianists Ann Powers, Harriet Wheatley, or Martha Sue Fitzsimmons (who were equally at home in sandlot baseball games). Songs don't seem to have meaningful, or even decipherable, lyrics anymore.

What does this all mean, we may well ask ourselves? If typewriters, fountain pens, penmanship, poems, songs, and oratory disappear, are words themselves on their way to oblivion? I feel certain the disappearance of a love of words is not caused by the disappearance of word carriers (typewriters or pens, poems or speeches). Such vehicles are indeed vanishing, but something other than their demise is causing the parallel decline in the love of written words. Their passing is an effect, not a cause.

But what does cause us to be at an increasing loss for words?

Is it stage fright, caused by the world getting more and more public and smaller and smaller—some inner instinct for not standing out in the crowd? Is it national senility, a feeling that everything worth saying has already been said, and "there is nothing new under the sun?" Is it a loss of standards, a feeling that speed is more important than form in handwriting, or that sound volume is more important than lyrics in music, or that a face is more important than ideas in oratory? Is it multiculturalism, providing so many competing languages in this nation of immigrants? Is it the lack of home or school influence?

I used to think that a love of words was linked somehow to a love of land, and that as land ownership declined, love of words would decline as well. That has come to pass, but I'm less sure of the cause-and-effect relation between land and poetry. Maybe there was a simplicity in agrarian America that bred a love for words. Maybe city life is too complex for words.

We may not know why we are at a loss for words, but we can lament the loss and say a few words in praise of words as they die.

November 23, 1992

SCHOOL TAXES

Our daughter has never been to Disney World. But she has been to Auschwitz.

She and her fellow performers in the Spartanburg High School Orchestra have just returned from 17 days in Europe. They visited Poland, the former Czechoslovakia, Germany, Austria, and France, and played seven concerts.

They saw Krakow and Innsbruck and Paris, stayed in one fine hotel and some that weren't so fine, stayed with families two days in Germany, received standing ovations, played encores at every concert, signed autographs, stretched their budgets to make ends meet, fantasized over the McDonald's burgers they would be able to buy at journey's end in Paris, learned a lot, and had an experience they can never forget. In Poland, distant relations of the conductor in his family's ancestral hometown made a concert especially poignant. Tears flowed freely.

These orchestra students have had the very good fortune of being educated in a superior public-school system. Many of them have been enrolled in its strings program since they were in the fourth grade. The strings and orchestra programs are parts of a larger music program which includes choral music and concert and marching bands.

Once orchestra members reach junior high school, they start saving funds for their trip abroad. They sell citrus fruits in November and December, and the school banks about five dollars a box for each musician. With a little work over several years, most orchestra members save enough to cover the cost of the trip. When they reach high school, they become eligible to go on the orchestra's European tour. Since high school is a three-year school, and since a summer tour is made every third year, each high school orchestra member has an opportunity to go on tour.

The same school district begins its language programs in the fourth grade as well. A student can get nine years of language training, either in one language or split among several. Many of the orchestra members have had extensive foreign language courses, and most find an opportunity to use their French, Spanish, or German on their tours. In Germany, our daughter lucked into rooming with the family of a French teacher of English and had good opportunities to use her French. In France, the orchestra conductor surprised her by asking her to translate for him to the audience.

Rome, once the center of the world, was built upon seven hills. Spartanburg is sort of a center of education, built upon seven school districts. Our county's schools are divided into seven districts, each with its own tax base and each with its own superintendent. Citizens in most of the districts have been willing, over the years, to pay slightly higher property taxes in order to make the schools good ones. They have succeeded. The music and language programs are available to all students. In addition, classes are offered that prepare college-bound students for advance-placement exams. A wide range of supervised student activities and extensive guidance programs makes for a very involved and invested student body. The teachers are excellent, dedicated, and hardworking; the curriculum is varied and substantial.

The emphasis upon education in this Carolina county—which also has five college campuses—makes it one of the very best places to rear children in this nation. In this it is aided by being a place of manageable size, with four distinct seasons, at the crossroads of two major interstate highways, and with easy access to the Smoky Mountains and to the Atlantic beaches.

But the K–12 public-education system here is what makes this one of the highest quality counties in the nation. What has made education succeed is a rugged and almost universal determination of many citizens, mostly African American and Caucasian natives, with a sprinkling of Asian Americans and first-generation Europeans, whether they have children in the schools or not, to go the extra tax mills for education. Educational quality is even more important to them than lower taxes, garbage collection, or sewers and streets.

They get great mileage out of their millage, because they address their tax assessments fundamentally toward quality education. Elsewhere myopic taxpayers see millage as a millstone around their checkbook. But here, millage is the way on, up, and out—through education. Quality taxpayers are producing quality education.

August 10, 1993

BOOKSTORES

While taking some new books out of a shopping bag today, it suddenly occurred to me that I had never been in a bookstore before I graduated from high school. Our speech teacher took a carload of us to a national tournament right after graduation in 1954, and we spent some time in New York City en route. We stayed in a shabby hotel near Times Square, and there was a bookstore nearby. It blew my mind, and I came back with a suitcase full of sale-book bargains.

Books weren't novelties to us, of course. We had a decent public library, and the high school had a little library in its study hall. The four local drugstores had paperback book sections (mostly of Westerns and detective mysteries, plus *Classics Illustrated* comics) up by the magazines and newspapers, next to the glass cigar case and the pinball machine. Our relatives ordered books for our birthdays and Christmases from Sears—lots of Bobbsey Twins, Hardy Boys, and Albert Payson Terhune dog books. The local schools usually had one book fair a year. And one local gift shop carried Bibles and inspirational books such as *A Man Called Peter* or *In His Steps.* We also had teachers who read Laura Ingalls Wilder and William Green Hill to us, or, in the case of our Bible school teacher, a biography of David Livingston.

Most of us book readers learned which neighbors had home libraries and depended upon them. Neighbors, especially older ones, were as a rule exceptionally generous about lending their books. I found Arthur and his knights and Rudyard Kipling that way.

Schoolteachers somehow managed to amass small libraries, too. Schoolteaching used to be dominated by single women who used books as bridges to their students but also as entrees into the women's social circles from which being employed and single otherwise excluded them. If we visit the homes of old families, we marvel at the collections of books passed on from those earlier generations. If we visit the used-book stores in any fair-sized city, we marvel at the collections of books printed before World War II and then acquired from estates.

So there were books to be had. If one would seek, one could surely find.

But bookstores? They were scarce back then—and still are today. Bookstores were—and are—big-time, big-town stuff, like colleges or museums. They are few and far between.

In the old days, bookstores were the hub of an American city. By 1750, Benjamin Franklin had made his fortune from printing books and selling them in Philadelphia. Any community of any ambition or size had at least one newspaper, and almost all newspaper publishers also published tracts and books. Out on the frontier when Indian raids were still a threat, Lexington, in Kentucky, which was only a few years past statehood in 1792, is said to have had more bookstores than bars or churches.

Many early bookstores combined their regular stock of books with coffeehouses, newspaper libraries, and literary societies. Because public life was male dominated in those days, bookstores had a musky male feel of mildew and leather. However, despite their invisibility and home-front presence, women probably read more than did the men. Men visited bookstores; women read books. Maybe the men bought books and brought them home as men today do flowers, jewelry, or candy—to atone for being out on the town so much and to establish alibis for where they had been. Women congregated in parlors to discuss their reading. Hundreds of literary guilds and review clubs survive even yet in America's small towns, populated with members whose great-grandmothers were grande dames of culture.

Is the shortage of bookstores a problem in our nation? Some argue that it is not a problem but merely a symptom. This view holds that bookstores, like ballparks, would be built if there were a real demand for them. The reason there are so few bookstores is that there are so few readers. For decades, as leisure activities have increased and television has assumed more importance, reading has been on the decline nationally. Most readers prefer to get their information from news commentators and talk shows or from scanning short articles in magazines. There just aren't the habits, reasons, or time for reading that there once were. There are more books in print than at any other time in history but fewer readers of them. Most bookstores have space enough only for those books most likely to sell, usually cookbooks or romance or mystery novels. Readers are rapidly on their way to becoming an endangered species. Their breeding grounds—the old-fashioned bookstore and the neighborhood library—are already disappearing.

I'm for saving whales, but I'd probably start by saving *Moby-Dick, Treasure Island, Mutiny on the Bounty, Two Years before the Mast,* and the travel journals of Captain Cook or Charles Darwin.

Reading them helps us understand why whales are worth saving and why bookstores are, too.

November 8, 1993

DAVID MATHEWS

On our kitchen wall hangs a piece of art we have lugged from home to home wherever we have moved the last twenty-five years. Created of various woods by a Tennessee artist, it is a representation of the Parable of the Sower. It shows a man scattering seeds, some falling on stones and some being eaten by birds, but others rooting and flourishing. Because my wife and I come from families intensely dedicated to bettering education and have devoted our own entire adult lives to educating, the artwork has personal significance for us, but it also reminds us of our larger family of friends and colleagues, most of whom are also in fields of education.

One educator for whom we have very special affection and admiration is a fellow named David Mathews. He comes from a line of rural public-school teachers in Alabama, and he was a sort of "Wunderkind" in his youth, having studied Greek at the University of Alabama when it no longer had a Greek department and later returning from graduate study at Columbia University to become president of Alabama at age thirty-four and to be selected as one of the "Ten Outstanding Young Men" in America soon afterward. He went on to become HEW secretary under Gerald Ford, and for the last decades he has been president of the Kettering Foundation in Dayton, Ohio.

The brilliance of his youthful career has survived into his senior years, and in that extended genius Mathews reminds us very much of the late

Robert Hutchins, innovative president of the University of Chicago and later head of an important think tank on democratic ideals. In other ways, he also reminds us of philosopher John Dewey and of two Mathews's mentors, writer Norman Cousins and educator Lawrence Cremins, all of whom were strikingly optimistic about the ability of people to take control of their lives and society and to make them better.

Ever conscious of his family's ties to the soil, Mathews gardens some on the side. He has an unusual knack for making things grow. His garden is multicultural, because it reflects his work, which takes him to China, Russia, and Latin America frequently. Exotic imported vegetables grow side-by-side with his turnip greens and asparagus. He is a fine gardener and an equally good improvisational cook.

Mathews's garden is a metaphor for his work. He is in the very serious business of sowing and nurturing ideas about our taking responsibility for ourselves and our world. Mathews believes we are better persons when we are participants rather than mere spectators, when we are producers rather than mere consumers of the public good, and when we do our own homework rather than letting "experts" and "pros" do it for us.

Of course, those aren't novel ideas. They've been around quite a while. Thomas Jefferson popularized them; Mathews nurtures them.

Public apathy is the price for progress. Our world has been increasing in size, diversity, snarling and intermeshing technique and technology, and specialization of functions. We try harder and harder to be parents, citizens, patriots, scholars, moralists, and volunteers while trying to hold down jobs and hold together households. It's an upstream swim all the way, and we aren't salmon.

Ever since this nation was founded it has fiddled around with answering the fundamental question of whether a democracy delegates its destiny to a few or educates the many to participate in nation making.

What Mathews has achieved is the creation of a network of thousands of people who believe in people taking back the public's life and who have set about setting up forums, study groups, investigations, dialogues, and education to make that happen. Some of what Mathews has learned and then turned into seeds to be sown can be found in his books, such as *Politics for People: Finding a Responsible Public Voice* (University of Illinois Press). In a time of growing feeling of public helplessness, his books and his Kettering Foundation synthesize well the literature and spirit of empowerment. They are a call and a door to public involvement.

Enabling people to enable themselves is a Herculean and often a Sisyphean enterprise. It requires strength and persistence. Some of what the sower sows gets eaten by the birds and some falls on rocky soil. But some takes root and grows. What David Mathews has given a lifetime to sowing and tilling may not see a full harvest in his lifetime, but if the crop survives (as democracy's survival demands it must), it will be in part a tribute to his stewardship.

February 6, 1994

SOUTHERN DIALECT

Cleanth Brooks, recently deceased, was one of the greatest English professors of our century. He studied at Vanderbilt and taught at LSU and Yale, was a collaborator with Robert Penn Warren on textbooks used by thousands of college students, and was an expert critic of southern fiction and poetry. His three volumes on William Faulkner are but a sample of the range and depth of his literary interests. Brooks was a gentle man, the son of a Methodist minister in western Tennessee and Kentucky. He was modest in demeanor, generous in his attentions to inquiring students, and perceptive in his judgments. He never lost his fascination with novel ways of seeing things, and there is throughout his works an abiding sense of discovery and an openness to revelation.

Brooks comes to mind just now for me because I am thinking about the disappearance of southern language. With the omnipresence of radio and television, the multiple dialects that characterized the South a half century ago are being homogenized into something more nearly approximating a national neutral norm. The norm, says Brooks, is becoming an academy's version of purged language replaced by the jargons of bureaucracy, psychology, and sociology, spread by business and politics and media.

Brooks resisted that tendency. He recognized how the great southern writers depended upon the peculiarities of southern language for their storytelling. Southern literature is southern storytelling put to paper; if the language and art of storytelling vanish, the creek of southern literature may dry up.

The southern language, Brooks said, has old English origins. In one amazing essay, he produced evidence that the Gullah dialect of Uncle Remus— dropping final g's and using *de, dis,* and *dat*—was a nigh-pure preservation of seventeenth-century Devonshire English that the English themselves gave up toward the end of the nineteenth century. In the South, which has always been a region of regions within regions—pockets of people—old English survived longer because of its isolations through country folk.

Brooks found two strata of southern language, both of them important to southern literature. There is an oral commonplace colloquial language of the court square and farmer's market and ballpark, and there is a more elitist and formal gentry language of courtroom, pulpit, and schoolhouse. One is oral, the other written. Paralleling these two types of southern language are two vehicles of literature. There are folktales and family histories passed on by the colloquial language, and there are books and poems passed on by formal traditions. The soul of southern language, Brooks preached, is its allegiance to both strata of its language heritage. If we lose our roots, it will be because we have lost our informal and our formal language.

This conservative bent of Brooks was illustrated by an essay in which he defended the old Book of Common Prayer at the time it was being replaced, amid controversy. The exchange made was a trade-off, he felt. For the sake of modern idiom and clarity, the believer was giving up a link to the past community of faith. Personal ease in understanding was being bought at the cost of the self-discipline of study and understanding of the past. Similar controversies surrounded the appearance of various revisions of translations of the Holy Bible, replacing the King James Version.

There is value, Brooks felt, to old language. Shakespeare would not be Shakespeare without his language, and we can appreciate his genius only by appreciating the language of his times. The same is true of appreciating Eudora Welty, William Faulkner, Robert Penn Warren, and the galaxy of southern writers who made southern literature in the twentieth century the South's most priceless treasure and its most precious gift to posterity.

Laziness in language, the temptation to surrender heritage for some bland and nondescript lowest common denominator, was a threat to history and to literature for Brooks. More even than the colossal and crass commercialism of the New South, the demise of language represented the death of southern distinctiveness for him. For a region that for so long had nothing else upon which to fall back than words, the loss of fussing over words meant a loss of soul.

February 13, 1995

DUKE AND VANDERBILT
AND WOFFORD

Modern psychology makes much of the Greek myth of Oedipus in which a son outshines his father. The Oedipus complex isn't limited just to humans. The compulsion to outshine a progenitor is also found in corporations, churches, and countries. Colleges and universities are not immune from it, either. The forgotten father figure of importance in the founding years of Vanderbilt and Duke was little Wofford College in Spartanburg, South Carolina.

Two thick university histories—Paul K. Conklin's 810-page *Gone with the Ivy: A Biography of Vanderbilt University* and Robert F. Durden's 572-page *The Launching of Duke University, 1924–1949*—show how Wofford helped get those superpower universities off their shaky launching pads.

According to Conklin, Vanderbilt's ambitious beginnings were modest and tentative. The campus almost folded in its first years. The partnership of Methodist bishop Holland N. McTyeire, a South Carolina native, with Commodore Vanderbilt, put the college on firmer ground. McTyeire, without much clear authority for handling Vanderbilt campus affairs, imposed himself on the campus significantly. The chancellor, Landon C. Garland, held severely circumscribed powers. Perhaps the most substantive contribution McTyeire made, beyond attracting Vanderbilt funds, was in rebuilding the faculty. He was, without office, the chief academic officer for the young college. McTyeire hired two young professors who would have lasting influence on the direction of Vanderbilt. Charles Forster Smith, a classicist, came from the University of Virginia but had earlier taught at Wofford. With Smith came his friend William M. Baskerville, who had replaced him at Wofford and had remained there. Both had Ph.D. degrees from Leipzig, in Germany. McTyeire liked their Methodist and South Carolina connections. In 1881, the year of their appointment, there was a young fellow, still an undergraduate student back at Wofford, named James H. Kirkland. He went on to graduate study at Leipzig, keeping in touch with his older friends Smith and Baskerville. He joined them at Vanderbilt in 1886.

The Wofford triumvirate hoped to replace Vanderbilt's chancellor Garland with Wofford's outstanding and long-time president James Carlisle, but Garland lingered on too long. Nonetheless, the three professors succeeded in reorganizing the academic program and elevating the standards that would make Vanderbilt distinctive in an impoverished South still lacking a major private university of the stature of Yale, Harvard, Columbia, or Princeton. Kirkland later became Vandy's most famous chancellor.

Over in North Carolina, a few years behind Vanderbilt's blossoming, three other Wofford men were transforming little Trinity College into Duke University. Like Vanderbilt, Duke would benefit from its Methodism, its reliance upon an available and affluent benefactor (the Duke family: Washington and his sons Ben and Buck), and the lack of major universities in the reconstructed South. In Duke's case, the evolution began with the accession of John Carlisle Kilgo to the presidency of Trinity College in 1894, two years after it moved to Durham. Kilgo was a dynamic Methodist preacher, a South Carolinian who had graduated from Wofford. The English and history departments, the library, and scholarly research received special attentions from Kilgo, along with his growing connection to the Dukes. Kilgo brought to Duke two other Wofford men. William H. Wannamaker, a Wofford alum with graduate studies at Harvard and in Germany, came in 1902 to teach German, soon rose to dean, and served until 1947. More important than anyone to the early Duke University was William Preston Few, a South Carolinian who graduated from Wofford in 1889, taught school, and then went to Harvard for his doctorate in English. The exposure to serious scholarship and to Harvard president Charles W. Eliot's educational reforms would influence Few's administrative career enormously. Arriving in Durham in 1896, active in founding the Southern Association accreditation agency, Few became dean of Duke (its first) in 1902, and when Kilgo became bishop in 1910, Few became the president, serving until his death in 1940.

As for Wofford College, the sire of the two trios that elevated Vanderbilt and Duke to national prominence, it chose to remain the proud father. It has been content to bask, like Man o'War, as a champion in its own race and as a father of subsequent champions. Over forty Wofford alumni have headed other campuses, as have a comparable number of non-alumni Wofford faculty members, and a couple of hundred Wofford alumni have become professors, carrying on the outreach impacts of Vanderbilt's Smith-Baskerville-Kirkland and Duke's Kilgo-Few-Wannamaker models.

January 8, 1996

Back in our high school days, our Latin teacher, Miss Mary Lou Diggs, was determined to prove to us that the language was not, as reputed to be, "a dead language." We had trouble believing her. Our range of experience didn't throw us into frequent contact with the local Catholic priest, and the *Classics Illustrated* comics that we used for our book reports weren't written in Latin, not even the one for "Julius Caesar." Besides, Miss Diggs (and her two sisters who all lived in a house with dormers that we called the House of Seven Gables) had snow-white hair and seemed past retirement age, leading us to think Latin wouldn't last much longer, if it was indeed still alive. When our high school suddenly dropped Latin III and Latin IV just as we finished Latin II, we knew we had been right about it being a dead language. The Catholic church itself seemed to confirm it shortly afterward, at Vatican II, when it permitted mass to be said in other languages.

Some of us have always lamented the lapse in Latin learning that seemed to coincide with the end of our puberty. We had visions of going on to college and being able to astound the professors by starting all of our essays with memorized epigrams in Latin. Some wanted to be able to write Latin epigrams in phone booths and on bathroom walls. Those thinking about becoming doctors assumed they had to be able to write prescriptions in Latin, and those aspiring to be lawyers assumed most legal cases would have important Latin phrases in them. The language seemed to have some practical uses. Yale's president still reads the citations for Ph.D. degrees at annual commencement ceremonies in Latin. The ability to pronounce it properly may even be a requisite for holding that office.

I am rapidly reaching that age in life where I can no longer depend upon my good looks, quick witticisms, and athletic prowess to impress others. (In fact, I passed that age long ago.) My children and friends express weariness with my faltering ability to recite whole Vachel Lindsay poems or sing Pat Boone's greatest hits. I have been lamenting, like Alexander the Great standing on the banks of the Indus River, that "there are no more worlds to conquer." "O tempora, o mores!" (Cicero, in *Catifinam,* 1.1; "What times! What manners!")

I am rediscovering Latin. It is not dead but only lost. My theory is that if I can make Latin bones rise again after forty-two years away from them, I can recapture my fast-fading family's and friends' attentions. In short, somehow a resurrection of dead Latin can be translated into a personal resurrection for me.

Alas, it is difficult for the language to "come back" with only a little prodding. The truth is that I never had enough proficiency; there's nothing to retrieve. All of us back then relied on "ponies" from which we painfully copied translations between the lines of the textbook and texts we were given. We didn't really read Caesar's *Gallic Wars;* we read pony translations of it we copied interlineally. (The Latin word that meant anything to me was a Latin derivative: "interlinear.") Glossaries in the rear of the text also helped.

I've always blamed my Latin deficiency on the school system for dropping it. Actually, I'm also tempted to blame Van Veazey Olds, a sophomore who sat in front of me in Latin I and who, every time Miss Diggs had her back to us, made me turn around and hold up my left arm for him to knuckle-punch in the upper muscle. But I never have claimed retrospective child abuse, and it wouldn't help to cry peer abuse at this late date against old Van, who otherwise was as decent a fellow as one could hope to know. The fault, dear Brutus, actually was in myself. I learned a few Latin rules about parsing, tense, conjugation, and declension that made me a better English major in college, but I didn't learn Latin. Oh, well, "Omnia fert aetas, animum quoque" ("Time takes away everything, including memory").

"Parturiunt montes, nascetur ridiculus mus," joked Horace (65–8 B.C.; "The mountains labor, but give birth only to a mouse"). But I say the opposite: with this Latin book, a mouse can labor and bring forth a mountain. With this little book in hand, I can turn any common letter into an art form, any ordinary little speech into a masterpiece. Simply throw in a Latin phrase and stun an audience into awed silence.

I could use a little help, however. I'm having trouble finding a good use for my favorite lines (from Quintus Ennius, 239–169 B.C., *Annals*): "Oscitat in campis caput a cervice revulsum / semianimesque micant oculi lucemque requirunt" which translates: "His head, severed at the neck, rolled down the field, the half alive eyes twitching and longing for light."

"Quo" should I "vadis?"

May 20, 1996

NURSERY RHYMES AND FAIRY TALES

Nursery rhymes, fairy tales, myths, and legends, along with the alphabet and some children's songs, have seemed to me to be the first block in a firm foundation for educating children well. Surrounded by those influences, a child develops curiosity, appreciation for stories, imagination, and a habit of listening and reading and talking, graduating from that into reading itself and applying for a library card.

One side of the ongoing controversy over television and movies believes that shows appealing to children sometimes displace the parents, to the detriment of the children. The true importance of fairy tales and nursery rhymes and bedtime stories is in their being passed on directly from parents to children. That way, a child gets the messages that he or she is important enough to claim time from the parent and that talking, reading, listening, and singing are important and fun things to do. Ten minutes spent reading a bedtime story just before a child drops off to sleep probably can help offset the six hours of television the average child is watching passively every day. The content of the stories is not as important for creating learning habits as is contact between parent and child. I doubt that children ponder the meanings of what they hear and repeat and learn to read in their preschool days. Contact is more important than content then.

But I know that adults remembering fondly the time their parents and grandparents spent telling them stories and reading to them sometime do wonder about what message those rhymes and stories carried. What lesson was there in the story of Tom, Tom, the Piper's Son, stealing a pie and running away with it and eating it? What lesson was there to the story of Goldilocks entering the Three Bears' house uninvited, breaking their chairs and beds, and eating their porridge, and then running away when about to be found? What message was there in the Old Testament story of David taking the throne of Israel away from Saul, his best friend's father? Is that where Absalom, David's son, learned to try to take the throne away from his own father? What message was there in the legend of Jesse James, stealing from the railroads and being hailed as a hero for doing it? What message was there in the tales of Robin Hood, stealing from the king and being idolized for it? What was the message about Robinson Crusoe's island survival? Was it about the means for surviving (stealing and cannibalism among them) or about the will to live?

Poet Robert Bly's book *The Sibling Society* has chapters in it in which Bly retells the Jack and the Beanstalk story in its original version and points out dangers in trying to make the story mean something too simple and other than what it was intended to mean. Jack and the Beanstalk is not a

Marxist indictment of remote corporate giants who live above us in castles loaded with loot, nor is it a Horatio Alger story of a young man climbing the ladder of success. It could be read as a Robin Hood or Goldilocks story of youngsters being led to steal and running away from being caught, but children don't seem to get that out of hearing it. It could just as easily be read as a story about children being foolish enough to be tricked into trading a cow for magic beans, a form of child abuse and exploitation. Or it could be a story about a young man's shouldering early responsibility for his widowed mother.

My own favorite interpretation is to see it as a version of the Prometheus story. In the Greek myth, Prometheus dares to steal the sacred fire from the gods on Mount Olympus. He is caught and shackled for eternity to a rock as punishment. But to humans, warmed by the fire he brought them, he is forever a hero. As for the remote gods, they are brought down to human level by Prometheus, and eventually they fade away and humans take over their own lives. Similarly, Jack invades the giant's domain high in the heavens and brings back a chicken that lays golden eggs and a singing harp and bags of gold. When the giant finally chases him, Jack slays him by cutting down the beanstalk. The giant is out of place on earth and dies, but Jack was out of place in the heavens and is applauded.

The meanings are not all that important. Good stories have many meanings. But we don't see hordes of kids running around stealing and citing fairy tales, nursery rhymes, or adventure stories as license to steal or lie. Stealing and lying are learned somewhere else than from parents putting children to bed at night. What is important is that their parents encourage their children to listen, to repeat in their own words, to use their imagination, to read, and to be curious about things. At the infancy stage, the color, the action, and the adventure in stories seem more affective for their future lives than do the layers and nuances of what the stories mean.

And if much later, when grown, these youngsters return to those stories and rhymes and find in them mixed signals about Good and Evil, Crime and Punishment, Hierarchies and Levelings, Privilege and Impertinence, then all the better. Those are precisely the dilemmas of life with which to wrestle in adulthood.

August 5, 1996

For almost all of the nineteenth century, college life was centered in "literary societies." Literary societies were organized and operated by students themselves, centers for intellectual activity in which students gained experience in public speaking, logical argumentation, formal debate, and social graces. They were training grounds for classroom recitations all students made and for commencement and examination speeches many students had to give. Usually wreathed in secrecy and exclusivity, occasionally societies opened their doors to the public for presentations by members or guest celebrities, especially to groups of chaperoned young ladies.

Every college had them. There were the Harvard Speaking Club, Princeton's Cliosophic and Whig Societies, Missouri's Athenaeum Literary Society, the Transylvania Philosophical Society, UNC—Chapel Hill's Dialectic and Philanthropic Societies, Georgia's Phi Kappas and Demosthenians, Tennessee's Chi Delta and Philomathesian and Dialectic Adelphick Societies, Vanderbilt's Philosophic and Dialectic Societies, and Williams's Philologian and Philotechnian Societies. Some antebellum colleges, such as Davidson, still have stately buildings of their societies on their campuses. College faculties embraced, encouraged, and endorsed literary societies fairly fully except when they became too secretive, too social, or too outspoken. The clubs gave students something constructive to do, especially on long weekend nights.

The societies didn't curb adolescent pranks entirely. Robert A. Law, an English professor in Texas, recalling Wofford College in South Carolina as it was in 1898, noted that the college bell still was rung at midnight and squawking hens were thrown into rival literary society meetings. Professor Henry Nelson Snyder's cow, painted by a member of the Class of 1898, licked the paint off and died (but Snyder survived as Wofford's president from 1902 to 1942).

The reminiscing professor in Texas recalled especially fondly Wofford's Calhoun and Preston Literary Societies. Every student was required to belong to one. "The society halls were comfortable, carpeted rooms, devoted solely to that purpose, were well lighted and furnished with attractive opera chairs, and their walls were ornamented with many oil paintings of distinguished alumni and professors. The president of the society sat on a high platform under a canopy, and he always wore a black gown. . . . Regular meetings were held each Friday night, beginning at seven-thirty o'clock and lasting frequently until midnight or later. . . . Half the society's members . . . came on duty to read essays, to declaim, or to debate each Friday night. Thus, if one was not on the program at one meeting, he was sure to be at the next one. . . . Before the end of his freshman year practically every student had gained some self-confidence in addressing the society. . . . The average Wofford graduate of that time would prove a readier speaker and a more skillful rough-and-tumble debater than the average male graduate of the University of Texas."

Wofford's luminary history professor, Lewis P. Jones, recalls that the two societies promoted good art. Members of Calhoun commissioned a painting of John C. Calhoun by the popular South Carolina artist Albert Capers Guerry, promising him $150. When the painting was done, the boys didn't have the money, so Guerry took the painting on tour. He copied it for the duplicate that hangs in the South Carolina House of Representatives. The rival group, the Preston Society, had paintings of W. C. Preston and of Wofford president James H. Carlisle also done by Guerry. They and other Guerry works still grace Wofford today.

Virtually all of the thousand colleges in America before the Civil War followed the pattern of the first one, Harvard, established in 1636. They were small liberal arts colleges, most of them for men, dedicated to preparing students to head toward careers in law, medicine, or the ministry, or to run their inherited family businesses or farms. Only a fifth of them survived the Civil War, and higher education took new roads thereafter, adding new fields to the curriculum and adding graduate schools and schools of engineering, education, business, law, medicine, and divinity. Extracurricular life changed just as radically. Fraternities flourished, as did intercollegiate athletics, providing social outlets that literary societies had tried to fill.

Professor Law had good reason to lament the demise of the societies. "These organizations furnished a training in the clash of opinion and a preparation for citizenship which, to my mind, are invaluable. That such literary societies seem everywhere to be passing away . . . is a source of profound regret." In these days of lectures, video, and the Internet, with their emphasis upon one-way data flow, where do students get experience in speaking in public, constructing arguments, and making presentations? Recitation, rhetoric, debate, parliamentary procedure, and dialogue are art forms relevant to making a living and to living good lives.

March 31, 1997

Waiting for Hurricane Bonnie to hit the Carolinas during the last week of August, inland residents found the humidity more horrible here than usual. The air was stifling, and normally healthy humans found themselves puffing and dragging while making their appointed rounds. Sweltering from day to day, I found myself turning the air-conditioning up and ceiling fans and bath water on more frequently. How did we cope with such weather in the early 1940s?

There were large tripod electric fans and funeral-home cardboard fans in the church sanctuary. Homes had screen doors and windows, and all of them were kept open. Some homes had screened porches, and ours had army bunks on which my brother and I slept. Older homes had high ceilings and heavy draperies. Farm homes had dogtrots (breezeways, some called them) between the rooms. The only air-conditioning I recall was in the Capitol Theater, although perhaps the less-visited Princess Theater also had it. Boys' clothing consisted of a pair of shorts and little else. Some few families sent their children to summer camps in the mountains of east Tennessee, western Carolina, or Arkansas, or to Minnesota lake camps. Church camps were popular refuges from summer heat, as were Boy Scout and Girl Scout camps. Usually I spent a couple of weeks each summer out at our grandparents' farmhouse. It had high ceilings, cases of Coca-Cola, and cool well water, and faced a huge wooded gully that was cool to wander through.

But most of the time, when the heat was the most oppressive, I hid out in the elementary school library just across the street from us. The Lee School summer library was located in Miss Mary Margaret Richardson's first-grade classroom and was usually staffed from nine to noon weekdays by one of the senior teachers—Miss Stella Dunn or Miss Valentine Cooper for sure and maybe Miss Rebecca Byers, Miss Alice Lampley, or Miss Opal Lashlee sometimes as well.

Each summer, this classroom was converted to a library with bookcases filled with books drawn from all the other classrooms and reading tables moved in. A visitor could read books in the high-ceilinged room with a couple of desk fans humming away, or take two or three books home.

As a special incentive, if the heat wasn't enough reason to drive us into the library's refuge, we got Reading Certificates. The summer librarian would carefully write the names of nine books we had read in spaces on a lovely suitable-for-framing certificate bearing our names, the librarian's signature, and the date. Some of our group competed with one another to see who could read the most. One summer I got through fifteen or so certificates of nine books each, and reached my peak when I once read nine books in one day and got a certificate for doing that.

I remember books about collies, airplane pilots, baseball players, Greek and Roman mythology, Bobbsey Twins, and Hardy Boys. Most of all, I remember orange and blue books of biographies, everyone from George Washington through John Quincy Adams and Abraham Lincoln.

Those were, of course, segregated days. I would not, being born when and where I was, have an African American classmate until I was in graduate school in 1960, and there was not much in the library about African American history either. But that little one-room makeshift library is where I was introduced to black educator Booker T. Washington and to black scientist George Washington Carver. I credit two books on them, in combination with a Sunday school picture of Jesus surrounded by children of all races and with my parents' refusal to allow the "n-word" in our home, for my later attitudes on race.

While I have dabbled at various hobbies over the years, the one hobby that has dominated my entire life has been reading. Looking back, I see now that I got hooked into reading by the heat that drove me into the summer school library.

September 1, 1998

HORACE HOLLEY

After a lifetime in higher education, I still hold on to a small pantheon of educational heroes. My list includes some professors and administrators under whom I have served, plus some big-name figures such as Charles W. Eliot of Harvard, Robert Hutchins at Chicago, and John Dewey. At the top of my list is an old-time college president of whom most folks have never heard. His name is Horace Holley, and from 1818 to 1827, he was president of Transylvania University in Lexington, Kentucky.

When Yale-educated Horace Holley left the pulpit of the Hollis Street South End Church in Boston to become president of little Transylvania out on the American frontier, he was only thirty-seven years old. Kentucky had been a state for only twenty-six years, and Lexington had been in existence only forty-three years. Transylvania had been chartered by Virginia in 1780, but had not gotten underway until 1787, and its history over the first few decades was one of ups and downs with few students enrolled; often it was bogged down by political battles for control between Presbyterians and nonsectarian civic leaders such as Henry Clay. With Holley's election as president, the nonsectarian Clay faction won temporary management of the fledgling college.

It was incredible to find a college that far west, in territory where some residents still remembered Daniel Boone. Yet, trade routes and primitive roads had made Lexington for the moment the star of the west, and Horace Holley made it the Athens of the West. Cincinnati, Nashville, and Louisville would speedily grow to rival it, but for a time, it was the western crossroads of trade and the center of education and culture.

From 1802 to 1818, Transylvania had granted degrees to only 22 students. In the next nine years, under Holley, it conferred over 600 degrees on 558 students. Enrollment when Holley got there—already inflated over previous years by news of his coming—was 110 students, taught by fewer professors than the fingers of a hand and in a one-year curriculum. Three years later its 282 students rivaled Yale's 319, Harvard's 286, Union's 264, Dartmouth's 222, and Princeton's 150. By 1826, there were 418 students from fourteen mostly-southern states, and a four-year program.

Holley fleshed out the embryonic medical department he inherited and created a medical college second in reputation only to the University of Pennsylvania. He operated a law school in which Henry Clay sometimes taught and which had as faculty the famous Jesse Bledsoe and William T. Barry, both U.S. senators from Kentucky. John J. Crittenden studied law there and went on to become a U.S. senator and Kentucky governor. All three of the famous Blairs—Francis Preston and sons Montgomery and Frank—studied law there. Undergraduate students in Holley's years included such future leaders as Albert Sidney Johnston and Jefferson Davis.

In the years that Jefferson Davis was in Washington as secretary of War or U.S. senator from Mississippi, there were seventeen of his Transylvania classmates in either the U.S. House of Representatives or the U.S. Senate. Among them were Iowa's senator George W. Jones, Indiana's senator Edward A. Hannegan, Louisiana's senator S. W. Downs, Kentucky's senator Joseph Underwood, and Missouri's senator David Rice Atchison (who served as president for a day, March 4, 1849, when Zachary Taylor refused to be inaugurated on a Sunday).

Holley's wife, Mary Austin, was the sister of Stephen F. Austin, famous in Texas history. Holley himself was befriended by ex-president John Adams and by Harvard's famous Edward Everett and by a circle of other eastern luminaries. He played host at Transylvania to President Monroe and to the Marquis de Lafayette.

Presbyterians attacking Holley made allies with Baptists and with anti-Clay Jacksonian Democrats, accused Holley and the college of promoting an aristocratic and elitist philosophy, and forced his resignation in 1827. He died at sea from yellow fever a few months after.

But in his nine years in Kentucky's bluegrass wilderness, Horace Holley set the educational standard and the pace for the whole South and Midwest. He left big footprints where he trod.

September 29, 1998

SOUTHERN FESTIVAL OF BOOKS

The irony of the Southern Festival of Books, an annual three-day gathering in Nashville, is obvious to all of the thousands who attend it. In the shadow of the Tennessee State Capitol, designed by the talented architect William Strickland, the Southern Festival of Books annually pitches an encampment of tents on the expansive War Memorial Plaza, and overflows into the Senate Chamber, War Memorial Building, and other state buildings for lectures and readings by famous authors.

The irony is that a book festival occupies space dedicated to commemorating war. This is space dotted by statues and ringed by lists of dead Tennesseans. Before it was a memorial, this space from 1862 to 1865 was occupied by federal armies that came into Nashville upon the heels of their victories at Forts Henry and Donelson. A book festival in a war memorial—it is a fitting paradox, testimony that perhaps, after all, the pen is indeed mightier than the sword, or that the purposes of war are to make peace and to elevate learning and the human estate.

Staged in perfect fall weather, the Southern Book Festivals offer the crowds a couple hundred authors and panelists—lecturing, conversing, and signing autographs. In a typical year, the most recognizable names included white-trash-fiction writer Dorothy Allison, prize-winning Edward Ball fresh from his slave-family work, Kentuckian Wendell Berry, crime novelist-reporter Jerry Bledsoe, versatile writer-television producer Stephen J.

Cannell, biographer Bruce Clayton, novelists Lee Smith and her husband Hal Crowther, the pseudonymic Ellen Douglas (Josephine Haxton), North Carolinian Clyde Edgerton, Oprah-choice Kaye Gibbons, intriguing neo-Confederacy chronicler Tony Horwitz, prolific late-bloomer Robert Inman, Terry Kay, essayist-turned-novelist James Kilgo, Jill McCorkle, Jay McInerney, and Robert Penn Warren Lecturer novelist Elizabeth Spencer.

Sheerly by chance, I sat at the banquet with Jimmy Faulkner, nephew of William Faulkner, who regaled us with his opinions ("commercial" and "inappropriate") about the controversial Faulkner sculpture on the Oxford, Mississippi, court square, and with recollections of his "Cuddin Will." Jimmy Faulkner's late father, John, wrote *My Brother, Bill* which the new Hill Street Press reprinted with Jimmy's foreword.

C-Span 2 viewers got some idea of the impressive festival by watching interviews from the Crowne Plaza Hotel that showed the tent city of book-publisher booths across the street in the background. University presses of Tennessee, Kentucky, Louisiana State, Vanderbilt, and Georgia were especially well represented. So, too, were premiere presses such as Algonquin Books of Chapel Hill, Harcourt Brace, Henry Holt, John F. Blair, Penguin, Putnam, Avon, and Random House. Several small presses, including religious presses, had booths. Food booths and music performances and poetry readings rounded out the enticing festival fare.

I ate a hotdog and sipped a lemonade while seated on a granite ledge in front of the Vietnam list of Tennesseans who died for us. I sat in front of the names beginning in the letter *C.* One of them, Vandiver L. Childs, had been a high school classmate. Another from my home and era was in the "M" list—Jerry Mustain. I sat with Buster's and Jerry's ghosts and listened to high school students read their poems from a stage next to bronze statues of three Vietnam soldiers. I thought of the Fugitive Poets of the 1920s, also from Nashville, some of whom wrote odes to the Confederate dead. I could see the columns of the memorial's colonnade rising above me to my right, and behind them I knew were lists of World War I dead Tennesseans, celebrated long ago by another poet with a poem about poppies growing in Flanders Field row on row.

What better tribute at the physical center of a state's government and at a massive memorial to the war dead than to find reading and writing, books and the human mind and spirit, thriving in the freedom the sacrificed lives bought us?

October 5, 1998

Looking for a graveyard to haunt this Halloween, we could choose worse than Cave Hill Cemetery in Louisville, Kentucky. It holds the remains of architect Gideon Shryock; artist Matthew Jouett; editorial cartoonist Hugh Haynie; Mark Twain's aunt Polly; 7 feet, 8 inches, tall "Kentucky Giant" Jim Porter; chicken-fryer and franchiser Col. Harland Sanders; and a host of Louisville notables with names such as Speed, Seelbach, Watterson, Bingham, Belknap, Galt, Ballard, Morton, and Brown.

Located on what used to be the eastern border of the downtown area, Cave Hill was purchased by the city for its quarries and in hopes the L&N railroad line would be running through it. The railroad bypassed it, and it became the city pesthouse, isolating patients suffering from contagious and congestive diseases. In 1846, the city decided to make a cemetery of the three hundred acres, and in 1848 Cave Hill Cemetery was dedicated.

Perhaps the pesthouse prehistory explains why one Cave Hill Cemetery resident is George Keats, who died of tuberculosis in 1841—as had his brother, John Keats, in 1821. George Keats could have died in the pesthouse and been buried there in the graveyard that preceded the city's Cave Hill green lawns.

John Keats, of course, was a bit more famous than his American brother, George. Born on Halloween, 1795, John Keats lived mostly in England, although he died—at age 25—in Rome, not far from places occupied by Lord Byron, Percy and Mary Shelley, Elizabeth Barrett Browning, and Hans Christian Andersen.

George Keats was born the last day of February in 1799. In June 1818, he left to seek his fortune in America, settling for a while in Henderson, Kentucky, down near where the Ohio River joins the Mississippi. Apparently he fell into the company of the famous naturalist and artist James John Audubon, who may have "bilked" George of his savings by selling him a boat and cargo that turned out to be submerged in the river. In 1820, having failed in his initial gambit, George and his wife returned to England, where he persuaded John Keats to give him John's inheritance from their grandmother's estate. Penniless poet John Keats moved to Rome later that year, and died there the next year.

George returned to Kentucky, settled in Louisville, and went through a fortune made in shipping, lumber, flour, and real estate. Keats Avenue in the old Clifton section of Louisville was named in his honor in 1828 because he was on a city charter committee. George Keats lived in a fashionable Greek Revival home on Walnut Street near the heart of the city. It later was used by Hampton College and then by the Elks' Club, and more recently it has been headquarters for Hilliard Lyons. Buried in Cave Hill Cemetery, for some reason George's remains were moved in 1879, to section O, lot 73.

John's letters to George and George's English wife, Georgiana—he called them Brother George and Sister George—are important documents in literary scholarship.

Recognition for John Keats came late: his poems were not collected and published until 1884. One, number 14, was "To My Brother George" and begins, "Many the wonders I this day have seen" and ends "But what, without the social thought of thee, / Would be the wonders of the sky and sea?" Another that he sent his brother began "Why did I laugh tonight? No voice will tell."

Knowing that he was dying, John Keats faced death in despair but with triumph. In his letters to George he elaborated on his theory of "negative capability," that is, an openness to irony and paradox that he felt marked Shakespeare but that Coleridge and Wordsworth resisted because of their craving systems and certainties. Keats disdained dogma and moralizing. A poet should have a completely open mind and should not have definitive ideas or character.

Scattered among great libraries and repositories of the globe—including Harvard's Widener Library, Louisville's Filson Historical Society, and Oxford University—are caches of John Keats's manuscripts and correspondence.

Posthumous though his fame may have been, some of John Keats's fame—as well as many an academic career that scholars have built upon it—is indebted to the forgotten brother, George Keats, whose bones are in Louisville but whose more valuable relics are in several John Keats collections in libraries.

And George's own fame, forgotten though he may be, rests in being the brother of the author of some of the world's greatest poetry: *Endymion,* "Ode on a Grecian Urn," To a Nightingale," among it.

"A thing of beauty is a joy forever."

October 6, 2002

Our administrative cabinet meets Monday afternoons. Of the dozen college officers there weekly, five of us are "wincers." We visibly wince when our colleagues make grammatical mistakes. The worst offense is the improper use of "I" and "me," as in "Mr. Jones went to town with George and I." We wincers are part of a loosely knit, not-so-secret society that (or which) finds commonality in being appalled by grammatical error.

Columnists such as William Safire and James Kilpatrick have catered to us nitpickers (not nick-pickers) by wallowing in the mire of declining public grammar. (Excuse my mixed metaphor.) Sometimes they arouse their readers to synchronized head wagging; other times they antagonize them because they sound elitist and pretentious. Discovering a linguist with more plebian humor and more engaging prose than Safire or Kilpatrick out in the Appalachian hinterlands (Berea, Kentucky) is a welcomed pleasure.

Thomas Parrish is actually a historian, with books on World War II, Roosevelt and George Marshall, and the Cold War to his credit. But Parrish has an unnamed friend, identified in the title of Parrish's most recent book as *The Grouchy Grammarian* (John Wiley and Sons, 2002), who has drawers overflowing with grammatical mistakes collected over the years. Rather than writing his own book, the grouch enlisted Parrish to produce "A How-Not-To Guide to the 47 Most Common Mistakes in English Made by Journalists, Broadcasters, and Others Who Should Know Better."

Because the errors are so abundant, Parrish had to be selective in his examples. He ignored material from small-town newspapers and local radio and television. The bigger public voices—National Public Radio, the *New York Times,* the Associated Press, the major television networks, the History Channel, and the largest newspaper chains—bear more public responsibility for good usage than do others.

Parrish organizes his carefully culled examples of poor English in descending order, from worst offenses to minor ones. The major offense is that people don't think enough about what they write. We write, "The car crashed while traveling at a high rate of speed." Speed is a rate. It is proper to say, "The car crashed while traveling at high speed." Or instead of "some people don't ascribe to the president's management style," thinkers would say "some people don't subscribe to the president's management style." And if FDR was "rarely seen in a wheelchair during his lifetime," does that mean he has been seen in one more frequently since he died? Parrish is particularly irked by users of singular nouns with plural verbs (or of plural nouns with singular verbs). An AP story tells us "if a show's ratings go up, so do the price of ads." Parrish asks, "It do? Really?" Consider what's wrong with "there's Boy Scouts everywhere."

He takes us through thickets of language—distinctions between "its" and "it's," between "somewhat" and "something," between "each" and "both," between "may" and "might," between "lie, lay, lain" and "lay, laid, laid," between "less" and "fewer," between "who" and "whom," and among "which, who, or that"—or the distinction between "between" and "among." When do we say "former President?" (When a former president is still living, such as "former presidents" Carter, Ford, Reagan, Bush, and Clinton, but never Presidents Washington, Lincoln, or Jefferson.) And what can we do about "sound-alike words" used wrongly, such as "diffuse" instead of "defuse," "compliment" instead of "complement," or "hordes" instead of "hoards?" Are we aware of the redundancy of "the reason why" when used with "because?" How often do we insert "of" unnecessarily, as in "I'm not that highbrow of a person?" Is "none" used as a subject singular or plural? (Answer: both.) Does "Congressional oversight" mean supervision or neglect? Does "bimonthly" mean "every other month" or "twice a month?"

Parrish's grouchy friend dates the "great eruption" and decline in proper English to the 1961 Webster's Third International, when a whole "passel" of colloquial words was (not "were") accepted into the language on the dubious grounds that a dictionary is descriptive and not prescriptive.

Our not-so-secret society of pessimists and pedagogues opts (not opt) for prescriptions. Reading aloud Parrish paragraphs is the next best thing to having my mother-in-law still around. My wife and our two daughters inherited her eye for peevish English improprieties.

April 20, 2003

FINAL EXAMS

Institutional histories of America's earliest colleges almost always mention early graduation exercises. In pre–Civil War days, colleges were few in number and scattered across the expanding girth of the nation. Many of them, seeking moral purity, were located in the wilderness, far from the vices of towns. Not only were college scarce, so were college graduates. Today, over half of each year's high school graduates go on to college—several millions of students each year. But in early times, higher education was available only to privileged white males, and they numbered a few thousand students each year.

Because of their remoteness physically and numerically from the masses of people, colleges were public curiosities, sort of intellectual Disney Worlds. Realizing that the Tree of Knowledge bore seductive fruits denied to most citizens, once a year colleges would open their doors and extend hospitality to the general public. Citizens of local communities and alumni of the colleges would flock to campuses, joining parents and large families of the graduates.

Having made their arduous trek to Eden, visitors were reluctant to leave. Often they parked their wagons for days on end, cooked their meals, listened to visiting clergymen, college presidents, distinguished alumni, and numerous graduating seniors for hours, with concerts and singings thrown in for good measure.

Commencements were the model for the Chautauqua forums that became popular nationwide. They were something like revival camp meetings, but with a bit more Latin and Greek. Bowing to the egalitarianism of the Jacksonian Era, the elitist knowledge and mysteries of higher education were "investigated" by the excluded masses, who were invited to cross-examine in public any of the graduates before they could receive their diplomas (or, fitting the agrarian setting, their "sheepskins").

The wonderful things about early college commencements were that they were celebrations of the Life of the Mind and that the celebrating was by many noneducated frontier folk and working people for whom higher education was at best an aspiration and at most a mystery.

Recent wire-service stories about the commencements of 2003 have been critical of them. They have, in some places, shoved the graduates and their achievements—and their families and friends and alumni—to marginal places in the ceremony. In many instances, the speakers selected are personages with political agendas. One wire-service story noted that in recent commencement speeches by President Bush and former president Clinton, the focus was on politics, never on the graduates or the educational process. Some campuses spent long portions of the programs citing the achievements of outsiders being given honorary degrees, but then neglected to call the graduates up by name.

Recalling the warmth of early community-spirited commencements and conscious of the short shrift increasingly shown to graduates on what should be "their day," I made a spur of the moment decision about the address I prepared for the Transylvania University 201st Commencement, which was held outdoors on the original site of the university.

Noting the forgotten practice of public gathering and cross-examination, I called for a revival of the practice symbolically. I asked David Marshall, an accounting major from Nicholasville, Kentucky, to stand and answer one question, pretending that a wrong answer would deny his 199 classmates their diplomas. (I had met Marshall at an alumni gathering a month earlier, so the choice was not entirely random on my part.) The question was "Who wrote the play, *Henry IV, Part I?*" To the relief of the entire class, Marshall answered correctly, "Shakespeare." Then, calling for a voice vote from parents, relatives, friends, and the faculty of the college to allow the seniors to graduate, a resounding "Aye" drowned out the sirens and hum of the city of Lexington.

That audience participation held the audience's attention another seven minutes while I quoted a passage from *Henry IV, Part I* in which Glendower claims he can call spirits from the vasty deep, and Hotspur replies that so can anyone, but that doesn't mean they will come if called. I then acted as a séance medium for the graduates to hear the collective voices of famous alumni and presidents and faculty saluting them for their academic achievements.

Politics were put aside, and the focus properly was placed upon the graduates, who responded enthusiastically and warmly. For a moment, Paradise was revisited. I haven't enjoyed a commencement so much in years.

June 1, 2003

BOOK SHELVING

A previous owner of our home, in which we have now lived more than twenty years, raised the roof. With four sons, more space was needed, and he built, out of the back half of the attic, two bedrooms and a bath connected by a hallway.

The bigger room, now our study, contains a computer and four walls of bookcases. The hallway, until recently, held three bookcases, and the corner bedroom has four bookcases. Below, on the main floor, we have floor-to-ceiling bookcases on both sides of the living-room fireplace, another on the den wall, two half-wall bookcases embracing a corner fireplace on the sun porch, a large bookcase in a daughter's vacant bedroom, and a short case under the phone in the hall. We ran out of bookshelves ten years back. Since then, we've been stacking books on the study floor, by the lounge chair, and beside the bed.

We have little of material value to show for forty-plus years of marriage, but we do have books—dozens of books, hundreds of books, probably two or even three thousand books.

Periodically, my ever-patient spouse, Betsy, would urge me to cull and give books away or to buy more bookcases. The local public library sometimes got boxes of novels and, once, even a complete 1971 set of encyclopedias. Still, the stacks grew faster than the cleansings, like algae. Books covered the entire carpeted floor, ten or more to a stack, with only a narrow pathway to the computer. When the ceiling in the den below the study creaked and appeared to be sagging, we knew time was running out for us.

One Saturday in June, we took down pictures and I installed bookcases down the upstairs hallway wall. Despite some false starts (miscounting the number of pine boards needed for shelving, running the electric screwdriver in reverse by error, buying twelve-inch metal triangles for ten-inch planks), I still succeeded in having the shelves in place in a day's time.

This will be a piece of cake, I foolishly thought to myself.

The hard part lay ahead, concealed by my false optimism. It took three weeks to finish what I had started.

First, I had to cull out give-away books from existing bookcases, which only added to the piles and piles on the study floor.

Then I had to decide on a system for grouping books into compatible categories: biography, Civil War, southern history, southern culture, race studies, southern literature, southern literary criticism, Appalachian studies, southern states' histories, etc. That meant moving books from other bookcases to new areas on bookcases and culling those hundreds on the floor by categories.

It also meant stretching muscles seldom used, and spending a lot of time on my knees on the floor.

Worst of all, it meant revisiting old friends I treasure and neglect. I found myself taking longer and longer breaks, leafing through forgotten unforgettable prose, relishing the variety and savoring the words as if I were salivating at a Sunday dinner on the grounds. Saying farewell to old friends became harder as I pored over books and sweat poured from me night after night.

In the end, the mayhem was over. Thirteen boxes of books went to the Wofford library, thanks to the sturdy backs of two student workers and the spacious rear of the librarian's station wagon (the axle of which survived the journey). Four boxes of Alabama books went to Alabamian exiles in Dayton and one box of Kentucky books to friends in Lexington. Five boxes of African American history, civil rights history, and women's studies works went to our graduate student daughter and four boxes of fiction to her Maryland sister.

We bade each box good-bye with the mixed emotions we had when we sent those daughters to college, joyful that the books would have far, far better lives in the hands of people actually reading them instead of hoarding them, but we sorrowfully acknowledged that we were losing members of our family.

The day after the last box left (like Browning's "Last Duchess"), our new *Oxford American* magazine arrived. Rick Bragg—whose books we kept—writes in it about the pain (mental and physical) of divesting oneself of books: "While books are more than just possessions, while they are much more than paper and ink and cardboard and cloth, they are also damned heavy." In his last move, "I found myself unwilling to part with almost anything. . . . Before I know it the only ones I'm willing to give away are the ones—like *To Kill a Mockingbird*—that I have two of."

We know that feeling.

July 13, 2003

A FEW MORE WORDS

The first Commencement was "In the Beginning"—
  heavens, earth, day, night, sky, water, lands and seas,
  planets, stars, birds, fish, animals, plants and trees,
      PLUS Adam and Eve!
  God spoke at that one.
      He said: "Not bad!"

Through microscope and telescope
  you've studied His whole creation.
Without any heart you could take it apart.
  But are you good at restoration?
      If you do dissect it, Can you resurrect it?

Maker of promises, which can you keep?
  Sower of dreams, what will you reap?
Hoarder of tomorrows, will you sell them cheap?
  Bearer of sheepskin, will you become a sheep?

Are you a robot programm'd for close encounters
  in our Earth-Star's wars,
or a Frankenstein creature stitch'd from snitch'd scraps,
  with nothing your own?
          Be neither!
Be neither automaton nor monster.
  Be a mortal touch'd by immortality.
  Be a "Not bad!" human touch'd by humanity.

Open our gifts:
  our food-for-thought upon which you've din'd,
    our insights into a world gone blind,
      our worn hardback "History of Man-Unkind,"
      our real rev'rence for the Life of the Mind—
              PLUS some old wounds we fail'd to bind,
                a few loose ends we couldn't wind,
                a Holy Grail we hope you find.

Out of schedules that caus'd you pain,
  out of beds where you've seldom lain,
    out of labs in which you've search'd,
      out of tests through which you've lurch'd,
        out of books into which you've peek'd,
          out of classes through which you've squeak'd,
line up, as we call you out:
            march on up—and haul on out!

Commencement, University of Tennessee, Knoxville, August 25, 1978

Chapter 4

PEOPLE
"FOR HIS NAME'S SAKE"

THOMAS HOLLEY CHIVERS

And the voice of that sweet Maiden,

From the Jasper Reeds, of Aiden,

With her lily-lips love-laden,

    Answered, "Yes! forever more!"

And the old-time Towers of Aiden

Echoed "Yes! forever more!"

Who would you guess wrote this? If your answer is Edgar Allen Poe, you are wrong. Well, half wrong anyway. The lines are from "The Vigil in Aiden," by Thomas Holley Chivers.

Chivers, like Poe, was a southern writer in the first half of the nineteenth century. For years an unresolved debate has simmered over whether Poe stole poetry from Chivers or whether Chivers stole from Poe. The only agreement scholars can reach is that they did influence one another. Yet, Poe received public immortality, while Chivers faded into near oblivion. There is no doubt the two knew each other, read and criticized each other's works, and kept up a steady flow of correspondence. When Poe died, Chivers was one of the first to write Poe's biography (but it was unnoticed until 1952, when University of Tennessee Professor Richard Beale Davis arranged its publication.) It's also a fact that Chivers claimed Poe had used his style and words— but that Chivers waited until Poe was dead before he made that claim, and never tried very hard to prove it. Duke University has a collection of his unpublished works, and there are a number of books in larger libraries, mostly published since 1952, that tell us more about this neglected Georgian poet.

The debate gets highly technical, and I find its primary value to be something other than the issue of authorship. Most poets are influenced by other poets, and both Chivers and Poe were clearly influenced by Tennyson, Keats, Shelley, Byron, the Bible and Shakespeare, among others. The real value of the literary debate is that it rescues Chivers from obscurity. He is an interesting southern poet on his own merits, read and reviewed critically by the New England and New York literary establishment of those pre–Civil War days, and read approvingly by Bayard Taylor, who shared his works with Swinburne in England. Joyce Kilmer and Vachel Lindsay read Chivers, as did the Rossettis and Rudyard Kipling.

Chivers, a son of a cotton planter and mill owner, was born in 1809 in Washington, Georgia. His part of the country was still next to Indian territory in his youth, and frontier revivalism was in its own youthful era. The influences of nature, Indians, and religious afterlife are apparent in his poems. He married at age nineteen, and his pregnant wife left him within a year. He then enrolled in medical college at Transylvania University in Kentucky, one of the best medical schools in the country. Graduating in 1830, Chivers returned to Georgia, wandered among Cherokees, published a book of poetry from his Kentucky years, wrote a verse drama on the Beauchamp-Sharpe murder case (the Kentucky tragedy that is the story in Robert Penn Warren's *World Enough and Time*), and sent some poems to the *Southern Literary Messenger* in 1835 that were rejected, but which may have influenced Poe, an editor.

An Indian-legends poem, "Nacoochee," was published in 1837, the year Chivers married a Massachusetts lady. Other works include "The Lost Pleiad," "Search after Truth," "Eonchs of Ruby," "Atlanta," "Memoralia," "Virginilia Birth-Day Song of Liberty," and "The Sons of Usna." He died in 1858. He had lost a sister, then his mother in 1838, a daughter in 1842, and his three remaining children in 1848.

With his medical training, he had a special faculty for describing deathbed scenes, and like Poe was often criticized for his preoccupation with dying. Like many educated Americans of this era, Chivers became enamored with Swedenborgianism, a mysticism that saw a correlation between things worldly and things otherworldly, between the natural world and the spiritual world. The two worlds coexist during a person's natural life span, but the spiritual remains once the material body is gone. The mystic often feels he is living more and more on the spiritual side as he matures, and feels he passes easily back and forth between the two. Poetry thus becomes a way of using worldly words to tell about the next world.

Most Chivers-Poe correspondence was during the 1840s. Poe was usually begging money to publish something, but Chivers was not taken in. Chivers wanted someone with whom to share ideas. His own lifestyle was simple. He spent little money, had strong religious convictions, and abstained from drink, in contrast to Poe. For many years it was fashionable to say the South had no poets or novelists before the 1920s. Chivers joins Poe, Sidney Lanier, William Gilmore Simms, and others in proving that untrue.

May 17, 1982

THOMAS JEFFERSON'S NEPHEWS

One scandal in Thomas Jefferson's family never mentioned anywhere in the thousands of letters and notes he left behind had to do with the murder of a slave in Kentucky by two of his nephews. It happened near Smithland, Kentucky, on December 15, 1811. Smithland is a river town located at the junction of the Ohio and Cumberland Rivers in western Kentucky. Col. Charles L. Lewis and his family, virtually destitute in Virginia, had moved there in 1808. Mrs. Lucy Lewis was Thomas Jefferson's sister.

Within two years after they arrived, Lucy died, leaving three daughters and Colonel Lewis to be cared for. The oldest son, Randolph, responsible for them and for a wife and eight children of his own, took charge. Then he died and a year later so did his wife. Family responsibility fell to the next son, Lilburn, whose own wife died and left him with five children. He remarried, perhaps unhappily. In debt and burdened with so much family and with several slaves, he apparently became bitter and took to drink. A younger brother, Isham, came to live there, too, after failing to find work in Natchez or St. Louis. Moodiness ran in the family. A cousin, Meriwether Lewis of Lewis and Clark fame committed suicide about this time on the Natchez Trace in Mississippi. Lilburn was probably depressed and irrational.

On December 15, 1811, Lilburn Lewis sent George, a seventeen-year-old slave, to fetch a pitcher of water. The pitcher was broken, and Lilburn, with all his troubles, decided to take out his frustrations on George. With Isham present, he called all the slaves into a cabin and killed George with a hatchet. Then he swore the slaves to secrecy and proceeded to destroy the evidence by burning the body in the fireplace. An incredible freak of nature that very same night led eventually to Lilburn's downfall.

The year 1811 was one of the most unusual in history. As Boynton Merrill, Jr., who bought part of the Lewis farm, tells the story in his book *Jefferson's Nephews: A Frontier Tragedy*, a flood early in the year delayed the crops, followed by a wave of sickness in the Ohio valley. In April, a great comet appeared and remained visible all year, growing brighter until October. In the summer, a drought wiped out what crops had grown, and a series of tornadoes and hurricanes swept all of the east. In August, the Indian chief Tecumseh came through the area, trying to get the southern Indians to unite with his northern tribes to overthrow the whites. Squirrels by the thousands left their forests and drowned trying to swim the Ohio, and fantastically large flocks of passenger pigeons descended and cleaned out the forest food. On September 17, there was a total eclipse of the sun. In November, the Prophet (Tecumseh's brother) led the tribes to defeat at Tippecanoe but killed many Kentuckians in the process. War with England seemed certain to break out soon (and did the next year, the War of 1812). During most of 1811, the first steamboat on the Ohio was traveling down-stream; it was near Smithland when the murder occurred December 15.

But the fantastic cap to all of these incredible events of 1811 was the earthquake at 2:00 A.M. on the morning of December 16, 1811, the same night the murder by Jefferson's nephews at Smithland occurred. It was the first of several continuing quakes that would last into 1812. The first shock from the New Madrid earthquake made rivers run backward and created new lakes and new hills where there once was only flatland. Cabins fell for hundreds of miles around, and hundreds of boats sank. Entire forests were uprooted. Time has since covered most traces of the quake, and the fron-tier was still too young for its full effect to have been recorded in newspa-pers. Some people said it was Tecumseh's curse, for he had told the southern Indians that when he returned to Detroit he would stamp his foot and cause the ground to tremble and houses to fall. Reelfoot Lake is the major remaining evidence of the quake.

At Lilburn Lewis's farm, the quake caused the stone chimney of the cabin to fall in and to smother the fire before the body of the murdered slave was consumed. Next day, Lilburn had the slaves rebuild the fireplace, but when they did, they covered up the pieces of the body with masonry. Two more severe earthquakes followed on January 23 and February 7, 1812. During one of these, the fireplace fell again. A dog found the head of the dead slave and dragged it off, and it was found and reported to the sheriff. Soon after, Lilburn's wife and newborn son left the farm. Lilburn and his brother were arrested and released on bail. On April 9, 1812, Lilburn wrote his will, and he and his brother, Isham, went to the family cemetery. They agreed to shoot each other with rifles. According to Isham, the suicide pact failed when Lilburn accidentally shot himself while explaining how to use the rifle alone if it should misfire. Isham was jailed but escaped and, according to legend, was killed at the Battle of New Orleans.

This story became a book-length poem, *Brother to Dragons,* by Robert Penn Warren.

May 31, 1982

FANNY WRIGHT

The myth that southern women are sugar-throated, helpless creatures doesn't die easily. Women tilled the farms and ran the plantations throughout the Civil War—and often, as widows, long afterward. They set up schools and shops that pulled the South out of Reconstruction. They led the crusade against lynching in the early part of this century and ran the farms and shops again during the Depression before becoming government workers, merchants, and riveters in World War II. The network of social service volunteers and welfare agencies in the South was women's handiwork. Behind the fluttering eyelashes of the stereotypical flirtatious southern belles spun busy brains of strong, businesslike, organizing women.

This backdrop of stoic and sensible southern womanhood is important if one is to appreciate the entrance of Fanny Wright into the southern scene in the 1820s. No one in America, north or south, had ever met a woman quite like Frances Wright. From the moment she arrived in New York in 1818 until she died in Ohio in 1852, she swept the nation off its feet with her insistent causes and persistent poses. She refused to accept the traditional roles of woman in either European or American society. She was at home in the fashionable salons of France or upon the saddle of a horse winding its way, unescorted, across Indiana, Ohio, and Pennsylvania.

Born into educated aristocracy in Scotland in 1795, Fanny Wright was orphaned before she was three and reared by a grandfather and aunt in London until she was eighteen, when she left to join her uncle's family on the University of Glasgow campus. She never had a real childhood, and never developed a sense of humor or the art of feminine flattery. She read voraciously from the university library—poetry, political science, philosophy, and everything she could find about the United States. Tall and withdrawn, she compensated for her lack of suitors by writing poetry and plays. She was particularly taken with the essays of the manufacturer-reformer Robert Owens about his experiments at nearby New Lanark.

At age twenty-one, she was back in London, in the midst of social reform movements, impatient because change came so slowly there compared with what she had read about changes elsewhere, especially in America and in Owens's factory-town. She sailed for America. She mixed with the cream of New York and Philadelphia society, saw her play produced on Broadway and in Philadelphia, and—most important—became interested in the slavery issue and made notes that would become a best-selling book when she published them back in England as *Views of Society and Manners in America.*

In England, the utilitarian philosopher Jeremy Bentham befriended her, and then, on business to Paris for him and for herself, she met Lafayette, then sixty-four years old. He took Fanny into his home, and until his death she was treated as one of his family, not without outcries of scandal in later years. She supposedly was doing research for a book on Lafayette's life. His family disliked her, and she was bold enough to propose marriage to him, which he gently refused. Then, in 1824, he prepared to leave for his triumphal tour of America, the "son of Washington," hero of two revolutions, and first honorary citizen of the United States. Fanny Wright solved the problem of whether she would go with him by going two weeks after him and then meeting him at various points along his tour, which lasted a year. As the days passed, she felt frozen out of his circle. She did get to Monticello, where she met Jefferson, who was only a year away from dying, and renewed her interest in slavery.

Encouraged (she thought) by Jefferson and others, she studied Robert Owens's experiments at a utopian commune in New Harmony, Indiana, and resolved to make a commune of her own farther south for the purpose of ending slavery.

From that came the fabled but short-lived Nashoba, twenty miles out from Memphis, a "plantation" hardly larger than a clearing, to which Wright and her followers brought slaves they purchased for the purposes of educating them and letting them buy their freedom by farming and learning skills.

From there, she moved northward and became a public spokeswoman for women's rights, for open marriage, for socialism, for the working class, and for uncensored speech and press. She kept, for years, her ability to move in the circles of the mighty, but as the years faded, so did her popularity. "Fanny-Wrightism" became a derisive term, the papers stopped sending reporters to hear her latest heresies, and she closed out her years in relative obscurity and poverty.

Two authors have captured something of her times and spirit. Celia Morris Eckhardt's *Fanny Wright: Rebel in America* (Harvard Press) is the most thorough, and John Egerton's *Visions of Utopia* (UT Press) catches Nashoba well.

January 28, 1985

WILLIAM MAXWELL MARTIN

In the old center of the historic Washington Street Cemetery in Columbia, South Carolina, a broken fluted column still draws visitors after 125 years. It reads: "William Maxwell Martin. Born 4th June, 1837. Died 21st Feb., 1861. 'The first Martyr to Southern Independence.' His death caused by exposure in defense of his native State, at Fort Moultrie."

A visitor might muse that Martin was the prototype for Charles Hamilton, Scarlett O'Hara's ill-fated first husband. He was much more than that. He left a mark other than his being the first southern soldier to die.

William Maxwell Martin was in Wofford College's Class of 1857. Historian Allen Stokes (Class of 1964) of the Caroliniana Library has uncovered a book by Maxwell, published posthumously by Southern Methodist Publishing House in 1861, consisting of eighty-four poems, fourteen short essays, two orations, and extracts of letters, all written between 1853 and 1861. Its title is *Lyrics and Sketches.*

The works are fairly good, promising better to come as a writer had Martin lived. These are youthful and romantic, full of idealized ladies, chivalry, nature, fame, and death. In cadence and style they evoke Poe, Timrod, Lanier, and Browning. One of the best is poignantly simple, about the death of Prof. James H. Carlisle's two-year-old daughter: "Sing, ye winds of evening, / Softly, sweetly low; / Lull her dreamless sleeping, / sighing as ye go."

His friend James Wood Davenport captured Martin's brief life well in the introduction to the book, and passages from two distinguished college presidents, A. B. Longstreet and William M. Wightman, under whom Martin had studied at South Carolina College and Wofford College, respectively, echo Davenport, and all are supported by editorial excerpts from several state newspapers. His budding genius was already being recognized at age twenty-three when he died so suddenly.

He had taught school from 1857 to 1860 and was entering law studies when the war came. Martin attended the December 20 secession convention and quickly enlisted soon afterward in the Columbia Artillery; it was sent to Fort Moultrie on January 2, 1861.

A week later the battery fired on the northern *Star of the West* as it tried to provision Fort Sumter. Then twenty days later the battery was called out to watch the shoreline and fired on two Pee Dee boats that turned out to be their own. During that mission, Martin caught a cold and was put to bed.

His last letter home was on January 31. Shortly afterward he was sent to a Columbia hospital, and on February 16 he was sent home. Five days later he died.

Martin wrote that he loved writing more than all else in the world. Davenport noted his great love for the sea and for the mountains, especially Caesar's Head. His essays show a quick wit, much humor, and terrible puns.

H. L. Mencken said southern writing before 1920 was a "Sahara." William M. Martin, had he lived, might have proved otherwise. The war took him as its first lost soldier, but it took some of the poetry out of the South, too.

November 11, 1985

JULIAN S. CARR

At Appomattox in 1865, Julian Shakespeare Carr was only nineteen and still a Confederate private after enlisting the year before, near the end of his sophomore year at the University of North Carolina. When he died in 1924, he was commander-in-chief of the United Confederate Veterans of America.

Today, Carr is virtually forgotten. Yet, in his sixty years of adulthood, he left footprints everywhere. He virtually invented international advertising as he moved a little tobacco business from a manual-labor mail-order shop to fame and a first fortune from his Bull Durham conglomerate. For decades, Carr was one of the wealthiest and most influential Methodist laymen; his support and management of little Trinity College meant there is a Duke University today.

Without Carr's financial help, a drifting young Chinese seaman called "Charlie Soon" would never have been educated at Trinity College and Vanderbilt University to return to China in 1886 as a native missionary, got involved in the Hung P'ang "Red Gang," become secretary-treasurer of Sun Yat-sen's party, prospered in flour mills and in Bible publishing, and fathered six children. One of them, T. V. Soon, became China's minister of finance; another, Ai-ling, married H. H. Kung, a descendant of Confucius of enormous wealth who also was minister of finance and of commerce and industry; another, Ching-ling, married Sun Yat-sen himself; and a fourth, May-ling, married a man who already had a wife and several concubines who was named Chiang Kai-shek.

Without "Jule" Carr, there would probably be no Durham, North Carolina, today, or the textile town of Carrboro. Carr also was responsible for the building of the Durham Public Library, the first library to be sustained by public funds. One of Carr's sons, Julian, Jr., introduced "industrial democracy" into his hosiery industry, with joint labor-management quality-control systems and "profit-sharing" for the workers.

The Carrs were connected by marriages and business partnerships, and even by rivalries, with the great families of the region, including the Moreheads, Cannons, and Dukes. The expansive grandeur of Carr's homes and farms rivaled those of the Vanderbilts' Biltmore Estate. He served on almost every civic and business board of any significance. He ran for governor and for U.S. senator, was mayor of Durham early in his career and a state legislator near its end, was offered as a favorite-son candidate for the Democratic vice presidential nomination in 1900, and tried to enlist in World War I and served instead as a public campaigner for the U.S. Food Administration program headed by Herbert Hoover.

The weddings of his children matched the extravaganzas of any belles of prominence. Carr was determined to prove that the South could rise phoenix-like above war, defeat, and reconstruction. In his jovial manner, high style of living, concern for working conditions and civic progress, Carr personified the New South, which was a vision of the Old South refinanced and a little more democratic. He was buried in 1924; twenty thousand people lined the streets, and he was attended by honor guards of Confederate veterans, the Elks, and the Masons, and a bishop and three ministers led a cortege of 150 automobiles to private services at the cemetery. Many of those present had attended a gigantic seventy-fifth birthday celebration for Carr in 1920.

Men of Carr's mold—paternalistic patriarchs who somehow climbed high without forgetting the common touch that, in his case, being a Confederate private and unemployed veteran gave—once dominated the South. Some are still around, in single-industry towns with long memories and old habits, but entrepreneurs are less conspicuous and managers more muted now. They served the South well in its infancy, and through the war and its second infancy. With the coming of the Depression and of World War II, people moved into another dependency, turning to federal agencies for fatherly help. After World War II, the adolescence of the South, so long deferred, finally came and was enjoyed by all who rushed into new employment and affluence. Now, with economic leadership and political leadership shifting back to the South, it remains to be seen whether southern people are ready to move into their maturity or back into youthful dependencies.

Jule Carr was born of southern aristocracy and bred a new one of his own. Carr money came and went, but the capacity to rule never ebbed. The greater portion of southern people never had that background or that drive, never acquired the habits or the opportunities to acquire them. Perhaps the times in which we live as this century ends will be times for uncovering and testing dormant southern instincts for leadership and cultural improvement. Those elevated to fuller responsibility in the newest version of the New South, at the millennium's end, could do worse than recall the civility, dignity, and faith in education and ethics shown by some past giants such as Julian S. Carr. Those, more than his birth, success, and wealth, were the real sources of his power.

March 23, 1987

CASSIUS CLAY

Mention Cassius Clay and most folks think of the boxer. The earlier bearer of the name was also a Kentuckian and just as famed in his own right as a fighter.

Every age needs its legends. In the pre–Civil War and postwar years, Cassius Clay filled a void left by the passing of the frontier and its Boones and Crocketts. He was a folk hero of a fiery sort, liked by few people but the subject of talk for many. Even today, Cassius Clay stories are retold, a saga of rugged individualism, freedom of the press, unpopular racial beliefs, violent self-defense, and unorthodox marriages. Lawyer William H. Townsend became famous for his recording and book about Clay. H. Edward Richardson gave a more balanced account in *Cassius Marcellus Clay: Firebrand of Freedom* (University Press of Kentucky).

Except for the Mexican War, diplomatic service as wartime ambassador in Russia, a short-term residency in Lexington as a newspaper editor, and a brief time in Washington mobilizing the local guard to defend the city and Mr. Lincoln, Clay spent his life from 1810 to 1903 at White Hall, an impressive mansion outside Richmond, Kentucky.

Pastoral as that farm life and locale may look, Clay was rarely isolated or idle. Bluegrass sentiment about the Union was split, but predominantly anti-Union and pro-slavery in blueblood circles. To that dominant society Cassius Marcellus Clay was linked by birth, by kinship with Henry Clay, by education at Yale, and by inherited status and wealth as the third child of six of a patriot father, Gen. Green Clay, formerly of Virginia.

But Clay was a rebel within his class. Doing the unexpected and the unacceptable was the stuff from which his legend was made. In a society of slaveholders he became a southern abolitionist. His aversion to the practice started early when he and his sister saw the bloody knife held by their slave nursemaid after she killed the overseer for attacking her. Though acquitted, she was sold and sent to the Deep South.

Cassius Clay was a member of the Kentucky House of Representatives in 1835–37 and 1840, edited a controversial newspaper opposed to slavery in 1845, served with distinction in the U.S. Army during the Mexican War, campaigned for Lincoln's nomination and election and sought the Republican nomination for vice president in 1860, was U.S. minister to Russia in 1861–62 and 1863–69 (primarily so Lincoln could get him out of the country), and was a general in the Union army during the Civil War. Probably the best-known southern antislavery man, Clay freed his own slaves in 1844.

As a young scholar, Clay attended Transylvania University and then Yale. Transylvania's main building burned down in 1829, and in 1898 Clay admitted that the fire was started by his body servant, whose tallow candle on the steps set them on fire when the servant fell asleep while blacking Clay's boots. When Transylvania, one of America's four best universities in Clay's student days, fell on hard times in 1838 and was split by sectarian squabbles, Clay was one of eleven Lexingtonians who sponsored a campaign to endow and save it.

At Yale, Clay showed the independent spirit that marked his entire career. Yale had an impressive southern enrollment, largely attracted there by the fact that a southern idol, John C. Calhoun, was a Yale graduate in 1804. A society of southerners was founded in 1819 and was active until just before the Civil War, but Clay proved to be an unusual southerner. From a slaveholding family and state, he was convinced by the antislavery speeches and writings of William Lloyd Garrison that slavery should be banished. Clay graduated from Yale in 1832 and married the same year. Chosen by his classmates to make the Washington Centennial Address in 1832, his oration was a plea for voluntary and immediate emancipation.

All this came before he was twenty-two and before the South pulled into itself in that long defensive era from Nat Turner's Rebellion on through Reconstruction. He was one of the founders of Berea College, the only integrated college in the prewar South, and a passionate spokesman for the Union and against slavery, a posture that became virtually untenable in his region and society.

Clay was particularly respected and remembered because he was quick to fight. Fresh out of college, he courted and married Mary Jane Warfield despite the animosity and threats of her father and family; it was not to be a happy marriage. Trouble began before the wedding day when father Warfield goaded a rejected suitor into taunting Clay into a duel, an event delayed twice until the wedding day, when the suitor followed the honeymooners to Louisville. Later fierce political battles between Clay and Robert Wickliffe, Jr., moved away from slavery issues to the field of honor.

The violence that marked his life escalated. In 1843 a paid assassin, Samuel M. Brown, attacked Clay at a rally at Russell's Cave near Lexington. Brown's shot went straight toward Clay's heart, but Clay pulled his Bowie knife and ripped Brown to shreds, continuing to slice even when mobbed by the pro-Wickliffe crowd. The bullet had struck Clay's knife scabbard.

He campaigned in the antislavery North for Henry Clay's presidency, fought and was imprisoned in the Mexican War, became the friend of influential editor Horace Greeley, became a fire-eating editor of Lexington's short-lived *True American* until a mob forced him into early retirement by shipping his press off to Cincinnati, and was mobbed and stabbed at another rally but killed his attacker.

Clay's support of Lincoln for president led him to believe he would be secretary of war. Lincoln sent him to Russia instead. There he was the hit of the court, keeping Russia on the side of the North in the war and later negotiating the American purchase of Alaska. Rumors of a ballerina mistress, affairs, and illegitimately sired children followed him to his grave. He and his wife separated in 1863 and divorced in 1878. After a flurry of political activity supporting Andrew Johnson's gentler Reconstruction over that of radical Republicans and opposing President Grant's corrupt cronies, he supported Democrats Greeley and Tilden in their unsuccessful presidential bids, and finally returned to the Republican Party to campaign for Blaine in 1884.

Late in life Clay was still a fighter. He found that the nurse for his adopted child, aided by her lover, was poisoning the child and stealing silver from the house. He sent the nurse packing and gave word to the lover to stay away; the man did not, and in a shootout, Clay killed him. When Clay's son and his friends were attacked and one of them killed for trying to vote, Clay marched black voters to the polls and faced down white Democrats who had threatened to kill him on sight. Three consecutive foremen of Clay's farms were killed by the Klan.

At age seventy-four, Clay offended his fellow citizens again, this time by taking a fifteen-year-old orphan as his bride. When the sheriff and seven men in a posse came to take child-bride Dora away, Clay greeted them with the two brass cannons he had kept loaded in his newspaper offices half a century earlier, shattering the water maple behind which they all took refuge. The couple divorced amicably two years later, and Dora married Riley Brock, but moved back to White Hall as housekeeper. In 1900, an armed party allegedly led by Brock broke into the house, and two of the party died from gunshot wounds.

After that Clay lived the life of an eccentric recluse, refusing to repair the house or to pay his taxes, talking to ghosts and portraits. As he lay dying in 1903, Kentuckians placed bets on whether Clay or the also-dying Pope Leo XIII would die first. Clay was delighted that "although not infallible," he outlived the pontiff. In Kentuckians' long memories, he yet does.

May 2, 1988

A friend nearly thirty years older than I has written me. I hesitate to call her an "old friend" because she is still young in her ideas, her ability to remember, and her affection for reading and writing. Her reason for writing was to correct me. I had written that a 1929 rematch of Centre College and Transylvania University celebrating the fiftieth anniversary of southern football was canceled because of the stock market crash and the coming of the Depression. She sent me her ticket from that game and a newspaper clipping, and she recalled details about her date, whom she later married. The game was played, and I stand happily corrected.

She mentioned in the same letter that, while reading about this year's Centennial of Washington State, she had noticed a description of the state tree, the western hemlock, was followed by the word "Raf." She was delighted to discover that it meant that the tree was scientifically classified way back in the 1820s by botanist Constantine Rafinesque, a familiar name for all Transylvania alumni.

Rafinesque was one of America's most brilliant and most forgotten scientists. Born in Constantinople in 1783, he wandered throughout Europe before arriving in Philadelphia in 1802, where he taught himself botany. After returning in 1805 to Sicily, where he did extensive study and writing for ten years, he came back to the United States in 1815. He accepted a teaching position at Transylvania University in 1818 under the college's best-known president, Horace Holley. On his way to his post, he detoured to Louisville to spend some time with the famous naturalist, John James Audubon. Audubon was awed by Rafinesque's knowledge of natural sciences and also a little irritated when awakened by Rafinesque running around the room naked, killing bats with Audubon's priceless Cremona violin.

Science itself was a new, and suspicious, subject in any college in those days. Add the peculiarity of the subject to that of its teacher, whose dress, speech, foreign origins, and personal habits clearly set him apart, and we have material for legend. Even those most likely to respect him, doctors and professors of medicine, could not communicate with him. He was totally absorbed in gathering and classifying specimens of plants and animals, one of the first professors to bring them into a classroom.

President Holley never knew if Rafinesque was going to show up for his classes. He would disappear, going unannounced on extended expeditions to find new specimens all over Kentucky.

One extended journey in 1825 to Washington, D.C., to obtain a patent pushed Holley too far. He ordered Rafinesque's personal effects and collections moved to another place. Rafinesque was furious when he returned, accusing Holley of evicting him, dumping his priceless collections in a heap, and depriving of him of his position as librarian and of his right to board at the college. He cursed Holley and Transylvania.

Rafinesque returned to Philadelphia and died there in abject poverty. But his curse lingered after him. Holley was dismissed as president of Transylvania in 1827 and died of yellow fever on his way back east. In 1829, the college burned to the ground. Witnesses to the fire saw a pigeon flying above the flames. As the fire was dying, the exhausted bird dropped into the flames. Was it one of Constantine Rafinesque's specimens?

In the 1920s some sentimental alumni of the college had Rafinesque's body exhumed from its potter's field grave in Philadelphia and reinterred in the college's main building, Morrison College, which had been built in 1833 to replace the burned main hall.

Old Morrison itself burned in 1969.

Rafinesque's tomb was untouched by the fire.

July 31, 1989

NELL WALDROP

One woman my whole family loves a great deal is Nell Waldrop. Our affection for her goes back to college days, when she was a tall, lanky girl from Alabama who followed her high school sweetheart north to Kentucky and married him. Wife Betsy and Nellie worked together in the same local junior high in Lexington.

Our paths crossed again some years later when we all lived on the same street in Tuscaloosa, Alabama. Her husband, Guy, was a minister there, and Nell and I worked at the university. We moved on to Tennessee and later to South Carolina, and the Waldrops back to Kentucky, to his church work and her social work. We've seen each other off and on at class reunions or elsewhere, enough for our daughters to call them Aunt Nell and Uncle Guy and for us to keep up with their older daughter and their twins.

The Waldrops are good folks who have admirable abilities to care about people and to care about improving the world. Sometimes those two things don't mix well, because of the intensity. Somehow they always have in this couple.

A few years back, Nellie discovered she has multiple sclerosis. Watching her deal with it as it slowly works its will upon her body, I want desperately to write something about her and about what it all means. But I don't know what to write.

I could write of progressive loss of physical controls, the stages of her odyssey from driving herself to work, to having to have a special vehicle, to having to have a driver, to having to quit work, to moving into a one-story home, to using a motor scooter, to having to change the furniture so that she could slide on to it, and on to the current stage of needing help in dressing and eating, but Dante has already written a description of the nine circles of Hell better than I can.

I could write of her personal courage, which matches the heroism in any war memoir or of any Medal of Honor winner.

I could write of her example, of how well she is teaching others to understand the mysteries of fate and disease and coping, even though this is not the kind of lesson that she was certified by the state to teach back thirty years ago when she robustly taught physical education.

I could write of her patience, not with her body or with its illness, but with people helpless to help her, torn into frustration between feelings of pity and ignorance, people whom she always puts quickly at ease.

I could write of her good humor, which seems to heighten the more her bodily control diminishes. If her laughter is a barometer, she is very, very far from being at wit's end.

I could write of her selflessness, of the inexplicable paradox that as the disease forces her inevitably to think of nothing else but herself simply to get the smallest things done, somehow she seems to think about and do more and more for others. They say that blindness or deafness is compensated for by increased powers in the other senses. In this case, as Nellie's entire body goes downhill, her spirit and mind are climbing higher and higher mountains.

I could write of how truly pale and petty are things which pester me compared with her pain and predicaments or how envious I am that, even with more with which to cope, she seems so much more capable of coping than do I.

I could write all those things and more about Nellie Waldrop, but still I wouldn't know really what I ought to write.

I don't believe God put this disease into Nellie: not as a punishment, not as a test, and not as an example. But when this nefarious thing did come, it must have been surprised to find how totally God had gotten there first.

August 14, 1989

FRANK A. ROSE

In 1954, I left the nest, college-bound. I knew very little about where I was going other than Transylvania College was very small, was church-related, and was noted for little except its being 175 years old at that time.

Two things happened soon afterward that left a permanent impression on me. The first was that the entire student body came down with food poisoning from banana pudding. The harness races were in town that week, and banners hailing "The Lexington Trots" were everywhere. Our particular group of students, having shared that distress, is probably still closer-knit than most alumni anywhere.

The second thing was getting to meet the college's president. Frank Rose was tall, dark, and dignified and, at age twenty-nine, was just beginning a long and successful career in college administration. His vigor and rhetoric put the college on the map, and before he was called in 1957 to become the president of the University of Alabama he was chosen one of the Ten Outstanding Young Men in America.

The University of Alabama was suffering when he arrived. Earlier attempts to integrate the campus had ended in chaos, state appropriations for education were among the lowest in the nation, and its football fortunes were at low ebb. Before Rose even moved into the President's Mansion in late 1957, he persuaded Paul "Bear" Bryant to "come home" to begin writing new record books. By 1963, the campus was integrated. State and federal aid was boosted. No matter how controversial the university became at times, Alabama became education-conscious and education-supportive.

From there, Rose moved in 1969 to Washington to carve out yet another niche by serving as counsel to congressmen and campuses, an intermediary promoting quality higher education and quality health care nationwide. He continued on an expanded scale what he had done well on the small campus in Kentucky and statewide in Alabama, being an outspoken gadfly for raising both the level of economic existence and the vision of hopes for the South, primarily through better education.

Back when our generation of students knew him, attendance was required at Wednesday chapels at which Frank Rose presided magisterially, robed in a black gown that matched his hair, which he wore long and parted down the center. Whatever visiting fireman was speaking that day, he inevitably would begin his introduction with the phrase, "It is a real and genuine pleasure to. . . ."

The measure of our affection for him as students came each May when he would announce tuition increases none of us could afford but were guaranteed to make the college superior to all others. On those annual occasions, we would shout, "It is a real and genuine pleasure!" and leap to our feet to give him a standing ovation.

With hair gray and parted on the side, Rose approached seventy still giving full-time to a mission that began when he left a Mississippi farm fifty years ago.

He had a double-sized pacemaker attached to him, he carried an oxygen tank since having a lung removed, and he used wheelchairs to get him from cabs to planes. But don't be deceived by appearances. His mind, his enthusiasm, and his determination, like Tennyson's aging Ulysses, were undiminished.

The entire southern region should applaud him. He has, indeed, been "a real and genuine pleasure."

September 4, 1989

IRVIN E. LUNGER

"Persistence pays off."

That adage is as familiar to us as "Genius is 1 percent inspiration and 99 percent perspiration" or "Early to bed, early to rise, makes a man healthy, wealthy, and wise."

The trouble with adages is that they are commonplace truths, and what we take for commonplace is usually what we also take for granted.

The stop-over revivalist in town gets more attention than the preacher who has watched his flock for decades. The passing-through circus gets more attention than the stay-put art gallery. The first-day aftermath of the hurricane or earthquake get more attention than the one hundredth–day aftermath.

We have abbreviated attention spans. We thrive on novelty, and we take the long run for granted. We are not tenacious enough observers to appreciate the unsung virtues of tenacity.

One of the best passages in "John Brown's Body" has Abraham Lincoln musing about how long and drawn out the war has been and how impatient and cantankerous people have become. Sometimes he feels he has been deserted, left alone to see the thing through. He compares the fickle fallen-away with scampering bird dogs, yelping and scattering across the countryside, and the role he must play is that of a tired old hound whose only virtue is that he plods along, keeping his nose to the scent.

Tenacity does not get its fair share of applause. It is an unrewarded virtue. Those who display it are doomed to do their work silently, out of unrequited love, not out of hope for recognition.

We see the tenacious everywhere about us but without really seeing them. They are the teachers, the courthouse clerks, the heads of banks and of hospitals, the aldermen, and the family businessmen with longevity. Only in rare moments of introspective retrospection do we glimpse their shadows and know that the pictures could not have been made had they not been there.

An example comes to mind in Dr. Irvin E. Lunger, who served little Transylvania University as president and president emeritus with hound-dog tenacity for over thirty years.

Probably only one building and one faculty member remain from the days when he arrived in 1955. His legacy is the survival and the transformation of a college, not an insignificant achievement for a lifetime of persistence.

Lunger weathered the death of his first wife during the move from Chicago to Kentucky and the deaths of their two daughters in the intervening years since, personal illnesses, the burning of the college's main building, years of meeting payrolls without visible means of support, reams of unsolicited advice, yelps of personal abuse from scampering cynics, having to attract private support in a city dominated by Rupp Arena and a major state university a few blocks away, and absence of appreciation for each block he put in place in reshaping and breathing new life into an aged institution.

Like Dilsey, the invisible family servant spanning the generations of William Faulkner's Compson family, Irvin Lunger "endured." And like Dilsey, by simply enduring, he "prevailed." And, again like Dilsey, the "family" would have disintegrated without him. He was the gray mortar for all its bricks.

Because he was able to weather so much for so long, his college endured. His tenacity, seen in retrospect, was its largest endowment fund; his persistence was its greatest asset. The old hound dog kept his nose to the scent.

It would be warming to think that generations yet unborn will arise and bless Dr. Irvin Lunger's name. That will not happen. He plodded for progress instead of yelping for attention.

He left a monument, but he insisted upon not signing it. The institution's posterity will not know how it is possible that it is where it is or how it profits from what he did. But his legacy is there, not a dead inscription on a stone in a desert such as Ozymandias left, but a living thriving institution. The buildings may bear names other than his, but what Irvin Lunger left is more important—tenacity. That touch gave an old college new life.

December 4, 1989

F. A. P. BARNARD

The University of Mississippi's Center for the Study of Southern Culture is in renovated quarters, the old F. A. P. Barnard Observatory near the center of campus. The building bears the name of the man who built it. F. A. P. Barnard was one of the greatest educators in America in the nineteenth century.

A New Englander who graduated from Yale in 1828, Barnard joined the faculty at the University of Alabama in 1838. For the next sixteen years he built a reputation for himself as one of the most innovative and outspoken professors and scientists in the nation. He was prominent in several national science associations, surveyed and settled the boundary line between Alabama and Florida, participated in a number of international expeditions on behalf of astronomy and geology, defended the university against legislative and gubernatorial encroachments, quietly made classes in the all-male college coeducational by admitting some local girls and daughters of faculty members to his classes, spoke out against excessive regulation of students, and began expressing ideas that later would blossom into full-grown definitions of a university (as distinguished from a college).

In 1854 he was lured from Tuscaloosa to the younger University of Mississippi in Oxford. Hired as a professor of mathematics, two years later

Barnard was made president and then chancellor of that campus. His national prominence increased through his scientific association memberships. Elected president of one in 1860, he was unable to preside over it until 1868 because the Civil War broke out.

Barnard was a highly respected educator. Attacked frequently for being a scientist, an Episcopalian, and a defender of blacks, and for advocating more legislative allocations to the university, he was supported strongly by the university trustees and by then-senator Jefferson Davis.

When secession came, Barnard told the university's board he could not remain in office because his sentiments and heritage were pro-Union. The board at first refused to accept his resignation. When the university had to discontinue operation, they proposed to send him to Virginia and other points east to advise school systems and to recruit students for the envisioned reopening of the campus.

Barnard requested state permission to pass through the Confederate lines to return north for the duration. It was denied on the grounds that such permission had to come from the president of the Confederacy in Richmond. Barnard traveled east to Richmond to get Davis's clearance to leave the South. Davis refused to grant the request and instead asked Barnard to undertake scientific work for the government. When Barnard discovered that the work would involve developing sulfur resources for munitions, he refused the offer. Instead he was assigned to service in Norfolk, at the shipping yards there. In 1862, Norfolk was captured by the Union armies and held by them thereafter. At that time, Barnard was finally able to cross the lines and return to New York.

In a few years he was elected president of Columbia College, later to become Columbia University, where he served for twenty-five years. During that time he introduced coeducation, created a number of professional schools around the liberal arts college hub, and built a major-model for what would define the best of universities in American higher education thereafter. Later the Columbia trustees honored Barnard by creating a women's college and naming it Barnard College, still in existence today.

When Barnard was at the University of Alabama he designed and built one of the first observatories in the country. At the University of Mississippi he built an even larger observatory building, the one that still stands and bears his name, and placed an order for the largest telescope lens in the country. War broke out before the lens could be shipped, and the manufacturer later sold it to a northern college.

Upon leaving Mississippi, Barnard packed up his personal library, a very extensive and valuable collection, and had it sent to Tuscaloosa for safekeeping on the University of Alabama campus. On April 5, 1865, General Croxton's units of the northern army, operating out of Nashville, where Gen. George Thomas was in command, moved against Tuscaloosa while other units pressed to attack Selma and Montgomery and Nathan B. Forrest.

Four cadets in the Alabama Cadet Corps at the University of Alabama buried the lens of the Barnard telescope somewhere on campus. Then the entire university cadet corps marched out to face the oncoming northern troops. The cadets who buried the telescope lens were all killed. The old observatory still stands, but no one knows where the lens is buried. The only other buildings left standing when the federal troops overran the cadets and burned the campus were a sentry's pillbox and the president's home. Barnard's library was also burned.

One of the innumerable tragedies of the Civil War was this loss to the South of two university telescopes, an important scientific library collection, an outstanding educator, and an entire university campus. The University of Alabama campus was burned needlessly only four days before Lee's surrender at Appomattox, Barnard's books and papers were destroyed by an army Barnard had resigned to support, and Alabama cadets died defending the Unionist's possessions and the telescope lens he had bought.

Local legend in Alabama has it that a century later Alabama's senator John Sparkman introduced legislation in Congress for "war reparations" to the university and succeeded in getting funds that were used to create Marshall Space Center and the University of Alabama's Huntsville campus.

The daughter of one of those Alabama Cadet Corps students was in her nineties when Frank A. Rose was the University of Alabama president (1957–1969). Early in his career there she presented him with a pair of brass cufflinks made from two of the buttons on the cadet uniform her father had worn a century earlier. Dr. Rose, who wore tailored shirts with French cuffs, wore the cuff links the rest of his life. Rose had been president of the college I attended in Kentucky. Later I served on his staff at Alabama in my first full-time administrative post after graduate school (where my dissertation included a study of Barnard).

Just before Christmas I had dinner with Mrs. Frank Rose, my mentor's widow. Tommye Rose is a marvelous and gracious one-of-a-kind Kentucky lady about whom legends abound quite independently of her late husband.

She gave me Rose's cadet cufflinks. Those entwined ironies and memories of Barnard and Rose, Alabama and Mississippi, flooded me when I opened the box.

Barnard was representative of the best of American culture, committed to high quality in learning that knows no sectional lines, and foremost among educational prophets and architects, and thus it is highly fitting that his name appears on buildings on the Alabama and Mississippi university campuses as well as in New York. His two southern telescope lenses may not be in place, but his academic farsightedness endures. Frank Rose helped that Barnard vision to survive.

The Mississippi building appropriately houses an important center whose research and outreach attract attention like that Barnard received in his times. Its young scholars from all over the world are telescopes looking at the South. Support for the center preserves Barnard's observatory and his academic spirit.

July 23, 1990, and January 11, 1993

F. W. OLIN

A philanthropist who died mid-century became as important for higher education in the second half of the twentieth century as Andrew Carnegie and his libraries were in the first. Franklin W. Olin's legacies are the F. W. Olin Foundation, Inc., and, since 1940, some sixty academic buildings on fifty American campuses.

Franklin W. Olin was born in Vermont in 1860 and reared in relative obscurity and hardship. His formal education consisted of only one year of school, but he studied on his own and qualified himself for admission to Cornell University in civil engineering. Olin taught school and repaired farm machinery to get funds to enroll and played professional baseball in the summers to pay his way through. His batting record was .316, and he was such a good player than he could have chosen a career in baseball. But he didn't.

Instead, Olin started off working for a patent attorney, then designed textile machinery, and then became superintendent of construction for a powder mill being built by a cousin in New Jersey. The cousin abandoned the project, and Olin took over, saving the project so much money that his bonus was as big as his salary. For the next five years, he built more powder mills on contract and then went into the powder manufacturing business for himself. He invented processes to lessen the danger of explosions, and he founded the Equitable Powder Mfg. Co. in East Alton, Illinois, in 1892. The DuPonts were impressed enough to buy heavily in his stock and then to offer him management of the Phoenix Powder Mfg. Co. in New Jersey and West Virginia.

As this century dawned, explosives were being transformed. Dynamite was becoming a major industry, and breech-loading shotguns were replacing muzzleloaders. Olin began making powder for shotgun shells, then expanded to making paper shell casings for his powder, and expanded again to make shot, primer, and wads for the shells. He prudently avoided heavy debt and escaped the fate of competitors who expanded too much in the euphoria after World War I. He bought the famous Winchester Arms Co. in New Haven, Connecticut, when it was in financial straits in 1931. He could then make guns as well as ammunition. Then came World War II, and Olin's United States Cartridge Co., a subsidiary, became the largest small-arms ammunition company in history, churning out 14 billion rounds. In 1944 all Olin companies were united into Western Cartridge Co. and the whole renamed Olin Industries, later Olin Corp.

Using personal funds, Olin established his foundation in 1938, added to its assets over the next thirteen years, and left the bulk of his estate to it in 1951. He turned over management of the foundation to three businessmen outside of his family who ran it in their spare time and without the aid of professionals. One of them, Charles L. Horn, was president of Federal Cartridge Corporation, once owned by Olin but transferred by him to his foundation.

Over the years, the foundation moved toward making building grants of considerable size to independent colleges and universities. It insisted on providing total costs, including furnishings, for each building funded. In the South alone, F. W. Olin Foundation provided buildings for Birmingham-Southern, Centre, Clemson (pre-1960), Hampton, Millsaps, Roanoke, Rollins, Vanderbilt, and Wake Forest.

A Franklin W. Olin Building at Wofford College cost $5.9 million. Its forty-six thousand square feet house faculty offices and classrooms for mathematics, computer sciences, and foreign languages, for visiting professors and for a summer program for talented students, and the very latest video, computer, and audio teaching equipment. The gift transformed Wofford. A catalyst for significant change, this building had already been revolutionary even before its doors opened early in 1992. No building is funded by the foundation for the sake of the building alone. Grants are made to institutions showing they can multiply a building's positive effects. A quest for a grant becomes an impetus for campus planning, for expanded alumni and trustee investment, for curriculum and teaching renewal, and for momentum and reform.

The foundation's president, Lawrence W. Milas, uses a metaphor of a planted seed to describe the blossoming and harvesting effects of a successful grant. Other metaphors come to mind: Rip Van Winkle wakened from a long sleep, or a middle-aged person getting back into shape by new diets and exercises. Because of the Franklin W. Olin Foundation, committed to a singular purpose, private colleges have shown resiliency and progress, surviving the runaway economy of the last fifty years to remain the adaptable model for undergraduate liberal arts education they have been in America since Harvard's 1636 founding.

That, even more than the Franklin W. Olin buildings, is quite a legacy for one man. It is a legacy of wizardry or alchemy. Bullets have been turned into buildings, and buildings into academic excellence.

October 28, 1991

FIREMEN

The success of Norman Maclean's *A River Runs through It* made possible publishing a second book, *Young Men and Fire*, after his death. Like the first, this is Maclean's attempt to gather and tie scattered strands of his long life. He calls upon his experiences as a researcher and scholar, writer and storyteller, and, before that, as a logger and Forest Service employee and firefighter. All of those perspectives focus for Maclean a scene he saw in 1949, a forest fire seen still burning soon after it trapped sixteen of the nation's top firefighters and destroyed thirteen of them only two hours after they jumped into it.

I wanted to read the book because Maclean wrote it. I also wanted to read it because it is about Montana, my mother-in-law's birthplace. That didn't prepare me for the surprise that hit me when I opened it.

The book's center section is a collection of sixteen photographs. The last one is a photo of a memorial plaque at Meriwether Campground. It reads, "To the 13 heroic young men who lost their lives . . . fighting the Mann Gulch Forest Fire 1 mile down the river on August 5, 1949." Then, in larger letters, it lists in alphabetical order the names of the 13 who were killed, along with their hometowns. Six are from Montana; seven are from six other states. ROBERT J. BENNETT — PARIS, TENNESSEE heads the list.

My hometown was Bennett's hometown.

A shiver ran down my spine when I saw the picture. Although in 1949 I was entering the eighth grade, this was a story I couldn't recall hearing. Yet something about it seemed familiar. I called home to check it out with my mother, whose memory is very much better than mine from having had more years to practice using it and from having never left home. With her help, things got clearer. She remembered the boy's sisters and reminded me that I used to know his father from around the courthouse.

Fire is a strange thing, simultaneously fascinating and frightening. My dad was a volunteer fireman, and we two sons of his never missed a chance to make a run with him when the siren sounded. My job while Daddy was pulling out his boots and slicker was to call and ask Tony Brown, the fire truck driver and only permanent employee on the squad, "Where is it?" I think the phone number we asked the telephone operator for was simply the single number "4." (Or was that the number for the local taxi? Something else to ask my mother.)

Last week we had a guest speaker on campus talk to a group of student volunteers from several colleges. He's a Methodist minister who has devoted many years to rebuilding dilapidated shacks and decaying shanties for subsistence-level families. He was telling us how he got started. His church was next to the fire station in one of the first small towns he was assigned to by the Methodist Conference, and he became a volunteer fireman. The rules were that the first volunteer to the truck got to drive it, and with his office so nearby he usually won the race. He was young then, and fires were fun, he said.

Sometimes he and his fellow firemen found themselves hoping the blaze was a big one, so they would get to use the equipment. (Back in Paris, real fires paid $3.00 a call, and false alarms paid $1.50. The farther away the volunteers were from the last payday at their regular jobs, the better real fires looked to them.) But our speaker's life changed the night the truck pulled up to a shanty already in full blaze, and they discovered that three little children were inside, left alone by a retarded mother and an alcoholic father. He's been repairing houses and twisting the arms of everyone he meets to help him ever since. I thought of him as I read Norman Maclean's meticulous research on a forest fire—and thirteen young men—that burned in his memory for half a century. He almost got its story told before he died himself.

In legend, the phoenix was a mythical creature that could consume itself by fire and rise from its own ashes. Life isn't always like that. We do wake and rise each day; we do shake ourselves and rise each time we fall; we do, often enough, bounce back from disappointments. But humans aren't always phoenixes. Sometimes we fall but can rise no more.

Those fallen do rise again when we remember them. Recalling those whom untimely fate has consumed is a sort of resurrection for them. They live on as long as we remember them; and maybe, too, subconsciously but selfishly grateful for our own good fortunes, we try to live a bit of our own lives for them.

There's a little of the phoenix and a lot of the best of the human in trying to do that.

February 8, 1993

JOE SUTTON

It may not be the 1940s, but I'm still a sucker for a story with a happy ending. *Bambi* and Bette Davis movies remain my favorites.

Down in Alabama we have a friend and former office colleague, now retired and over seventy, who has won a major prize in the lottery of life. Dr. Joe Sutton has a Ph.D. in psychology from Vanderbilt. He was for many years a vice president at the University of Alabama and afterward, until retirement, headed the Alabama Commission on Higher Education.

Soon after retiring, Joe developed a case of shingles. That was around July of 1991. He didn't think much about it. Shingles occur frequently among people in their seventies. A few months later Joe and his wife, Frances, trekked northward from their Opelika home to visit their daughter and her husband in Knoxville for Thanksgiving. They had big plans for camping out in the Tennessee hills. But out in the woods, Joe was suddenly seized with some mysterious symptoms.

They rushed him to the University of Tennessee medical center, which fortunately was located only a stone's throw from the daughter's condo on the Tennessee River across from the UT campus. The diagnosis was Guillain Barré syndrome.

Named for two French neurologists, Guillain Barré is "an acute neurological disorder of unknown cause, involving partial paralysis of several muscle groups and occurring rarely after certain viral infections and vaccinations."

I had seen Guillain Barré before. After the swine flu scare of 1976 a professor (also with a Ph.D. in psychology) at the campus we then served developed a case that temporarily affected his ability to walk. I have seen it again recently. My local doctor developed a mild case of it last year but continued to function fairly normally.

Joe's case was more severe. It rapidly spread to his entire body. Scholar that he is, he knew exactly what was happening to him and what he might expect in a worst-case scenario. In severe cases of Guillain Barré a person can lose the ability to write, move, or speak. The nerve endings are stripped and virtual paralysis occurs. Fatalities are rare but possible when other internal systems are aggravated while the victim lies helpless.

With remarkable foresight as the symptoms spread throughout his body, Joe worked out with his son-in-law a system for communicating. It consisted of an alphabet held by whomever was in attendance. Joe could blink as the assistant scanned the chart, and slowly spelled out words. Months later he and his wife could laugh about his perfectionist insistence upon making complete sentences.

For a few months Joe had the most severe case of Guillain Barré imaginable. He was completely paralyzed and dependent. Yet his mind continued to function perfectly normally. It must have been like being half-awake at dawn, that time when one feels one's body but at the same time seems to be in a mental world above and apart from it, a feeling that you are two instead of one.

Then, after months in limbo, came recovery. Every muscle command and every bodily function had to be learned all over again. It was like what happens when an electric outage or lightning erases a computer's program system; the body has to be reprogrammed.

He's become something of a celebrity for the intelligence and willpower he has brought to his ordeal. Early accounts of his road back described the hours it took to learn how to shave again. Friends who saw him recently tell us that except for a slight high-stepping in one leg, he is back to his old self.

Joe and Frances are about the kindest folks one can hope to meet. There was a natural tendency when Joe was stricken for their friends to shake heads and ponder how or why something so awful could happen to someone so good. But in a slightly perverse way, if Guillain Barré at its worst had to strike someone, it couldn't have picked a better victim. Joe has always been a person of intense and wide-ranging intellectual curiosity. After an enormously active academic career, a traditional retirement would have been very inappropriate for him. One can't picture him on a tour bus or asking for a senior discount at a restaurant.

When Joe Sutton reached retirement age, he found a mysterious world waiting and a psychology experiment that topped any he had studied or taught.

In the process, he took self-discovery to new plateaus of definition.

I hope he writes it all down for the AARP magazine. We need our heroes.

July 13, 1993

CHANCE ENCOUNTERS

The L. L. Bean headquarters store is way up in Freeport, Maine. Remote as it is, the store is open twenty-four hours a day.

The president of the college where I work had never been to the L. L. Bean store, nor to Maine itself, for that matter. Attending an educators' meeting up there, he and his wife drove over to L. L. Bean after dinner one evening.

Wonder of wonders, the very first person they saw when they entered L. L. Bean for the very first time, and at 10:00 P.M. at that, was a fellow history professor from Wofford College, a relatively small college located some thousand miles away.

Statisticians can cite figures of probability on such coincidences happening. The odds are against them; they are practically impossible.

Yet it seems to us that such incidents happen all the time—so frequently in fact that it is hard to believe there is much "accidental" about them at all.

It is almost as if some invisible hand was out there guiding our paths to intersect with one another, disguised as "coincidence" and "chance" but actually something "as meant to be" and "destined."

Everywhere we turn someone has a story to tell about the most mystifying encounters and coincidences. Our youngest daughter is in Washington for the summer, working for the National Folklife Festival at the Smithsonian

It turns out that the supervisor is the daughter of a man from the same small Tennessee hometown, small high school, and small church and the same small undergraduate college in Kentucky as I. I'd known my daughter's supervisor's daddy all of my adult life, and my mother allegedly babysat with him and his four brothers over seventy years ago. He died very recently, and I had the obituary lying on my office desk when our daughter reported the supervisor's name.

Business took me to New York City for two days back in April. Three surprises there verify that even in crowded New York, the world is still a small one.

Reading the *New York Times* at breakfast, I stumbled upon a review of a play, *The Heiress,* an adaptation of a Henry James' novel. The review was very complimentary, especially of the play's leading actress, a young woman named Cherry Jones. Cherry Jones is indeed a talented actress. She is also a native of Paris, Tennessee. We share the same hometown, and I've known her parents, Joan Cherry and Jack Jones, an English teacher and a florist, for years, and knew her grandparents as well. We also shared the same speech and drama coach, the late Ruby Krider, Paris's sterling answer to Sarah Bernhardt and Mother Teresa. I wished in vain for another night in New York, so I could see Cherry perform. Six weeks later I did see her, on television, receiving a Tony Award as Best Actress. Not bad for a Paris girl, but no less than Miss Ruby expected of her.

After breakfast that morning, I walked two blocks to a rare-book store located on the third floor of an old building. One has to press a buzzer to be admitted; once inside, a grizzled salesman, wearing an old maroon cardigan sweater and a tieless plaid shirt, asked where I worked. When I told him the name of our South Carolina college, he replied that some of his best customers were from that state, and proceeded to name two whom he said he had been serving for thirty-seven years now. I happened to know them both. The father is a former governor and university president, and the son is a state senator, and the son had begun buying leather-bound books there back when he was in prep school. I brought greetings back to them from their old New York friend.

My path back to the hotel from the bookshop took me by St. Thomas Church, an Episcopal cathedral. The bulletin board on the steps of the gothic structure caught my eye, announcing a forthcoming organ recital at 5:15 P.M. on Palm Sunday (two days hence) by someone named Quentin Lane. Some twenty-five years ago, when I was working at the University of Alabama, I had known a talented student named Quentin Lane, an African American National Merit Scholar from Selma, who had demonstrated impressive music ability. I recalled that he had won a fellowship for graduate study at the

Eastman School of Music in Rochester. I rushed into the church, where I heard someone tuning the organ. It was not Lane, but a brochure in the narthex told me that Lane was from Birmingham. Back at work, a call to the Alabama alumni office provided me with an address, and I wrote the Quentin Lane I had known. Shortly afterward, he phoned, delighted that I had tracked him down and that we could renew our acquaintance. He has had a distinguished career in church music in England and this country.

These chance encounters demonstrate that I am a typical small-town southerner. Most southerners have some inbred radar that guides them through mass and anonymous society to familiar faces and names. It is a commonly held southern gift, and I have no more portion of it than do most other southerners.

It has proved to be a blessing, and I marvel that it has been given us. Anything that can make an enormous metropolis such as New York seem personal is quite a gift.

Given the high number of unlikely connections we see being made everywhere around us, it is difficult to believe so much happenstance is really happening.

I'm not much of a determinist nor a fatalist, but goodness gracious, it is hard to deny that Something or Someone Other Than Us is in charge of things, or at the least jiggling the controls a little. There are just too many missing class rings turning up in the bellies of fish after twenty-five years of absence and too many unplanned reunions in the Atlanta airport to believe otherwise.

We southerners take these "connections" more seriously than others. Southerners, unlike other Americans, are entirely fearless about asking complete strangers "Where are you from?" or "What do you do?" or "Who are your folks?"

We scan guest books at motels and monuments, and we squint at auto license tags, looking for what Thomas Wolfe called "the great Lost Leaf," the connecting ties between us and others that we are totally and unswervingly convinced exist if we only ask enough questions to find the links.

It's an old, old habit, started when much of the South was barely settled wilderness before the Civil War and sustained through the Civil War, Reconstruction, and the Depression, this making assets out of each other when we have nothing else than each other upon whom to depend.

May 30, 1994, and June 12, 1995

Knowing my interest in unexplored back roads of southern history, my next-door neighbor told me about one of his ancestors, Miss Lulu Hurst (Mrs. Paul Atkinson). For two years in her youth, Lulu captured the public eye, was hailed as "the Georgia Wonder" (and sometimes as "Laughing Lulu"), and traveled the lecture circuit of America.

Lulu Hurst was born in 1869. Her father was a farmer, a Tennessee Baptist deacon who was wounded at Murfreesboro as a Confederate artillery officer and who took up farming in Georgia where he met and married a Baptist minister's daughter. In 1883, at the age of fourteen, Lulu and a visiting cousin were sharing a bed at the family farm near Cedartown. An electric storm raged outside, and the cousins were awakened by strange popping noises which seemed to come from inside the house. The popping and rapping resumed the next night, and neighbors were called in to see if their source could be found. Convinced that some "force" was causing them, one neighbor asked "it" questions which the soundings "answered." The phenomenon continued over the next week with more and more curiosity seekers coming to the house. By then, the noisemaking had progressed to the point that furniture and articles of clothing were being made to move without apparent human effort.

It soon became evident that somehow the mysterious "force" was linked to Lulu Hurst. A delegation of leading local citizens (educators, lawyers, bankers, editors, legislators, and others) investigated and certified that Miss Hurst was indeed the conduit for the mysterious force. With some reluctance, she and her father agreed to have an exhibition. It consisted of three tests. Strong men from the audience were invited to try to wrest from her an umbrella, to hold on to a chair or cane as she was touching it, and to try to lower a chair to the floor while she touched it. In all cases, they were unable to do those simple feats. They usually wound up being thrown about the stage.

Word began to spread and more exhibitions and investigations followed, from Cedartown to Rome, then on to Atlanta and Chattanooga, to Mercer University and the University of Georgia and the Medical College at Augusta, and to Columbus. From there, it was on to Charleston and Columbia in South Carolina and to Jacksonville, Florida, before moving to the more urbane centers of the east. Other tests were added to the show. Everywhere she met the rich and the famous, playing to crowds averaging several thousand. Lillie Langtry saw her, as did Smithsonian scientists and congressmen and governors. There was Washington, then Baltimore, Pennsylvania, and New Jersey, and then New York, Boston, Providence, New York's inland cities, and the resorts at Saratoga, Newport, and Long Branch, and Brooklyn (where she downed Matsada, a popular Japanese wrestler). Moving west, San Francisco, Sacramento, and Denver marveled at her performances. Chicago, Milwaukee, Missouri, and Illinois, were just as receptive.

Then suddenly, after two years on the road, she halted her exhibitions, canceling a tour of Europe and giving a last performance in Knoxville, Tennessee. She was only sixteen then. Lulu was, she wrote in her biography in 1897, overcome by the great superstition she was stirring in the public mind. So she quit.

Her own interest in her abilities did not end there, however. She believed that reason can explain everything, that every natural effect had some natural cause that could be explained, no matter how mysterious it might seem for a while. In later years, Lulu Hurst came to see that her abilities could be explained by physics. Her power came from simple principles of leverage. She did not exercise mass hypnosis over her audience, but there was a self-willed hypnosis that crowds seemed to impose on themselves, blinding them to principles of countervailing physical forces. The rigid position of the men holding the chairs, canes, umbrellas, and billiard sticks in the exhibitions rendered them vulnerable to simple leverage from her. She simply shunted it back against them. Ten years after her "retirement" she could see and explain that what she had done was "to deflect" the direction of the men's pushing. Her abiding concern in her book was to expose the public willingness to attribute natural events to occult and supernatural forces. She found that mass public superstition and emotional public movements can be dangerous to society. It scared her out of her work and fame.

The only tricks of her trade were the very first ones, the poppings and rappings in her house. Lulu admitted that she did these by moving the bed's footboard and by pushing hatpins into the feather mattress, and that she persisted solely for the entertainment of family and neighbors. But that attention led to the discovery of the chair phenomena and the several tests of physical skill that made her reputation. She was as much taken in by these "powers" and "forces" as were her audiences.

August 20, 1995

One Saturday night in 1996 seven people, three adults and four children, drowned in John D. Long Lake near Union, South Carolina. The tragedy was news in itself, but its national poignancy came from its happening exactly where Susan Smith, now in prison for life, let her two children drown in 1994.

In a bizarre and irony-wrought sequel to the Smith horror, a 1987 Civic Suburban rolled past the granite monument to Michael and Alex Smith and into the lake and into twenty feet of water eighty feet from shore, and turned over. The four children and the driver inside were dead, as were two other adult passengers who were outside the car when it rolled but who dived after it trying to save the children. The ignition key was still on; the gearshift was in park.

Much speculation surrounding the event focuses on why the group was there in the first place. The simplest answer seems to be the most logical. It is a pleasant summer evening, the party had been to a Saturday cookout, it was still early when it ended, and the lake was only ten miles away from the cookout.

Curiosity and time to waste probably drew them there as they will draw others to the place they died. The nature of human beings is to be fascinated with death places.

Battlefields at Gettysburg and Shiloh, Manassas and Antietam, Little Big Horn and the Alamo, attract millions of visitors each year. So do cemeteries and monuments. Thousands visit Ford's Theater in Washington where Lincoln died, the Texas Book Depository in Dallas from which John Kennedy was shot, the motel in Memphis where Martin Luther King, Jr., was killed, and the Little White House in Warm Springs, Georgia, where FDR died. The altar of the chapel at Washington and Lee University is a full-sized recumbent statue of General Lee, who actually rests in a mausoleum beneath the chapel. Visitors to this tomb can also visit Lee's horse, buried outside and next to the chapel now after many years of being displayed downstairs as a skeleton, and Stonewall Jackson's grave is only a few blocks away. The waiting lines to walk by the shag-carpeted bathroom of Graceland where Elvis died are still long, years after his death, as are the lines at the Roy Rogers museum in California wherein are displayed Roy's stuffed horse, Trigger, Dale Evans's stuffed horse, Buttermilk, and Roy's stuffed dog, Bullet. Goodness knows where Roy and Dale will wind up.

Over in merry Britain, a venerable university requires that a respected scholar, Jeremy Bentham, attend meetings of the governing board. Bentham died in 1832, but his preserved body duly makes an annual appearance—seated.

I have never visited Graceland, nor wanted to, but a few summers ago my wife and I drove six hundred miles to Memphis to view the coffin of an Egyptian pharaoh. And come next summer, we'll drive it again to see relics dredged up from the Titanic. Those of us who drive Interstate 40 across Tennessee regularly know by heart where to look for the white crosses or decorated cedar trees marking fatal accidents, placed by bereaved relatives or friends. In a short story recently published, elderly couples of the near future tour America in RV clubs, visiting the canyons and debris piles left after a global nuclear war.

What is this attraction the macabre holds for us?

I have a theory that seems a plausible explanation. It is stimulated by having seen the Halloween merchandise being put out at the local Wal-Mart during Labor Day weekend.

Most of us grew up hearing and telling ghost stories. Around the Cub Scout, Brownie, and Sunday evening church-youth-group campfires of our impressionable youth, we heard of dead girls dressed in white graduation dresses reappearing on lonely nighttime highways and of headless horsemen chasing teachers out of town. We early become accustomed to death and to hooking it to hovering spirits and misty evenings.

Charles Dickens's *A Christmas Carol* is actually a ghost story, in which Marley's Ghost is followed by the Ghosts of Christmases Past, Present, and Yet To Come into Scrooge's bedroom and imagination, and the most riveting scene of all takes place at his imagined grave.

Early childhood fantasies and horror tales linger with us as we age, even when we become educated, logical, skeptical, and seemingly in control of our emotions. Spirits still beckon, their crooked fingers snaring us like fish drawn to hooks.

There's seldom any thing personal in our human curiosity. Appalled by the grotesque and the ghastly, we are drawn to them by human nature.

September 30, 1996

OSEOLA MCCARTY

When I drove my bride-to-be from Louisville to west Tennessee to meet her future in-laws in 1961, I almost scared the betrothals out of her by listing penny-wise household maxims with which I had been reared. I can still recall her eyes widening as she pondered what fate awaited her once I delivered her into my family's hands. My family was far from unusual in those days. Young people today pretty much miss out on the homespun economic wisdom of past generations of southerners accustomed to "getting by" on farms and small towns.

An eighty-five-year-old lady built her life and a small fortune out of simple maxims. She took common sense literally and made of it something other than platitudes.

Her name is Oseola (a variation of the Indian Osceola) McCarty, and she has lived all of her life in Hattiesburg, Mississippi. For nearly seventy-five of her eighty-eight years, from age eight to eighty-six, Ms. McCarty worked as a laundress for others. At age twelve, she dropped out of school in the sixth grade because of her aunt's illness. She cared for the aunt until 1967 and helped support her grandmother until 1944 and mother until 1964. Outside of those three women, she had few family members or friends. Except for Sunday church, her laundering consumed her time, sometimes stretching well past midnight.

Oseola McCarty never forgot the education of which she was deprived. She never traveled, she never had or wanted many possessions, and she took her religion (into which she was baptized at age thirteen) very seriously. She saved and saved and saved. In 1994, age and infirmity forced her to retire from laundering. She had kept her money in savings at the local Trustmark Bank, and they approached her about setting up trust funds to care for her health care and property disposition. She surprised the bank and then the world by dispersing her savings, which amazingly had grown to $280,000. Some went to the church and some to family, but a great big chunk—$150,000, in fact—went to set up an endowed scholarship at the University of Southern Mississippi.

Since then, Ms. McCarty has received an honorary doctorate from Harvard, visited with President Clinton, appeared on several national television networks, accepted medals and other awards, and gone a long way to becoming a modern-day folk hero. She thinks back over her life, ironically, as neither isolated or deprived, but as what she calls "rich living."

Ask her for advice, and you'll hear things like these taken from *Oseola McCarty's Simple Wisdom for Rich Living* (Longstreet Press):

> I go to the store once a week for groceries. I buy clothes once or twice a year. If something like detergent comes in two sizes, I buy the larger one.

> I'd go to the bank once a month, hold out enough to cover my expenses, and put the rest into my savings account. Every month I'd save the same and put it away. I was consistent.

> The secret to building a fortune is compounding interest.

> I keep everything—clothes, furniture, housewares—until it wears out. Usefulness often outlasts style.

> My black and white television set only gets one channel. I don't care because I don't watch it often. I have never subscribed to a newspaper because it cost too much. There's a difference between needing and wanting.

Last August, Stephanie Bullock became the first Oseola McCarty Scholarship recipient. An African American honor graduate of Hattiesburg High School and eighteen years old, she is getting an education denied Oseola McCarty, the "Best Drop-Out of 1920."

Ms. McCarty may also be returning to school. She has registered for a computer course at USM.

If anyone personifies the abiding message of the love of God expressing itself through love of others, unselfishly, it is this Deep South lady. Her dignity, her simplicity, her scale of values, and her self-sufficiency are Old South lessons from which our brash and greedy New South could profit in its new next century.

January 13, 1997

SIR AND MA'AM

In the days of kings and courts and of lords and ladies, a man of authority was addressed as "sire" and his wife as "madam." As society moved from baronies into boroughs and from castles into cities, the practice went with them. With people congregating and commoners becoming citizens, lords and ladies became difficult to distinguish. The safe thing to do when addressing one's seniors was simply to call them "sires" or "madams." Those honorifics, of course, became abbreviated with usage. "Sire" became "sir" and "madam" became "ma'am."

Like most southern boys, I was trained forcefully and early by my parents and reinforced by aunts and uncles, always to say "sir" and "ma'am" to my elders.

The trouble for me has been that, in growing old, there are fewer and fewer people around for me to call "sir" or "madam." Whenever I do get a chance to say it, it always makes me feel younger, probably because I subconsciously recall how young I was when I started saying it.

And for quite a few years now, I have been hearing younger folk calling me "sir." That makes me feel old, and I look around each time it is said to me just to be certain it isn't being addressed to someone else. But being called "sir" also makes me feel good. It tells me instantly something about what sort of training and parents the young addresser must have had, and it reassures me that good manners and civility are not totally gone in an age when most other social grace moorings have been loosened.

I was taking my car through the car wash downtown recently, and when I turned my keys over to the young hourly-wage man who was to vacuum its interior, I instinctively addressed him as "sir." You would have thought I had knighted him! He grinned so widely and genuinely it would have put a jack-o'-lantern to shame. He threw his shoulders back, shed his shuffle, and hustled into the car. I thought about that the whole time I was waiting for the car to emerge. I liked what a simple word had done, like magic, for the car washer, and I liked what his reaction had done for me.

The rest of the week I very deliberately addressed each person I saw as "sir" or "ma'am." Most of them were students, but there were also servers in the buffet line, grounds crew members on the lawns, clerks in the post office, secretaries, nurses at the hospital next door, and a rainbow of phone callers. Half the time, there was no reaction at all, of course. But the other half, there was a blink or a smile or a pause, some slight acknowledgment that the gesture was both unexpected and was welcomed.

What rule is there that "sir" and "ma'am" have to be reserved for our elders? Why not use it for anyone, regardless of age or station in life? Why not, especially in this mass society where we no longer know names or bloodlines, assume that any one we meet deserves our respect until they prove otherwise?

Long ago, I recall being told by a teacher not to call a woman a lady until she had demonstrated she was one. "All ladies are women, but not all women are ladies" was the rule. My mother, however, said the teacher was wrong. She said that we should *assume* all grown-up women are ladies, until they did something to prove they weren't. The teacher may have had logic on her side, but my mother had common sense and good manners on hers.

My car wash experiment was so successful that a new habit formed quickly. Not that I am ready to move on to spreading my coat on mud puddles, but I do call everyone "sir" or "ma'am" now, even babies who spit up when I am drilling into them these passwords to civilization.

April 28, 1997

SOUTHERN ASIAN AMERICANS

Except for Native Americans (and even they may have migrated here from Asia across the Bering Strait centuries ago), all Americans are immigrants or descendants of immigrants. Watching the Atlanta Braves sweltering through three games in Cincinnati in 109-degree weather and noticing the ethnic composition of the teams—Asian American, Caucasian, African American, Hispanic, Slavic—it struck us forcefully that America is still the world's great melting pot. It's the people more than the heat that makes that the case.

Down in Mississippi the Wong family began migrating to the Delta from China in the 1930s, when the patriarch, Wong, opened a grocery. His son, Kim Wong, came over in 1949 and operated a restaurant, a grocery, and a karate school in Clarksdale. In 1961 he met and married a Hong Kong lady, Jean, and brought her to Mississippi. She made the biscuits for the restaurant, rendering her own lard. Sometimes she would cook the cracklings for her husband. Kim put some of the cracklings in plastic bags and gave them away, and they were so well received that pretty soon he began marketing business for them. Kim's Fried Pork Rinds and Kim's Seasoned Pork Cracklings took off, and his plant uses about fifty-five thousand pounds of pork skin each month to satisfy the appetites of his customers nationwide.

The Wongs weren't the first Chinese in the Delta. The Chow family, which was a centerpiece at a recent National Folklife Festival in Washington exhibiting their cooking and arts skills, has been there since 1850. Listen to them talk, and you would swear you were hearing Shelby Foote or Eudora Welty.

There are pockets of displaced Vietnamese all around the South. In the Greenville-Spartanburg area, where international companies are clustering, one is as likely in a Wal-Mart line to hear French or German as English. Any town over twenty-five thousand in population now has an array of international restaurants—Mexican, Thai, Japanese, Chinese, Hungarian, German, Italian, Indian, French—along the strips that used to offer only fast-food hamburgers and homogenized seafood and barbecue. In the larger metropolises, there are even more esoteric food (and clothing) options, especially savory African specialties and even some Native American places. Our music is changing, our literature is expanding, our art is being enriched, bilingualism is not uncommon now, and our social life is being transformed. All across the South, the mix of people is changing, moving toward more and more diversity.

In the small-town South of fifty years ago, there was usually one or maybe two Jewish families, but that has changed. Asians have come as tourists and stayed on as citizens. There are Honda, Toyota, Nissan, and Hyundai factories where they are concentrated, but also they can be seen conspicuously when one looks at university graduate students in medicine and science and technology fields. Mexicans came as migrant workers and stayed on, following the familiar upward mobility path from hourly wage labor to owning storefront restaurants and yard services to the next generation going to college.

In California today, Caucasians have become a minority. No group has a majority; it is a pattern very likely to become the national one. California and New England and New York, being centers of population and of transportation, have always led the way in diversification.

The cotton-poor Deep South finally woke up to the fact that it could not survive, much less prosper, on a single crop. The tobacco-dependent Upper South is finding the same truth. With diversification of the economy and of politics has come diversity of population. After centuries of cultural isolationism and standoffish "go away and leave us alone" practices, the South in World War II opened its doors to the world, and the world since has worked its way South.

Among the South's natural resources (water, sunshine, and changing seasons) are hospitality and civility. It has shown a marvelous ability to absorb newcomers and even to give them a southern accent. Its welcome mat has become as big as the world. Ironic, is it not? This region that tried to secede has endured and succeeded. Now it has become that "Light on a Hill" that America has always claimed to be for the rest of the globe.

July 28, 1997

WILL CAMPBELL

The first time I saw Will Campbell, around 1963, when he spoke to us students at Yale Divinity School, he already looked old. Southern-weathered, bald (except for the fringe on sides and back which he let grow long, prophetlike), and dressed very casually, he was then about forty years old.

Now, many years later, Campbell hasn't aged at all. He has gone from being a boy on an impoverished Mississippi farm to being a Southern Baptist student at Louisiana College to being a soldier in the closing days of World War II back to being a college student (this time at Wake Forest, where he wed his Louisiana College sweetheart) to being a graduate student at Tulane to being a seminarian at nondenominational Yale Divinity School to being a minister at a small Southern Baptist church in Louisiana to being director of religious life at the University of Mississippi to being director of racial and cultural relations for the National Council of Churches to being head of the Fellowship of Southern Churchmen and publisher of its magazine (which he suspended in 1983) to being an unaffiliated Christian spokesman.

From his Mt. Juliet farm in middle Tennessee, where he has lived and worked since 1963, Campbell churns out book after book. In each one, his writing improves. The first I recall, prophetic in its times, *Race and the Renewal of the Church,* was in 1962. Then came *Up to Our Steeples in Politics* (1970), *The Failure and the Hope: Essays of Southern Churchmen* (1972), *". . . and the criminals with him . . ."* (1973), *Callings* (1974), *The Glad River* (1982), *Cecilia's Sin* (1983), *God on Earth: The Lord's Prayer for Our Time* (1983), *The Convention: A Parable* (1988), *Covenant* (1989), *Chester and Chun Ling* (1989).

My personal favorites have been *Brother to a Dragonfly* (1977), *Forty Acres and a Goat* (1986), *Providence* (1992), and the new *And Also with You* (1998).

Merrill M. Hawkins, Jr., made Campbell the subject of his doctoral dissertation. In *Will Campbell: Radical Prophet of the South* (Mercer University Press), Hawkins provides a helpful summary of Campbell's colorful career before launching into a deeper inspection of Campbell's theology and his use of autobiography as a method of proclamation.

Campbell is "radical" in his religion only in refusing to be bound by institutional forms of faith and in being a minister both to African Americans and to Klansmen. Beneath that uncommon calling lies a bedrock of faith, an understanding of grace in which good works are essential, not as a means to grace but as responses to it. What is especially moving about Campbell's work is that it is focused on other people. He is a great observer, great listener, great storyteller, and great appreciator of others who have faith, talent, and selflessness. He finds parables in hound dogs, mules, drug addicts, and shacks, and he passes on in unsurpassed prose the stories and the points they make.

When sculptors look for native models of ancient prophets, they could do worse than to ask Will Campbell to pose: work clothes, shaggy fringed hair, and hiking stick and all. He has made a career of beckoning us to be better and of tolerating our failures to succeed at it. He has loved his South enough to live in it and to try to improve it.

February 2, 1998

PARIS, TENNESSEE

After sixty-two years, most of it spent in places from which I did not start out, I remain convinced that little Paris, Tennessee, where I did start out, is the center of the universe. I bump into it everywhere I go.

Take today, for example. It has come up three times already, and it isn't even noon.

This morning a fellow worker was trying to decipher a cryptic message from her husband about preparing to celebrate their anniversary. From clues he gave her, we guessed they would be going to Asheville, North Carolina, for a luxurious weekend at Grove Park Inn. Now, Grove Park Inn was built about 1912 by Dr. E. W. Grove, a Paris, Tennessee, native for whom our high school was named and who founded the Paris Medical Company and invented wonderful things such as Grove's Chill Tonic, Bromo-Quinine, and the Four-Way Cold Tablet, later sold to a St. Louis pharmaceutical firm.

Then came a phone call from Mrs. Lois Stembridge, a retiree living twenty miles from us in Tryon, North Carolina. She is the widow of H. H. Stembridge, pastor of First Baptist Church in Paris, Tennessee, about the time of World War II. The Stembridges had gone on from Paris to churches in Paducah, Kentucky, Forest City, North Carolina, and Lynchburg, Virginia, before moving to San Francisco and then back to his native

Georgia. Their daughter, Jane Shelton Stembridge, was my closest friend in the first grade, when we were classmates in Miss Valentine Cooper's class in 1942 at Robert E. Lee Elementary School. Jane Shelton was such a Pied Piper of a companion that I even enrolled in the Sunbeams youth group at the Baptist church, although I was not a Baptist, just to be around her.

In a long list of southern race relations books, I have run across the name Jane Stembridge. For example, Bob Moses, Hamilton College and Harvard University graduate and Mississippi civil rights leader, talks about Jane Stembridge being "a short, peppy blond with piercing blue eyes, a fiery spirit, and a crazy haystack of unruly hair" who was "a southern girl, a minister's daughter, who had left Union Theological Seminary to become the Student Non-Violent Coordinating Committee's first executive secretary, a job she carried out with dispatch from her desk stuck in a corner of the SCLC office" (Southern Christian Leadership Conference in Atlanta). Jane made a major impact in the race relations transformation of the South. In some way, Paris, Tennessee, made a contribution to her work.

In the third Paris coincidence of the day, I was doing some filing, and I ran across some civics materials having to do with race relations, freedom of speech, religious liberties, and social change that had been authored or sponsored by a fellow named John Buchanan. This John Buchanan is a man with whom I have worked occasionally for twenty years and of whom I knew back in Alabama in the 1960s. About seventy-five years ago, John's father was a minister at the same First Baptist Church of Paris, Tennessee, in which H. H. Stembridge later served a quarter century afterward.

John H. Buchanan, Jr., was born in Paris, Tennessee, in 1928. He is an ordained Baptist minister, a graduate of Samford and of Southwestern Seminary who served eight terms as a Republican congressman from Birmingham, Alabama. He was a founder of the Congressional Sunbelt Council, chaired the board for the Fund for Improvement of Post-Secondary Education, chaired the controversial People for the American Way, chairs the Council for the Advancement of Citizenship, and has been a pillar of an integrated Baptist church in Washington. As was the case with Jane Stembridge, surely John Buchanan's formative years in Paris, Tennessee, had something to do with the good he has done for his nation, for race relations, and for the South.

I'll bet, if pressed hard enough, Jane and John will recall having to take tablespoons of Grove's Chill Tonic as children. People from Paris, Tennessee, seem to turn out well, are malaria-free, and do good things.

July 6, 1998

Tennessee joined the Union as its sixteenth state in 1796. Indian land between the Tennessee and Mississippi Rivers was annexed October 19, 1818. On November 7, 1821, the General Assembly of Tennessee created Henry County, the fourth county in west Tennessee. It reputedly was named for Patrick Henry. But why?

Patrick Henry was born May 29, 1736, in Hanover County, Virginia. He taught himself law. Three years after entering practice, he involved himself in the 1763 Parson's Cause lawsuit. His plea was one of the first acts of resistance to the English Crown. Two years later, at age twenty-nine, he was elected to the Virginia House of Burgesses, serving ten years, from 1765 to 1775. England's Stamp Act in 1765 laid a tax upon anything being printed or embossed, and Henry introduced resolutions opposing the Stamp Act. In making his case, Henry concluded with words that would be oft quoted. "Caesar had his Brutus, Charles the First his Cromwell, and George the Third"—here some of the delegates shouted, "Treason! Treason!"— "and George the Third," Henry repeated, "may profit by their example—if this be treason make the most of it."

Henry was a delegate to Virginia's second convention and in charge of the Virginia militia. The convention convened in St. John's Church in Richmond on March 20, 1775. Henry pleaded for the colony to arm itself. He gave the "Liberty or Death" speech that made him immortal, closing with "Is life so dear, or peace so sweet, as to be purchased at the price of chains and slavery? Forbid it, Almighty God! I know not what course others may take; but as for me, give me liberty or give me death!"

Henry became Virginia's first governor, serving three one-year terms from 1776 to 1779 and two more from 1784 to 1786. He refused offers from President Washington to be secretary of state and to be chief justice of the Supreme Court. Patrick Henry died on June 6, 1799, at the age of sixty-three. Why, twenty-two years after he died, never having lived in Tennessee, would a county be named for him?

Mary Sue Dunn, who taught American history in Henry County for years, said Patrick Henry had six sisters, and one supposedly lived in Henry County in 1821. Each of Miss Dunn's classes was assigned the task of finding out who this sister was and where she is buried. Some of us have been searching for fifty years. Some thought the Henry County sister was a

McCampbell, buried in sight of the high school, but those early McCampbells do not seem to have had Henry ties.

A study of family genealogy charts for Patrick Henry on the Internet and through Mormon records reveals that Patrick Henry actually may have had seven sisters, not six: Jane Meredith, Sarah Thomas, Susanna Maddison, Mary Bowyer, Anne Christian, Elizabeth Russell, and Lucy Wood. We suspect that none of Patrick's sisters lived in west Tennessee. They would have been very old by 1821, when the county was named.

Local historian Raymond Van Dyke, on the other hand, has a different theory. He says, without documentation, "The county was named for the Revolutionary War patriot-orator Patrick Henry, one of whose daughters lived and died in West Tennessee." He traces the naming to a daughter, not a sister, and he places her only in west Tennessee, not explicitly in Henry County.

Here genealogy charts help. Patrick Henry had sixteen children, six by his first wife, Sarah Shelton, and ten by his second wife, Dorothea Dandridge. A few sons and grandsons moved from Virginia to Tennessee, settling primarily in Sevier, Blount, Rutherford, and Rhea Counties. Patrick Henry daughters are more difficult to trace than his sons. From his first marriage, there were three daughters: Martha (who married Col. John Fontaine), Anne (who married Judge Spencer Roane), and Elizabeth (who married Phillip Aylett). From his second marriage, there were three more: Dorothea Spotswood (who married George D. Winston, her cousin), Sarah (who married Alexander Scott), and Martha (who married Edward Henry, her cousin).

Perhaps it was daughters, not sisters, we should have been searching for. Daughters born to Patrick Henry anywhere from 1757 to 1780 would have been between forty and sixty-five years old, a much more likely age at which to move to west Tennessee at the time of its settlement in 1819–21 than the eighty to ninety years of age Henry's sisters would have been.

Thanks to an obscure little note tucked away in one of the genealogy charts, we feel closer to finding Patrick Henry's lost kin than ever before. Our best suspect is Mrs. George D. Winston, the former Dorothea Spotswood Henry, buried in Elmwood Cemetery in Memphis and fourth daughter of Patrick Henry. We are not yet prepared to close the files on this lingering mystery, but we may be nearer.

November 7, 1999

Nine or so people waving Confederate battle flags like animated "Forget, Hell!" bumper-sticker characters gather Friday afternoons at the local Chamber of Commerce to "rally 'round the flag" that until recently flew over the South Carolina state capitol. (They have retreated to Thursday protests after American flag wavers gathered on the corner across from them to taunt and protest them.)

Old feuds die hard. The Civil War ended in 1865. It should be over but apparently is not. Memories and media feed our instincts to keep on feuding. We love long fights—brief encounters magnify into Hundred Years' Wars in our imaginations.

Wire services reported in mid-October a revival of the classic feud—that of the Hatfields and McCoys. Hatfield relative John Vance denied McCoys and the public access to a cemetery where three McCoy boys were executed in 1882. The story was a bit sensationalized. Rusty old squirrel rifles of the two clans were not taken down from over cabin fireplaces. McCoy folk are trying verbal persuasion first but are prepared to escalate to legal wrangling. No one is talking about shooting.

Some historians track the feud's beginnings back to William Anderson "Devil Anse" Hatfield, a Confederate mountain man accused of killing Asa Harmon, a McCoy and Union soldier, January 7, 1865. His antagonist over the ensuing year was Randolph McCoy, but no retaliations followed immediately. Then in 1878, "Ol' Randell" McCoy accused Devil Anse's cousin, Floyd Hatfield, of stealing one of his razorback hogs. A jury of six McCoys and six Hatfields decided against Randell. The deciding votes were from Randell's nephew and cousin, both of whom moved away to escape Randolph McCoy's wrath. The nephew, Bill Staton, got in a gun battle with two other nephews of Randell, Sam and Paris McCoy, and Sam shot and killed Staton. Sam was acquitted and released.

In 1880, elections threw Hatfields and McCoys together at a polling place, and Devil Anse's son, Johnse, and Randolph McCoy's daughter, Roseanne, fell in love there. When they got back from sneaking away from the polls, everyone was gone, and Roseanne went home with Johnse. Roseanne, forbidden by Devil Anse to wed his son and fearing her own father's anger, went to live with her aunt Betty, and Johnse visited regularly. The McCoys arrested Johnse, but Roseanne ran off, borrowed a horse, and carried the alarm to Devil Anse and the Hatfields who surrounded the McCoys and rescued Johnse. The pregnant and unwed Roseanne gave birth to a daughter, but Johnse Hatfield married Roseanne's cousin, Nancy McCoy. At another election, in 1882, brothers Tolmer, Pharmer, and Randolph, Jr., sons of Randolph McCoy, fought and seriously wounded with knives and gun Ellison Hatfield, Devil Anse's brother. The McCoy brothers were captured and, when Ellison died, were marched into Kentucky, tied to pawpaw trees, and shot.

Things escalated thereafter: more shootings, a shootout at Randolph McCoy's home, surrounded by twenty Hatfields, retaliatory raids on Hatfields by McCoys, and then a major shootout between nineteen McCoys and thirteen Hatfields at Grapevine Creek in 1888. Finally, the governors of West Virginia and Kentucky got into the act. At an 1889 trial, eight Hatfields were sentenced to life imprisonment and "Cotton Top" Ellison Mounts, a Hatfield, was sentenced to die. After five thousand folks watched him hang in 1890, Hatfield-McCoy warfare waned.

Historian Altina L. Waller's book *Feud: Hatfields, McCoys, and Social Change in Appalachia, 1860–1900* (UNC Press), documents this colorful chapter in American history. The real victims, she shows, are the American people, led by the romanticizing of the Hatfield-McCoy saga into stereotyping Appalachian mountain people as indolent, ignorant, and vengeful.

The globe is filled with Hatfield-McCoy feuds: hatreds between Muslims and Jews, between India and Pakistan, between mainland and nationalist China, between Czechs and Slavs, between the two Koreas and thousands of other "Forget, Hell!" rivals. Sometimes one wishes, and even prays, for social amnesia to rid the world of memory scars that refuse to heal and feuds that refuse to end.

November 11, 2001

COLONEL WILLIAM O. SNYDER

He was eighty-two when he died February 25; I had known him since he was fifty. When he visited in 1986, I realized we barely had scratched the surface in knowing each other. We knew him when he owned a men's store. An earlier career as an army officer with the engineers was in other times and places, and we had never talked about it. We had in common a love of education, of helping students, of college athletics, for our daughters, for model trains, for coffee, for barbecue, and for kidding. Considering his age, I had assumed he had been in Korea. In the course of his visit, we idly asked where he had served.

It was as if we had opened a bottle of warm cola that had been shaken for five minutes. His memories gushed out nonstop for over an hour while we listened mesmerized, wishing for a tape recorder to capture the word-pictures he dredged from his past. (We felt like Robert Penn Warren sitting in childhood at the feet of a Civil War grandfather, filled with vicarious exhilaration at being invited into his world.)

His war was World War II, not Korea. In Ancient Mariner style, he skipped tales of induction, training, and North Africa, and went straight to the action, starting with Monte Cassino in Italy and ending with luncheon with generals in Hitler's Berchtesgarten bunker on V-E Day.

The group he commanded was so highly skilled it could build bridges under heavy enemy fire in minutes and make roads almost as rapidly. Theirs was a wedding of men and machines that bred inventiveness, adaptation, and efficiency, bio-machines of steel and blood that took Italy, landed in southern France, and raced across Europe and stored memories for future reference, to recall later, after first assuring there would be a future.

He arrived in Dachau two hours after it was liberated. With him was a Jewish photographer who found his own mother and father there, still alive amid the railway cars and ovens. That's a glimpse into what our friend carried with him all these years. We'll not repeat his stories here. They were his, rightfully earned, tightly held. We are grateful—no, humbled—that he shared them, but they had an intimacy that defies description, as if for a moment a hidden soul exposes itself. One cannot, ought not, go public with a friend's nakedness.

He recalled dates and places as if he were still there, and he remembered each man's name or death or wound as if it were flashing on a screen in his mind. Ravines, upended trucks and jeeps, potholes, night battles, a day as a POW, encounters with greats like Mark Clark and then-colonel Goodpasture and especially with his men: he recalled them in microscopic details. To hear it, to watch his eyes in telling it, was an experience we never got from history books and war movies.

Perhaps "you have to have been there to understand it." Perhaps. But because he was there, with hundreds of others like him in the early 1940s, perhaps we are here now. And perhaps he was saying, "Try to keep from ever having to be there."

By the time his wife could get him to leave, both he and I were crying. The tears come again each time I think of that hour he gave us, a gift from the very bowels of history and of eternity. We write of him now with a lump in our throat.

Had it taken him almost a century to be able to face and articulate his memories? And if so, how long does it take a whole world that subjects its young men and women to such experiences to come to grips with its own huge scrapbook of horrors?

He was only twenty-five when his war ended. Now we know why he loved life and people so ferociously and buoyantly. That war never ended for him, and, engineer that he was, he spent the rest of his life bio-engineering faith, hope, and love.

They buried Colonel William Oscar Snyder of Martin, Tennessee, Spartanburg, South Carolina, and Europe with full military honors in Arlington National Cemetery on March 18, 2002.

March 24, 2002

Chapter 5

CONFLICT
"THROUGH THE VALLEY OF THE SHADOW"

IN PRAISE OF IRONY

Guitars are becoming albatrosses around our necks. Outside the South, especially in the myth manufactories of television, people are repeating their oft-made mistake of thinking we in the South are all alike. The stereotypes they have held of a South unanimously in favor of Civil War, followed by a South that voted for one party, have been extended unto the present generations. We all supposedly dress like derivations of *Tobacco Road* and *The Beverly Hillbillies* or else like Colonel Sanders, a derivation of *Gone with the Wind.* If you are to believe the pictures made of us, we bootleg booze, race stockcars, fix elections, and whip up on one another during the week, play our guitars and sing sad songs about adultery and divorce on Saturdays, and baptize and sing gospel music on Sundays.

We know better. Our response to such melting-pot mentality has been the best one we could have made: we laugh at our mockers. We even take on some traits they think typical of us, when they are around, so we won't appear discourteous to our tourist-guests whose wallets we are happy to lighten. They may think we are laughing with them at ourselves, but we are usually laughing at them for being so naive and ignorant.

The truth of the matter is, it's unsouthern for southerners to think or act alike. What we do have in common in the South is a fierce pride in individualism, independence, and variety. When W. J. Cash was writing *The Mind of the South* he thought seriously of making "Mind" plural. There are as many Souths as there are southerners. The protection of our rights to disagree, to appear eccentric, and to change our minds has always been the southerners' sense of irony.

"Irony," of course, involves a sense of humor, which all southerners have had since the beginning. The closest the South came to losing its sense of humor was in the period after the Missouri Compromise of 1850 and on until the end of the Civil War in 1865. We let ourselves be baited into becoming too serious about what others said of us in those days, and the real blessing of Appomattox for the South, other than that of an end to the losses of young life, was the recovery immediately of our collective sense of humor and irony. Everyone was more or less in the same pickle barrel then, so they made a picnic of it and found the courage to see the humor and paradox of the situation.

Looking back to those days now, when the South was more solid and serious than it had ever been or ever has been since, there are many ironies that show we were far from being of one mind even then. For example, in the 1820s there were more antislavery societies in the South than in the North. Also, in proportion to the population, more southern men fought for the Union in the Mexican War before the Civil War and in the Spanish-American War afterward than did northern men. In the Civil War itself, at least fifty-four thousand soldiers from seceded states fought on the Union side, more than Lee had in almost any of his battles. Over one hundred Union generals and admirals were from seceded states, says Carl Degler in *The Other South.*

Winston County, Alabama, seceded from Alabama after Alabama seceded from the Union. Numerous east Tennessee, western Carolina, west Tennessee, and north Alabama counties were pro-Union throughout the war. West Virginia carved itself into a state within the Union in 1863 out of such mixed sentiments. After the war, over twenty-two thousand southerners filed war claims with the federal government and presented evidence of pro-Union loyalty. Even in these most "solid" of times for the South, there was strong evidence of independence of thought and action. Several states voted against secession several times, even after Fort Sumter, and finally yielded only after Lincoln called up seventy-five thousand Union troops.

One of the most striking ironies of that day can be seen in old photographs. When Jefferson Davis became U.S. secretary of war under Franklin Pierce, in 1853, one of his duties was to select the statue to go on top of the Capitol dome, just getting under construction. All through the war and all through the dome's work, Davis's statue sat in two halves on the Capitol lawn. Photos of the Capitol during Lincoln's first term show the dome nearing completion at about the same pace as the war. At the war's end, just as South and North were being reunited, the statue's halves were hoisted and joined atop the dome. The symbolism was unintended but conspicuous nonetheless, and separate work of Davis and of Lincoln—ironically born about one hundred miles apart in Kentucky—became a whole.

The war was full of such ironies. The Robert Anderson who surrendered Fort Sumter in 1861 was the same one who raised the flag there after the fort was recaptured in 1864. The Edmund Ruffin who supposedly fired the first cannon shot at Fort Sumter in 1861 was also the Ruffin who shot himself a few weeks after the last troops (out in Texas) surrendered.

Lee, Grant, and Davis were all West Point graduates and Mexican War veterans, and many officers on both sides had been West Point classmates. The whole war seems like a family feud when one studies the kinships and friendships among the officers. One of Davis's staff officers on his flight at the war's end was the son of his favorite general, Albert Sidney Johnston, a Transylvania College and West Point classmate killed at Shiloh. Davis's fierce quarrels with General Joe Johnston during and after the war began at West Point over a girl both courted. The western army Davis fled toward in Alabama and Mississippi after Lee and Johnston surrendered in the east was headed by Richard Taylor, brother of Davis's first wife and son of Zachary Taylor. Both Lincoln and Davis had young sons to die in the two White Houses. Another ironic parallel between Lincoln and Davis is Lincoln's secret entrance into Washington in 1861 in cape and cap disguise and Davis's flight from Richmond and his eventual capture near Irvinton, south of Abbeville, Georgia, wearing his wife's rain cape and shawl.

Defeat itself may be what gave the South back its lost sense of perspective, according to historian C. Vann Woodward in his well-wrought *Burden of Southern History.* Woodward says that military defeat gave the South a way of looking at reality that the rest of America has never had and probably could use. The rest of America, unlike any place else in the world, had never lost its innocence. Consequently, it was easy for the rest of the country to keep on believing that progress is automatic, that morality is simple, that wars are unlosable. Southerners, in their crucibles of hard experience, share some of that feeling, but don't find it contradictory at all to be a little more skeptical about resources being unlimited, affluence being predestined, or people in power being well intentioned. In short, southerners have their sense of irony. Whether the inconclusiveness of Vietnam or the mysteries of the current economy will make Americans a little more southern in outlook remains to be seen.

Historical irony is a wonderful thing. When Grant moved into Richmond after Davis and the Confederacy evacuated it, he slept in a bed that Lee was said to have slept in the night before. (The innkeeper lied; Lee had been elsewhere.) When Mrs. Lincoln found her husband had gone to Richmond after its fall without her, she commandeered the *River Queen* and went on her own, her party including abolitionist Charles Sumner, the congressman who had been caned nine years earlier by South Carolina's Preston Brooks. Sumner slipped the ivory gavel of the Confederate Congress into his pocket and made off with it. By one account, the surrender table used by Lee and Grant at Appomattox was bought by General Sheridan and presented as a gift to General George A. Custer's wife; another account says there were two tables, one for each general, and that General Ord bought Lee's for forty dollars and Sheridan bought Grant's for twenty, but owner Wilbur McLean (who had moved to Appomattox after a shell smashed into his former home at Bull Run) threw the money on the floor and refused to sell anything. Everything disappeared anyway.

Lincoln being shot on Good Friday, dying in a tailor's house and being succeeded by a tailor, two southern presidents named Johnson coming to office through assassinations—the ironies go on and on. They breathe life into history.

You can make your own list of the peculiar paradoxes in the South, the coexistence within the South and within yourself of many "minds" and many ironies. Irony is as southern as Scarlett O'Hara, that thrice-wed greedy belle so many people think of as the typical southern woman. Irony is as southern as "Dixie," which was written by a northerner and not sung in the South at all until midway through the war. As long as southerners still snicker at their stereotypes, they're safe. Only when they believe them themselves do they become a crowd of Senator Cleghorns or a race of racecar addicts guzzling beer and gasoline and wearing guitar necklaces.

April 19, 1982, and August 26, 1985

Robert Penn Warren's writings often have a southern setting, but one book from the tall seventy-eight-year-old Kentuckian takes place in the Far West. *Chief Joseph of the Nez Perce* (Random House) is the narrative celebration of the tragic exodus of a peaceful tribe of Indians, driven from their homeland at Wallowa in northeastern Oregon. They were led by Chief Joseph, and the viewpoint of the poem is primarily his.

The facts are pretty simple. The white man became aware of the Nez Perce tribe through Lewis and Clark, who were hosted by these pacific people during their great expedition. The Nez Perce moved around a bit, but "home" was where their ancestors were buried, at Wallowa. In 1855, the federal government guaranteed the Nez Perce Indians the right to their homelands. Then, in 1863, the government proposed a new treaty that would take away those rights and place the tribe on a reservation in Idaho, at Lapwai. Some subtribes signed, but others refused to do so, including the band led by Joseph. President Grant, in 1873, agreed in writing to let Chief Joseph's tribe stay in Wallowa; then he changed his mind.

Joseph's people were given thirty days to move, and they started toward the reservation. Federal groups attacked them as they were trying to obey the federal law. On June 17, 1877, began what white men called "Chief Joseph's War," but what Joseph himself saw only as an effort to escape to Canada. In the next three months, the Indians never attacked the white man's troops, but several defensive battles were fought as three armies— under General O. O. Howard, Colonel Miles, and Colonel Sturgis—pursued them. Finally, almost in sight of the safe border of Canada in eastern Montana, Joseph surrendered to Miles, with a promise from Miles to let the tribe live in good high country in Washington State. That surrender agreement was soon broken by General W. T. Sherman, head of the U.S. Army, and for several years Joseph waged a campaign of petitions and words to make the government honor the promise it had made. In the process he met Presidents Rutherford Hayes and Teddy Roosevelt, rode beside Buffalo Bill to Grant's burial, and finally—with great help from Miles—won the right for the survivors to go to the promised mountains. Joseph died there in 1904.

Reading Warren's poetic version of this story recalls other flights, such as the flight of the Hebrews under Moses from Egypt. Moses, like Joseph, never got to enter Canaan—or Canada—but his people did. The tragedy for Chief

Joseph was in never returning to Wallawa, never getting into Canada, and having to beg for years to get the promised land in Washington State. Chief Joseph's own words are just as eloquent as those of the poet. When he surrenders in 1877 to Miles and Howard, he says, "I am tired of fighting. . . . It is cold and we have no blankets. Our little children are freezing to death. I want time to look for my children and see how many of them I may find. Maybe I shall find them among the dead. Hear me, my chiefs, I am tired. My heart is sick and sad. From where the sun now stands, I will fight no more forever."

What has all this, from a southern-born poet, to do with the South? It has both direct and indirect bearings. It involves generals (Howard, Miles, Custer, Sherman, Grant) who fought the same seek-and-destroy battles against western Indians they learned to fight against southern rebels. Another Joseph, General Joe Johnston, led a retreat from Lookout Mountain, Tennessee, to Atlanta, Georgia, from the pursuing Sherman. A southerner who knows about the shelling of Vicksburg or the burning of Atlanta can understand the raids upon the Indian villages and the firing of teepees. A piece of the country that endured reconstruction and imposed legislatures and troops of occupation can understand the Indian reaction to gold-rush settlers and frontier forts upon their sacred graveyards.

This story is an echo of a universal lament. Israelites, in Babylonian captivity, wept and hung up their lyres in the willows, unable to sing their homeland song in a foreign land. So was it with Africans brought here in slavery, with southerners who lost a horrible war that still leaves scars, with six million Jews herded into boxcars in our own century, and with the boat people of Vietnam, Cambodia, and Cuba.

C. Vann Woodward was right. The thing that makes southerners more a part of the whole world and more in the mainstream of history than our Yankee cousins is that our northern kin have never known defeat and occupation and dispossession. It is touchingly ironical that southerners, who cleared away all Indians east of the Mississippi with no more second thoughts than clearing logs for farms, should be the Americans most likely to understand Indian history. But the South's greatness has been its sense of irony, something the New England Puritans could have used. What Yankee could appreciate, as Robert Penn Warren does, the ironical fact that General William Tecumseh Sherman said the only good Indian was a dead one, and yet he was named for one of the greatest Indian chiefs, Tecumseh?

June 6, 1983

On all sides of the little town of Gettysburg, Pennsylvania, one day last July, the rolling, lush, green farmland was bathed in sunlight; but the battlefield at the center was gray, with stones and fog and a misty rain. It seemed fitting.

The only way to even remotely understand the mystery of Gettysburg is to visit it. Some 121 years after it entered history, it still tells its own story, still teaches tough lessons. Like an inanimate Socrates, it raises more questions than it answers. The guidebooks and tape-recorded messages are not its textbooks. Like Golgotha, it bears its own messages. Lincoln was right to say so little when he saw it that November 19, 1863. Man's words are inadequate for this place. Perhaps only the words spoken from the cross fit: "My God, why has thou forsaken. . . ."

From atop Little Round Top, where Hood tried to come up on the North's left flank and was stopped by Warren's quick actions, one looks down upon Devil's Den, a ravine of boulders behind and around which but-ternut-clad boys once swarmed; they are more natural monuments to the 43,733 men lost here than all the impressive status, pillars, and gravestones that ring the field. The Peach Orchard, where some of the worst fighting took place, was left in splinters, as if a tornado had touched down in Eden. Between them, the two armies lost 33 generals; but it is the other 43,700 men whose ghosts walk the fields of Gettysburg and who filter through the sightseer's inner eye. Mr. Lincoln knew that oratory was not right for that place. Nor do all the fine books about the battle, even with maps and daguerreotypes, do it justice. Gettysburg is Paradise Lost as not even John Milton could have described it.

A month before we went, television brought us ceremonies from the for-tieth anniversary of D-Day at Normandy Beach. Here, one sees immediately the link between Gettysburg and Omaha Beach. Perhaps that is why General Eisenhower chose it for his retirement home. The reason for studying history is not to glory in it, but to learn from it.

What a "terrible swift sword" is war: so many lost young lives, "unfin-ished," to use Mr. Lincoln's word, so few of them old enough to have left descendants, without whom our nation has to be weakened for centuries because it was deprived of so many ancestors.

Here Union General Reynolds and Confederate General Barksdale both died, only months after they were exchanged for one another in a swap of prisoners of war. Here Hancock and Armistead, West Point classmates and eternal friends separated for years by war, were reunited; Armistead led a charge at the Bloody Angle and was killed in sight of the wounded Hancock on the other side of the defenders' parapet. Here an inevitable collision of two great armies came by accident, when Lee's soldiers, looking for shoes, found Meade's men instead. One shoemaker, the seventy-two-year-old John L. Burns, picked up a rifle, joined the Union forces, was thrice wounded, and then captured and released. Here one woman died. Jenny Wade, volunteering as cook and nurse, was struck by a stray bullet that had come through a building.

Here a rebel soldier named Culp died, charging up Culp's Hill, the farm he had left to go South and join the army.

The official tour begins and ends at the national cemetery that Lincoln said he could not consecrate because it had already been consecrated by those who died there. The small stones there are laid out in neat long rows. Over in the famous Wheatfield, which changed hands several times that July 2, the new wheat blows in its own neat rows.

In the mist of Gettysburg, amid its ghosts, one dreams of a world that someday will find a way to avoid treating its boys as it does its wheat, lining them up to be scythed and ground for the rest of us.

November 19, 1984

LINCOLN

Congress tells us presidents have birthdays only on Mondays. I continue to observe those anniversaries on their true dates, even on a Tuesday where Lincoln's happens to be or a Friday as Washington's is this year. Lincoln comes to mind as we are watching General Westmoreland's lawsuit against CBS-TV. The network had reported that the general deliberately underestimated the numbers of enemy troops in Vietnam, and the general took issue with that report.

Someone once asked Lincoln how many troops the "Rebels" had. He replied that he had a precise count of 1,200,000. The inquirer gasped and asked how Lincoln could be so sure of his figure. Lincoln smiled, and said his generals always reported after each defeat that they were out-numbered 3 to 1, and since there were 400,000 Federal troops, there had to be 1,200,000 Confederates.

One of the paradoxes of American history is that the best president ever technically presided over only half a nation. Lincoln was fond of using the word "Providence" to refer to divine power. He invoked Providence in his speeches, his letters, and his calls for days of thanksgiving. The greatest act of Providence may have been in sending Lincoln to the White House for the time it took to mend the rip in the fabric of the country.

Lincoln endured the most vicious name calling, buck passing, and blame placing the nation ever saw, with more of it from his own "allies" in the North than ever from the South. He refused to call southerners "enemies." To Lincoln, the South never left the Union, and the people of the South were always the brothers and cousins of the people of the North. His view of the war was that of a quarreling family that Providence, in time, would cool and reunite.

He often seemed unable to select and control his generals. Perhaps Providence was at work in that failing, too. Had the war ended earlier, it would have been only a draw, to be resumed later. It had to go on to its tragic conclusion. Even then, the scars would remain for decades longer. The sense Lincoln had of the war as tragedy, outside the control of those who were dying in it, set him apart as a president. He had duties to fulfill, armies to assemble, constituents to rally, a public with an ebbing morale to lift, and a nation to administer. Yet, he had a tragic vision that put him above and beyond his duties.

He was a man *of* the people, placed *by* the people in a position to be *for* the people. Tragedies do not come to machinery, or buildings, or even to land. Tragedies come only to people. The feel Lincoln had for people, as their best representative, was a feel for their tragedy, something he could grasp and express better than any of the people themselves. His Gettysburg Address and his two inaugural addresses are literary masterpieces, equal to the Homer and Shakespeare and Bible that Lincoln read over and over and quoted from memory. They are better addresses than most because they were penned by one who had the tragic vision to match the gift of using words.

We think of Lincoln as the ultimate American. Carl Sandburg's flattering biography makes him too much the Illinois lawyer. Lincoln was a Kentuckian before he was an Illinois or Indiana resident. He was never a local, provincial figure. His thoughts and hopes were on too grand a scale to be contained by a particular town or state or by a specific time. The war he was in had its origin in the world's past and its significance in the globe's future. The tragedy Lincoln knew was the shortsightedness of past and future that consumed everyone else in the flames of the moment.

He fought the tragedy more fiercely than he fought the war. From the first shot at Fort Sumter until the one that killed him in Ford's Theatre, Lincoln was always looking beyond the war. All wars eventually end: even the Hundred Years' War ended. The hard part is not the fighting: it is the living together afterward that is always mankind's greatest challenge.

Those around him vilified him for his humor, for telling parables and making puns in the midst of carnage and chaos. He had a ready reply for such critics: "If I do not laugh, then I must weep."

What day his birthday is celebrated never would have disturbed Abe Lincoln at all. Any day or every day of the year is appropriate. Washington may have been the "Father of His Country," but without Lincoln, it could have been a nation that died prematurely at its own hands at age eighty-five. Lincoln made Washington great by preserving Washington's offspring. We salute his courage, his steadfastness, his humility, his humor, his vision, his choice of words, his touch with Providence, and his affection for all of us, even those of us whom he never met, as members of his family.

February 11, 1985

MANNERS

The Book-of-the-Month Club sent me a free copy of Judith Martin's lectures at Harvard, *Common Courtesy,* in which Miss Manners tries to solve the problem Jefferson couldn't: what kind of manners are appropriate in a democracy where everyone is equal. The problem is caused by American democracy retaining class distinctions. Class lines have been clearest in the South, except perhaps in Boston.

For a long time Americans didn't know there were class lines. Andy Jackson was a brawling backwoodsman whose friends stood on the White House chairs, but he was also an aristocrat who built a mansion and kept a permanent portrait painter in his employ.

So much attention had to be given to creating a code of etiquette between the races, a *caste code,* that class manners never got much attention. That caste code started breaking down when southern congressman Preston

Brooks caned Yankee senator Charles Sumner because southerners had run out of patience and words. The *caste code* is still changing, and whites and blacks alike are designing new ways of being civil with one another.

The *class code* of manners changed a bit later. It was the reason so many small farmers and merchants were willing to follow traditional landowner leaders into the Civil War. They had hunted together and accepted their separated roles since frontier days. Small farmers deferred to big planters. After the war, the economy changed, and towns grew and industries came, and people spent more and more time together. Manners had to change because men were working together more often. The change was symbolized in Faulkner's books when Ab Snopes stepped into the manure pile and then walked into old Major DeSpain's hallway and wiped his feet on a hundred-dollar French rug. DeSpain was as shocked by Snopes coming in the front door as by anything else.

After World War II, manners really changed. Men who fought together and women who riveted together weren't about to go back to the old high-low class manners. They became better paid and better educated, and those upper classes unwilling to accept the mass equality of all the changes had to retreat. Some of them moved to exclusive and guarded neighborhoods, sent their children to private academies, and confined friendships to country-club acquaintances. The majority of the folks stayed with the public schools, lived in ranch houses and mobile homes, and congregated at shopping malls and high school ballgames.

But there are lots of problems in the world that need the attention of people in all classes. Unless they find ways to meet and tackle those problems together, the class gap will widen instead of narrowing, and chaos or dictatorship will follow as it has in other nations where classes have clashed.

There has to be a new etiquette, invented and followed by all parties, that recognizes legitimate claims of both upper and lower classes. The problems of school quality, unacceptable minimum incomes and unemployment statistics, illiteracy, infant mortality, racism, and welfare dependency have to be attended to by everyone.

No one has the right to withdraw from the hard work of being civil to one another. Everyone has the duty to help invent rules that get us all in the front door to the same table to talk without shouting or pouting.

February 10, 1986

WILLIAM GOEBEL AND EDWARD CARMACK

Frock-tailed statues stand in the front of the state capitol buildings of both Kentucky and Tennessee. Most tourists, and even some employees within the buildings, don't know whom the statues honor. Appropriately, the two men pedestaled for posterity were politicians. But they held something else in common as well.

Both Edward Ward Carmack of Tennessee and William Goebel of Kentucky were shot to death in the first decade of this century.

Goebel died of a rifle shot fired on January 30, 1900, from the secretary of state's office in the capitol as he walked toward the building in Frankfort. Carmack died on Seventh Avenue in Nashville, in sight of the capitol, from three shots fired on November 9, 1908, by Robin Cooper, who had been struck by two bullets fired by Carmack.

William Goebel was born in Pennsylvania to German immigrants who moved on to Kentucky in his youth. He studied law in the offices of a prominent northern Kentucky politician. Practicing in Covington, Goebel moved from local politics into state activity, serving in the state senate and also in the constitutional convention of 1890. His ambition was to head the Democratic Party of the state, and in 1900 he ran for governor. Goebel had built a reputation as "defender of the little man" and had taken on the text-book companies and the L&N Railroad. The campaign was a bitter one, and the Republican candidate was declared the winner amid shrill charges of election frauds. Charges circulated of Republican ballot-box stuffing, especially in eastern Kentucky counties where it was claimed that even the trees were given names and allowed to vote alongside the residents of grave-yards. Boatloads of armed mountaineers poured down the Kentucky River and trainloads rolled down the L&N tracks, bent on seeing their winner installed and their honor upheld. Goebel lingered on for four days, during which time the legislature convened, controlled by Democrats, and Goebel was declared the winner of the election and the Republican candidate fled the state. Two men were arrested and imprisoned for the shooting, but neither confessed. To this day, the killer of William Goebel, who won a lost election by dying, is unknown.

Edward Ward Carmack was born in 1858 at Castalian Springs, Tennessee, and was left fatherless at the age of three, at the outset of the Civil War. He attended Culleoka Institute, where he was a favorite student of William Robert Webb, the headmaster whose school would later become famous as Webb School of Bellbuckle. Webb suspended Carmack for two weeks when he was seventeen, and Carmack refused to return. The stubborn drama of this event was a sign of Carmack's turbulent later life.

Like Goebel, Carmack "read law" under a local attorney and was admitted to the bar. He served as city attorney, justice of the peace, and local magistrate of the county court, and then spent a term as a state representative in Nashville. Meanwhile, he found his niche in the public eye by becoming a journalist, starting out as an editorial writer in Columbia and moving at age twenty-seven to Nashville. He became a statewide spokesman for the old-line "Bourbon Democrats." Col. Duncan Brown Cooper, also of Columbia, controlled the Nashville paper and selected Carmack as his assistant. Ironically, it was Cooper at whom Carmack shot twenty-two years later, and Cooper's son who shot Carmack. In the interim, Carmack edited three major papers, including the forerunner of the Memphis *Commercial-Appeal*, became an ardent free-silver advocate and later a prohibitionist, was elected to Congress by four hundred contested votes and finally seated by an eighteen-vote margin of the House of Representatives, and served one term as U.S. senator. In a typically vitriolic campaign in 1908, Carmack ran for governor, losing by six thousand votes. He immediately became editor of the new Nashville *Tennessean,* whence he fought (again like Goebel) the L&N Railroad. His attacks upon Colonel Cooper, his longtime friend whom Carmack felt had deserted him in the 1906 senate race, led to his death a few weeks later, again like Goebel, shortly after a gubernatorial loss and within view of the office building he coveted.

Their monuments are to their mutual martyrdom.

December 28, 1987

WEST POINT AND THE CIVIL WAR

The real fighting of the War between the States came after the war was over; it still goes on today. Mostly it has been a war among southerners themselves.

Once the rebel officers who survived found niches of employment, their memoirs began to roll off the presses. The rationalizations and finger-pointings, the self-congratulations and partisan denouncements, do not make for an attractive finale in the legends of the fallen. Only a few had the grace to stand above the continuing fray. Lee retired to Washington College and refused to replay the game in print or in public. Ewell shut up his critics by saying "it took a dozen blunders to lose the battle of Gettysburg and I committed a good many of them." One former officer delighted in introducing himself as a former private at Confederate reunions as his way of putting down the large number of "self-promoted colonels" that suddenly populated the South after the War.

One of the aftermath battles has been a debate over the West Point–educated leadership of southern forces. Most historians believe the war would have been lost in months rather than years had not so many Point men sided with the South. Others believe that Davis and Lee relied far too heavily upon the Pointers, keeping incompetents and cowards (George Pickett is a favorite target) around while discouraging the rise of venturesome officers who lacked West Point credentials.

There were 306 U.S. Military Academy graduates in the southern forces. Among them were Albert S. Johnston, Class of '26, Leonidas Polk, Class of '27, Jefferson Davis, Class of '28, Robert E. Lee, Class of '29, Braxton Bragg, Class of '37, Jubal A. Early, Class of '37, P. G. T. Beauregard, Class of '38, William J. Hardee, Class of '38, Daniel H. Hill, Class of '42, James Longstreet, Class of '42, Thomas J. Jackson, Class of '46, Ambrose P. Hill, Class of '47, John Bell Hood, Class of '53, Custis Lee, Class of '54, J. E. B. Stuart, Class of '54, and Fitzhugh Lee, Class of '56. About a fourth of West Point's alumni went with the South. For those of them already serving in the U.S. Army as professionals when war came, it was a daring thing they did. For all they knew, defeat would mean trial and execution as deserters. At the least it would mean unemployment in their chosen profession. Only three of them were ever taken back into the federal service—Fitzhugh Lee, Tom Rosser, and Joe Wheeler.

Of the 306 Academy southerners, about a third served under Lee at one time or another, and 28 of that group died before the war ended. In all, on all fronts, some 72 West Point men died in southern service.

Upon their shoulders rested most of the responsibility for organizing and drilling green troops and teaching rudiments of military strategy and procedures. Laymen could not do that. And having "regimented" their men, it fell their lot to lead them, too. Most of them took leading literally and fell in battle, often at the head of their charges. It was when this irreplaceable group of professionals dwindled that the South had its problems of command. There was no reservoir to tap for new Academy alumni just as there was none for food, clothing, frontline troops, horses, and medicine.

Gerard A. Patterson has told a bit of the West Point–South story in *Rebels from West Point;* but by concentrating on only some 38 key figures in North Virginia, his book is a shadow of the unwritten story of the role of West Point in the war. The topic begs for fuller treatment. Patterson whets our appetite.

These were men who lived in the same barracks and drank at the same tables at Benny Havens Tavern, dated and married one another's sisters and girlfriends, studied out of the same textbooks and under the same professors, fought in Mexico and out west together, and lent money to each other.

They knew each other, or knew others who did, and it subtracts nothing from the glory due non-Academy troopers of both sides to observe that the War between the States was in large degree an Academy matter.

February 15, 1988

JACKSON AND LEE: THE LAST MEETING

Sometimes in looking for the unusual we overlook the obvious.

My office here at Wofford College is next to a reception hall. In it last year and again over the last few weeks a large painting has been on display. While I have enjoyed having it as a neighbor, I haven't really thought much about what a well-known work of art it is. It needed a place to be, and the ceiling in the room is about one inch higher than the enormous frame.

You'd recognize the painting instantly. You've seen copies of it in textbooks, probably from an engraving of it that circulated in the tens of thousands after 1872. The painting is called "The Last Meeting of Lee and Jackson," and it shows those two generals on their horses, Traveller and Little Sorrel, shortly before Jackson was killed at Chancellorsville. In the background are staff aides of the generals and a clump of trees. This original has been privately owned for its entire history. Painted by St. Louis artist Everett B. D. Julio in 1869, it was intended as a gift for General Lee, who by then was president of Washington College (now Washington and Lee). Lee declined the gift, and Julio took it south to sell in New Orleans.

As it worked its way down the Mississippi, it was placed on display in Memphis, where Jefferson Davis saw it and wrote a letter to the artist commending the work. Efforts to sell it in New Orleans failed. Lotteries and subscriptions and sales of the engravings of it were equally unsuccessful.

Further efforts to get New York buyers to purchase it for Washington and Lee were just as futile. The president of LSU did buy a copy, and Julio used the money to go to Europe for further art study.

Julio died in 1879 without having sold the piece. A New Orleans gallery to which he owed money claimed the painting. Col. John B. Richardson, a veteran of the famous Washington Artillery of that city, bought it and hung it in the armory of that company down in the French Quarter. It was there from 1872 to 1910, and Mark Twain saw it there in 1883 and wrote critically of the Sir Walter Scott and southern chivalry myth it represented in his *Life on the Mississippi.*

In 1909, Richardson's widow offered the painting for sale, and in 1910 another veteran, James Butterfield Sinnott, bought it for eighteen hundred dollars. It hung in Sinnott's home on St. Charles for the next fourteen years, and then the family lent it to the Louisiana State Museum for the next thirty-two years. They retrieved it in 1956 and held it until 1986.

Then a Spartanburg art dealer took it to Washington, D.C., for careful restoration, which uncovered surprises such as the scarlet of Jackson's cape and a heretofore-hidden valley of soldiers, tents, and campfires in the background of the picture. Today the painting is valued at several million dollars.

The frame is almost as interesting as the painting. If a very big and very old antique four-poster bed were laid flat, with the painting where the mattress would be, one would get some idea of the rich woods and size of this frame. Made mostly of walnut, it is assembled in sections, like nineteenth-century wardrobes. Rising from a heavy pedestal at the base are two side columns with carved coats of arms for Jackson and Lee capped by a wooden crown with a wooden seal of Virginia in the center, above which perches a gilded eagle with wings spread wide. The frame is thirteen feet, ten and three-quarter inches high and nine feet, seven inches wide, hardly a living-room piece for most homes.

As for the painting itself, the influence of painters of General Washington at Yorktown (Rembrandt Peale) and at the Delaware (Thomas Sully) seems evident. The family links between the Lees and Washington are well known, and this painting plays upon them. That family tie is reinforced in this Julio painting by the fact that most Confederate theoreticians saw the Civil War as a repetition of the Revolution.

But in those early portraits of Washington the viewer's emotion is upbeat: victory is inevitable and Washington is destined and demi-divine. In the Julio picture, however, the moods are of sadness and of finality, a prophecy that the war is about to be lost that very day in Jackson's death. In fact, some historians have said that Gettysburg and the war itself were lost because Jackson wasn't there.

Interesting neighbors, these two. Jackson and Lee, bigger than life both while living and in the eyes of history and of a painter.

April 17, 1989

EARL K. LONG

Paul Newman is a great actor, but he would probably be the first to admit that his screen portrayals of historical figures—such as Billy the Kid, Judge Roy Bean, General Leslie Groves, and Earl Long—are not intended to be historically accurate. At least, they trigger interest in character, and, at best, they prompt us to read more about the histories behind the characters.

On the heels of Newman's film about Earl Long, scholars Michael L. Kurtz and Morgan D. Peoples provided a timely biography in *Earl K. Long: The Saga of Uncle Earl and Louisiana Politics* (LSU Press).

It is difficult for the brother of a famous man to become famous himself—as Edward Kennedy probably knows. Earl Long had the good and the bad fortune to be Huey Long's brother. But the mantle of Louisiana politics did not pass as automatically to him by inheritance after Huey's assassination in 1935 as is sometimes supposed. He captured it as it was slipping away, by being elected lieutenant governor in 1936 and appointed governor in 1939, almost lost it in his unsuccessful races for governor in 1940 and 1944, and redonned it on his own again in his election in 1948 and again in 1954.

Uncle Earl's career as a populist, who did succeed in instituting many programs of benefit to masses of citizens and also as a crafty and probably corrupt manipulator, paralleled that of his older brother in many ways. What made Earl Long memorable for a later generation too young to remember Huey Long were the bizarre and well-publicized events at the end of his career, especially in 1959: trysts with Blaze Starr, bouts with alcohol and drugs, being locked in his room in the Governor's Mansion after a harangue of the legislature intended as a speech of apology, time in a Galveston psychiatric clinic, his self-dismissal from that place and return to Baton Rouge, his capture there and lunacy hearing in the courthouse parking lot, removal to the state hospital at Mandeville, retention of gubernatorial power while there, his suit for separation from his wife in order to deprive her of powers to act for him (or against him, for that matter), his dismissal of the hospital director and acting superintendent and appointment of new ones who dismissed him and thereby cancelled a large sanity hearing in Covington, his announcement for reelection, and his eighteen-day whirlwind "vacation" to Texas and points west.

Unable to succeed himself, Long ran for lieutenant governor and was defeated in 1959 but bounced back to run for Congress in 1960. Elected to Congress on August 27, one day after his sixty-fifth birthday, he entered the hospital the same day, and there he died on September 5, 1960. But the memories linger on; Blaze Starr and Candy Cane are hard names to forget.

April 1, 1990

JAMES JOHNSTON PETTIGREW

A Civil War vacuum slowly being filled is the lack of knowledge about many officers on both sides whose stories have been neglected. It was a war that produced many generals, many of whom died early or were forgotten. But as time passes, more is discovered about some of them. One such biography is provided by Clyde N. Wilson in *Carolina Cavalier. The Life and Mind of James Johnston Pettigrew* (University of Georgia Press).

Pettigrew was a brilliant North Carolinian. Born in 1828, he attended the best school in the state, Bingham Academy, and then went on to the University of North Carolina, where he compiled a perfect academic record. He moved to Baltimore and worked for the Naval Observatory under the famous Matthew F. Maury, studied law there, and then moved to Charleston.

Befriended by a wealthy North Carolina planter and bachelor for whom he had been named, and by an older cousin of much fame in South Carolina, James L. Petigru, Pettigrew was able to travel extensively and to study in Europe. He had ambitions to spend ten years in Spain as a scholar and to write a definitive history of Spain but never achieved that goal. He did succeed in writing in 1860 and in publishing the next year a book titled *Notes on Spain and the Spaniards*.

Like his benefactor, a bachelor, Pettigrew burned with ambition for recognition and honors. He served in numerous public and civic offices, wrote an effective treatise opposing the reopening of the slave trade, tried to enlist in the Sardinian army in Europe, and was a much-touted leader of the local militia. Pettigrew was universally hailed as a young man of extraordinary genius. One admirer went so far as to claim him capable of holding supreme command of all southern armies instead of Lee. After heading the Charleston militia through the fall of Fort Sumter, he commanded a regiment on the Potomac, a brigade at Seven Pines (where he was wounded and captured), and operations in eastern North Carolina.

In June 1863 he and his troops became part of Lee's invasion army into Pennsylvania. He led successful charges the first day at Gettysburg, and on the third day his men formed the major portion of the line which history has misnamed "Pickett's Charge." A third of the fourteen thousand Confederates in the charge on July 3 were Pettigrew's. His horse was hit in the charge, and Pettigrew dismounted, his right hand's fingers smashed by grapeshot. He was one of the last men to leave the field that day.

As it turned out, he was also one of the last Confederates to leave northern soil. In the retreat to Virginia, his troops brought up the rear. At Hagerstown, Maryland, they fought off federal cavalry on July 10. On July 14, they camped on the Potomac, ready to cross into Virginia. A group of fifty federal cavalrymen recklessly charged him in a garden there. All fifty were killed, but not before they had wounded Pettigrew for the fifth time in his military career. With a pistol wound in the chest, he was carried across the river into Virginia and died three days later.

Wilson believes that Pettigrew epitomized the ideal of the southern cavalier, but Wilson's biographical evidence is otherwise. Pettigrew was not a representative figure at all. In intellect, in patronage, in lifestyle, and even in his ambitions, he was cut from cloth quite different from most planter-aristocrats of the South. That is why this biography makes such interesting reading—a welcome discovery and valued footnote to antebellum and Civil War histories.

What Pettigrew does represent, all too well, is the effect of war upon a nation's intellectual resources. Recognized as one of the few truly brilliant minds in the South, he was only thirty-five years old when he died in 1863. In a war that cost the nation one million men, his loss was multiplied many times over, and no nation can suffer such a loss of young leaders without paying an awful price centuries afterward.

September 1, 1990

[Legendary coach Robert E. "Bob" Lee broke his self-imposed silence for this interview.]

Southern Seen: Coach, everyone talks about your great '62–'63 season. Can you summarize it? Why was it great?

Lee: "It was our best year. We won at Seven Pines at the end of May, tied at Malvern Hill in June, went on to a pretty easy win at Second Bull Run in August, pulled a tie at Antietam in September, had a big win at Fredericksburg in December, and had a good one at Chancellorsville in May, except for losing our star, Stonewall. We were playing at home most of those games, a definite advantage, and we had the best quarterback in the nation in Jackson. He ran the option like he invented it—sweeping end runs, hidden-ball tricks, fake passes.

"The amazing thing was that our team was made up of nonscholarship walk-ons. We had a good recruiting year, hard boys eager to fight who didn't mind drills and marches and who loved being first-string. That was before our AD, Jeff Davis, had to establish the draft, of course, when boys still didn't care about getting paid, or laundry, or cars to get around in. The uniforms were embarrassing, but they wore them anyway; they believed and we were winning.

"We ran a great offense that year. Lean and quick. The other side never seemed to get its act together. They just couldn't hold on to the ball whenever they got it, which wasn't often, and on defense we intimidated them so badly that they never knew the meaning of teamwork. They always wound up with every man for himself when we were marching down the field. On offense, they would fold at the first sight of blood. Look at their injury lists and low yardage gained, and you get the picture. And, of course, all those coaching changes didn't help them at all. They switched from McDowell to McClellan to Pope to McClellan to Burnside to Hooker, all in one year! The first time McClellan was coaching he drilled his team to prime condition but wouldn't play any practice games. His green recruits were in condition when they did show up on the field but didn't know what to do once they were there. And then, when he was coaching the second time, we lost our playbook, and he found it, and even with that, he couldn't manage more than a tie."

Southern Seen: So what happened? There you were at the end of the '62–'63 season: national coach of the year with the national champion team, and two years later you were out.

Lee: "It's hard to pick any one thing. I lost my right arm at Chancellorsville when we lost Jackson, as I said. Then we headed for the bowl game at Gettysburg. We weren't ready for the game. I had sent Stuart out on a scouting trip, and he got lost and didn't report back, so I didn't have good information on who was coaching—it was Meade—or what kind of reserves he had or what kind of line he would be using. Once the game got under way, I never felt I was in control of it. They just stood there, and every time we would punch part of the line, they would just move fresh players into it. Longstreet was moving slowly at halfback, and we never got the whole line moving at the same time. Pickett and Pettigrew got chewed up by their defense. But I take the responsibility myself. Probably we shouldn't have accepted the bowl game at all, except we needed the gate receipts so badly, to pay for the next season. Their AD, that Lincoln fellow, called it a tie. Jumped all over Meade for not going for the goal on the last play. But looking back, we lost it, and that loss set us up for the others later.

"The '63–'64 season the next year looks better on the record books than it really was. We held our own at the Wilderness, at Spotsylvania, and Cold Harbor, but by then we had had so many injuries and lost so many veterans and were doing so poorly in recruiting that even the water boys were giving up. They had this new coach, Grant, who was a Lombardi type. Winning was everything to him. He didn't care how many of his players got hurt or how much money it cost. Up against that type of philosophy, the fun was gone. It wasn't Civil anymore. Playing was just another job, sort of a funny depression in which there wasn't any food or clothing or money to be had, but everyone kept on working anyway.

"We didn't want to play the '64–'65 schedule the final year at all. The game at Petersburg went on so long we had nothing left. The teams out in Atlanta, Nashville, and the Valley got all of the headlines. If we could have pooled our teams, maybe we could have lasted longer. We tried to get out of the contract for Appomattox, but they wouldn't release us. So in April '65, I got my walking papers. Joe Johnston finished out the season. Then they dropped the sport. Went to hunting, fishing, and playing baseball, all stuff you could do out around the farms when you could get some free time from plowing. They gave me a watch and sent me off. I'd been coaching so long, I didn't have a home to go to. I found this administrative job at this college in Lexington. I don't even keep the watch wound; it's stopped on three o'clock. That's when Pickett made his stab at their line on July 3, '63."

Southern Seen: That '62–'63 season that was so great for you. Is that when you got your nickname, "The General"?

Lee: "Yes. I've always been proud of it. I had it all to myself for years. They almost retired it, but folks in Tennessee used it later for a fellow named Neyland. I would have picked that Bryant fellow myself. I was his fore-Bear."

September 3, 1990

WEST VIRGINIA AND THE USSR

Is West Virginia really a state?

This is one of those questions that occasionally pop up to be pursued sometime when we have more free time.

Here's why it piques my curiosity. West Virginia became a state during the Civil War. It was encouraged to do so by the federal government, including President Lincoln, but it became a state by seceding from Virginia. Right in the middle of a major war being fought to uphold the principle that states had no legal right to secede from the Union, the government upholding that principle was contradicting itself by encouraging a state to secede. (Slavery wasn't an issue, yet, because West Virginia was admitted as a slave-holding state.) Most historians beg the question of West Virginia's secession by taking a southern historian perspective, referring to battles in that region as "western Virginia" rather than as in "West Virginia."

If the federal government put itself into contradiction with itself by permitting secession for one state while resisting it for eleven others, the Confederate government was in a dilemma, too. Defending the right of states to secede, it could hardly argue that West Virginia's secession and creation were illegal. It might have tried to rationalize that the creation of West Virginia was illegal because many of the voting citizens were in the southern armies and not home to vote, or because the territory was occupied by federal troops at the time. But history books say little about how either the southern government or Virginia's government took this secession.

Suppose the war had ended with southern secessions assured, either by southern victories or by a negotiated stalemate settlement. Would the issue of West Virginia's status have come up then? And if so, how would it likely have been resolved? Would it have become part of Virginia again, or stayed with the Union?

Most of the states of the nation were formed out of new territories like the Northwest Territory or Louisiana Purchase or Mexican war booty as the nation expanded westward. Few were carved from existing states, and then only with the official permission of the home state, North Carolina sponsoring Tennessee, Virginia sponsoring Kentucky, etc. There was provision for future internal carving in the case of Texas, for the admission charter provided that Texas could be carved into as many as five states sometime in the future, if desired. But the fact that such a provision had to be stated so explicitly in the Texas case indicates that dividing a state was not an implicit right or likelihood in other established states.

At any rate, West Virginia statehood is a rather fascinating historical footnote for some scholar to pursue. It may be a moot point anyway. We don't hear many West Virginians demanding to be readmitted to Virginian citizenship, nor do we hear many Virginians threatening to take West Virginia back into statehood. The topic, however, is not irrelevant to modern society. All over the Union of Soviet Socialist Republics, individual republics are asserting their independence from the larger union. They are in fact seceding. One would do well to study hard the history of the United States for the years from 1830 to 1861 in order to see the kinds of questions of authority and autonomy that the Soviet break-up raises.

Hard-line southerners who have never conceded the right of the central government to supersede the secession rights of the separate states will find themselves opposed to the militaristic right wing of the USSR as it asserts nationwide martial law and suppresses state rights to preserve its union. But meanwhile, the president and State Department, if acting consistently with the principle of antisecession and the means of enforcement of the principle by the federal government in our own civil war, would have to declare its sympathy with the central union's preservation, even by the use of force.

Consistency in principle has never been a requisite for our government or in our history as a nation.

What happens there will certainly have enormous consequences for our own future. And if I lived in West Virginia, I would be watching USSR developments especially closely.

June 17, 1991

WAR REPARATIONS

Growing up in west Tennessee, one of the grand old men who ruled over our court square in those paradise times before malls and suburbs was a loveable pharmacist, Charles Trevathan. Mr. Charlie's family had been important in that little town almost from its beginnings, and he carried on the tradition by being mayor and on all the important boards and committees. Mr. Charlie's daughter, Cara, sent me a copy of a bill she has framed in her home. Back during the Civil War, once Fort Donelson had fallen in 1862, the Yankees intermittently occupied our hometown. Mr. Charlie's father and uncle owned a drugstore in town, founded sometime before 1856, and Yankee troops betimes supplemented their supplies with goods from the store. A careful record of purchases was kept, and over a two-year period various colonels ran up a bill of $867.95.

In 1862, the bill included "60 Meals for Co. Lowe's command @25 cts, $15.00; feeding Co. horses at different times for Same @ 25 cts, $15.00; 1-1/2 BBls Cider by Col. Lowes Men @5.00, $750.00." The bill for 1863 showed "120 lbs Salt Pork @7c, $8.40; 1 Saddle Taken by Same, $15.00; 1 Coffee Pot & Wash Pan by Same, $.75; Dinner for 12 Men & Horses, $6.00; 1 Mule by Col. Lowes command, $150.00; 1 Mule Returned, -$150.00; Expenses on his return, $5.00; 1 horse, $75.00; 1 Mule, $150.00; 1 Horse returned, -$75.00; Expenses in getting horse home, $10.00." (The Trevathans must have operated an Avis-Rent-A-Mule franchise.) In 1864 the 2d New Jersey Regiment consumed "15 Ton hay, @25/a ton, $375.00; 1 Log Chain, $6.00; 100 lbs Salt Pork, @8 cts, $8.00, 100 lbs Sausage Meat, @15 cts, $15.00; 1 Skillet, $1.50; 1 Bee gum, $3.00."

The best we can tell, the bill was never fully paid, although it was reduced by some small amount. Cara figures that as of 1989, with interest at 6 percent accrued annually, by 1989 the U.S. government owed her something in the neighborhood of $895,450.85. I'll round it off to $900,000. The unfortunate thing for Cara is that so far the government hasn't offered to settle its debts. The government is very quick to unleash its agents when someone understates an income tax form by a hundred dollars, but it has no bevy of agents out trying to see that people get what is owed them. Cara must ponder occasionally how one goes politely but effectively about getting her money from her government. We are trying to help her.

If Cara's $900,000 is included in the national debt figures, it is but a miniscule amount in that total and would never be missed if paid in full. If that doesn't work, she could incorporate herself as a defense contractor (which is what the Trevathans were, in effect) and submit the bill to the Pentagon. Defense contractors seem to have no trouble at all in getting their billings paid. She might have to inflate it considerably to get their attention because $900,000 may not fit their computers, which can't handle bills under a million dollars.

She could also withhold payment of her annual income tax, subtracting whatever is due each year from the amount the government owes her. This is the most considerate approach for her to take, saving the government a lot of time and paperwork, plus doing them the patriotic service of not hitting them up for the whole bundle in one year. However, since Miss Cara is approaching retirement age, it would take an impossible number of years for her withholdings to pay the bill in full.

The only other option that occurs to me is to suggest that she enlist her two South Carolina U.S. senators, and the two Tennessee U.S. Senators, all four of whom speak her native southern tongue and who are pledged to honor southern women and to help them in wartime distress. They could easily introduce some special legislation for redress, perhaps of the sort Native American tribes have been successful in securing for confiscation of their properties.

I want to see justice done Miss Cara. She comes from decent, hard-working, civic-serving stock. She also comes from Paris, Tennessee, a truly fine little town in which not a single citizen has ever gotten all he or she truly deserved and most folks have gotten less. No foreign nations have ever offered to buy it; no one from Publishers Clearing House has ever visited there. It would do the morale of that ol' hometown more good than a recount of its last U.S. census to see one of its own finally "hit it big." Miss Cara deserves it, and so does her hometown.

If she does get it, I hope the very first thing she does is to find her daddy's beautiful old mahogany and marble soda fountain and install it, fully operative, in the county historical society headquarters. Let justice and good times roll!

November 4, 1991

Remember Pearl Harbor? How could we forget it, even though it was a full half century ago? Everyone my age and older remembers where they were and what they were doing that Sunday afternoon, December 7, 1941. What I can't remember are the words to a song that we were all singing soon afterward. In my mind's eye, I can see the white bouncing ball on the movie screen, jumping atop each syllable as we all joined in singing it before the main feature started. But I can't remember the words. Its opening line was "Just re-mem-ber Pear-ul Har-bor." I think it was sung to the tune of Yale's "Boolah-Boolah." And I remember that after the show, we could buy war stamps with a minuteman pictured on them for ten cents each. I think they were green, but memory plays tricks.

Actually we remember Pearl Harbor more clearly today than we did at the time. Few of us then knew where Pearl Harbor was. We had to buy maps to find it. Lacking television, what little we could picture of it came weeks later, from *Life* magazine photos and *Movietone* newsreels. It took historians years to piece together the fuller report from official records of both Japan and our own government and from eyewitness recollections.

It was probably just as well that there were such delays in details. What the country heard about and reacted to was almost more than it could absorb, and Pearl Harbor needed no immediate elaboration. Suddenly on a Sunday the world turned upside down and went into reverse for America. Suddenly on a Sunday a nation that had pledged to stay out of a world war that had been raging since the 1930s was in it. Suddenly on a Sunday we found ourselves with our backs against a wall we had built around ourselves. We tore down our wall of isolationism after Pearl Harbor, sucked ourselves in long enough to draw a deep breath, and then sailed out.

The wall had been the keystone of American policy since the Revolutionary War. We had sneaked over it a bit during the Spanish-American War a hundred years later and then had come out in force and quickly for the last years of World War I. But then we rejected Wilson's League of Nations and patched the wall instead. But with Pearl Harbor, our wall finally came tumbling down forever. Henceforth, we would never be the same. There would be no turning back to "normalcy." America went forth into the rest of the world and has stayed there ever since. When the Berlin Wall was destroyed not long ago, what we were celebrating as much as the liberation of the East German and Russian people was the revival of memories of the day our own wall fell. We remember Pearl Harbor. That was the day the little bouncing ball on the screen stopped beating out "The Good Ship Lollipop" and started jumping along the words to "Don't Fence Me In" instead.

We sang that the lights had gone out "all over the world." But truth was that for America the lights just came on with Pearl Harbor. The dark day of Japanese "infamy" brought us into world consciousness, into industrial expansion, and into national unity such as we had not known possible. It redefined "duty" for us. The slumbering giant heard the rumble of planes and felt upon its eyelids the heat of the bombs from far away, and stirred and then awoke; it has not slept again since.

The list of those who died at Pearl Harbor seemed long back then. But as the war lengthened, the list seemed to shorten. Longer lists came, and remembering the first few who fell became harder. We even argued, in post-war years, whether their deaths had been "necessary." But historians had had the same arguments about the Alamo and the sinking of the *Maine*. We have not forgotten them.

If in time we forget the names of the men and women killed there, they and their Pearl Harbor will still be remembered. They were the vanguard of America's awakening, these fallen warriors in front of the wall of isolationism that came down behind them. They were the first eyewitnesses to an engulfing transformation of a nation such as the world had never seen or known, still being transformed fifty years afterward.

They were admittedly, as the young and lean Frank Sinatra sang it back then, "long ago, and far away." Yet how could we forget them? They are with us today more than ever before, in what we have become and are yet becoming because of their Sunday in the sun.

December 2, 1991

NATIONAL UNIVERSITY OF WORLD WAR II HISTORY

We knew America was at war when the World War I field gun in City Park disappeared, shipped off for scrap for bigger weapons for a bigger war.

Our hometown paper regularly prints a popular column of excerpted local news from fifty years ago. A few weeks ago, recounting a day in December 1941, it reported the first death of a local boy in World War II.

Already now, in my mind's eye, I can recall other names that will be appearing between now and August of 1995. They are names that were mimeographed and pasted in the inside covers of our church hymnals and that were posted and changed regularly down at the front of the sanctuary and, augmented by names from the rest of the county, were painted in black letters on white plywood fastened to the northern front of the county courthouse in center square of town.

The list of names was long; the plywood boards covered most of the courthouse facade. We learned to read and to alphabetize from them. They were more real to us than the silly boy and girl and their dog, Spot, in Miss Valentine Cooper's first-grade reader. Later on, the plywood came down and the names were chiseled into granite for the gates of the memorial football field up near the high school. The high school consolidated years ago, and the stone markers have become relics like the statue of the Confederate soldier. Today's young have little reason to visit them.

When we were youngsters in the 1940s, a few Union and Confederate soldiers were yet alive across the country. We looked upon them with awe, knew their names and ages, and saluted each as he passed on, until finally there were none. It is a tribute to American standards of living and the health-care profession that thousands of World War II veterans are still around to observe the fiftieth anniversary of their big moment in history. As they sift through scrapbooks and letters, try to fit in moth-eaten uniforms, handle souvenirs, gather in reunion clusters, and revisit their pasts these next four years, they deserve an audience. They have the potential of being living textbooks for a whole generation of younger folk who do not know what global warfare was like.

At the time, World War II with its radar, sonar, atomic bombs, snorkels, and long-distance bombers seemed to be the apex of technological achievement. Surely nothing that would come afterward could top the inventions that war stimulated, we thought. Half a century later, with Desert Storm's machines fresh on our minds, World War II now seems primitive. More and more, World War II is seen as a battle of peoples for whom weaponry and gadgetry were still secondary.

At its heart, World War II was what Bill Maudlin pictured: Willie and Joe in muddy foxholes pushing foot by foot against French hedgerows and across Pacific atolls. It was what Ernie Pyle described in words: slush and drought, plodding and pounding, ordinary men and women lined up against ordinary men and women, slugging and patching repetitively.

Most of the local wars that have spotted the globe since have involved eye-to-eye battle. The only things that have changed have been the scope and scale of war. But Desert Storm was the vanguard of something new, and before the old warfare fades and disappears, the young need to hear from the old about what personalized suffering and dying were like and why progress means preventing them from happening again. The young need to ask to hear the war stories of the erstwhile warriors whom they know only as retirees, grandparents, salesmen, and factory workers. And as they listen, they need to be prepared for uncontrollable emotions.

There are some World War II veterans who have never spoken about their war, and this anniversary may unblock their memories and unseal their lips for the first time. There are others who have not missed a day remembering and reflecting. Many of them have bodily scars to remind them of how it was. All of them have mental scars. One moment they will be laughing at some obscure moment of pleasure; the next they will weep because a face or name long forgotten unexpectedly flashes up on the screen of memories.

The young need to listen hard. They ought to make 1991–95 the most universal university of all time. The young need to carry the war stories with them into the next millennium that begins at the end of this decade. They need to chew on them, digest them, and be nurtured by them. Then, when their own time for battle rolls around, as history shows it usually does, they can live off their grandparents' legacies of legends of war and maybe never have to create their own—the reason why the old folks and those listed on the courthouse plywood who died and are forever young fought in the first place.

February 3, 1992

GIRL SCOUT COOKIES AND TAXES

Two things we did with our free time this month: prepared our 1992 income tax return and waited for our Girl Scout cookies to arrive. The two are connected more than it may appear. Every year when itemizing our deductions, we have to ponder whether Girl Scout cookies are an allowable charitable deduction. We have the same question about Christmas wrapping paper purchased from the elementary school and fruit from the high school orchestra. The law allows donors to deduct that portion of the price which exceeds the actual cost of the goods or services provided. Not knowing exactly how much of the purchase price for these benefits is allowable, we usually just wind up leaving them off our claims list.

Putting together a tax return is a humbling experience. The IRS has tried to help us by simplifying the form but, even though my wife and I are college graduates, we still can't understand the instructions. We use a tax firm to verify our records and to fill out the form. The only simplification we have noted is that many of the things we used to be able to deduct no longer are deductible. We are always surprised at filing time at how much we are paying out in interest to the mortgage company (deductible) and for credit cards (nondeductible) and how little is going to reduce the principal on our home loan. We are always surprised, too, to find that we haven't been as generous to United Way and other charities as we had intended to be.

What really alarmed us this year was how much we paid out for health care. Even after paying high premiums for group insurance and supplemental hospital insurance, we wound up paying hundreds of dollars for eye, dental, and medical care not covered by insurance. No single item on our five-page list of health expenses seemed unreasonable, but when all were added together, our family opinion was that we have all died from rampant unhealthiness and no one has bothered to tell us. We feel like those voters in Georgia that President Carter tells about: they are legally allowed to continue voting for three years after their demise. We don't know if the Clintons will find solutions to the health-care-costs crisis in our country, but we applaud them for trying.

Nor do we mind being asked as a middle-income family to make a sacrifice by paying higher taxes, whether through our annual income tax return or through our property taxes. It has always struck us as a privilege, not a penalty, to support our country. If we all do our part, we can each chip away (or melt, if we each "light just one little candle") a sliver of the titanic iceberg of trillion-dollar debts that threatens our children's voyage into the next millennium, only seven years away now. We can talk about how much better health care is in Sweden or how much cheaper or better Japanese-produced goods are than our own, but the bottom line is this: everything considered, living in America is still the best bargain on the globe. Compared to the tax bills citizens in other countries pay, ours seems relatively to be a real buy for the privileges and services received. In most other countries, people would steal to have a box of Girl Scout cookies. Look at the pictures of those street urchins in Bosnia and Somalia if you want to see why American taxes are a bargain.

For our tastes, there are too many outspoken good-income soreheads picking gnats in editorial letters and television opinion spots about having to pay taxes. They seem to think, even more adamantly than do professional welfare recipients at the other end of the ladder, that living in a free society means it ought to be free to them. The mark of their patriotic pride is that they boast openly and loudly of how much they "beat Uncle Sam out of last year."

That's not a mark of patriotism; it's the mark of Cain. Some of them spend more money finding loopholes and tax shelters than the taxes they would have had to pay. We often feel that our position—that it is a pleasure and a privilege to pay our taxes—is admittedly optimistic and idealistic and is somewhat a minority opinion. We aren't so naive as not to be indignant about the indecent government skims and scams, wastes and wantonness, that Mike Wallace and a legion of others call to our frequent attention. But, overall, the considerable (for us) amount of money we hand over to our country each April 15 strikes us as a very sound investment. We remain high on buying America. It's the best investment we make for ourselves and our children's futures.

March 22, 1993

INTERSTATE FLOWERS

Circumstances brought us into North Carolina several different times in the month of May. Usually our treks were into the mountainous western section along I-26 and I-40, but one occasion took us on I-85 clear across the state.

North Carolina has become a pacesetting national leader for planting wildflower beds near the cloverleaves and rest stops of her interstate highways. This year there are acres of white daisies and golden brown-eyed Susans, some occasional plots of mixed-color poppies, and frequent patches of blue and purple flowers not easily named. But the eye-catchers of the summer in North Carolina were the red poppies. There were millions of them. They dominated the landscapes and flamed across the travelers' eyes, beckoning like the pillars of fire the Hebrews followed out of Egypt.

As both Memorial Day and D-Day approached, the choice of red poppies as the prevailing flower of choice in North Carolina struck us as peculiarly appropriate this year. Red poppies remind us of the American war dead in Europe. For those of us whose exposure to them has been in occasional purchases of the paper ones sold for veterans' causes, this epidemic appearance in North Carolina has been something at which to gasp in wonder. Flanders Field itself surely would look like a tiny home garden if set down among these miles and miles of North Carolina blossoms.

All through May the television channels became increasingly filled with D-Day "Fiftieth Anniversary" programs; somehow the highway poppies seemed a perfect fit for this occasion. The world actually knows more about D-Day fifty years after it happened than it knew then. Military censorship was so important and so effective at the time that the statistics and sweep of the greatest invasion since the 1066 Battle of Hastings were not disclosed. It has taken decades to piece together the facts. Consequently, with D-Day so belatedly entering our psyche, the weeks leading up to the memorial services this anniversary on June 6 produced unprecedented and unpredictable national mourning.

One interview made this point directly. It was a video recording of one veteran's very first conversation about what happened to him half a century ago. All of those years, he had kept bottled up inside himself the horror of what happened and of how he personally behaved under his first fire. But then, on camera, he revisited Omaha Beach and relived those minutes. Even though he had later fought bravely and won medals for his heroism, his self-image of a single first hour of cowardice, in which he had played dead on the beach, had warped his life ever afterward. For that man, the commemoration of a distant day has become a catharsis. His healing was as moving to watch as Stephen Crane's *Red Badge of Courage,* which is the very same story, is to read.

What moves us as observers of catharsis, perhaps, is a need for our own catharsis. Some impulse in the psyche of many Americans calls all of us to a collective purging. Unless there is indeed some impulse for national catharsis, it is difficult to explain why so many of us would sit so many hours glued to our television sets, or why so many others of us would make pilgrimages to Normandy beaches this D-Day.

What strikes me in all the D-Day interviews, but also in watching the behavior of us—the watchers and bystanders—is how long it takes for grief to arrive. We watch old men and women weeping who have lived half a century with dry eyes. It's almost as if life has been so busy and so consuming that we have not had time to tally our losses and costs and to reflect upon them seriously. It's almost if we could not stand the pain of remembering until now. We needed fifty years to get ready to grieve.

There is also much more than all of that to this national need to feel sad in order to feel good. When we see pictures of a whole lost generation of young men laid out upon the sands of Normandy and along the hedgerows and the French village streets, we grieve for them because they are lost as are we, lost in our own ways upon beaches and streets just as real but less noted and dramatic. Youth and innocence, one way or another, are always taken from us, and they turn out to be the possessions we remember best, rue losing most, and lament the longest and loudest.

In the fading photos and movie reels this D-Day what is truly being revealed is our simplicity. What saddens us is the realization that amid so much death, life went on, but never again as simply, courageously, and cleanly as then. There are Native American, African, and Amish peoples who refuse to be photographed, for fear the camera will capture their souls. They may have been right all along. We may have left our souls in D-Day pictures.

Or in red poppies along the busy interstates of our lives.

June 13, 1994

CONFUSING CONSERVATISM

Between "liberal" and "conservative" I have been nearer the conservative pole than the liberal.

First, I believe in learning from history. Taking history into account slows down one's activism. It is too complex to teach simple lessons.

Second, I believe that many small steps make for more effective forward motion than do a few giant leaps. Any movement forward causes unforeseen ripples somewhere else. Taking incremental steps, over the long haul, is less damaging to society than gigantic dramatic strides. Between enduring effectiveness and drama, I choose effectiveness. Punch a pillow hard and it puffs out somewhere else, but pat it gently and it has fewer lumps. Or, to choose a better metaphor, you don't see a portrait restorer doing his work with a paint roller: he uses a small brush and light strokes.

Third, I believe that conserving something implies saving it rather than destroying it. Our institutions, our laws, our ways of doing things, and our mores evolved; we didn't build this Rome, decadent though we are told it has become, in a day. We may have had cataclysmic moments along the way, time-outs for revolutions and civil war, for Depression and the civil rights movements, but progress in America (and elsewhere as well) has overall been evolutionary rather than revolutionary. One is very reluctant to trade the familiar for the unfamiliar. Generally speaking, you don't get to the artistic sculpture inside a block of marble by using a sledgehammer; you chip away patiently, deliberately, with a vision and plan and sensitivity to the grain of the rock to guide you.

Fourth, I believe in both the universal frailty of human beings and in their infinite but difficult possibilities. I think weakness, error, bad luck, and unpredictability of nature and exterior forces acting upon us make us all vulnerable, so universally so that it is easy to see why the doctrine of Original Sin has such enduring attraction. The acknowledgment of human frailty, I have believed, is a conservative trait, offsetting the stereotype of simplistic perfectibility.

Those four basic beliefs have been my self-justification for calling myself a conservative, even when I have found labels politically restrictive and debasing.

But now I am confused. The fixed order of the social universe in which I practiced my conservatism has been abruptly interrupted by others who also call themselves conservatives. In the twinkling of an eye, whether you count that as the time since the November elections or as "The Hundred Days Revolution," everything has changed. Old signposts have been removed, and old maps no longer guide. Miles of red tape have been unraveled suddenly, and its disappearance has left something sticky on everything. We find ourselves in a nation and under a government as astonishingly novel and unknown as any recently released former Communist bloc nation. All things are new, and all things have to be invented.

The most vocal spokesmen for the current social and political revolution underway in our country claim to be marching under the banner of conservatism. What troubles me is that we share the banner, but disagree on the rudimentary principles which make it meaningful. Their view of history is not mine. They don't respect history for its lessons, but for its rhetoric. To them, history is a well from which to draw selected anecdotes of past foibles in making a case for radical change. Their view of progress is not mine. They believe speed and sweeping change are more important than widespread deliberation and judgment. Their methodology is not mine. They choose the paint roller (and the steamroller) over the brush, the sledgehammer over the chisel. Their view of humanity is not mine. They see human frailty as something Darwin solved years ago through the doctrines of survival of the fittest and of species selectivity. The strong succeed, and the strong rule, and it is in the self interest of the many to let them do their thing. Ordinary people, whom Marx called the masses and whom spokesmen for conservatism as redefined today treat as herds, are there to be followers acted upon and for by a few select leaders, not to think or to act as participants.

My more sanguine friends, sensing my disorientation, try to reassure me. "The pendulum always swings back," they tell me. "Time will correct all things." "Give them enough rope and they'll hang themselves." I'm trying very hard to follow their advice. I'm trying hard to "see things in their brightest light" and to "roll with the punches" and to "put the best face on things." But my four basic beliefs have been challenged, and I am at sea in this strange new world where what I called conservative is now called liberal and what conservative spokesmen call conservative strikes me as radical, revolutionary, and risky.

July 17, 1995

SMALL COLLEGE AND BIG-TIME SPORTS

Among America's thirty-four hundred campuses, Wofford College with its enrollment of eleven hundred students is, by numerical standards, relatively small potatoes. It may be the smallest NCAA Division I member. Yet its basketball team opened its season this winter against Missouri, Vanderbilt, and North Carolina State, and will face Auburn, Army, South Carolina, Clemson, and Navy by February. The first preseason polls ranked Wofford 305th, at the very bottom of the list. The next ones, still before the season started, moved them into a three-way tie for 301st place. For sheer bravery in scheduling alone, it deserves to be 300th or better.

The courage of the diminutive campus for playing Little David against Goliaths of basketball such as Georgia Tech, Wake Forest, Tennessee, and Colorado in 1995, many of them nationally ranked, has been duly applauded. In most cases, Wofford makes respectable showings. For example, against second-ranked Wake Forest, Tim Duncan was held to under ten points for the only time this year. Game after game, the Terriers hurl slingshot pebbles at giants; usually, they are sent back to playing their harps.

However, there is an anomaly in their record. Against the military schools they have faced thus far—Navy (on Pearl Harbor Day), Army, and

Virginia Military Institute—they have actually won! On Washington's birthday (himself a military leader), they play Air Force. The football team started the trend of defeating the military schools by beating the Citadel in November near the end of its season, just as the basketball team was beginning fall practice. That streak of victories against the military academies is cause for pause. How is it possible for a little college, fresh out of NCAA Division II and new in Division I circles, to do so well against institutions that enjoy the full backing of the U.S. Department of Defense? What do four consecutive defeats at a minor power's hands tell us about the condition of the nation's military preparedness?

The British used to boast that their wars were won on the playing fields of Eton, the prep school from which many leaders went on to Sandhurst, their military academy. A great many of the great names among our own nation's generals and admirals played some sport or another at one of our nation's military academies.

And, to be truthful, those institutions have not really fared poorly in overall wins and losses in their sports schedules. Wofford's winning streak against the military is a quirk.

What the American defense establishment has been learning ever since Korea—in the Falklands, Vietnam, Iraq, or Bosnia—is that small wars in small nations have replaced global world wars as a way of warring.

Complex and large though they were, World Wars I and II (which Lawrence Welk called "World War i-i"), like Grant's campaign to take Richmond in the Civil War, caused us to plan and act in massive mobilization terms. In large wars, throw enough men and matériel into the conflict, and sheer weight of numbers will soon silence the enemy.

Such truisms of warfare don't always hold when geography and objectives of battle are more limited. The British learned that when they sent ranks of well-dressed, well-drilled, and well-fed soldiers against scruffy, retreating, American volunteers in the Revolution and in the War of 1812. The North learned that in the 1860s, when it took four years to end a war that most northerners thought would be over in six months.

Perhaps the point to be made is that the nation and the world need to brace themselves for a far different kind of warring in the twenty-first century than it knew from Napoleon's days through World War II. The inevitable wars that lie ahead—much as all of us pray that there will be none—are likely to involve small, little-known opponents who use restraint, patience, and diplomacy as weapons as well as men and armaments.

I doubt that the defense establishment has learned that lesson from its military academies suffering defeat at the hands of little Wofford College. But perhaps the pattern of Wofford's winning streak can serve them and us as a symbol of our need nationally to be vigilant and armed, but flexible and patient as well. Little underdogs like the Terriers can pack vicious bites, and even when they seem to be losing, they keep coming back for more.

December 3, 1995, and February 17, 1997

FRANKLIN DELANO ROOSEVELT

America waited almost too long before it finally put up a monument to Franklin Roosevelt. Fifty-two years have passed since he died and sixty-four years since he took office. The number of us who remember him is dwindling fast. The FDR Memorial has been a matter of controversy for years. Early on, there were squabbles about whether to have a memorial at all. FDR himself had said he didn't want one, and if there was to be one, then it ought to be a block of stone about the size of his desk. Designs were submitted, only to get lost somewhere in committee.

Now the memorial is at last in place, appropriately near the Jefferson Memorial. Jefferson and FDR are the bookends of the Democratic Party, and it is well that they are saluted together. The FDR site is also appropriately near the river, for FDR was assistant secretary of the navy in World War I and always considered himself a seaman. The design seems fittingly spacious and inspiring, despite detractors who want FDR's seldom-seen wheelchair displayed conspicuously or his omnipresent cigarette holder in his statue's hand or his crushed hat on his head,

FDR would relish the bickering. He often stirred it up himself.

Marble monument aside, FDR built and left his own monument. The whole nation was his legacy and tribute. He saw it through its roughest times: the Great Depression that wasn't so great for those alive then, and World War II.

My first recollection of FDR is of a photo of him over the double bed (with feather mattress) in my grandparents' living room. Actually, their living room had two double beds, their own and one for guests, with cane-bottom chairs nearer the fireplace for sitting. The other room of the house, across a dogtrot that had become the central hall, was a second bedroom with fireplace, reserved for two bachelor uncles. A dining room and kitchen had been tacked on to the back, making the house L-shaped. One washed-up on the back porch, bathed in a galvanized tub in the yard in summer and in the dining room in winter. There was no indoor plumbing or electricity. The only wire to the house led to a crank phone, hung by the fireplace. About five o'clock each evening my grandfather would hook up a radio to a Delco battery and listen to the news.

But then came TVA. That framed picture of FDR was stuck into a corner of a map of TVA. The farmhouse was five miles from the Tennessee River, the part of it turned into Kentucky Lake by TVA dams. After TVA, another wire came into the house, and there was then a single ceiling light suspended in the middle of the bedroom–living room. My grandfather was a lifelong Democrat, county chairman of the party for thirty-three years and a delegate to the 1944 convention that nominated FDR and Harry Truman. He was on a first-name basis with Jim Farley, FDR's party chairman and postmaster general. The naked lightbulb burning after sundown was more of a symbol than a utility. I suspect it was the monument my grandfather installed to honor FDR. With it turned on, one could see that picture of FDR at night.

FDR is remembered not only for TVA but also for a whole parade of alphabet agencies he initiated in his crusade to end the Depression. Many of them failed, of course, but what was most praiseworthy was his willingness, with life at a standstill and slipping backward in America, to try anything to restore people's self-confidence and to get momentum going again. People knew that he cared and that he was trying, and they elected him again and again. His encouraging words lifted the nation (as Churchill's did war-torn Britain) more than did his agencies.

FDR had been president three years by the time I was born, and I was almost nine when he died in April 1945, a month before Germany surrendered. We were living in town across from an old elementary school, and I sat listening to the funeral descriptions coming over the radio. Arthur Godfrey was one of the commentators. Looking out the front door as I listened, I seemed to see FDR's profile in the accidental design formed by the bricks of the schoolhouse lunchroom. Last year I drove over to that now-vacant Lee School building. The design is still there—or perhaps it is there only in my mind, transposed upon the bricks.

The radio that April day played FDR's favorite song over and over. It was "Home on the Range." I pondered for years why this wheelchair-using easterner who loved the sea would have made a western horse-riding song his favorite. The opening of the FDR Memorial gave me the answer. It is the song's second line: "Where seldom is heard a discouraging word, and the skies are not cloudy all day."

June 2, 1997

CONFEDERATE FLAG CONTROVERSY

My reason for wanting the Confederate battle flag removed from the South Carolina capitol is personal and not compelling. Two great-great-grandfathers fought and four great-great-great uncles were killed for the South, but when the war ended their families rejoiced. In later years they hated South Carolina for seceding and starting the war almost as much as they hated Yankees. Most Confederates that fought had not voted to secede. The flag today is a symbol to many true-blue southern families of the price the South paid for fire-eating extremism. Many Confederate descendants want that symbol of South Carolina rashness removed. But that is only an emotional opinion and therefore not a valid reason for its removal.

The battle over the Confederate battle flag atop the South Carolina capitol building (but only since 1962) has created a war of extremes rivaling the real Civil War in which that flag flew and was furled. One side says the flag is a painful reminder of slavery, or that flying it is causing non-Carolina industries not to establish themselves in the state, or that tourists and conventions are boycotting the state and hurting the economy, or that the South surrendered the flag when it lost in 1865 and has no legal right to fly it, or that it is one of several battle flags of the Confederacy and not the official national flag, or that the heritage of the flag has been soiled by inappropriate postwar uses by supremacists or profit-making companies pandering to truck-stop sales. The other side says the flag has nothing to do with race or slavery (and that the war didn't either), or that it commemorates dead and wounded who sacrificed themselves in that war, or that it is a symbol of states' rights, or that removing it would place economic pressure over principle.

We are talking here about a piece of cloth and about the awful polarization between normally peaceful and compatible people it is causing. Symbols are very potent things: many of us despised the swastika of Germany and the rising sun of Japan in World War II; the unlighted Statue of Liberty became a symbol as we fought for "lights to go on again, all over the world." Historians tell how the Mongol invasion of the west was halted when a pope carrying a cross met the invaders. Duke fans go bananas over being in Cameron Field House. Symbols are powerful.

Both extremes are "rallying around the flag," but when careful observers of this new civil war count noses, what they report is that most people are not enlisting on either side. Most thoughtful folks, and folks are increasingly thoughtful about this issue, are anxious for a compromise that removes this issue from public acrimony and anger, perhaps by removing the flag from the building but displaying it at some appropriate heritage site or among all the flags that have flown over the state. Most people want peace, not a symbolic war.

The best argument for removing the flag is not that it is a symbol of either racism or of heroes, but that it is a symbol of our present-day inability to get along with one another. Polarization is paralyzing public progress and preventing the creating of a civil, caring community. Real issues of substance—educating our children, sharing prosperity, erasing crime, repairing roads and infrastructures, being global good citizens, facing ecological disaster, electing better public officials—are going unattended while a war of words escalates into a war of worlds.

This isn't a football game or a childhood "Capture the Flag" game where we choose sides and then get together afterward to cook hot dogs or drink Kool-Aid. The stakes are much higher. The Confederate flag has never been dishonored as much as it is when we let it come between us as a symbol for twenty-first-century divisiveness and self-destructive delay in building a better society.

Whatever spectacular Confederate charges and stands you recall, remember that there was enormous thanksgiving on both sides when the war ended, and that veterans remembered gratefully being allowed to keep their horses for plowing and their rifles for hunting. They honored their furled flag by setting about building a better South. They honored it by getting on with creating schools and churches and jobs and government.

"We" lost the war; don't lose the peace. For peace's sake, let the flag rest in peace.

February 27, 2000

THE CSS HUNLEY

Around 9:00 P.M. on February 17, 1864, the USS *Housatonic,* a 207-foot Union sloop of war bearing twelve large guns at rest three miles out past the breakers near Charleston Harbor, was rocked by an explosion and capsized and sank with a loss of two officers and three seamen.

It was sunk by an explosive attached to its hull by men aboard the CSS *Hunley,* one of the first successful war submarines. Its mission successfully completed, the *Hunley* made for its dock at Breach Inlet. Its signal of return was sighted, but it never arrived. Discovered off Charleston Bay in 1995, the *Hunley's* raising this month has captured the nation's imagination.

During the Civil War at least two dozen submarines were designed and built by both sides. As with other Civil War evolutions—including repeating rifles, trench warfare, land mines, underwater mines, battlefield telegraphs, railway networks for moving troops and supplies, and observation balloons—submarines presaged a seismic shift in warfare as the world would discover almost half a century later. Submarine warfare would be critical in both World Wars.

The *Hunley* had sunk at least twice before its final sinking. Built in Mobile, it was launched in July 1863, with successful subsequent demonstrations of its potential value. The submarine was transferred to Charleston, which was commanded by General P. G. T. Beauregard. By late August it was being tested and manned by sailors and soldiers rather than civilians. On August 29, commanded by Lt. John Payne and manned by eight other seamen, an accident occurred that caused the submarine to rise and then sink, drowning five of the men. On September 13, the vessel was raised. Supervisory command passed to one of the *Hunley's* original designers and owners, Horace Hunley, a Tennessean who had been involved in submarine work at New Orleans and Mobile. Hunley arrived from Mobile with a crew of volunteers, men who had built and then tested the vessel. On October 15, Capt. Hunley took the boat out for another in a series of tests. Hunley and seven men died when the submarine sank again. Hunley was not even supposed to be in command. Lt. George E. Dixon was in charge of tests and operations but was absent that morning.

Raised again, this time on November 7, the CSS *Hunley* received its name, honored the dead Horace Hunley, and passed into the hands of Lieutenant Dixon. After training and tests at the nation's first submarine school in Mount Pleasant, South Carolina, it was declared ready for service on December 14, 1863. Its blasting device was redesigned, involving a spar on the boat's box rather than an explosive trolled by a line. Two months later, in its first battle mission, the *Hunley*, with Lieutenant Dixon commanding, sank. All hands were lost. When the *Hunley* is X-rayed and then opened in its new resting place on shore, they may be found.

Oddly enough, these first submarines were viewed by most authorities as "infernal" and illegal instruments of war, weapons beyond the realm of conventional "civilized" warfare and their crews punishable by death. (What war was ever "civilized"? Sherman would have laughed at the concept.) In retrospect, after more grisly warfare in the twentieth century with submarine fleets becoming commonplace, that view has changed.

The CSS *Hunley* and its drowned crews from its three sinkings are subjects of some awe now. The courage of perhaps as many as forty drowned men, some of whom had seen bodies recovered from previous sinkings of their ill-fated craft, willing to enter the deep waters and to risk their lives and futures astonishes us decades after the event.

Psalm 107 foretells such naval gallantry and seemingly foolhardy daring as that on the *Hunley:* "Some went down to the sea in ships. . . . They mounted up to heaven, they went down to the depths; their courage melted away in their evil plight; they reeled and staggered like drunken men, and were at their wits' end. Then they cried to the Lord in their trouble. . . ."

The sailors in the psalm were rescued when they called upon God. Those in the *Hunley* had no such happy ending, except perhaps belated salutes they are receiving this year.

August 13, 2000

QUEST FOR IDEALISM

Last year a "Man of the Century" was chosen for the twentieth century. I can't recall if it was Albert Einstein or Adolph Hitler. I had nominated Franklin Roosevelt. But who should we pick as the main figure of the last thousand years? With the second millennium ending and the third beginning, who should we pick as the "Man (or Woman) of the Millennium"? After much thought, I've settled on a man who wasn't even a real person but a character from fiction.

Don Quixote.

Most folks recognize Quixote as the Man of la Mancha who sang of dreaming the impossible dream and fighting the unbeatable foe. The Broadway musical Quixote was drawn from Cervantes's epic story, a story of astonishing influence on many of the great writers of our world. Flaubert drew heavily on the bumbling knight for *Madam Bovary;* Dostoyevsky patterned Prince Myshkin after him in *The Idiot;* Faulkner uses him over and over again, especially in *Light in August,* the "Hunting Stories," *The Sound and the Fury,* and a dozen memorable characters; Mark Twain made Huckleberry Finn a quixotic embodiment and Tom Sawyer his interpreter; the Nashville Agrarians bent upon salvaging the best of the Old South from the debris of modern industrialism implicitly depended upon Quixote; Walker Percy uses him in several works, including *The Last Gentleman;* and he is even influential in Ralph Ellison's *Invisible Man.*

Beyond literature, Don Quixote's importance is that he is the symbol of all well-intentioned idealists, symbolic in his willingness to don in old age the rusted armor from his youth and to go forth to do battle for righteous causes such as chivalry, civility, honor, and dignity, and symbolic in his self-delusion that he is able to set all things right.

Quixote challenges each of us as much as he challenges a windmill that he mistakes for a giant or a herd of sheep that he mistakes for an army. He raises the troubling questions of our humanity: what things are worth doing battle for? Is honor possible in a compromising and crass world? Do the good guys always lose, and what is meant by "losing" anyways?

The best people of the last thousand years have been those with ideals and a willingness to take risks for those ideals. More often than not, even the best people have fallen short in living up to their ideals. The more important thing has been getting up and trying again, jousting for justice and swashbuckling for sensitivity, crusading for conscience and reconnoitering for rationality.

Don Quixote reminds us that to err is human, but that it is also human to try to do one's best, to try to leave a footprint of nobility upon the scarred world, to try to make a difference for good. He falls but rises again. Even when his bones creak as loudly as his rusty armor, he tries.

Keep honor alive. Life without daily crusades for the right is not worth living.

December 31, 2000

SOUTHERN BLACK CONSCRIPTION

Recent controversy over the Confederate flag reignited a smoldering debate. The question at issue is whether the South seceded from the Union in order to preserve slavery. The issue has been around for one-and-a-third centuries, and the answer to the question of whether the Confederacy was formed to protect slavery is both "yes" and "no."

Today's debaters might consider a little-noted chapter of Confederate history. When the South's eastern army was trying to recover from its crushing defeat at Gettysburg and its western army was retreating from Chattanooga toward Atlanta, Major General Patrick R. Cleburne drafted a "Proposal to Make Soldiers of Slaves and Guarantee Freedom to All Loyal Negroes."

Cleburne was considered one of the best southern generals. Irish-born, Cleburne had joined the British army in order to have a livelihood and had seen military duty for several years. He and his family migrated to America during the great Irish famines, and he settled in Helena, Arkansas, as a pharmacist and then as a lawyer. When the Civil War came, Cleburne was elected colonel of the 1st Arkansas, later designated the 15th Arkansas. Conspicuous gallantry and military ability led to steady rise in rank, and after Ringgold, Georgia, where he and a small unit of soldiers held a gap that allowed the rebel army to escape, he was the "Stonewall of the West."

He had been wounded three times by then. His bravery and patriotism were unquestioned, and his records at Shiloh, Perryville, Chickamauga, and in other battles were sterling. He was in line to be a corps commander like Jackson and Longstreet. His career was stalemated after his January 2, 1864, proposal to arm slaves and to free them and their families.

Cleburne wrote his proposal during a time of great gloom. Major defeats in 1863 at Gettysburg and Vicksburg were followed by the loss of Chattanooga. Union forces by then occupied a third of the southern territory, desertions were high and army morale was low, supplies and arms and means for transporting them were almost exhausted, and England and France had refused to recognize the South. Cleburne knew that if the South played out its losing cards, the game was over. Cleburne maintained that the cause for which he and hundreds of thousands of other nonslaveholding southerners had been fighting was independence. He saw the war, as did many, as like that of the colonies seeking independence from England.

As the war escalated, it became clear that southern independence and southern slaveholding were twisted together in ways almost impossible to separate. Cleburne's proposal was an attempt to separate them. Freeing slaves would increase the manpower of the diminished armies, would hasten recognition by England and Europe, would remove the North's major motivation for fighting, would remove the fear of slave uprisings from the army's rear, and would secure southern independence as a separate nation.

Most of Cleburne's own officers endorsed the proposal, and it was given a hearing by the top officers of the western army headed by Joseph Johnston. Opinion was divided, and some called it "treason." Johnston ordered the proposal tabled, but General William H. T. Walker disobeyed Johnston and sent a copy to President Jefferson Davis. Davis forbade debate on grounds that slavery was a matter for each state to consider, not the central government.

Ironically, a year later Robert E. Lee advocated an almost identical plan. By then governors of Louisiana and Virginia and many others were favoring Cleburne's plan, and in January 1865 Lee revived and endorsed Cleburne's idea. As late as April 2, a week before he surrendered, Lee was still pushing the reluctant Davis to adopt it. It was too little, too late.

Cleburne did not live to taunt his fire-eater enemies with "I told you so." Obedient to orders, he ceased discussion of his proposal and followed Hood into the folly of Franklin, where he and five other Confederate generals died.

January 21, 2001

Chapter 6

FOOD
"THOU PREPAREST A TABLE FOR ME"

PIGS

Are you one of us who gets sentimental about hog-killing season? Hog-killing season is fast becoming a country memory that sets city mouths to watering and longing to go back to the farms their fathers left. It is a season of friendships around the boiling pots, a romantic season that distance embellishes.

Hog-killing time is that season of the year after the first frosts when most people are talking about Thanksgiving and Christmas, furnaces, leaf raking, antifreeze, and pumpkin pies. For others of us, however, it's a time of chitlings, souse, crackling bread, fatback, lard, sausage, hams, pork chops, and barbecue. From a safe distance, one can see the steam from the boiling pots of water where the hog-killing teams do their work. I emphasize distance because the process and odors aren't much to get all sentimental about.

The lone hog-killing I attended was at my grandparents' place one November. I've spent too many years forgetting the details to share them with you now. In fact, although the products of that process are in very good taste, the details aren't, so consider yourself spared. If you want to stay sentimental about good ol' hog-killing season, stay away from hog-killings.

Like most hog-killing sentimentalists, I pretend to enjoy chitlings and souse. The truth is that I think it is a southern form of social snobbery to eat them, just like those New Yorkers smack their lips about eating escargot. Do people really enjoy chitlings or snails? Maybe so; to each his own. In my own limited taste range, however, nothing compares with slow-smoked barbecue or a baked two-year smoked ham. Fried country ham center cuts with biscuits and red-eye gravy are for people who also like grits. I'll hold out for baked old ham, please. And for holidays, add yeast rolls and oyster casserole.

My problem is that some fox has been in the smokehouses and all the two-year hams and most of the one-year ones are gone. No ham is decent eating until it has hung and dripped itself out through a "summer sweat." The best ones have little white spots in them. A friend of mine sent two old hams north to some folks who had entertained him. They wrote back that they appreciated the gift, but had to throw both hams away because they had white spots in them. That's as bad as the northern visitor who tells the southern waitress he'd like to order "a grit."

With the smokehouses empty, I have learned to settle for those quick-cure hams that have been pressurized and painted with liquid smoke. There's just enough flavor to one of those to make me daydream fondly of that one time in Kentucky when our host served a five-year ham that literally melted when placed on a tongue. The only strange thing about Kentuckian ham habits, incidentally, is that they serve it with something called "beaten biscuit," little biscuits so hard they must have been petrified in a sailing ship voyage around Cape Horn a century ago and saved to serve today. Kentucky spoon bread, on the other hand, is something extra special.

As for pork barbecue, I must have been forty before I realized that barbecue came in any form other than pork. When I was a high school carhop, we shouted "pig in a poke" to order a barbecue pork sandwich in a paper bag to go. I tried that phrase at a take-out restaurant recently, and the order boy said, "How about beef? Ain't got no po'k." No po'k? I'll concede that other things, swabbed with store-bought sauce, are called barbecue. I've gnawed my share of mutton and goat and ripped chicken off its bones with a gusto that matches that of Henry VIII. Maybe a rose by any other name is still a rose, but barbecue is pork, or it just isn't barbecue.

When meat rationing ended after World War II, homefolks rushed to build backyard barbecue pits.

Actually, they weren't "pits" at all. Most "pit barbecue" never gets anywhere near a pit. These were open-hearth constructs on top of the ground. These first-effort homemade postwar pits were usually inverted U-shaped affairs of two sides of stones or cinder blocks about three feet high, cemented together, with a chimney in the bend of the U. Metal bars were laid across the stones half-way up, and a grill could be made by placing metal sheets or mesh on top of the bars. A wood fire would be stoked on the open ground beneath the grill, and once it had burned down and charcoal bricks had been added to it, the cooking could begin. More sophisticated techniques replaced these do-it-yourself fireplaces. One favorite device was a fifty-four-gallon oil drum, sliced vertically in two halves, then hinged on one seam and mounted on metal legs, with mesh grill on the bottom half, a precursor of expensive commercial smokers and of inexpensive metal saucer-shaped grills popular today. My recollection of those 1940s pits is that the food cooked far too rapidly and usually flamed and charred. It also tasted strongly of charcoal-lighter fluid. Side dishes of pork 'n' beans, coleslaw, potato salad, watermelon, pound cake, and hand-churned ice cream tended to outshine hamburgers, hot dogs, steaks, ribs, and chickens cremated on homemade grills.

Real barbecuing in those days was in the hands of professionals, men and women whose families had made their living by cooking for others for generations. I worked through high school days for one such entrepreneur. Once a week we would stoke with hickory logs a huge metal oven in a shed and baste pork butts all day long. He spoiled it all by insisting on chopping the barbecue into little cubes and soaking it in red tomato sauce. It was delicious pulled loose and fresh off the pit and eaten with one's fingers, but awful stuff when prepared for sandwiches. On our days off, we would disloyally use our hoarded tip money to buy better barbecue at Redmond's or the River Road Inn.

In the summer months, we also occasionally catered huge annual picnics for several hundred employees of the local carburetor plant or for members of the Farm Bureau, as well as smaller feasts for the Rotary Club and its spouses. On those occasions, we did indeed dig pits for barbecuing. Actually the pits were long trenches about eighteen inches wide and six inches deep with mesh wire across the tops. On them, we mostly simmered and basted chicken halves for about eight or ten hours, although we also used them to cook corn on the cob and to reheat pre-prepared barbecued pork. The secret of the barbecuing taste, of course, is in the simmering, the hickory smoke, and the basting. Most amateur backyard cooks just don't have the equipment or the patience to let the meat cook slowly enough, and it winds up with hard exteriors and cold interiors. True barbecue will literally fall off the bone of its own accord.

While there may be few expert barbecue cooks left—and their number dwindles daily, faster than tailors and plumbers—the southland is filled with people who know their barbecue eating. I have friends aplenty who can be blindfolded and fed assorted samples of barbecued pork and iden-tify not only from whence came the barbecue but often who barbecued it. Southerners may only play at being wine connoisseurs, but they take their barbecue seriously; it is a high art form. The diversity of barbecue tastes is astounding. Regional cook-offs have become more competitive than trac-tor pulls or county-fair baking contests, and may have replaced baseball as the South's national sport or church as the region's religion. Arguments between vinegar-based, tomato-based, and mustard-based pork proponents are more heated than old-time court square squabbles among Methodists, Baptists, and Campbellites. That doesn't even get into the more esoteric side of the debates—over the alleged virtues of beef or mutton versus pork, or over the apostasies of barbecuing shrimp, trout, or possum.

Yet despite the splits among us that barbecue arguments cause, its most miraculous quality is its ability to pull us together. Again, the religious metaphor helps us understand this mystery. We may each have our own idea of God, and we may align ourselves with particular denominations, but when pressed really hard, we overcome our particularities and come together as one in believing in God. We may have particular and even peculiar tastes in barbecue, but press southerners hard enough and we will admit that it is one surefire thing we all love in common despite its variety of forms.

So, at this Thanksgiving and hog-killing time of the year, I want to pause in grateful salute to the Porkys and Petunias of the world that have made my good taste possible and made a pig out of me. Thermopylae and the Alamo sacrifices are small in numbers compared to all the mamma pigs that have cast their swine before pearly teeth.

November 8, 1982, and July 8, 1996

MINT JULEPS

Northerners think we all drink juleps before and after three meals of grits a day.

A great debate in the South centers on the correct way to make a mint julep. I recently acquired two rare little books on mint juleps and a modern recipe from a member of the bar. At the same time, I uncovered a forsaken mint bed growing by our backdoor. With fear and trembling upon entering a controversy I can't win, I shall distill (pardon the term) some of what I have read about this uniquely southern drink, the mint julep, rivaled only by iced tea and moonshine as the South's national beverage.

Scholars disagree on its age and its place of birth. The most definitive study of the mint julep is a little book by Richard Barksdale Harwell called *The Mint Julep,* first published in a very limited edition in the mid-1960s by the Beehive Press of Savannah and reprinted in 1975 by the University Press of Virginia. Harwell finds variations of the word "julep" in almost every language. Usually it just means "simple syrup," which all old sodajerks will recognize as thick syrup made from sugar and warm water.

The late Joseph C. Graves, an amateur printer from Lexington, Kentucky, claimed "the classical receipt" was that of J. Soule Smith, Lexington lawyer and journalist (1848–1904), first published in the 1890s in *Kentucky Whiskies.* Graves published this version in a handsome version on his Gravesend Press in 1949:

Take from the cold spring some water, pure as angels are; mix it
with sugar until it seems like oil. Then take a glass and crush your
mint within it with a spoon—crush it around the borders of the
glass and leave no place untouched. Then throw the mint away, it
is a sacrifice. Fill with cracked ice the glass; pour in the quantity
of Bourbon which you want. It trickles slowly through the ice. Let
it have time to cool, then pour your sugared water over it. No
spoon is needed, no stirring is allowed—just let it stand a
moment. Then around the brim place sprigs of mint, so that the
one who drinks may find a taste and odor at one draught.

A friend who is a member of the bar in Rock Hill, South Carolina, uses Bill Samuels's formula (Mr. Samuels being the owner of Maker's Mark bourbon): "Pile small mint leaves, no stems or large leaves, in a big pile on an old, well-washed tee shirt. No other cloth works as well. Make a simple syrup by boiling two cups of sugar in a cup of water. Pour some bourbon in a separate container. Pour the syrup in the bottle with the remaining bourbon, seven parts bourbon to one of syrup. Pick up the tee shirt to form a ball and dip it in the poured bourbon removed earlier. Then squeeze the saturated ball several times over a bowl to get mint drops. Pour some of this extract into the bottle of bourbon and syrup, until it meets your taste. Put the bottle in the freezer until it gets thick. Fill glasses with crushed ice and stick sprigs of mint into the ice, and then pour the bourbon mix over it."

Traditionally, juleps are served in silver cups. Harwell thinks the silver cup tradition began when William Heyward Trappier of South Carolina visited New College at Oxford University in 1845, introduced students to mint juleps, endowed an annual Mint Julep Day at New College (each June 1), and left an engraved silver cup (five and a half inches high) from which the students could drink. A more likely story is that drinkers in horse-racing country (Kentucky and Virginia) had to do something with the silver cups they won at horse shows and races.

Pre–Civil War versions of the drink used every kind of liquor—rum, brandy, apricot, and peach liqueurs. After the war, southerners had to rely on homemade liquor, and corn whiskey was the most available; that has become the only acceptable standard. Heated and extended arguments have raged over the right liquor to use, the proper amount of syrup to add, whether to crush the leaves or not, the kind of water and shape of ice and choice of glass or cup. *Gourmet* magazine carried on a readership debate for five years, from 1963 to 1968, when other magazines were devoted to Vietnam or campus turmoil.

Harwell thinks the definitive word on mint juleps came from "Marse Henry" Watterson, a famous Louisville editor: "Pluck the mint gently from its bed, just as the dew of the evening is about to form upon it. Select the choicer sprigs only, but do not rinse them. Prepare the simple syrup and measure out a half tumbler of whiskey. Pour the whiskey into a well-frosted silver cup. Throw the other ingredients away and drink the whiskey."

July 12, 1983

SODA FOUNTAINS

"Doc" Lawson, a pharmacist here for decades, passed away last month. With him passed a living history book. He embodied the town's business and memory, a man who had spent a lifetime talking and listening to his fellow citizens at his drugstore. There was a time in Dr. Lawson's heyday, not long ago, when drugstore tables at soda fountains served local communities in the same way cracker barrels and potbellied stoves in general stores used to serve rural communities.

Drugstores were gathering places for the community, male or female, where the news was shared and interpreted, and even where news was prophesied and fulfilled. They were forums for democracy, places where people met and conducted the important function of expressing opinions, setting the civic tone, and reaching consensus. They were places where doctor met patient on neutral ground, where minister and local agnostic traded coffee and repartee with impunity, and where local youngsters on the counter stools or in the back booths were kept under surveillance as they courted under the public eye. The "cowboys" at the pinball machine stood away from the coffee crowd.

They served other functions, of course—one went there to get a bottle of Evening in Paris for one's mother at Christmas, or to get free medical advice from the pharmacist, or to catch a quick lunch, but the real business in the drugstore business was the service as a community center. Other places served a similar purpose but not quite as well. Courthouse benches were gathering places but were occupied mostly by retired men and never by any of the ladies of the town. The same was true of barbershops, although the men were more mixed in age, or of beauty parlors for the womenfolk. But drugstores were open to both sexes, to young and old, and were visited daily rather than just every other week.

In the early days of America, there was in most towns something similar to drugstores. Usually the local apothecary was in a store next to a community reading room with its small library and current newspapers. Both the reading room and the apothecary were near a coffeehouse. As time passed, the three functions combined to become drugstores. At the front of the store were magazine racks and newspaper counters. The old reading-room habit of reading there persisted, despite the sign warning people to buy rather than read the literature located there. Get information up front, and talk it over in the back. Between the newsstand up front and the back tables were the marble and mahogany soda fountain and six to ten revolving stools. Soda fountains were works of art, beautifully built, sort of indoor fairyland fantasies come true. And the confections and concoctions that came across the marble counter were also works of art. One of the best I recall was Candyland, in Nashville.

My own fantasy is to get one of these fountains and to turn my basement into an old-fashioned ice-cream parlor, complete with small marble-top tables and wire-back ice-cream chairs. A less selfish fantasy, however, is to dream of drugstores returning to downtown, as all the towns continue their current sincere efforts at restoring local architecture and at reviving downtown shop business. Most of the new malls out at the edges of towns are modern, miniature court squares. But they don't serve the same function for the community. Turnover of customers is more important than customers who just sit, sip, and gossip.

Maybe the economy doesn't allow our society the luxury of drugstore gathering places anymore. They do take up space, which costs a lot to own or rent, and regular customers buy very little except a cup of coffee or a cherry coke. But what they meant in conducting the business of the community, by involving so many people in sharing their public concerns and private lives with one another, is something lost that badly needs replacing. The pharmacist served the physical health of the town, and his soda fountain served its spiritual, intellectual, and governmental health—an irreplaceable combination of health services. So, to my list of meeting places to revive in America—such as passenger trains, tent meetings, neighborhood post offices, downtown libraries, graveyard cleanings, and wakes—I put downtown soda fountains as a top priority.

Banana splits may be the cure to community splits.

January 2, 1984

COUNTRY COOKING

We love country cooking, and we love people who share that love and heritage. A freshman student from Kentucky showed up this fall to enroll in our college; having been in touch with her, her mother, and her grandmother, I was startled to find three gift bags from them—one of packaged minced country ham, one of country ham trimmings for cooking with vegetables, and the third a big center cut of country ham—all from Broadbent Hams of Cadiz, Kentucky, the perennial Kentucky State Fair winner for best country hams. The prize Broadbent ham this year allegedly sold for eighty thousand dollars, so I estimated this gift was worth about fifteen hundred dollars. After tasting it, I knew it was. A senior student's mother periodically sends me home-baked bread. The most recent loaf arrived just in time to eat with the last slab of ham. Because the food is so great, I love the hands that prepare it.

A longtime friend from my hometown gave us a whole ham when we moved from Tennessee to South Carolina, and I hung it in our basement to cure a bit longer. By the time I got around to cooking it, it was twelve years old. If a two-year-old ham is a treasure, I could hardly wait to see how good my twelve-year-old ham was. We boiled it and baked it and did all the right things, and after trimming its outer fat, I set in to slicing it. The knife broke. After breaking a barbecue fork and another knife, I discovered that the ham had petrified; it had turned to stone.

In today's fast-food and frozen-food world, country cooking has become a rare art form, and efforts to imitate it and resurrect it often turn to stone, but it is a cause worth fighting to preserve. The recent war-like atmosphere of our lives dregs up memories of other times and other sacrifices. In all of them, food played important roles. Those of us young during World War II rationing recall how scarce were things like Hershey bars and ice cream.

Those of us with grandparents and parents who lived through the Depression recall how independent of grocery stores and restaurants our ancestors were. In times when there were no autos to be bought or gasoline on hand to operate them, life focused on family and food. My grandmother never bought anything from grocery stores except flour, sugar, salt, pepper, and baking powder. The milk, corn meal, meats, poultry, eggs, vegetables, fruits, and syrups were all homegrown. Sunday dinner at grandmother's, now that it is no longer available and old age and infirmity won't allow us to eat that well, is my idea of what Heaven must be. What made each Sunday dinner perfect was not the taste but its constancy—something to count on in an uncertain world, a linking of family generations with one another even as they linked with earlier generations long dead or family members living too far away to be there, as well as strangers drifting in and out. In our memories, we devour anew the love at that huge table—love of food and love of family.

In memory, we dine again on white-specked slices of baked old ham laid next to turkey piled upon dressing and drenched in giblet gravy surrounded by a wagon train of sweet potatoes, new potatoes in cream, turnip greens, butter beans, corn, greasy beans, spiced peaches, cornbread sticks, biscuits, and churned butter, followed by pecan and egg custard pies, fruit cobblers and pound cake and boiled custard.

In memory, too, we dine together—four of us daily in town, and twenty-four of us on Sundays out in the country. Never alone, never in a car seat at a drive-through, never at a TV tray. There is no more lonely and meaningless act than eating alone. The great social events of our lives today are eating with people who relish the same foods and memories of foods past that we have.

A friend and I, returning from a funeral in Georgia, hit Atlanta at lunchtime, and I introduced him to Mary Mac's, a country-cooking restaurant nestled amid skyscrapers. The waiter brought two plates with samples of the fourteen vegetables—fried green tomatoes, creamed fresh corn, squash, macaroni, butter beans, green beans, black-eyed peas. We devoured the samples, then stuffed ourselves with country fried steak and two more vegetables, cornbread, and yeast rolls—and sweet potato cobbler for dessert. Gluttony seemed exactly the right thing to balance grief, a groping for love, and we understood something we had grown up knowing—that food and funerals go together because family and friends gather for both.

My favorite local restaurant is short on atmosphere but long on home cooking. The only way my wife will agree to go there is to promise her she can order chicken livers. Last week, when she was out of town, I went alone. I like the greasy vegetables and cornbread. At the entrance is a bulletin board. A gourmet restaurant would post that day's menu there. This place uses the space for a poster called "First Aid for Choking."

I have never been there when there wasn't a crowd. The place would never win a prize for décor or ventilation. The only thing that keeps the flies away is that the customers don't leave room for them. The secret of its success is fast service of home-style food. Biscuits, gravy, cornbread, three meats, ten vegetables, three pies, and quart-sized iced-tea glasses (refills free). Nothing fancy. Shirt-sleeve trade. Over the years the customers have gotten to know one another pretty well, so the noise of dishes banging and children crying is no different from that of a family reunion.

More and more, people are eating out, usually carrying their own trays and standing in lines to order. The hash houses I haunt are sort of halfway houses between meals at home or under the golden arches. Variety is the spice of life. I like that "bigger family" menu and atmosphere. The only other places I seem to find it are at truck stops, but there one feels like an outsider if one doesn't drive a semi and talk CB code.

This restaurant I favor is the country farm kitchen come to town and gone commercial. Prices are cheap, people are friendly, and the help lets you alone if you want to read the paper. They keep about twelve waiters and waitresses hustling, but somehow all of them seem to enjoy their work and have honed the art of public service to a fine edge. Older citizens get special attention there. They tend to be a little finicky about wanting to have half portions or to substitute menu items; but within reason, the management is very flexible about catering to personal tastes. Widows and widowers like to be there, and often it is the place they bring their grandchildren after they give up cooking at home three times a day.

Sit-down, simple-fare, low-cost restaurants are important to building community spirit. They are the common man's country clubs where the affairs of the town get discussed and chewed over. They are, of course, among the many nonchain, small businesses that are being pressed into oblivion in our society. Local communities that want to promote a healthy civic life and public spirit need to give them encouragement and incentives to keep their burners going. They are educational institutions as much as they are eateries. The staff is young, high school and college age. One of the most important, and neglected, aspects of education is learning how to deal with the public. Waiting tables and washing dishes can teach a bright youngster more about management techniques, human nature, the arts of listening, and group dynamics than any course in college.

The scripture says we should take no thought for what we eat. I think that was meant for those of us who make eating too central to our lives. A better thought is that we should think some about what we eat and where we eat.

Eating may not be central, but it ought not be peripheral in our community life together. After all, "communion" originally meant coming together for a common meal and sharing both bread and conversation.

Our oldest daughter is grown and gone. We've been saying that about her ever since she took her first full-time job. Before that she was away for five years in college and graduate study, but we dated her departure from the time she got her own apartment and full-time job. She still checks in regularly by phone and E-mail and always gets home for Christmas. So we have been gingerly inching our way into admitting her absence.

When she lived 150 miles away, the full realization that she was in fact grown and gone struck me full in the face when I stopped by her apartment once. I was not prepared to find it clean and orderly, a break in the long-standing pattern of disarray. But what aged me overnight was going out to lunch with her. She insisted on driving, used her own car, and picked the restaurant herself.

Then, once we had eaten, she insisted on paying for lunch. I did not realize that anyone could age as quickly as I did in that instant at the restaurant cash register. If your daughter is old enough to buy you lunch, how long will it be before she is putting you into a nursing home? This is the little girl whom I would not let cross the highway without holding my hand until she was twelve. This is the little girl with whom I agonized for hours over English themes and history dissertations. Now she handles pages of stories for a good-sized newspaper each day. This is the little girl whose checking account never balanced and was in constant need of fiscal transfusions. Now she has enough money saved up to fly to a cousin's wedding and to talk about a vacation in California or Europe.

In my own childhood, the end of a visit with my grandparents was a walk to the country store where my grandfather would buy me a half of a pint box of vanilla ice cream, sliced with the store's cheese knife. Even after they moved to town and he was in his eighties, he still would pay when we ate lunch together. My own father was the same way. The only meals of his I ever paid for were those my wife served in our own house. It was important to him that he pay the restaurant bill even though he had given up morning coffee breaks on principle when the price of a cup of coffee went up to ten cents.

There is much irony here. The only way to give our offspring their independence is to give up some of our own, to accept dependence upon those who were for years our dependents. Most of us resist it. The habit of having our children depend upon us is deeply ingrained. The pride of being responsible for them is gigantic, and so a graceful acceptance of reversed roles is awkward. Worst of all is the psychological shock of realizing they are free of us. Parents have enormous pride of authorship. These grown-up children of ours are our creations. We gave them birth and then molded their lives. Parents are as creative as famous inventors, writers, artists, and architects. Most of us do fairly well at being parents. There aren't too many Frankenstein monsters running around. We have some right to be proud of our creations. But when the creation becomes independent of its creators, parental pride takes a fall. Godlike parents that we are, a declaration of independence from a child has to seem as unexpected as Adam and Eve chomping on the forbidden apple. We are accustomed to thinking that our children's transitions into adulthood and freedom come easily and routinely through graduations and weddings. But then we stumble suddenly onto hard evidence that they are really grown and gone.

The turnip greens, creamed corn, black-eyed peas, cornbread, chess pie, and iced tea at the truck stop to which our daughter took me were super. But it was the revelation at the cash register that floored me. I think I know

now how Paul felt on the road to Damascus. Somehow I wish I had gotten her to autograph, date, and frame the greasy menu or the little green meal ticket. And I wish she had asked me to make an after-lunch commencement speech full of all the stored-up advice that I had assumed I would be giving her for years to come. What a glorious blessing it was to be needed those years. We are proud of our creation and selfish about surrendering it.

August 13, 1984, October 29, 1990, and October 28, 2001

COCA-COLA™

During World War II, when local baseball struck out for lack of players, I was a batboy for my mother's softball team. I wore white shorts, white cap, and white T-shirt. On the cap and T-shirt were lovingly sewn the round badges of the team's sponsor: Coca-Cola™ (Trademark Registered).

Years later, home for the summers from college, I coached two consecutive championship Babe Ruth baseball teams. The team members got heavy red wool athletic jackets, and I got one, too. I still wear it. On the back was the round white badge with red lettering of the team sponsor: Coca-Cola™.

Out in the country, the water bucket and gourd dipper sat on the back porch table of my grandparents' house next to two cases of six-ounce bottles (the only legitimate size in my estimation) of, you guessed it: Coca-Cola. They didn't have a refrigerator. They didn't even have electricity until TVA ran a line in after the war. Why, then, do I recall how icy-cold those Cokes were?

Yet alive in the South today, there are hundreds of people who drink Cokes instead of coffee for breakfast. Are they of that age that got addicted before the unknown Keepers of the Formula took out the cocaine that gave the drink its nicknames of Coke and Dope?

For four years, I jerked sodas. I could add cherry or vanilla to a fountain Coke, even chocolate or lemon, and stock the bottle box with the best of them. I was always grateful that I retired before the era of king-size and caffeine-free, cans and liters, and Diet Coke. The old silver and red bottle opener in our kitchen is rusty from not being used. I was a dinosaur in the new land of Coke by the time I was twenty. Lately I've been waiting for the new Cherry Coke to get to the local groceries, even though I've been warned that it isn't the same as the old fountain Coke with cherry added.

And now, even before that newest twist arrives, I am told that the Formula itself is being changed; it's as if someone finally found the lost Ark of the Covenant and changed one of the Ten Commandments in it. I wish I had known in advance. That empty basement of ours that guests say would make a fine wine cellar would make a great Coke cellar if I could borrow enough money to stock it with the Real Thing.

I've learned to pretend a lot as I've aged. I buy Coke in three-liter plastic bottles, but serve it in Coke glasses given me years ago by Hardy Graham, a connoisseur-dealer who remembers the old days. I pretend the ice from the icemaker is cracked ice I chipped myself with my handy Coca-Cola ice pick. I look at the bottom of the clear (not green) plastic bottle to see if the address of the bottler is circled there. I drain the juice from the maraschino cherry bottle left from Christmas to pour in my guests' cokes. I can even pretend that the big plastic straws squirreled away from MacDonald's are thinner and made of paper.

I wonder what J.P., Jimmy Vincent, and High Pockets ("Hip") Rawls from the old hometown bottling plant would think of all these Coke changes?

In third grade we wrote on Coca-Cola tablets with Coca-Cola pencils, copying our script letters from Coca-Cola–furnished cardboard samples tacked above the tops of the blackboards under colored prints of enemy planes provided by Coca-Cola for us to use as volunteer air-raid wardens. With the help of Coca-Cola^{TM}, we prevented the invasion of the country. But we are helpless to prevent the invasion of the Formula.

Let it come. They can't conquer our memories, which are ^{TM} (Trademark Registered).

May 27, 1985

COOKBOOK

The most spellbinding southern book since *Gone with the Wind* (Macmillan) 1935 is not about war or sex, but about food. John Egerton has written the south's most tasteful book: *Southern Food* (Knopf). If he had written a book this gripping about sex instead of about southern eating, the book would have been banned, and he would have been arrested for catering to prurient interests.

The next best thing to a banquet of all the dishes Egerton describes is digesting the book itself; it is a movable feast of good eating. Egerton catches and preserves for posterity the elusive mandrake root of southern culture, the mysterious secret that explains best what it is to be southern: its food.

Armies may march on their stomachs, but so do civilizations. To read these menus and recipes is to understand that for which starving Confederates fought and for which hordes of tenant farmers plowed. At the end of the struggle was a shared vision of good southern eating. The southern empire has not belonged to mighty planters or to conspicuous politicos or to captains of banking and industry. The only counting rooms which have counted the most consistently throughout southern history are its kitchens, ruled by cooks and chefs who have turned common fare into ecstasy.

What makes the South a separate civilization is our long-shared taste for well-prepared country ham, barbecue, catfish, oysters, turnip greens, butter beans, cornbread, biscuits, molasses, chess pie, pound cake, and 1,001 other culinary pleasures, several hundred of which Egerton has found yet alive—if not well—across the region.

Southern Food is written in two main parts, one on eating out and one on eating at home. In addition, Egerton offers side dishes of wonderful quotations about southern food, comments on the history of southern food in the context of the region's whole history, bibliographies of good cookbooks, recipes, and state-by-state guides to good places to eat.

"Eating Out" is a discriminating report on the best eating Egerton found in eight exhausting but unforgettable months of travel to the South's best restaurants—"best" being a matter of taste, and certainly not of price or of advertising. There are places like Montgomery's Elite Cafe, Tuscaloosa's Waysider, and Centerville's Twix 'n' Tween in Alabama, and places such as Duke's Barbecue in Orangeburg, Country's Barbecue in Columbus, and Mrs. Wilkes' Boarding House in Savannah. The range in Louisiana is from Galatoire's of New Orleans to Dwyer's Cafe in Lafayette. Kentucky's Beaumont Inn has the nation's best baked ham, and the barbecues of a dozen stops like the Moonlite in the western end of that state and Bozo's in west Tennessee may be unbeatable even in the superb pit stops of the Carolinas. Egerton covered eleven states, ate at 335 carefully preselected places, and reports on 200 of the best.

For the "Eating In" half of this masterpiece, Egerton and his wife moved into their kitchen. The result was a test of over 400 recipes, and a mouthwatering selection of 160 of those "broadly representative of Southern cookery at its best." If time and enthusiasm permit, our family friends will be given watermelon rind pickles or pickled peaches for Christmas this year, made from these recipes. If not, we'll give the book itself, probably a better choice.

Despite its joy in southern cooking, *Southern Food* is a rather sad book, rather like uncovering dusty mementos in an attic. The art of cooking is leaving the region as inevitably as Rhett left Scarlett. Egerton has captured in print the barbecue pits and beaten biscuits that are the tombstones of our regional minds, before they become illegible and topple. Such an ending need not be inevitable. Losing our tastes is not necessarily predestined. Surely preserving southern cooking is as important as saving the whales.

Before the door of our collective past is slammed and our identity as a civilization apart stalks out into the mists, there is yet time to save and savor, to protect and tell about, what our senses of texture, smell, sight, and taste have found unique about the South. We thank John Egerton for witnessing that we are what we used to eat and for warning that we are becoming what we grab on the run to eat these days.

July 13, 1987

MOM'S BIRTHDAY CAKE

It all started with the best of intentions.

Wife Betsy and daughter Molly had gone off for a few days during Molly's spring break. I was alone when it occurred to me that Mother's seventy-fifth birthday was coming up. That's not a big enough number to rate a Willard Scott salute, but I felt a special mother deserved something extra special for enduring three-fourths of this century.

Birthdays mean birthday cakes. A seventy-fifth birthday warrants something other than a bakery cake. What could better tell a mother what she has meant to a son than his baking her seventy-fifth birthday cake for her? I chose pound cake—my favorite. The ingredients are few and simple, it's heavy and ships well, and a quick nibble will tell if it turned out right. Besides, its name fits Mother better than does, say, prune cake. I found about thirty different pound-cake recipes, but used my secretary's fail-safe one. My plan was to make three small cakes instead of one regular-sized one.

Alone and intending to "honor thy mother" as the scriptures order, I entered Betsy's sacrosanct kitchen, territory forbidden to me when she is at home. I found the bowls, mixers, scrapers, measuring cups and spoons, and pans I needed.

The recipe calls for five eggs. I had four. A quick drive to the grocery solved that. But once there, which eggs? Large, extra large, or super large? White or brown? I chose super brown ones because they look more country-like.

Back home again, the recipe called for three cups of flour. I found only one in the house. Back to the grocery. But again a dilemma. Plain, self-rising, or cake flour? The three housewives I stopped to ask for advice all claimed they never bake. I chose self-rising; surely Martha White wouldn't let me down. Home again. Recipe calls for three cups of sugar. Including little paper packages from restaurants, I found enough for nearly two cups. Back to the grocery.

Home again, home again, jiggety-jog. This time I read the recipe all the way through to see if some grocery trips could be combined into one. They could. I could get the real butter (plain or lightly salted?) and the vanilla flavoring (imitation or extract?) in one trip.

The batter came out looking perfect. I poured the three pans half-full, stuck them in the cold oven, and set the temperature at 325 degrees and the timer for ninety minutes as the recipe says to do. Sixty minutes later the lovely aroma of pound cake baking wafted into the den where I was watching the NCAA tournament. It was followed by billowing fogs of smoke. Wishing for a gas-mask, I waved my way across the kitchen, parting the smoke like Moses in the Red Sea, and threw open the oven, despite the recipe's warning not to open it for another thirty minutes. All three cakes had self-risen and over-flowed, and charred batter hung from the shelf wires like moss on Spanish oaks.

I salvaged the cakes. Trimming off the crusts, they were just fine inside. Cleaning took another two hours of scrubbing the kitchen and opening all the windows to air out the house while the self-cleaning stove reduced the self-risen cake residue to a large pile of gray ashes, which I sucked out with Betsy's dust-buster. I had just finished washing the last window and rinsing the last bowl when I noticed that I couldn't get the hot water tap turned off. I took it apart, but couldn't fix it, and finally turned it off at the control valve and called a plumber.

The plumber came, fixed the valve in about sixty seconds, and then showed me some rust particles causing the problem. Stirred up by all the hot water I had used for cleaning the kitchen, the rust came from the bottom of our water heater. Next thing I knew I had bought a new one. Then I made the mistake of asking him, as long as he was there anyway, to adjust the floater ball in Molly's toilet so we wouldn't have to jiggle the handle after every flushing. Thirty minutes later, with the whole toilet spread out neatly like a dissembled robot in its separate parts, it was obvious that the toilet had to be replaced.

Next morning, the water heater and toilet were rapidly installed. As the plumbers drove away, promising to mail me the bill, I waved a fond farewell.

But the dominoes hadn't stopped toppling yet.

When I turned on the hose in the basement to wash away the mud the plumbers had tracked in, the water rushed merrily toward the floor drain next to the washer. Then it stopped and backed up. An inch deep. The drain didn't drain.

Wading out of the basement, I went to do the one thing Betsy had left explicit instructions to be done—clean out the cat's litter box. I checked the box carefully, even shaking the litter to be sure. There was nothing there to clean. I panicked and ran all over the house. This cat had been locked up in the house for three full days. Yet my full senses of sight and smell found no sign anywhere that she had been to the bathroom at all in that whole time. But, I thought, maybe she's just shy or only goes when Betsy's home. Or maybe she's so well trained she went in the old toilet the plumbers had just hauled away.

Then I suddenly realized that I hadn't seen the cat at all since the plumbers arrived that morning. I looked everywhere again. The cat had skeedaddled. Catastrophe; Doom loomed. Betsy was due back in only a few hours. Should I go the pound and try to find a duplicate of the cat?

Discouraged, I trudged back into the kitchen where all this had begun. The hot water was dripping again. Fortunately, I had the plumber's number.

The cat's back, and so is Betsy, and the water works. So far, my mother's birthday cake—which the delivery service took to the wrong address, I have since learned—has cost me over five hundred dollars, including grocery ingredients and gasoline, faucet repair, heater, toilet, and shipping. She's worth every penny, and more.

But she can buy her own candles. I've seen enough smoke. Come to think of it, why didn't those smoke alarms Mother gave me for *my* birthday work?

May 1, 1989

THE BOUGHT CAKE

Last fall, after a lifetime of political neutrality, my octogenarian mother got excited by the elections. It was a strange interest for someone who had always maintained that politics corrupt.

Well, she was right all along; it corrupted her.

A few weeks after the election, she came for her annual Christmas visit. Her regular job when she arrives is to bake the traditional coconut cake. Sometimes her cakes lean to one side a bit or the icing drips or slides off, but they are good, nonetheless, because they are homemade by her. My annual assignment is to break open the coconut for her. I do that in the basement with a hammer.

But this past year I wasn't asked to crack a coconut. My mother and my wife told me that the coconut crop wasn't very good this year and that the grocery's coconuts were smaller than oranges, and that my mother had used coconut "every bit as good" from a plastic bag from the grocery's frozen foods bin. When I pulled out the cake to cut the first slice, it was something else to behold. Instead of the usual two-layer yellow cake, this was a white cake, four layers high, so tall it barely fit in the big plastic cake container. It was absolutely symmetrical, so perfect that it could have made the cover of *Southern Living* magazine.

Trouble was, it didn't taste all that great. It was dry, and it tasted like bought birthday cake. But when she asked how it was, I did what a good son should do; I lied to my mother. I kept nibbling at it for the next three weeks, thinking that the coconut juice would ferment and make it better with time. But it didn't improve. I took to eating it with a slice of baked country ham to improve the taste. Sometimes I crumbled it into a glass of boiled custard. And all the while I kept on lying about how good it was.

It was getting close to time for her to go home, and we went out for dinner one night. Over their protests, I took my mother and wife to a little place that serves health food sandwiches, soups, and salads. While we waited for our order to arrive, I wandered over to the bakery displays in the restaurant. Nestled in the midst of Snickers pies and Millionaire cookies was a big coconut cake. It was the twin of my mother's cake. I went back to the table and told her she could probably get a baking job at that place.

Now, one would think that someone born before World War I would have forgotten how to blush. Not my mother. The twenty-five-watt lightbulb in my head went off when I saw her face. She and my wife had bought our Christmas cake right there. And then they both lied to me. They might as well have told me straight out that there is no Santa Claus.

What worries me most is, what happens next? Their lies led me to lie back to them. One lie leads to another, and once you get on that road, it's hard to turn back. What will they come up with next Christmas? We already make boiled custard from instant vanilla pudding mix. Will they empty fruit slices out of a grocery jar into glass bowls and call it ambrosia? Were those black things in the sweet potatoes really raisins? Did the oyster casserole have any oysters in it? Will they try to substitute instant coffee for the real stuff, like they do on that commercial taped in New Orleans's best restaurant?

More important, whom can a son trust if he can't trust his own mother?

Age isn't to blame in this case. Sons think their mothers are ageless anyway. Mine still drives and keeps house for herself, and I wouldn't have been surprised to hear in the Great Blizzard last month that she was out on her nearby hill on one of our old sleds. Besides, Helen Hayes just died at age ninety-two, and Lillian Gish at nearly one hundred, and I'd bet they both baked coconut cakes last December.

Husbands expect lies from wives. But sons expect more from mothers, and usually get it. Sons expect to be told how perfect they are, how young they look, and how thoughtful they have been over the years—and other such plain honest truths. They don't expect their mothers to fake coconut cake.

So there's really no one to blame for my mother's speaking with a forked tongue about my cake except the politicians. She went to the polls for her first time in November and came to see us in December; the lying started then. It's a simple case of cause and effect. Politics pollute. Just look at what my mother caught in that dirty polling booth.

Maybe it's not too late for her. Maybe she'll get the point when she opens the coconut I mailed her for her present this year. I just pray they don't take away her Medicare for lying.

March 29, 1993

HAND-ME-DOWN RECIPES

Back at the year's beginning, we reported my mother's misguided attempt to pass off a bakery-produced coconut cake as her annual homemade Christmas gift to me the year before. That led to a year of phone calls and mail for her. One hate-mail man held her personally responsible, because of her innocent fib, for the recent collapse of western civilization, family values, the schools, and public morals. Most of the callers were just curious, wanting to know if she had repented and planned to return to cooking her own cakes this Christmas.

We are happy to report that things are almost back to normal. I cracked the coconut myself and watched her dig out the coconut meat. She did compromise some, to the extent of confining herself to the icing and letting my wife cook the cake. My wife, unfortunately, elected to use a Betty Crocker mix, but I would never criticize my wife for that as I did my mother. After all, I do have to live with her.

Sometime last fall, all that continuing interest in the now-infamous "Store-Bought Coconut Cake of '92" opened up another chain of events. Our youngest daughter, a freshman at Davidson College, took an anthropology class, a portion of which was devoted to a study of foodways. It is absolutely amazing how much anthropology can be learned simply by concentrating on people's eating habits. Recalling the cake episode, our daughter called her grandmother several times (phone bill evidence produced upon request) to interview her about recipes, favorite dishes, and memories of how and what her own mother and grandmother cooked. That led our daughter to a search, first for one of my grandmother's eight missing Calumet Baking Powder cans in which date-nut bread was baked each Christmas, and then for the missing cookbook of the other grandmother.

Old wounds reopened as cousins accused others of confiscating cans, cookbooks, flatware, a pickled-peaches bowl, a pie safe, and a feather mattress. The blood shed by phone over a month's time had the happy result of producing one of the missing cans and a copy of an aunt's recipe book into which she had copied some of the recipes from the missing cookbook. Alas, it also unleashed the broken hearts and tortured memories of a goodly number of relatives, all of whom recalled at length (phone bill evidence available upon request) favorite dishes prepared often and lovingly "from scratch" by our mutual and long-gone grandmothers. Just as we had almost learned to live with living without, the sadness of recalling meals gone forever undid us. Our memories are attached to our tongues.

Frustrated by nostalgia and unsatiated palates of the mind, I enlisted my daughter in a futile effort to duplicate one grandmother's recipe for corn light bread. Unfortunately, cornmeal isn't what it once was, electric stoves cook differently from log-burning ones, and one person's "pinch" or "scant teaspoon" is not another's. She made an A on her foodways project and wound up with a fairly good genealogy of her family, but we failed to save home cooking from its modern oblivion.

One very bright star shone in the darkness, like a light over a stable. For decades now, my mother's sister, Aunt Dorothy, has been the undisputed Last Great Cook of our families. She has baked enough yeast rolls and pecan pies to have kept the Confederate army going, and she and her stove seem almost inseparable. Our taste buds aquiver from our daughter's painstaking but painful foodways project, I asked her if she would fix us one of the blackberry jam cakes with caramel icing that my mother and I recall so vividly from Christmases past. Aunt Dorothy came through like a champion—or, more correctly, like a saint. Straight from her phone that mid-November day, she went to her oven, and by day's end had produced a masterpiece. Then she froze it until she found a ride for it from Brownsville, Tennessee, to my mother in Paris, Tennessee, at Thanksgiving. My mother, to her credit, resisting temptations which befall aging ladies who relish food and who live alone, kept it frozen until she could join us for Christmas.

My wife, who has an irrational belief that Christmas food should not be opened or eaten before Christmas, kept Aunt Dorothy's jam cake in the basement until we returned from midnight Christmas Eve services. Then, at 1:00 A.M. on Christmas morning, we cut it. It was food fit for angels. We can swear we heard them singing as we ate. Then we turned out all the lights and hid the half cake remaining, greatly afraid that we would be besieged by hordes of shepherds and Magi demanding to share it.

January 10, 1994

FRUITCAKES

Fruitcake season has rolled around. Crates of commercial loaf fruitcakes have been opened and passed out among civic club salesmen. Grocery display tables are stacked with nuts and citron fruits for those who continue to bake their own. (Ever see a citron tree?)

About this time last year, a news item reported that someone who had inherited a 160-year-old fruitcake had sliced a sliver from it and pronounced it still tasty.

Before the season gathers steam and we get too carried away, a word of caution may be appropriate: in this age of political correctness, when we are all being extra careful not to give offense to others in what we say, one neglected victim is the oft-maligned fruitcake. Let's face it, do we really think about this? Can we imagine how a fruitcake must feel when it overhears us describing some weirdo "acting nutty as a fruitcake?"

There are endless fruitcake jokes. We resurrect each holiday season old stories about the fruitcake that couldn't die, spending eternity being passed from relative to relative, or about the old prospector in a canyon out west who built his house of fruitcakes. Some of us, more tasteless than others, give fruitcakes for gifts with cards that read "Christmas Doorstop." Some of us have called them an evil plot cooked up by dentists to build trade.

No doubt about it, fruitcakes are battered victims.

They need an advocacy group to plead their cause and protect their rights. One of the problems in uniting for action is that there are few fruitcake lovers willing to come out of the closet and admit they like fruitcakes. A related problem is that, even among the few fruitcake bakers left in the world, there is great dissension over definitions. No two fruitcake cooks agree about how to make a fruitcake. There are all sorts of disagreements over proper shapes, the ages and sources of the recipes, "secret" ingredients, basic ingredients, soaking time, appropriate stove, best temperature, et cetera.

Religion, race, and color get into the controversy, too. Recipes have been passed on from New England Puritans, Virginia Episcopalians, Eastern Orthodox immigrants, Pennsylvania Amish, and West Africans—among many others. Every nation and every creed has a fruitcake. There is also great debate over the proper color—white or dark. We have even seen families split over whether to include figs in the cakes, leading to Seed and No-Seed schisms that finally got resolved by baking two cakes, one with figs and one without. The same divisions occur over whether or not to "soak the fruitcake," a euphemism meaning to "add liquor." The first big question is whether to add liquor at all. For those deciding to do so, the next debate is over whether to add it to the batter and cook it in the cake, or to wrap the baked cake in swaddling clothes and soak the cloth. Then the debate degenerates into what alcohol to use: wine, bourbon, or brandy. That argument can lead, in turn, to disagreeing over whether to use the cheapest or most expensive brands of alcohol.

Alas, the poor persecuted fruitcakes! How seldom we hear anything good said about them! Not one of "The Twelve Days of Christmas" celebrates them, although less-deserving "lords a-leaping" and "maids a-milking" certainly get plenty of attention.

Fruitcakes are round pegs trying to fit into a square society and finding resistance at every corner. Yet for decades they have quietly and unselfishly shuttled about, carrying our season's greetings from one to another. They have adorned the tables of festive holiday balls and Christmas Eve dinners—not to mention December covers of *Southern Living* magazine. They have said to a million employees who get them instead of cash bonuses that their employers do care.

What would the winter holidays be without fruitcakes? One might as well forgo eggnog or ban Bing Crosby or kill Tiny Tim.

If you can't say something nice about fruitcakes this year, just don't say anything at all.

Less said, the better.

But as for me and my house, there will always be a fruitcake in our family.

November 7, 1994

JARS

One of the inconveniences of modern living is the shortage of jars.

Used to be every household had a shelf full of emptied Mason, Kerr, or Ball jars. You know the type: round or square clear or blue glass jars with flat metal tops held down by screw-on metal lids.

In other days, before foods were easier to get fresh, frozen, boxed, in cans, or in pry-off bottles in supermarkets, folks did their own canning. (Actually, what they did was "jarring," since cans weren't really involved, but it was called canning anyway.)

I recall in one grandmother's attic a whole closet of Mason jars that contained blackberries, green beans, tomatoes, peaches, and a dozen other delicacies hoarded for winters. She even canned her own grape juice which, with a little luck, occasionally fermented. The other grandmother canned, too. When I was two and staying with her while my mother was in the hospital having my brother, I backed a goat cart up in the backyard and fell out into a seated position atop a hot charcoal bucket she used for canning beans. I wound up on my stomach in the hospital bed alongside my mother. The vanishing art of canning is burned into my memory.

There's an antique shop in town that I visit simply because it has an impressive display of canned foods neatly lined up in rows in an old pie safe. It strikes me as the perfect family altar to the memory of tastes of tireless grandmothers. I annually ask if the exhibit is for sale and am always disappointed that it isn't. In the absence of such a shrine in our house, I made do a while with a quart of peaches our thoughtful eldest daughter gave me for my birthday. I held out seven months before opening the jar for Christmas dinner.

I can accept the fact that transportation and food processing progress have changed the canning industry. Leaving aside any debate over how its taste compares with that made at home by our grandmothers, there seems to be plenty of food, but it is prepared by distant hands. It's just that the emptied jars came in so handy. That's why I mourn their loss.

Mason, Ball, and Kerr jars were useful. They held assorted screws, left-over paint from the bottom of a gallon bucket, and soap powder for the washer. And nails. Nails were big business. Thomas Jefferson even built and operated a nail factory at Monticello. Remember when nails came in wooden barrels and bins and you filled paper sacks with handfuls of them, paid for them by weight, rushed home before the sack bottoms fell out, and stored them in glass jars? A ten-penny nail was three inches long and originally sold for ten cents (or pence) a hundred. Nowadays, of course, they're prepackaged in little plastic or cardboard boxes, cluttering our drawers and shelves, begging for container jars.

Fruit jars were especially good, with their lids punched, for storing lightning bugs (aka in the North and in cities as "fireflies").

Farmers who found their corn too bulky to haul to distant markets came up with the profitable enterprise of distilling it and transporting it in jars. In some sections of the South that was the primary support of the economy for many years.

Fruit jars were their most colorful when we used them to dye Easter eggs and to store assorted shirt and skirt buttons. Iced tea, lemonade, or water taste better when drunk from fruit jars.

No poet has yet written a fitting ode to fruit jars. They lie in pauper's fields, under tons of landfill, unsung.

We miss them, don't we? Almost as much as cigar boxes.

March 6, 1995

STRAWBERRIES

Old-timers tell us that our home was built on the strawberry patch of Andrews Farm. Mowing the back lawn, I find clumps of wild strawberry descendants. Living in a strawberry patch is a good omen for me. I've never met a strawberry I didn't like. English author William Butler (1535–1618) was quite right: "Doubtless God could have made a better berry, but doubtless God never did."

My appetite for strawberries is insatiable, but some are better than others. California now grows 80 percent of the nation's crop because the season there stretches from January until October, but the huge imported berries in our local groceries are almost tasteless.

The strawberries of my youth were from west Tennessee, where Humboldt has an annual Strawberry Festival as old as I am. They were modest-sized, juicy, harmonious blends of tartness and sweetness. Unfortunately, like other local crops such as okra and sweet potatoes, they are almost extinct. Strawberry season there is only during May, and the yield varies because of weather changes. Two of the old patches from the past are still in operation: the Wells patch near South Fulton, and the Wade patch near Kenton. I have been eating Wade's berries for decades now, and I salute Tom, Jr., and his son, Will, for carrying on the family business, if not for profit then as a historical symbol of west Tennessee's former greatness. Here in the Carolinas, I've found medium-sized berries that are better than California imports and close enough to the Wade's Tennessee tastiness to satisfy. I eke by each May, despite the absence of the abundance and access of bygone days.

Strawberries aren't named for their winter straw covering. The berries are "strewn" about on the plants, and "strewnberry" eventually became "strawberry." They are from the rose family and are not berries or fruit at all but enlarged ends of the plant's stamen. Strawberry seeds are on the outer skin, instead of in the inner berry, at about two hundred seeds per berry. The berries are nonfat and low in calories, rich in vitamin C, potassium, folic acid, fiber, and vitamin B6. The Alpine strawberries of thirteenth century France were used in medicines. They have been used for sunburn, discolored teeth, digestion, and gout. Newlyweds in France used them in soup as aphrodisiacs. Served at medieval state events, they symbolized prosperity, peace, and perfection. The most famous public eating of strawberries is at Wimbledon each year when strawberries and cream are consumed between tennis matches by the properly attired English. Russian empresses and tsars also loved them.

American Indians allegedly invented strawberry shortcake, mashing berries in meal to make bread the colonists enjoyed. They must have used wild strawberries since strawberries have been cultivated in America only since 1835. The Hoveg variety was imported into Massachusetts from

France in 1834. Strawberry festivals in the South—in addition to Humboldt in Tennessee—beckon us to Ashland, Virginia, Buckhannon, West Virginia, Ponchatoula, Louisiana, Portland, Tennessee, Poteet, Texas— and several in Florida. Plant City, Florida, is the Winter Strawberry Capital of the World.

There are references to them as far back as ancient Rome. The Fraser clan in Scotland derived its name from French immigrants named Strawberry (Fraise) who came with William the Conqueror in 1066. Musicians, novelists, and poets celebrate strawberries: Shakespeare in *Henry V* and *Richard III,* Ingmar Bergman in a classic film called *Wild Strawberries* in 1957, and the Beatles in a hit song "Strawberry Fields Forever."

Strawberries have a noble past, but do they have a future?

Would a world without strawberries still be called a world?

June 15, 1998

PEANUTS

This is that humid time of the year when I hunger and thirst for a five-cent cellophane bag of salted peanuts and an old-fashioned twelve-ounce return-able nickel bottle of RC Cola into which to pour them.

For younger folk, the word "goobers" probably brings to mind expensive cardboard boxes of chocolate-covered peanuts bought at movie-house concession stands. For others, "Goober" is the nickname of a service-station character in Mayberry on the old Andy Griffith television series. Even younger folk may associate goobers with President Jimmy Carter and Plains, Georgia.

For me, the word brings to mind folksinger Burl Ives singing "Goober Peas":

Sittin' by the roadside on a summer's day,
Chattin' with my messmates, passing time away,
Lying in the shadows, underneath the trees—
Goodness, how delicious, eatin' goober peas!
CHORUS: Peas! Peas! Peas! Eatin' goober peas!
Goodness, how delicious, eatin' goober peas!

It is a Civil War song, and in the next stanzas a Reb general mistakes the sound of Georgia militia eating goober peas for Yankee rifle fire, and the singer ends with:

I wish this war was over, when free from rags and fleas,

We'd kiss our wives and sweethearts and gobble goober peas!

Other than that song, there isn't much in Civil War history books about peanuts. More common foodstuffs for Confederates were cornmeal, green corn, apples, ersatz coffee made from roots, and occasional slices of infested fatback. Apparently peanuts have been around quite some time, however. Ancient Peruvians buried pots of them with their dead to nurture them in their life hereafter. The word "goober," like the word "banjo," allegedly came from Africa through the slave trade and is supposedly from the Bantu word "nguba." Other sources say African peanuts came from South America first, where they were exchanged for slaves.

In my own mind, I always associate peanuts with George Washington Carver. Born at the end of the Civil War, this African American scientist from Missouri made his career in research at Tuskegee Institute in Alabama from 1896 (ironically the year of the *Plessy vs. Ferguson* "separate but equal" Supreme Court decision) until his death in 1943. Carver developed there 325 peanuts products (and 108 sweet potato products and 75 pecan products, plus a substitute for rubber and 500 paints and dyes). All of us owe George Washington Carver an immeasurable debt. I wish the Planters people would put his picture on their products instead of that peculiar English-looking Mr. Peanut with his monocle and top hat, neither of which are very southern.

The United States has only 3 percent of the world's peanut acreage but produces 10 percent of the world's peanuts. Half of the world's peanuts are grown in India and China where rice is the stereotypical primary crop. There are four types of peanuts: the dominant Runner (in Georgia, Alabama, Florida, Texas, and Oklahoma); the snack nut Spanish (in Oklahoma and Texas); the red-skinned favorite for boiling Valencia (in New Mexico), and the large-shelled Virginia (in southeastern Virginia and northeastern North Carolina). The Florunner variety, developed since the 1970s, is uniform and abundant, and 54 percent of them go into peanut butter.

The most common commercial peanuts are sold roasted in and out of their shells, in bags or cans or bottles, but boiled peanuts are also sometimes considered delicacies. One sees roadside stands of them in Georgia and the

Carolinas. A major outlet in Columbia, South Carolina, Cromer's, advertises itself as having the "Worst Peanuts in the World." Personally, I think boiled peanuts are slimy and repulsive, but probably appetizing to people who also like grits and stockcar racing. I also think that baseball cannot be watched adequately without a bag of the unshelled, salted roasted ones. Nor can riverbank fishing on hot days be successful without a bag of salted goobers in a big RC Cola.

August 25, 1998

LOCAL BOTTLERS

Among freshmen and parents at the moving-in reception here at Wofford College last year was a family from Mount Sterling, Kentucky. I warned them to find a way to keep their son supplied with "Ale-8-One," since it isn't sold in South Carolina. Their surprising response was "We've got a whole cooler iced in the car trunk. Want one?"

Ale-8-One is a popular soft drink in the Bluegrass, somewhat akin to ginger ale, bottled in Winchester, Kentucky. Its name supposedly comes from workers at day's end asking one another, "How about having *a late one?*" The loyalty of local citizens to local soft drinks is a common phenomenon in this country. On a regionwide basis, Royal Crown Cola and Dr. Pepper are southern-based drinks of choice. When I was in graduate school in Connecticut I brought car trunks of Dr. Pepper to exiled southerners.

But there are drinks that have an even more limited geographical scope. Here in South Carolina, Blenheim Ale, bottled down by a creek in a cinderblock building south of Bennettsville, is a treasured refresher. People gift wrap six-packs of its hot, mild, or diet versions for Christmas presents.

Cheerwine and Double Cola are other regional options, and there are probably a hundred or more most of us never even heard of. Someone ought to do a national map of local soft-drink bottlers, just as local winery associations have begun doing for wine producers who limit their production quantity and their range of sales, or as local beer breweries have done, citing specialty beers in St. Louis, Milwaukee, Cincinnati, New Orleans, and a hundred other American cities.

In our Religion in America class this spring, students worked on "Other Gods before Me" projects, studying worldly things to which people give so much time, money, and attention that they seem to make religions of them—things such as Elvis, NASCAR racing, baseball, professional wrestling, collecting (Christmas houses, Disney products, spoons, etc.), or Civil War reenactments.

David Hoyle, a sophomore from Shelby, North Carolina, studied Sun Drop Cola. Energetic and unintimidated, a child of the television era with video camera and microphone in hand, Hoyle marched fearlessly into Wal-Marts, banks, high schools, a drum corps, quick-stop stores, a domestic-violence center, an Episcopal priest's church, and the president's office of the national headquarters of Sun Drop's parent company, Choice USA.

Articulate interviewees cheerfully testified to their reliance on Sun Drop as a means of staying alert during studies or avoiding headaches at work. Travelers from the Shelby-Charlotte-Gastonia areas told of not daring to leave home to visit New York or Disney World without a six-pack or twelve-pack with them. One lady limits her consumption to one bottle a day, taken "religiously" at 9:15 every morning. Another drinks "an average" of one two-liter bottle every day and "sometimes more." Others testified to the citrus flavor, "lighter than most colas."

A traveling salesman first made the drink popular, selling it as a soda-fountain syrup along his route from Shelby westward to Missouri. C. B. Nanney bought the formula and sold it to independent bottlers throughout the two Carolinas and the Tennessee Valley, several of which are still in business and which account for 85 percent of the drink's sales. A quick-stop store-owner says 40 percent of his soda sales are Sun Drop. First sold at Bridges Barbecue in Shelby, it spread by truck sales to mills throughout the Carolinas: long work hours and heavy labor made it ideal for helping make it through the day.

A priest says those most loyal to Sun Drop would probably resist calling their loyalty "religious," but notes that it does have rituals—drunk at certain hours and in certain places—and theological-like debates between those who swear by the regular Sun Drop versus those who prefer the diet version, or those who like smaller bottles and cans versus others satisfied with larger plastic containers. It is "religious," student Hoyle points out, in the broader sense used by poet Kahlil Gibran, who sees all things as religious, or in the sense that the priest points out of people tending to make religions of houses or money or "things." "Submission to external power" is a religious theme, and in our fierce loyalties of local products, whether colas, barbecue, or football teams, we do appear, as Hoyle demonstrates with a local soft drink with a strong local following, to invest things with religious-like seriousness.

June 11, 2000

PIMENTO CHEESE

Listening to South Carolina historian Walter Edgar's public radio talk show one Friday, I longed for a phone-in number. Edgar, while interviewing someone who has done research on where the best pimento burgers are around the South, kept insisting that pimento burgers began right there in Columbia. I felt his evidence was provincial and poor, and I wanted to correct him. (A Kentucky friend, however, agrees with Edgar, citing her childhood rearing that referred to pimento cheese as "Palmetto cheese."

Originating pimento burgers is a distinction that could be claimed by any fast-food place that ever served pimento cheese sandwiches and hamburgers. When I was a carhop in 1950, making $1.50 a night plus tips and a meal, I often smeared a thick topping of pimento cheese on an otherwise pedestrian hamburger. We can speculate without much danger of contradiction that similar mergers occurred in hundreds of home kitchens and drive-in restaurants.

Pimento cheese is one of those major southern distinguishing institutions, right up there as a subject for ferocious debate with religion, politics, barbecue, biscuits, gravy, mint juleps, and the proper age and curing of country hams.

Before she gave up her kitchen, my mother made pimento cheese regularly, and her former minister would drive all the way from Indianapolis to west Tennessee to eat it. My mother makes her pimento cheese with a block of American cheese, but my wife uses Velveeta. Most purists would feel they are both wrong, and that pimento cheese can only be made with sharp cheddar or "rat cheese." Some pimento preparers blend cheddar and one or more other cheeses.

Other debates focus on what brand of mayonnaise to use (or whether to make your own), whether to drain the pimientos and leave the juice, whether to mix the concoction with utensils or with your hands or feed it through a meat grinder, whether to add sugar or how much, whether to throw in olives or jalapeños, whether to use chopped pimientos or whole or sliced ones and how many to use, whether to add milk or cream cheese or lemon juice or salt or Tabasco or onions or garlic or vinegar—or Worcestershire sauce (as Elvis did).

There are even debates about how to spell it or pronounce it. Most recipes and menus call it *pimento* cheese, but technically it is made with *pimiento* peppers. *Pimiento* is Spanish for pepper. Upper-class consumers spread it on celery stalks or gourmet crackers and call it "puh-mintah," but most folks mumble it and call it "p'minnah."

In America, Georgia is the biggest producer. According to the Southern Foodways Alliance (based at Ole Miss, and one of my favorite organizations), prepared pimento cheese was available in southern groceries as far back as 1915, and in 1916 George Reigel of Pomona Products Company started canning Sunshine Pimentos in Griffin, Georgia, which spread to kitchens everywhere.

Perhaps they serve pimento cheese sandwiches at the Masters Tournament in Augusta because of that Georgia connection. We bet there are more pimientos grown in Georgia than peaches, and that as long as they are redesigning their state flag there, they might as well change their nickname from "The Peach State" to "The Pimento State."

Southerners tired of debating the multitudinous varieties of barbecue turned their attention for the summer to pimento cheese. (It sure beats being consumed by debates on the economy.)

Southern Foodways Alliance, the Southeast Dairy Association, and Web site http://www.ilovecheese.com teamed up to collect pimento cheese recipes and memories. Their enticing announcement included these instructions:

> Tell us about how your mother always hand-grated her cheese. Let the world know about how your father's homemade mayonnaise made all the difference. Tell us a story of 100 or so words about what pimento cheese has meant to you and your people. Include a recipe and please detail the recipe's provenance.

> Deadline for entries is July 31. Three finalists will be announced on August 31. The winner will receive a free trip to the Southern Foodways Symposium . . . October 2–5 in Oxford, Mississippi . . . , a monster jar of pimentos and a wheel of delicious sharp cheddar cheese . . . (and) chef Louis Osteen of Louis's at Pawley's will feature their [sic] recipe on his menu for the month of November.

If I can find out what "provenance" means in this invitation, I may enter.

June 15, 2003

Chapter 7

PLAY
"MY CUP RUNNETH OVER"

SPITTING

For a long while I thought what was missing from televised baseball games was probably real grass, the feel of summer heat, the pressing together and sharing of the game by a crowd, or the smell of hot dogs. Then I decided the missing ingredient was player identification. As we age, we no longer know the players' names, numbers, stats, and line-up sequences. Failing to identify the players, we can't identify with them. In all of these theories, however, I have been overlooking the obvious.

Spitting.

I never expected expectoration to be the missing ingredient. No other vanishing symbol marks the passing of baseball as does the disappearance of spitting. Not even the coming of electrified scoreboards invisibly operated, replacing boys perched on ledges who hooked on metal plates each half-inning, has so radically changed the face of baseball as has the passing of spitting. If the television camera catches a player in the act of chewing, chances are nine in ten that he is chewing gum. Sometimes you even see a bubble being blown, but not a player spitting. The extinction of expectoration is a major cultural phenomenon and one not confined to baseball. When you think about it, the disappearance of spitting may be the most significant line between the Old South and the New South.

Spitting has been swallowed up, or down, by progress. In older days, when every house had open fireplaces or topless molasses buckets in every room, there were snuff cans on every mantel and tobacco twists hanging in every smokehouse. Trains and buses, themselves symbols of progress, had signs at both ends of every coach, warning that spitting was prohibited by law, especially in the aisles. But now spitting has gone the way of the Saturday curb market and the mule, the cotton gin and the feed store, the one-pump country-store porch and the cane-bottomed chair, the woodpile and the back porch water bucket.

The only relics are the white circles of chewing tobacco cans on the seats of faded blue jeans worn by high school boys trying to live up to their daddies' reputations. The scandal of baseball is not that Pete Rose has clay feet but that he chews gum and is never shown spitting. In that transition is contained all the others that mark the game's changes from what made it what it was. Without spitting, why not play on carpet instead of grass? Why not watch from inside your house instead of out at the park? Why not eat microwave dinners instead of hot dogs? Why not open a jar of honey-roasted peanuts instead of cracking your own from their shells? Why not grasp, dry-handed, the controls of a video game instead of spitting in your palms to grasp the adhesive-wrapped handle of a wooden bat or spitting on a sight of a rifle to improve your firing?

The cuspidors we find only in flea markets and antique shops today are the containers of our past. Time has muted their pings.

June 12, 1989

BASEBALL'S GHOSTS

In our culture, movie houses are about the only place males can cry. They are dark, and unless you call attention to yourself by sobbing, no one need ever know you have shed tears.

I thoroughly enjoyed my birthday last month. My wife and our youngest daughter took me to see *Field of Dreams*. It's about a midwestern farmer who hears a voice telling him to clear away his cornfield and build a baseball field. He does, and ghosts of the banned Chicago Black Sox arrive to play upon it, followed by the ghosts of a doctor who played one half-inning in the majors without ever getting to bat and of the farmer's father, who was a semipro catcher who never made it to the big time and who never got to play catch with the son.

Only true believers in the magic of baseball can see the ghosts playing, but that's no problem. People drive there from all over the country and pay twenty dollars a head to watch, saving the farm and the field from bankruptcy. Here were all the forgotten players, the dreamers whose careers never developed or were cut short, pitted against giants of the game like Gil Hodges who never gave it up. Here was the All-American Everyman's dream come true, the chance to sparkle on the diamond, to slide into glory, to catch the golden ring, and to fulfill a father's fondest hopes for himself and for his sons.

I don't understand the modern fantasies that have replaced baseball. I fail to see how today's soap operas or Disney parks or shopping malls offer illusions anywhere comparable to what baseball once did. Baseball's spell is a mystery. Football and basketball may have passed it in gate receipts but not in sheer sentimentality. Some veterans tell me that World War II came close to giving them in reality the feelings baseball gave them in fantasy, but that even it fell short. Incidentally, the game got its real start when the troops took it away from Abner Doubleday in the Civil War, so maybe the link between it and fighting for a cause is closer than one would think.

I'm an educator, and some of my colleagues have trouble understanding why Bart Giamatti would give up being president of Yale University to become commissioner of baseball. I don't have any trouble understanding that at all, other than having a little envy of him for getting the promotion. All of the faded photographs of family albums, all of the warm feelings of Christmas, and all of the forgotten dreams of growing up can be wrapped up in a white horsehide ball stitched in red. If you ever want to take up a collection that really means something at the end of a man's career, put the offering on a home plate.

The movie is a real eye-washer. When it was over and the house lights came up while the credits were being shown, none of the men in the audience got up and left.

We didn't want it to end.

Perhaps it is well that it did while we still had a few unshed tears to spare. When they are all used up, perhaps baseball will finally be over. This way, we're left aching for more, and the game can go on.

June 19, 1989

WOMEN'S SOFTBALL

The first casualty of World War II was semipro baseball. The war carted away the men and boys who made up the little company teams that covered the prewar South like ants at picnics. The lighted fields which had become the pride and gathering places of the small towns stood vacant but only for a short while. The women of the South came to the rescue, just as they already had by replacing their absent men as salesclerks and factory hands. Women's softball was born. Until the male base runners came home, it would have to do. As it turned out, it did a whole lot more than just fill a void.

I was reminded of those summer evenings by an old photograph of the Coca-Cola team on which our mother played. "High-Pockets" Rawls, who worked for years for the bottling plant, back when Cokes came in six-ounce green glass bottles in twenty-four-bottle wooden cases, made a special trip to bring it to me when I was home visiting. The women are lined up, wearing their white shorts and their white T-shirts and caps with the team logo patches stitched on them. My brother and I and Billy Dyer, the team mascots whom the entire team served as babysitters, are down in front of them, wearing the same outfits.

The faces in the picture, which must date back to 1943 or 1944, are ageless. Most of the team is still alive, and when I meet some of them today I instantly see each as we saw her back then. Chicken and Pickin', the pitcher and catcher dynamic duo, made Bob Feller and Yogi Berra look like amateurs. Backing them up on the bases and out in the outfield were housewives of every conceivable shape and talent. The survivors still talk about the peculiar way this infielder threw or that outfielder, arms extended sideways, chased a fly ball. The most popular umpire was a mute. It was just as well that he couldn't shout back, because he never would have gotten a word in anyway. (Later on, when I was older and playing baseball myself, the same man would call some of our games, and I learned fast from him that neither authority nor profanity needs words to get a message across clearly.)

Crowds came to see them, just as they had come to see the men before the war. Women's teams filled a community need, for they were the town's entertainment in that pretelevision period on nights when there were no church prayer meetings or when everyone had already seen the local movies, which changed twice a week. More than that, they were a way the town could get together to say it was holding on until the war could end and the boys came home. Little did this home guard know that in holding on they were a vanguard of change. Once they traded dusting their parlors for the dirt of the diamond and the night lights of the stadium, things would never be the same again.

Women had come out in public, knees showing and civic spirit soaring, and they would never go back in. They pioneered just as surely as had the wives of Daniel Boone and Davy Crockett and, while keeping the home plates burning, had made a place for themselves in a business and professional world that had scorned them until then. Leave it to the ladies to do just that. They always make the world better.

September 11, 1989

TIED GAME

It's pretty late to be saying what needed saying back in October (1991), but it's been festering ever since and needs releasing. What happened in the World Series last year was wrong. It was wrong for the Series to go beyond the ninth inning of the seventh game. The Series should have been declared a tie. It was wrong that it wasn't. The Twins and Braves should have been declared cochampions. It is wrong that they weren't.

By the ninth inning of the seventh day, everything that really matters had been decided. The teams were equal, both were winners, there were no losers, and the real championship was for the game itself. Baseball had proven again why it has always been the national game, why it is the sun around which all other sports are but revolving planets borrowing its light. Things should have been left there. The extra inning proved nothing. Or if it did, it proved the wrong things—that winning is everything, that there always has to be a loser, that declaring a victor is more important than celebrating the game itself, that civilization has not progressed at all from the days of gladiators and thumbs-down spectators, or that drawing blood is more important than a drawn game.

Frank Kinsella, the man who wrote *Field of Dreams,* understands better than most how reason and passion, each at its best, meet on the baseball diamond. He pictures the batter's box as a point in time from which the first and third baselines diverge endlessly, on past first and third, on past right and left fields, on through the puny picket arc of a fence, so defenseless to stop them—ever onward, rationally moving in perfectly straight geometric lines outward to encompass the universe and all of time with all of its rules and laws of solar system regularities and certainties, glimpses of which the game going on back where the lines begin provides.

In the rationality and immensity of it all comes awe, in the microcosm and motion of a baseball game come mystery and emotion. And when, in a rare moment, such diverging evokes convergence of mind and heart, of reason and passion, as the end of the ninth in the end of the seventh did, that moment ought not be disturbed lest the universe it embodies be disturbed as well. To require an ending to perfection, as that unnecessary and irreverent tenth inning did, is to deny the existence of infinity and the promise of eternity, and that is wrong.

Had the game ended in the tie it was, the game would have gone on forever, would have been unending and unended. But as it was, everything unfolding from the batter's box in the first inning of the first game collapsed back into it in the top of the tenth. The analogy of eternity being reached was destroyed, and The Game became just a game. We needed the analogy more than we needed to break the tie. Our natural analogies have been taken from us, for we no longer live in nature. Like zoo cages, asphalt and linoleum separate us from the dirt, streets and sidewalks from the grass, buildings and freeways from the trees, smog and lights from the heavens—and a tiebreaker from the universe.

Like all series, this 1991 one too will be remembered, but not as it could have been had the tie been allowed to stand. In needing to declare a winner, we all lost. And now another season is beginning. Each season's beginning resurrects hopes for perfection, and perfection does not choose sides. The perfect game comes not in the pitcher's no-hit, no-run victory but in the drawing of the best from all the players and spectators alike. It came in an instant last October at the end of the ninth on the seventh day. We made it into a Halley's Comet we couldn't see; it may not come again in our lifetime.

On that seventh day, we should have rested then and there and looked around us and seen that it was good. But instead we are left with regret that we didn't and with hope that in the cycle of seasons imitative of forgotten nature we may even yet learn and have the chance again to do just that.

It was a fielder's choice, and we dropped the ball.

April 6, 1992

Baltimore. Is it possible this is the city which Lincoln had to bypass lest he be assassinated on his way to taking office? Is this the city which mobbed New England troops hastening south to Washington to protect it from being taken by green rebel troops converging on it after the fall of Fort Sumter?

Now, some 131 years later, Baltimore is a city of history. Behind its awesome waterfront of glistening skyscrapers, its harbor, its aquarium, and its convention center are narrower streets and older homes and storefronts that testify to its age. But the reason for my being there two days in August is in Baltimore's heart—tying old and new together where avenues, Amtrak, rail express, interstates, and airport converge, meeting and emptying themselves—in a baseball park. The whole inner city seems built around it.

It is not just any major league baseball stadium. It is an extraordinary place, probably the best big league baseball park on the continent (and hence in the world, since baseball is uniquely North America's possession). And what makes Oriole Park at Camden Yards in Baltimore so extraordinary is that it seems so ordinary. Oriole Park was designed for baseball fans. In fact, it was designed by baseball fans. It was designed for no other games, no other events, no other purposes than the appreciation of baseball. It has an outfield carpeted with rich green grass and an infield of real dirt.

There is no artificial turf beneath the players' feet and no manmade dome over their heads. Oriole Park has no protective inner wall between the fans in the stands and the game on the field. First-row patrons can lean over the fences and reach for bouncing fouls and 360-feet flies, talk with and taunt the players, shake a hand and get an autograph, and see real dirt and grass stains on uniforms. Early birds (appropriate for "Orioles") can see batting practice from a centerfield veranda or picnic behind the pitching bullpen in left centerfield before the gates open.

Over forty-seven thousand spectators can crowd into the park and not feel crowded. In its three tiers of seats, there isn't a bad seat to be found. The windows to the press box and announcers' booths are open, for their occupants are also part of the crowd. Even the army of ushers, concessionaires, groundskeepers, and officials are part of the family of fans, greeting strangers as they would friends, engrossed in the game even as they go about their repetitious work, blending into the ambience of the architecture.

This is big-time baseball architecture at its finest. In a century which has seen Ebbets Field and Sportsman Park, and other monuments once thought imperishable, disappear like the desert statue of Ozymandias, here is one that promises to take baseball in its highest glory into the twenty-first century. In its modernity, it has its inevitable electronic scoreboard, its instant replays, its escalators, its multiple hallway lounges and television sets, its stereophonic sound system, its hidden video cameras, and its carpeted and richly appointed VIP boxes. But such accoutrements are inconspicuous, tastefully woven into the whole, and happily secondary. What are primary are the game on the field and the spirit of the crowd.

This is no Disney World. No one escapes reality in today's theme parks, nor even in many of more recent big-city arenas. But in Oriole Park, one can almost escape. Miles away, even as we watched Baltimore lose a good one 10-8 and win a closer one 2-1 against Seattle, the Republican Convention was assembled in Texas. The contrasts of the people and the programs and the mood were self-evident. In the Astrodome, the talk was about recharging the national batteries for the pursuit of happiness. But in Oriole Park, some forty-five thousand of us felt we had already found happiness.

Probably what we actually found was more symbol than substance. Maybe the park is a vestige of a bygone age of dinosaurs. Maybe the America that gave birth to and was synonymous with baseball is extinct, and with it the sport, killed by the glacier of World War II industrial and economic growth and mobility. Maybe America's pastime has become something left behind in America's "past time." Certainly the sport has changed. The "pros" have been redefined in terms of big money and legal negotiating, unfree free agents, and television receipts. It has been taken away from the players and from the fans and delivered to the Pharisees.

Wherever baseball does survive, it testifies to an era and aura where rules were clear and were held and observed in common by mutual consent, where civil discourse chattered around the infield, where everyone who wanted to could be on a team. Baseball survives in its purest form in remnant small towns where, on sandlots at sunset, sticks still swat balls of twine wrapped in friction tape. And up in the majors, it survives best in Baltimore.

September 7, 1992

TY COBB

Nearly eighty years after the event, Wofford College, a Phi Beta Kappa campus in Spartanburg, South Carolina, has good reason to remember baseball great, Ty Cobb. A campus visit by the Georgia Peach in 1913 turned out to be almost as exciting and as bloody as the Great War, which followed it four years later. The *Spartanburg Journal* of Saturday, April 4, 1913, under a headline, "Ty Cobb's Bunch Play Here Today," announced "the much heralded game between Ty Cobb's famous bunch of All-Stars and the Wofford Invincibles, who have yet to taste defeat this season," and predicted a victory for the professionals but a lively contest nonetheless.

Reporting the next Tuesday, April 7, the same paper noted that Cobb's bunch won a close one, 9-8, but that the ninth inning proved especially "amusing." "Osborne, a Wofford player, was coaching on the third baseline and Ty was pitching. What passed between the man and the child could not be heard in the stands, but the Wofford boy bristled up like a Bantam rooster and wanted to fight. He was just so small and Cobb just so big that the whole incident was really amusing. After the words, Cobb stated that he would see the player after the game. About 613 boys gathered about Cobb intent upon killing him, or doing something else equally as harmful, and the prompt arrival of officers saved Cobb's life."

Notice the ambiguous accuracy of the reporting: "about 613 boys" (not "about 600"). Notice also the imaginative understatement of the mob's intent: "bent on killing him, or something else equally as harmful." (What could possibly be "equally as harmful" as being killed?)

But the story didn't end on the field. Two days later, on Thursday, April 9, the *Spartanburg Herald* headlined: "Tyrus Cobb and Wofford Player Fight in Hotel." Both Wofford and Cobb's All-Stars were in Greenville to play Furman University on Monday, April 6. Traveling salesmen brought to Spartanburg the suppressed news of a fistfight between Rutledge Osborne, a Wofford student from Anderson, and Tyrus Cobb. "One report was that Osborne publicly cursed Cobb in the dining room of the hotel; another was that Osborne drew a pistol, which was wrested from him." The *Spartanburg Journal* of the same day reported that Dr. Henry Nelson Snyder, president of Wofford College, who lectured the boys, that is, the student body, "deplores the affair," but would not bring charges against the student or team.

The full story came out in the *Spartanburg Herald* of Saturday, April 11, 1913:

> Mr. Osborne yesterday admitted that he drew a pistol when
> attacked by Cobb, but justified it on the ground that Cobb was
> much larger than he and had made threats against him.

After his trouble with Osborne in Spartanburg Saturday, Cobb, it is said, declared he would 'beat Osborne's face into jelly' when they met on Monday in Greenville. Osborne said that he borrowed the pistol to protect himself, but tried to avoid the difficulty.

. . . Cobb went to [Wofford] Coach McCarthy's room and asked my name. When I was told this, just before dinner, I slipped up to my room and put the pistol in my pocket.

When dinner was over, one of my teammates and I took the elevator for the room to dress. As the elevator started, Cobb and one of his men stepped in. When we arrived at the stop, he grasped me by the collar and pulled me out into his room, my companion going to the first floor for the rest of the team. I was thus alone with Cobb, Coles, McMillan and another member of Cobb's team. He struck at me and I naturally drew the gun. This made him release me, but Cad Coles slipped up behind me and wrenched the gun from my hand. Cobb then jumped on me and it was an easy matter for a man of his size to beat me up considerably. I did not hunt a scrap and I hated to be mixed up in one. Cobb acted cowardly and overbearing, and I, being only a boy, acted on the impulse of the moment.

How's that for excitement!

Osborne later transferred to the University of South Carolina and graduated in 1916. Years later, he served as chairman of its Board of Trustees, and the USC central administration building was named for him.

Cobb, on the other hand, never dared return to Wofford.

November 30, 1992

REFORMING BASEBALL

Six weeks ago our family concern was how our daughters' mother (aka my wife) would adjust to having no children at home after twenty-eight years. Free at last, would she know what to do with liberty? All in all, after a slow start, she has coped fairly well. The first week she papered the bathroom and scrubbed sticky stuff left by old tape off of walls, doors, and desks. The first three weeks she mailed our absentee nestlings letters or cards every day. Then she took to roaming Wal-Mart for "little things they may need" and mailing them things like dental floss, lightbulbs, and artificial leaves. Last week she found a half-time job.

She was developing a vacant look around the eyes, and she was so unused to not having the phone ring constantly that she would talk with anyone unfortunate enough to call. She doted on wrong numbers who get her by mistake; they obviously need her motherly help. She refused to hang up on magazine or credit-card salesmen who call at suppertime each evening. She mastered the art of having personalized ten-minute conversations about *Time* or VisaGold. She can ferret out the life story of any Tom, Dick, or Harry who calls and that of any Jason and Sheila, Shondra, and Geneva, as well.

But she has exercised self-discipline, too. When she found herself talking back to Oprah and Alex Trebek on television and trying to remember birth dates for characters on *Days of Our Lives,* she forced herself to stop watching.

And that's when an amazing thing happened. Salvation comes in unsuspected ways, and so it did in this case. She flipped channels to TBS, and a miracle came along. She adopted the Atlanta Braves. When she stumbled across them on Turner Broadcasting, the Braves were a miserable lot. They were hopelessly marooned behind the Giants, too far gone ever to catch up. But then our daughters' mother (aka my wife) found them. This motheringless mother took the Braves to her aching bosom and brought them back to life.

Loving baseball requires a fascination with statistics and detail. There is a special vocabulary that has to be learned: words like "bunt," "balk," "fade," "fly," and "ground." There are RBIs, HPs, ERAs, W-Ls, and DUIs that need to be memorized and then updated instantaneously; she learned the game quickly, but she has brought to the game a whole new dimension. She can tell you the names of most the Braves players, whether or not they are married (and, if not, whether they are engaged), which ones scratch themselves in public, which ones refuse to shave on road trips, which ones chew gum and which others are secretly chewing tobacco in the dugout when the camera isn't on them, which ones read a lot, and what the likely SAT scores would be for each.

She thinks Jeff Blauser is very intelligent and has a great sense of humor, that Mark Lemke is loveable, that David Justice is a hunk, and that Steve Avery needs someone like her to take care of him. Otis Nixon is experienced and dependable, and she thinks I could learn a lot from him about aging well. In between games she does strange things, like reading the sports page each morning before even getting her coffee or going to the dentist's office often to read *Sports Illustrated* (Although, as noted above, she knows all their phone salesmen on a first name basis, we don't subscribe. She thinks the swimsuit edition is too overdone.)

The awful thing is that when she discovered this tribe of orphans, they were about 12 games behind the Giants in the division race. Actually, that was what attracted her in the first place. These were obviously young men in need, and Jane Fonda just wasn't getting the job done. Pretty soon after she started watching the Braves, they started climbing in the ratings, and by late September they were three games ahead. She is convinced she is the reason. It is almost to the superstition point. When she misses a game, they lose. When she skips an inning to microwave our dinner, the other team scores. We miss parties and concerts in order to watch the Braves. She is sort of a reverse Oral Roberts; she sends power back through the TV set. By her reckoning, she came along just in time. The Braves needed her, she heeded the call, and she has mothered them along very well indeed. I haven't got the heart to tell her that when she adopted them and they started winning was also about the time they acquired Fred McGriff.

Her latest baseball cause is reforming the rules. She keeps a running list of her proposed "improvements" for the game. For example, she thinks the statisticians are unfair. A pitcher can leave the game after, say, seven innings with the team ahead. Then in the eighth inning, the relief pitcher blows the lead, but in the ninth, a third pitcher gets it back. The last pitcher gets credited with the win, for only one inning's work, while the starter who lasted and led for seven innings gets nothing. Betsy thinks that is a numerical crime worth redressing.

She also frets about the arbitrariness of classifying fielding errors. One man's bobble is an error, but another's is counted as a hit. She has the same concerns about inequities of strike zones. Taller players have bigger spaces between the knees and bottoms of their uniforms' lettering which puts the shorter players like Mordecai, Lemke, and Belliard at an advantage in batting. She thinks there ought to be some electronic device that could make the strike zone the same for all batters.

Others things simply puzzle her. Much of it has to do with "insider" information. What constitutes an infield fly? Why do runners have to tag up after a fly ball is caught? Why does a batter have to hold the trademark of his bat up? How do they select batboys (or bat persons)? How far do you have to be outside the baseline to be called out? Why do so many baseball players spit and scratch in public? How does the TV camera know exactly when a player is going to mouth some obscenity? Why aren't players required as part of their contracts to give autographs and be pleasant to fans? If right-handed batters run the bases counterclockwise, why can't left-handed batters run them clockwise? Do you have to be a descendant or relative of Harry Caray to get a sportscasting job? Why can't the umpires call technical fouls against the crowd? Isn't a "ground ball" really a "grounded" ball?

What has her bamboozled the most, being the former college newspaper editor and English teacher she is, is the use of the past tense of "fly." It bothers her to no end that a batter "flied out" to left field. The past tense of "fly" in her grammar book is "flew," and she feels strongly that announcers should be saying "Klesko flew out to left field."

There is a logical explanation for using "flied," I tell her. Actually what the announcer is saying is that "Klesko hit a fly ball to left field, where it was apprehended." Life and innings are too short for long sentences like that. Common usage takes the adjective (not a verb), "fly," and turns it from "fly ball" into a noun, a "fly." Then the noun is turned into a verb: Klesko "flies" (hits a ball in the air "on the fly" and not on the ground) out to left field; Klesko "flied" (not "flew") out to left field; Klesko "has flied" (not "has flown").

That may explain it, she responds, but explaining it doesn't make it right. After all, she says, you don't say the batter "striked out"; you say he "struck out." If "strike" becomes "struck," then "fly" ought to be "flew," she reasons. The more serious problem, she says, is that baseball hasn't had anyone literate in charge since Bart Giamatti died. Anyone who could get rid of Pete Rose, she reasons, could correct poor grammar by sportscasters. But, alas, baseball blew (not "blied") its best hope for reforms when Giamatti died so prematurely; baseball is the poorer for that loss.

October 4, 1993, and August 19, 1996

LACED-UP LEATHER

I was whisked to the hospital in mid-March with no more preparation time than that Kansas tornado gave Dorothy. Despite surgery to repair an aorta ruptured by an aneurysm, my past six weeks in recovery have not been without irony and fun. Now I am well enough to finish the essay I was writing when interrupted.

The NCAA basketball tournament had just ended, and I was lamenting the loss of real leather basketballs and footballs with real leather lacings and rubberized air bags (that could be patched if necessary). I was recalling the smell of the leather and the feel of the lacing on the fingertips, and the clunky thud sound the balls made on the ground when there wasn't enough air in them. Those recollections were triggering, too, memories of the smell of neat's-foot oil on fielders' gloves and old-time baseballs. Even the team shoes were leather back then.

Those were leather-and-lacings days. They have been gone for decades, but for some of us, today's footballs and basketballs still just don't feel real. They lack the shape and the feel and the smell of authenticity. These "modern-day" substitutes, universal though they have become, seem even yet to be some sort of ersatz athletic equipment forced upon us by wartime rationing, not real or permanent at all.

But, alas, the real reality is just the opposite. In order to show my own children what "real" basketballs and footballs were, we have to visit glassed-in college trophy cases where deflated old leather balls with bowl-game scores painted on them or long-dead teams' autographs fading on them gather dust.

That's about as far as I had gotten in my leather-reverie before they wheeled me off into surgery. When I awoke, I had stitchings of my own that easily rivaled those on the old leather footballs and baseballs, and I had an abdomen as deflated as one of them. I also had a new Dacron aorta in place of my own fifty-eight-year-old model. With that last addition came a change in attitude. Maybe new products that keep the game going aren't such bad things after all!

How truly important is it that football be played on grass outdoors instead of on artificial turf indoors, or that game balls be stitched and laced rather than melted and molded, or that the national anthem be sung live rather than on a recording? Those and a hundred other personal preferences all of us love to debate and recall are all matters of "druthers." Given a choice, we'd "druther" play games certain ways than other ways, and usually our druthers are linked to our memories of how we used to play those games ourselves.

But when push gets down to shove, we need to be grateful that the games get to go on, despite all the adaptations and changes changing times impose upon them. I sure as heck don't like the attitudes of most of the own-ers of big-time teams these days, nor do I like the salary packages, or the easy trading that takes place. But I sure am grateful that we still have baseball teams and parks and uniforms. Despite their modern perversions and aber-rations, modern sports still have a long, long way to go before I am willing to drop them altogether. I am a little more willing to compromise with changes, if they involve survival, than I once was.

If I can live with an artificial aorta, but not without it, surely I can learn to live with artificial turf and with synthetic rather than true-leather game balls, so long as the game gets to go on.

May 2, 1994

ORGANIZED SPORTS

William J. Hardee, one of the more distinguished generals in the ill-fated western army of the Confederacy, had been a U.S. soldier for twenty-five years when war came. In 1853, seeking to modernize its tactics in con-formity with French army procedures, Hardee was asked by Jefferson Davis, then secretary of war, to write a new manual for the light infantry and to revise the cavalry manual. It would be used by both sides when the Civil War came. I have before me a reprint of an 1862 *Hardee's Rifle and Light Infantry Tactics,* printed in New York, a compilation of many procedures designed to do away with soldierly independence and to forge units of mil-itary mass into mobile units. There is some debate about whether or not Hardee actually wrote the manual. Hardee went to the other side, but the U.S. army was not too proud to keep using his work. He had risen slowly through the army's ranks, and by 1860 he was commandant of West Point, from which he had graduated in 1838.

On the northern side was another general and West Pointer, Abner Doubleday. Doubleday had been at Fort Sumter when war came and later gained fame for capturing General Archer and many rebels at Gettysburg. But Doubleday is remembered most as the inventor of baseball. The most popular version of the invention's legend is that he devised it as a game to relieve boredom for Yankee troops. Another version of that myth has him at Cooperstown, New York, in 1839, where a rambunctious ballgame between Otsego Academy and Green's Select School inspired him to draw up rules on the spot. The truth is, Doubleday was at West Point and couldn't have been at Cooperstown in 1839, but legend is more important than truth.

So here we have two Civil War generals of some considerable fame, each credited with a pre–Civil War codification of rules of conduct, one for military units drilling and on fields of battle, and the other for baseball teams warring on another field.

What comes across this season of the year, as the World Series returns to our hearts and consciousness after a year's hiatus, is the civility and discipline of the baseball contest, not unlike romanticized versions of the Civil War. Behind the uniforms of baseball players and soldiers is a uniformity of which Hardee and Doubleday are the alleged authors. In the Civil War, southern soldiers were less disciplined than northern ones. They had come from isolated farms and plantations and hamlets and were unaccustomed to following orders. Northern soldiers came from regimented factories and large cities and were accustomed to being commanded. U.S. General McClellan thought the rules were so important that he devoted almost a year, while Abe Lincoln fretted, to training troops after McDowell (a classmate of Hardee) lost at the First Battle of Bull Run. Southern troops accepted only a minimum of discipline, improvised to find food and to clothe themselves, and were reluctant to march in step. Some critics think their improvisational skills and reluctance to be disciplined is why the war went on as long as it did. Their individualism and inventiveness is what gave them hope and "a sporting chance."

In my youth, Little League baseball came to our town too late for me. I had grown up playing on sandlots with balls made of twine and wrapped in tape, with teams from the neighborhood that more often than not included both sexes, and without rulebooks and practices. What rules and baselines we had, we made up ourselves. We just chose sides and played. My brother, two years younger, was on one of the first Little League teams, playing on a new field with stadium seating, fences, lines, bases, umpires, and uniforms. At the time, I envied him. In my old age, watching the predictability and professionalism of regulated major league baseball, I am having second thoughts; something is missing.

The zaniness, the flexibility, and the individualistic style of crackerjack players like Dizzy Dean and Satchel Paige and Babe Ruth just aren't there. The game is interesting but boring and usually forgettable simply because it relies so much upon tested rules and habitual responses. The game has become so professional, so routine, and so regulated, it's hard to understand why it's still called a "sport." The "heaven" of a ballpark that Kevin Costner builds in *Field of Dreams* is in the middle of an Iowa cornfield and not in a city. There is a difference between choreography and free dance, between formal art and impressionism, between running against the marathon masses and running against one's own clock, between playing to win and playing for the sheer joy of playing without a scoreboard or record book, and between a machine and a human.

Generals Hardee and Doubleday need to answer for what they did. The applause they deserve for outlawing chaos for troops and teams is offset somewhat by the loss of individualism and free expression that we used to call sport.

October 15, 1995

GOLF

I am ignorant about the methods and meanings of golf. In my college days, my roommate was big into golfing (and also into Glenn Miller music) and tried to make me share his enthusiasm. I trudged along with him over his hometown course a few times, wondering what drove men to hit a little ball, chase it over kingdom come, and then come back for more. I even took to visiting Picadome Par Three Golf Course and Driving Range out behind the Campbell House hotel in Lexington, Kentucky. It had night lights and was open until midnight. Playing in the fog once a week did nothing to motivate me to want to be a golfer.

Years later, I walked a Kentucky course with my father and brother a few times, but still with no aspirations. I had more fun fishing for abandoned balls at edges of water hazards than in playing the game. When our daughters always beat me in assorted Putt-Putt centers in Gatlinburg and state parks, I decided golfing wasn't my game. I did take up doubles tennis, until weight and angina made me give it up about eight years ago.

A recent bypass operation has filled me with new life and resolve. For some mysterious reason, I feel fit enough to start playing golf and actually find myself wanting to. I'm not as old as Arnold Palmer and only a few years older than Jack Nicklaus, and I have delusions of grandeur about how to have fun in my sixties. A monumental downtown restoration project is planning to put in a nine-hole par three course just across the railroad tracks from my office, and I figure that I may turn out to be one of its best customers. In my fantasies, after hard practicing for a couple of years, I'll periodically grab a trio of unsuspecting Wofford College students and take them to the cleaners at the new course next door.

Jim Barrett, a very good friend who is a superb golfer and who has made pilgrimages to golf courses in both Scotland and Ireland (playing in Ireland with an owner of the Pittsburgh Steelers) has given me his own first set of golf clubs. They are in my basement, and I daily take out a club and give it some practice swings. I'm still in heart rehab, and it's winter, so it'll be a couple of months before I can actually practice.

Meanwhile, he's told me that selecting a putter is a very personal thing, and so I visit various sports stores to try some out. I favor old-style putters that one bends over instead of newer tall jobs that one uses standing erect. My barber sells custom-made clubs on the side, and I have long talks with him about stainless steel and graphite shafts; it beats talking about Newt Gingrich, government intrusions, or pro football.

While waiting for warm weather and my rejuvenated leg and arm muscles, I am working on golfing philosophy. I tried reading golf instruction books and watching some golf instruction videotapes, but they were about as exciting as reading a cookbook without getting to taste the dishes. But I did read and get inspired by a moving book about a golfing son taking his dying father, also a golfer, to Scotland: James Dodson's *Final Rounds* (Bantam). It prepared me admirably to read another book, one on golfing as a form of transcendental mysticism, thoughtfully given me by our eldest daughter. It is Michael Murphy's *Golf in the Kingdom* (Viking). The hero of the book is an unorthodox golfer in Scotland named Shivas Irons, whom Murphy met at Burningbush (a fictional name).

To Irons, golfing was a unique, almost religious, way of life. Irons was given to saying things like: "Driving downwind, follow the shot to infinity" or "Imagine the golf ball as a hole in space." Most of all, "learn to take your time in playing the game and reaching your goal," he counseled. He also said that trying too hard is the best way to ruin your game, and don't be under any illusions that you will ever be a better man for all your practicing and playing. To Irons, the whole world was a mess of paradoxes, and learning to live happily with paradox, the unexpected, and the prodding and petty things of life is distilled into how one approaches golfing. I have illusions that I can learn to sit cross-legged in silent meditation and then arise to break par.

I have a long way to go before that spiritual release comes. Right now, I worry a lot about the warping effects that my wearing trifocals will have on my hitting the ball squarely. You don't see many golfers or baseball batters wearing glasses. Even so, despite eyesight and age, my intuition tells me I am a golfing natural.

After all, my ancestors were Scottish. Besides that, I grew up just 125 miles from Memphis's Cary Middlecoff. How can I miss?

January 20, 1997

GREAT BALLPARKS

The first time we saw Atlanta–Fulton County Stadium, which was torn down this month, was in the spring of '66. A flight from New York was late, making us miss our connection to Tuscaloosa and forcing us to spend the night in Atlanta. We stayed at the Georgia Tech Motel, and the cab ride to it took us past the stadium, then less than a year old. Atlanta was less packed in those days, and the stadium seemed to rise in free space, a rather majestic sight on a site that was better known for having been leveled by General Sherman 102 years earlier.

The Beatles had been there before us, in the summer of '65, playing to thirty-four thousand screaming fans who paid $5.50 to be there. In later years, Billy Graham would preach to three hundred thousand people there (in summer '73), and the following April of '74, Hank Aaron hit his 715th home run there. Near the end of its life, the stadium hosted the sixth game of the '95 World Series, when the Braves beat the Indians 1-0 and became world champions. It was August of '96 before we actually went to a game there. An anniversary present from our daughter took us high into the upper deck, above the pigeons. Our reward was seeing a short losing streak broken, as the Braves won. The stadium closed its gates a few weeks later.

In July of '97 we motored to the new Turner Field. The old stadium was still there, next door, awaiting the twelve hundred synchronized dynamite blasts that, on August 2, would make it crumble like a circle of dominoes in twenty seconds. As ballparks go (literally go), Atlanta–Fulton Stadium, dead at age thirty-two, wasn't much of a place to get nostalgic over. It didn't have the atmosphere of older ballparks such as Ebbets Field, the Polo Grounds, or Sportsman's Park, or even of newer and friendlier parks such as Camden Yards.

Its replacement strikes us as no vast improvement. Turner Field is little different from what it replaced. Our upper deck seats were a little closer to home plate than last year's third base seats but no lower. Both times we felt we needed oxygen masks, and both times we knew we would have seen more on television than we did at such real-life distances. Both times the traffic flow around the place was a psychic and physical challenge. It's a once-a-year Disney place to visit, not an every-home-game second home.

If one wants to see great ballparks, one has to view videos or read picture books. The great ones are history now: Baker Bowl, Philadelphia, 1887–1938; Braves Field, Boston, 1915–52; Comiskey Park, Chicago, 1910–90; Crosley Field, Cincinnati, 1884–1970; Ebbets Field, Brooklyn, 1913–57; Forbes Field, Pittsburgh, 1909–70; Griffith Stadium, Washington, 1903–61; League Park, Cleveland, 1891–1946; Municipal Stadium, Kansas City, 1923–72; the Polo Grounds, New York, 1891–1963; Shibe Park, Philadelphia, 1909–70; and Sportsman's Park, St. Louis, 1902–66.

They looked and smelled like ballparks. Maybe what made them great was their longevity. More likely what made them great was that baseball was still a game in their day. Today it's just another billion-dollar industry. It once was affordable, accessible, visible, audible, sweaty, dusty, and democratic.

Baseball was every boy's game, and baseball players were every boy's heroes. Boys learned math by keeping baseball statistics, learned physics by swinging a bat or chasing a fly ball, learned psychology by outwitting opponents, learned folklore by listening to old-timers, learned law and parliamentary procedure by knowing baseball rulebooks, and learned religion by observing baseball rituals. Would today's street gangs be transformed today if they had uniforms and mitts and swung clubs at cowhide balls instead of at each other? Who wouldn't rather steal second than steal a car? Something was lost in the translation of mid-century America into century-end America. Great fallen ballparks are symbols of loss.

Atlanta–Fulton County Stadium fell for a parking lot for Turner Field, its clone. (In truth, it went because Turner was built for the Olympics and had to be used afterward.) We live in a throwaway society. Ball players make millions and retire at age thirty; expensive ballparks have a life expectancy of three decades. Fast-food trash is more easily tossed than saved, so why not everything else—hospital supplies, cars, clothes, television ratings, and people—and ballparks and amateur nights? Easy come, easy go.

What about Flavian Amphitheater? Is it next in line to go? It seats forty-five thousand, stands four stories high, is 600 feet long and 500 feet wide, has awnings to protect spectators, is adorned with half columns and arched windows on three stories and rectangle windows and flat columns on the fourth, and forms an oval around a field 282 feet long and 207 feet wide. Concrete supported seats slope gently to the field. In its early days, when not in use for athletic events, it could be flooded for water shows. Thousands of visitors trek to it each year. Flavian Amphitheater is 1,917 years old this year.

Sometimes it's called by its other name, the Coliseum of Rome.

August 4, 1997

WOMEN AND FOOTBALL

At age eleven, our eldest daughter decided to be the first female NFL quarterback. Wearing a complete Minnesota Vikings dazzling purple uniform, shoulder pads and helmet, with Fran Tarkenton's number on the jersey, she practiced handing off and passing on the side lawn all fall long.

She gave it up after getting shin splints and taking up the trumpet. The closest she got to realizing her dream was getting a Tarkenton autograph. I also gave her my own treasured pass to Alabama football practices, personally signed by Bear Bryant in 1966.

Twenty years later, in Durham, North Carolina, a female student at Duke filed charges against the university and its football coach for sex discrimination.

After trying out for placekicker as a walk-on for two years, she alleged the coach told her the previous spring in the presence of the team that she could suit up in the regular season but that he later reneged on the offer during preseason summer practices.

In high school, the same girl had received all-state honors as the placekicker on an otherwise all-male team. As a Blue Devils walk-on, the young student kicked the winning field goal in the annual Blue-White game. Had she been added to the team roster, she would have become the first woman to play NCAA Division I football.

Duke University has distinguished itself for exceptionally high academic standards and for the success of its men's basketball program in both athletic and scholastic rankings. Both men's and women's basketball teams at Duke rank highly among the top universities for players' academic achievements. Basketball teams at Duke consistently make top-ten lists for graduation rates.

By contrast, Duke football within recent memory has not been conspicuous in either athletic or academic top twenty-five listings. Duke football would not likely risk a national crown, an AAC conference title, or a high academic ranking if it suited up the girl.

The coach's defense allegedly was that the girl's presence would be distracting. He would have had a stronger case had he allowed her to play a game and reached that judgment after the fact and with evidence on videotape to prove it. The university's defense is that the suit was "frivolous" and that a head coach's prerogative to sign and play whomever he (in football, not "he or she") pleases is absolute.

The coach and university will win this one. Regardless of the lawsuit, the girl is a senior, and the season likely will be over by the time the court acts.

But Duke will also lose.

Duke football has forfeited its best recent chance to be first in the nation in something. This is another postponement of the day of gender reckoning in college sports that has already been passed in admission of women to the armed services, to the national military academies and recently to VMI and the Citadel as well, to almost all careers, to government service, to the U.S. Senate dining room, and to Little League baseball teams.

Most women's and men's sports pair off in separated but equivalent teams: basketball, soccer, golf, tennis, track, swimming, gymnastics, etc. In the absence of separate but equal female football teams, football stands conspicuously apart.

Duke has not had a good internal controversy since the mid-1970s. The portrait of its most famous alumnus, a president of the United States, hung prominently in the Duke Law School. Chagrined alumni petitioned to have it removed.

The difference between that controversy and the current one was that Richard M. Nixon had had his day on the field and was being judged post-Watergate, but Heather Sue Mercer did not have her day and was judged preseason.

Judgment and justice are not always the same thing.

September 29, 1997

PROFESSIONAL WRESTLING

Approaching graduations sent me scurrying to the local mall in search of gifts.

What shocked me in assorted gift emporiums was the dominance of two categories of items. Huge displays of Star Wars items, timed to coincide with the release of the movie, were everywhere in evidence. But more shocking were titanic stacks of professional wrestling items: plastic figurines, games, T-shirts, books, posters, videos, plastic cups, belts, collector cards, and even underwear.

Chuck Garner, one of my students, made a serious study of this pro wrestling (he calls it "rasslin'") phenomenon, which rivals religion as a mass movement demanding zealous allegiance. Chuck found evidence that 35 million people each week watch professional wrestling in the twelve hours it is on television. The two rival wrestling empires were the World Wrestling Federation and World Championship Wrestling. On Monday night alone, some 15 million people watch pro wrestling, and the two Monday programs ranked first and second in cable ratings viewership, outdrawing *The Simpsons, Ally McBeal, The X-Files, Friends,* and fall's *Monday Night Football.* On pay-TV, monthly matches commanded viewer fees as high as thirty-five dollars a show and drew 850,000 viewers. Appearing in prime time, the most popular wrestling shows assume the youngsters of the households are already in bed, and their televised fare is an abrasive and ribald mixture of soap opera, cultism, and satire.

Garner had several interesting hypotheses to explain wrestling's popularity. One explanation is that we live in a highly technological world, closed off from one another in our autos, offices, homes, and computers, and that people hunger for touches with old-fashioned humanity. Wrestling involves real-live people, both on the mats and in the audiences. A more compelling argument that Garner makes is that, for most of us, the world is a battleground between Good and Evil, between Ups and Downs, between Optimists and Pessimists, and that wrestling is a low-cost way of translating the cosmological struggle into human symbols. In the same way that earlier generations could reduce moral issues to Cowboys and Indians, Allies and Axis, and God and Satan, so the wrestling phenomenon divides mankind and the universe into simplistic symbols of the forces of light and darkness. The good and evil contests of "orthodox" sports—football, basketball, baseball—pale beside wrestling.

There is, Garner thinks, a natural human inclination to want to see the world in such dualistic terms. Mankind has to have someone to adulate, and also has to have someone to hate. Wrestling provides both. Simultaneously with this good/evil dichotomy in wrestling, there is a Jerry Springer kind of fascination with bad language, bad manners, and perverse exhibitionism that also attracts throngs of viewers.

Further, there is a sort of Homeric *Odyssey* and Horatio Alger success-story theme in wrestling, as week after week some hunky hero moves like Hercules another step further in a personal quest to find and to assert himself, to become a superhero. And, finally, Garner shows us, wrestling is a participatory sport. True wrestling fans get into it with a vengeance, chanting for and emulating their favorites, buying all that assortment of memorabilia, viewing the shows religiously, and sharing vicariously in their favorites' fates. The wrestling Web sites number in the thousands. In one year's time, ratings for viewers with four or more years of college leapt 156 percent, and for households with over fifty thousand dollars annual income they climbed 111 percent.

We haven't seen anything like this since the Beatles or Elvis, though wrestling has been around since history began being recorded. Jacob wrestled God early on in the Old Testament, the first Olympics included wrestling, it was a dominant sport in ancient Greece and Rome, and there are Egyptian hieroglyphics of wrestlers. But television has elevated it to a man-centered and this-worldly religion, and also into a major business.

In an early film about the young Abe Lincoln, probably starring Henry Fonda or Raymond Massey, Lincoln wrestles a bully in frontier Illinois. Wrestling was popular in early America. Legends were built about Mike Fink riverboat characters, half-man half-alligator, willing to wrestle any man. A whole county would turn out for a good fight, and Mark Twain and other storytellers wrote wrestling into their stories regularly. Paul Bryant, before his fame as a football coach, first gained Arkansas fame for wrestling a bear, and was "Bear" ever after.

The Civil War was a watershed of sorts for wrestling. War's horrors made civilian wrestling seem tame—although diaries and letters from common soldiers describe campground wrestling as diversion rivaled only by baseball, snowball fights, prayer meetings, parade reviews, and executions of deserters. Around the beginning of this century, wrestling was revived in the form of commercial sport, mostly in the North. Even then, it was still "wrestling for real": unrehearsed, bloody and raw, but also impossible to keep exciting. Wrestlers circling each other endlessly bored the crowds, and the sport declined. "Real wrestling" was soon replaced by "professional wrestling," and the type of wrestling watched avidly on television by millions of people today was born in the staged, rehearsed, barnstorming, wrestling circuits of the North in the 1920s and blossomed when it moved to television and moved South after World War II.

According to Louis M. Kyriakoudes and Peter A. Coclanis (in a *Southern Cultures* journal essay), once television came up with Chicago wrestling and "Gorgeous George" on Wednesday and Saturday nights (ABC and DuMont networks), it became a major entertainment form. It moved South in the 1930s, when Milo Sternborn toured the Southeast, and it rooted in Charlotte in the 1950s in Jim Crockett's National Wrestling Alliance, a Carolinas-Virginia circuit, "the hotbed of professional wrestling." Dick Sternborn, Milo's son, operated the Gulf Coast Championship Wrestling circuit in Alabama and Florida. Big circuits sprang up in Texas and in west Tennessee. In the North, pro football replaced pro wrestling in public attention, but in the South it prospered.

I recall well the frequent renting of the City Auditorium in little Paris, Tennessee, to wrestlers who always seemed to be named Roberts or Welch or Jerry. Posters on light poles advertised major matches down the road in Jackson, Tennessee. Edward Welch, who wrestled as Buddy Fuller, had two sons in the business, Robert and Ronald. (Robert is now known as Col. Robert Parker, a promoter who dresses like Colonel Sanders and Elvis's Col. Tom Parker.) Dusty Rhodes was popular, and his son Dustin followed in dad's steps. Big-time wrestling came in the 1980s, when the World Wrestling Federation moved South, featured Hulk Hogan and Sting and Lex Lugar, and bought time on Ted Turner's WTBS in 1984, then sold the time slot to Jim Crockett's NWA, who in turn sold NWA to Ted Turner himself, who renamed it World Championship Wrestling.

Winners, in case you haven't suspected, are predetermined. Fights are quick and wonderfully staged. They are not unlike early Christian morality plays, in which good and evil players vie and in which good more often triumphs than evil (although it's been found that it pays to let evil win often enough to guarantee rematches and to get audiences back for the rest of the season). Promoters play on our southern biases, too: whites against blacks, rednecks against yankees, soldiers and marines against Russians, cowboys against Indians, macho men against homosexuals.

In 1995, the WWF grossed $58.4 million, and the WCW took in $48.1 million in pay-per-view cable revenues alone. Twenty percent of the audience were males under 18, and 44 percent were males 18 to 54, with women about 36 percent. 75 percent of the viewers have a high school education or less, and 70 percent have incomes under forty-thousand dollars a year. As wrestling declines in American popularity it is moving internationally, both in wrestlers and in audiences, with international audience making up 15 percent of viewers.

In its heyday, now probably ending, professional wrestling was a southern religion rivaling Elvis, but now the sawdust is old and the tents are frayed.

October 13, 1997, and May 10, 1999

MODEL TRAINS

My mother tires of my reminding her that I didn't get an electric train when growing up.

Truth is, there weren't any to be had. Our growing-up time was during World War II, and Lionel, like everyone else, had chugged off to the defense industry. We made do by visiting families with older boys who had gotten trains in the prewar years and who let us play with them.

It wasn't only electric trains that were in short supply in those years. The toy section of Woolworth's, visited religiously every Saturday on the way to and from the Saturday cowboy movies at the Capitol Theater, was pretty sparse.

No balloons were to be had since their materials were needed for tires and anti-aircraft blimps. The cap pistols we needed to reenact scenes from the latest, or recycled, Roy Rogers or Gene Autry film had gone to make army firearms.

We made do, anyway, and loved it. Parcheesi, Monopoly, and Chinese Checkers board games could be found in the older kids' homes as could wooden (not plastic) croquet sets. We made baseballs last by friction-taping old ones. One fellow considerably older than us had a lead soldier mold, and he would melt down old soldiers to show us how to make new ones. A cousin had an electric wood-burning instrument he would bring out when we visited. Harriet Wheatley, up the street, had a bicycle she shared with a dozen of us and also had a set of Authors playing cards. Some older kids passed on their BB guns and used bikes as they outgrew them or when they got drafted.

We envied older boys who had patience and skill to make model airplanes out of tissue paper and balsa wood, some with actual motors and others with rubber bands. They inevitably crashed the first day out, weeks of work wrecked in an instant. The closest we came to their skill were our kites made of newspapers, with paste from flour and water, using old sheet strips for tails.

Most of us took up fishing. Bamboo poles were available, as were hoarded hooks, and worms were as close as a backyard. There were ponds and little lakes scattered around within gas-stamp driving range, and for real excursions, Kentucky Lake was opening up on the Tennessee River at the county's eastern border.

And always, when all else was unavailable, there were books: King Arthur and the Hardy Boys, lots of books about collies, plenty of comic books. We knew the book titles in every house in a two-block radius.

When we had grown and left home, I bought—allegedly for our daughter but actually for myself—a Lionel train like the ones we had seen and played with in grade-school days. I passed it on when she graduated from college and went to work, and she displays it proudly for Christmas every year.

To make up for the loss of "my" Lionel, which looked exactly like the L&N freight trains that I remember running near our house on the line for which several of our relatives had worked, I bought a little N-gauge train. It's hooked up on my office desk. We stumbled across a model train shop in a nearby shopping mall and found an N-gauge L&N freight car and engine to add to it. A colleague at Wofford College presented me with a Lionel watch. I almost wept when I opened it. It is battery-operated with a little Lionel train circling the face. When I press a little button on the side, it makes chugging, puffing, and crossing-bell noises.

As I fondle the two-and-one-half-inch L&N engine nostalgically and play the train noises on my watch, I ponder how the monster steam engine I once rode in the switchyard has diminished over half a century to these little symbolic pieces. In the midst of the worst of times, with the Depression just ending and World War II raging and no electric trains to be had, we had the very best of happy childhoods. Everything today seems so small by comparison.

Fascination with trains is something we never lose. A few years back, in Chattanooga for a meeting, we stayed at the Choo-Choo in a red-carpeted club car that had a brass bed and brass fixtures. We have two brass wall lamps from club cars or diner cars burning warmly in our home. We took Amtrak from Fulton, Kentucky, to Louisiana back in the 1970s, and we rode it from South Carolina to Washington, D.C., more recently. When worse comes to worse, we can still drive to a crossing in town and wait for a freight train to come through.

March 30, 1998

SHOELESS JOE

A *New York Times* news item reports a dinner in Greenville, South Carolina, was attended by South Carolina governor Jim Hodges and baseball legends Ted Williams and Tommy Lasorda in support of pardoning Shoeless Joe Jackson and putting him in the Hall of Fame.

Ted Williams has been on this crusade for months. Suspicious folks think Williams may be a front man for Pete Rose, and that a hidden agenda here is to get Rose into the Hall after Jackson is allowed in. Less suspicious people think that Jackson ought to be admitted simply because justice and mercy require it. My wife, who suddenly knows more baseball than do I, finds Jackson innocent, simply because he said he was.

Truth to tell, even though he was barred from the game for life, Jackson was never tried and convicted. He did admit he received five thousand dollars in the 1919 "Black Sox" scandal but claimed he tried to return it and that he reported it to Sox owner Charles Comisky. The strongest evidence for Jackson was his performance in the World Series that the White Sox lost in six games. Jackson had 12 hits, including six RBIs and one homer, and no errors. Even though he was legally acquitted, Commissioner Kennesaw Mountain Landis banned him from baseball. Bart Giamatti, in his brief tenure as commissioner (long enough to ban Pete Rose), refused to pardon Jackson.

Once banned, Shoeless Joe quietly took his record—a .356 lifetime batting average that is third in the record books behind Rogers Hornsby and Ty Cobb—and came South to Savannah and then back to Greenville. He operated a liquor store and pool hall and never discussed the scandal. He died mid-century, thirty years after the 1919 scandal.

One of eight children, born in 1888 in Pickens in the South Carolina upstate near the Georgia line, Joseph Jefferson Wofford Jackson and his family left farming for the steadier pay of the cotton mills, moving to Greenville, where he swept floors for Brandon Mill at the age of seven. He joined the mill's baseball team when he was thirteen and then moved on to a minor league team, the Greenville Spinners. When his new baseball shoes rubbed blisters on his feet, he played a game in his socks and got his nickname from a fan after hitting a triple while shoeless. In 1908, he went to the majors with the Philadelphia Athletics, and he went to the Chicago White Sox in 1916.

The problem comes down to a lack of information. We have books and newspaper clippings and even movies aplenty about the 1919 White Sox and the thrown World Series, and yet the facts are never clear enough to be called facts. Lacking hard evidence and details, fans line up on both sides purely on emotional grounds. The bottom line is that hard-line, letter-of-the-law, guilty-until-proved-innocent folks decide one way, while gray-area, moral-ambiguity, mercy-tending, innocent-until-proved-guilty folks tend to favor Jackson.

Lacking the facts, I tend to the sentimentalist view. I know for a fact that Babe Ruth and Ty Cobb did far more reprehensible things than Shoeless Joe Jackson ever did, but those didn't keep them out of Coopers-town. I also know for a fact that even Richard Nixon was pardoned, and very soon after leaving his workplace, and that Shoeless Joe's alleged offense pales by comparison.

When the news broke in 1919, legend has it that a young lad shouted to Jackson, "Say it ain't so, Joe." Joe kept his mouth shut for thirty years. Just before he died, he said in an interview in the Columbia (S.C.) *State,* "My conscience is clear." He left the call for us to make. Personally I choose to pardon him, but don't take me as an authority. I also want to forgive Bill Clinton.

Those of us inclined to pardon Joe and admit him into the Hall of Fame are being urged by Chicago attorney Louis Hegeman, who drafted Ted Williams's fifty-three-page appeal that was filed with new commissioner Bud Selig, to join in the petition and to contact Selig. Prospects for that strategy aren't too bright; similar appeals in 1989 failed.

If fans really want Joe Jackson redeemed, however, they should sic the Adidas, Nike, and Reebok companies on Commissioner Selig. What more powerful and fitting voices could be raised for Shoeless than those of shoe companies that pay superstars more than Jackson supposedly got on the side in the 1919 scandal?

We can't give Joe Jackson back the years he lost playing the game, but we could replace the 1919 scandal with a 1999 "time-served" sandal to wear through the Cooperstown door. It's solely a matter of soul.

December 6, 1998

WOODEN BASEBALL BATS

We live our lives in contradictions and paradoxes. We crave fresh air but pollute with cars. We care deeply about the poor but not enough to sell our worldly goods. We know that overeating is bad, but food tastes good. We love our neighbors but lock our doors. We are caught in webs of our own making, "hoist[ed]" (Will Shakespeare would say) "with [our] own petar." We try to have many things both ways. Paradox is part of us.

We were reminded of this when we visited the Hillerich and Bradsby's Louisville Slugger Museum and Factory in Louisville, Kentucky.

The only authentic baseball bats are made of wood. Aluminum alloy bats are required by the NCAA and used by Little League, Babe Ruth League, and others, but I am a Luddite on this matter. If metal bats are doing the hitting, it isn't baseball. "Progress" can't mean metal bats.

We saw craftsmen turn out wooden Louisville Sluggers (1.4 million wooden bats a year, an average of 72 bats per player per year in the majors). Watching wood turned on lathes created momentary ambivalence in my adamant stance on wooden bats.

On the one hand, it is exhilarating to learn that wooden bats are still so much in demand and use. They are a long way from going the way of dodo birds, fountain pens, manual typewriters, and icehouses.

On the other hand, wooden bats are made from trees. A love of trees and a rigorous defense of forests conflict with our love of wooden bats (and also with our love of wooden furniture, houses, and even paneled station wagons).

The museum tour guide didn't tell us how many white ash trees give their lives annually to become Louisville Slugger bats, nor did he tell us if H&B owns timberland on which it grows replacement trees. I didn't ask because I didn't really want to know. I believe in trees, but I believe in wooden bats more.

There is no nobler sacrifice for a white ash tree to make than to become wooden baseball bats.

The first time a wooden bat was made by what would become Hillerich and Bradsby was in 1884, when young Bud Hillerich, playing hooky from apprenticing in his father's woodworking shop, saw Pete Browning of the Louisville Eclipse team of the American Association break his favorite bat. Hillerich took Browning to the shop and turned out a bat, and next day Browning went three-for-three with it.

Hillerich's father, turning out wooden bowling balls and pins, churns, and bedposts, scoffed at making bats, but Bud persisted. The "Falls City Slugger" became the Louisville Slugger in 1894. Soon the company was engraving names of players on their bats, each made to user's specifications. Over seventy-eight hundred patterns are on file, with those of John McGraw and Honus Wagner among the first.

Bud Hillerich was made a partner in the company in 1897, and when the company burned and was rebuilt in 1911, J. F. Hillerich and Son Co. hired Frank W. Bradsby from St. Louis to do its marketing. By 1916, Bradsby had become a partner and the company became Hillerich and Bradsby Company. The elder Hillerich died in 1924 after slipping on ice, Frank Bradsby died in 1937 after combating flood damage to the company in the Great Flood, and Bud Hillerich died in 1946. A son took over the company, but died three years later, and his brother replaced him. When he died in 1969, his son succeeded him. The company diversified, first with golf clubs in 1916, then providing war matériel in World War II, and later adding hockey sticks, baseball gloves and mitts, and finally (alas!) aluminum bats: a million a year, made in Canada. The Jefferson, Indiana, plant moved to Louisville's Main Street in 1995, and the World's Largest Baseball Bat, a mammoth sculpture (but not made of wood) marks its location.

H&B's look pretty much the same as they did fifty years ago when my peers and I were swinging them. (Except we painstakingly wrapped the handles with friction tape or adhesive tape, and some of ours had nails driven in to repair broken or cracked bats we cherished or were too poor to replace.)

One change I don't like is that the brand, that oval trademark one should always "hold up" when swinging, no longer reads Hillerich and Bradsby, but simply Louisville Slugger. I also dislike the hollowed out upper ends of many bats.

My learned friends, the few of them who don't worship at baseball shrines as do I, and most of my other friends, say we are "batty" for lamenting the passing of wooden bats.

But what do they know? I'll settle for a Mickey Vernon H&B Louisville Slugger any day . . . and give praise to the tree that made it possible.

June 25, 2000

What can we discover about ourselves out of the avalanche of public grief marking the death of NASCAR driver Dale Earnhardt?

The sustained outpourings of shock and sorrow remind us of other tragic moments when the public arose and was heard: the assassinations of President Kennedy, Martin Luther King, Jr., and Robert Kennedy, the death of Elvis Presley, the explosion of the space shuttle, or the Oklahoma bombing.

But tragedy alone is not enough to explain sustained grieving. Thirty thousand people can die in a flood in India, or ten thousand in a mudslide in South America, or ten on a foggy interstate highway and, within a day's time, shock will fade, and the dead will be forgotten. In Earnhardt's case, sorrow is prolonged.

In racing, death is not totally unexpected. The very nature of racing is risk of life, watched by thousands of people accustomed to spinning cars and menacing concrete walls. Yet, likely as death is, the public is shocked to learn that immortals are mortal.

One revelation from Earnhardt's demise is that NASCAR racing is a far bigger sport than suspected. Earnhardt stories report that the auto-racing followers represent anywhere from the fourth largest to the first largest body of fans for any sport in the world.

Another revelation is that these millions of fans take their devotion seriously, almost making a religion of it. They subscribe to NASCAR magazines, buy NASCAR clothing and mugs and miniature cars, choose NASCAR heroes and villains, name their children for NASCAR racers, lobby for more space for NASCAR on the sports pages of newspapers, pour out millions of dollars to spend weekends and wages at the races, know the names of pit-crew workers and the numbers of the cars, and have extensive information on what their chosen champions eat, who they marry, their children, and their lifestyles. Weeks after Earnhardt's death, there are over one thousand Earnhardt items for sale through Internet shops and over forty-six hundred Earnhardt collectibles available on Internet auction.

Another revelation is that the NASCAR phenomenon is more regional than national. In the South, newspapers gave extensive coverage to Earnhardt's death and the reactions of fans. In South Carolina, the state's major newspaper devoted its entire front page to the death, and the Spartanburg paper ended a full week of daily stories with a special Sunday supplement that had eight hundred fans forming a figure "3" on a football field as a collective memorial, while television stations devoted large blocks of evening news shows to the incident and then produced half-hour specials as well. But in Boston, the accident got a short notice on page 4 of the newspaper. Fans of racing are nationwide, but they are concentrated in the South, where auto racing rivals church membership in loyalties.

Another revelation from this extraordinary event is that the American public is segmented in its allegiances. For every NASCAR fan, there is another citizen blithely unaware of the sport. The claim upon the public's attention span never draws universal audiences. Half the registered voters don't vote. Our religious affiliations number over twenty-five hundred options where fifty years ago there were two hundred. Our local cable-television service offers over eight hundred channels where twenty years ago there were three. Our local shopping malls and order-by-mail-or-online options number in the thousands, where not so long ago a town was lucky to have a dozen shops and retail outlets. NASCAR followings are a specialized segment among countless claims on our loyalties and attention. This body of believers has its own language, its own rituals, its own symbols, its own uniforms, and its own subculture.

Another revelation is that we hunger for heroes. Educator Arthur Levine, describing college students, wrote a book, *When Dreams and Heroes Died,* about the absence of heroes since the 1960s. There is a big black hole in our society. Because we have few heroes, we make our own to fill the vacuum.

Media coverage and relativistic standards remove the aura of mystery that once surrounded public figures. Other presidents before Bill Clinton "fooled around," but today we are obsessed with finding faults and flaws. We have become a nation of *National Inquirer* believers, taking tabloid trash for truth and hooked to seedy talk shows staged for prurient-loving spectators. We topple leaders even more than we elevate them.

Dale Earnhardt was a public hero because the public fills its own vacuum of short-supply heroes as best it can. When mass culture unmasks heroes, the people manufacture their own.

March 4, 2001

Chapter 8

RELIGION
"IN THE HOUSE OF THE LORD"

FRONTIER HYMNALS

A kindly lady in Louisville, Kentucky, several years back gave me a hymnal that I've treasured. Bound in brown tooled calfskin, the hymnal is about two inches wide, four inches long, and about two inches thick. It is 552 pages long, and it contains 606 hymns. Its cover says *Methodist Hymns,* but the title page elaborates this into "A Collection of Hymns for the Use of the Methodist Episcopal Church, Principally from the Collection of The Rev. John Wesley, M.A., Late of Lincoln College, Oxford," quotes Psalm 104:33 and 1 Corinthians 14:15, and identifies the publisher as J. Emory and E. Waugh and the printer as J. Collord, all of New York. Printed in 1829, my copy once belonged to Rev. Jacob Ditzler and to Mary M. Ditzler and then to Anna C. Cox.

It may have been a practical joke. It was well known that I couldn't carry a tune, and this tiny package that fits so well into the palm of a hand or into a coat pocket provided over six hundred I could now carry. The hymns are grouped in sections, such as "Penitential," "Prospect of Heaven," "The Christian's Warfare," and my personal favorite, "Backsliding" (hymns 82 to 102). The hymns and faith packed into such a wee volume are all out of proportion to the book's size. I may not know how many angels you can get on the head of a pen, but I have some idea, from this hymnal, how many words of praise can come off the point of a pen.

Faith is always surprising when it comes in unexpected small packages. Maybe Jesus wasn't surprised to spot little Zacchaeus up in the tree, but I'm surprised at the immense amount of faith that comes out of little-known people, little crossroads churches, and little foot-pump church organs. Maybe one thing my little hymnal teaches is that folks who have or want very little of a material nature must have a mighty big faith.

The little hymnal also tells me that faith is something transportable. Here are hundreds of hymns "Late of Lincoln College, Oxford," probably written in the late eighteenth century, that worked their way to New York for printing in 1829, and then moved west across another century to wind up in my hand in Kentucky. Other hands have carried them to me, for the leather is worn smooth and is soothing to the touch.

When I hold the book, visions of plain-suited circuit riders and frontier women in homespun dresses and bonnets come to mind. How many generations has such faith outlived and through how many hands has it been passed? Where is it bound from here? Will its containers shrink to a microdot or a microfiche card? Can any computer retrieval system be designed to be as efficient as this book in bringing it instantly to hand?

Mine is only one of many such volumes. My wife has one the same size, an Episcopal hymnal and Book of Common Prayer printed in 1907 and presented to her mother, out in Montana, in 1911. When one multiplies our two books by all the hymnals, Bibles, sermons, interpretative lessons, and testimonials in print, the sheer magnitude of faith is crushing, even as it is uplifting.

This impressiveness expands when one realizes how little was in written form until Gutenberg's press came along. For centuries the records and writings were kept in Middle East libraries and European monasteries. That they survived is amazing grace itself, but that they spread around the world in the last five centuries to the extent they did enhances the drama of it all.

Putting faith into print was not the only effect caused by the printing press. An even greater effect was what it did to promote literacy. In order for people to be able to understand what was written, they first had to be able to read. As late as the Civil War, there were very few schools, and illiteracy increased along with the population. A survey by Samuel J. Mills around 1800 found that only about 10 percent of Americans were church members. In a nation that emphasized the individual's freedom to think, speak, and worship as the individual pleased and that was suspicious of authorities who controlled individuals, literacy became more than a vehicle to status. It became the protector of the individual's freedom and the instrument for his own unmediated encounter with faith. With freedom came mobility, and the little hymnals and pocket Bibles allowed people to take their faith with them quickly and lightly. The books themselves were not faith, but carrying them was evidence of it.

Faith is "the substance of things hoped for, the evidence of things not seen." My little hymnal and its many replicas are reminders of things hoped for by countless people and are strong evidence of things not seen.

April 5, 1982

CHRISTMAS ORANGE

Christmas morning, there will be a nickel and a small orange in the toe of my stocking. My wife and daughters see to that project every year. I'm to blame for it; each year I wax eloquent on how all we got for Christmas back in the Depression and Second World War years was an orange and a nickel and sometimes a box of raisins. There's not a word of truth in the story, and they know it.

Actually that story is my father's, who grew up on a farm in World War I days. He did admit that he also got a pair of black stockings each year. For some reason, I never doubted his story the way his granddaughters doubt mine. This year, however, I decided to check up on my father's story. I went to the library to see what Christmas was like down on the farm in the South in bygone days. The historical Christmas records I found seem to divide into two groups. There are several accounts, especially in travel journals and diaries, of lavish Christmas celebrations, often a week long, on the big plantations in the days before the Civil War. The other accounts describe Christmas on small southern farms, especially after the Civil War.

Thomas D. Clark, longtime historian at the University of Kentucky, explains that southern farm Christmases from 1870 to 1910 were shaped by the phenomenal number of crossroads country stores in existence then, when the South depended upon northern wares sent to southern store-keepers, before department stores became common in the county seats and roads were improved enough for people to get to town often.

During Christmas season, the little country stores stocked up on barrels of candy, bags of coconuts, and boxes of oranges. Kegs of liquor, barrels of apples, and boxes of fireworks appeared, and toys were hung on nails and wires from the ceiling rafters, next to the horse collars and buckets. Jars of peppermint sticks were on the counters, and bushel baskets of nuts lined the aisles. Mackerel, salmon, sardines, and especially oysters were all in demand. So were hoops of cheese.

To pay for Christmas, the women of the South started setting aside eggs to sell as early as September, trying to save up forty dozen or so to trade for presents and a few to use for special cooking. Meanwhile, outdoors, the men hauled crossties, cordwood, or the last of the cotton crop to get the where-withal for Christmas. Interestingly, few country-store inventory records show much demand for decorations and tree ornaments. Christmas trees are a relatively recent American tradition, imported from Germany (along with Saint Nick) in the nineteenth century. There were some Christmas trees in rural areas, but usually they were found in community centers where every-one added something to the decorating, and often they were used for parties for young couples who were altar bound.

Fireworks were especially popular. Tales of Roman-candle battles are still told today by seventy-year-olds. Fathers of homes without fireworks often fired the family shotgun or pistol as a substitute. Gunpowder and shells sold well at Christmas, not only as noisemakers but as providers of meat for the Christmas table.

But why oranges? Later generations know oranges as something avail-able year-round and having something to do with Florida or California, but not with Christmas. Professor Clark quotes H. C. Nixon's book *Possum-Trot* (University of Oklahoma Press) on oranges: "I still think of Christmas when I smell oranges in the country." So does my father, and so do I, and so now my children.

We may all be removed from the family farms, squeezed into towns and cities, and scattered like wedding rice across the fifty states, but the family tie is hard to break. The scent of an orange at Christmas is a hint of a past that time and distance and new ways of living cannot easily remove. It may be our children's only link to great-grandparents they never met or to great challenges they never faced.

When I roll the orange out of my stocking's toe this Christmas, I'll have a sweet taste of maudlin sentimentality, a magic moment when distant or disappeared hearts gather round our hearth and around us, perhaps only for a delicious instant, but worth waiting for all year.

December 20, 1982

GINGERBREAD HOUSES

When Elizabeth was Molly's age, and Molly was still a baby, I was in D.C. on business just before Christmas. Suzanne and Jim Wilder offered to drive me to the airport that afternoon. I was booked to fly out to St. Louis and then catch another plane back to Paducah, Kentucky, where my car was parked for the remaining sixty-five-mile drive home.

The Wilders dropped me at the airport, bid me "Merry Christmas," and drove away. I had arrived earlier than usual because holiday lines at the check-in counter were long with servicemen, students, and grandparents on their ways to hearths and hearts. As I sat outside the gate, waiting for my flight to be called, a voice on the loudspeaker paged me, telling me to pick up one of the desk phones for a message. Visions of emergencies back home danced through my head.

The message was for me to return to the ticket counter. I rushed to see what was the matter, and there were my Wilder friends. They held a gigantic gingerbread house wrapped in clear plastic and resting on a cardboard box top. They shoved it into my arms, yelled "Merry Christmas" again, and were gone in the twinkling of an eye. Left holding the bag, so to speak, I rushed back toward my plane, scheduled to leave in the next five minutes.

The lady at the security check gate was the first person to stop me. She said the house was too big to fit under the seat in front of me and that I couldn't carry it aboard. She said I'd have to leave it, or buy a separate ticket for it, or box it and ship it. Fortunately, the guard standing behind her played Bob Cratchit to her Scrooge. He suggested that they consider it a babe in arms and let me hold it in my lap on the flight. If I was lucky, he said, there would be an empty seat by me, and it would ride there.

Back in the waiting room I was greeted with the news that the flight would be an hour late. I sat the house down in a windowsill and sat there myself, for all the seats were taken. I needed to go to the washroom but was afraid to leave the house unguarded. A gentleman reading a *New York Times* looked honest, so I asked him to watch my house for me. He looked a little puzzled but kindly agreed. When I returned, a small crowd was gathered where my house was. A dozen snowsuited children and bespectacled grandmothers surrounded my house and the man I had left in charge. Up until we boarded the plane, the crowd got bigger and bigger.

There was no vacant seat on the plane, so it rested on my lap the whole way. All the way to St. Louis, people marched by me, pretending to be going to the rear but stopping to examine the minute detail of the exquisite house. It was covered with gumdrops and hard candies, and icicle frosting hung from its eaves. Green candy trees stood on its white drifts of frosted yard, and wisps of cotton candy billowed from its chimney.

In St. Louis there was a two-hour wait for my next flight. Again, the children congregated, and the adults, who seem to save a little of their own childhood to spend each Christmas, followed them. The same laughter and happy conversation took place again on the plane to Paducah. It was crisp, a clear night for flying, and the young man next to me was a riverboat pilot, headed home for the first time in six months, where a daughter whom he had yet to see had been born in September.

By eleven o'clock I was home, and our own two daughters were in my lap, the lap that had carried Christmas all the way from Washington, D.C.

Eat your hearts out, Hansel and Gretel! There's never been a gingerbread house like that one.

December 5, 1983

CHRISTMAS TRAINS

Back then, between two grandfathers' houses 150 miles apart, Christmas stretched for miles and for days like a strip of inner tube lashed to the forked tips of a slingshot. Both grandfathers bore old scars. One, a farmer politician, lost an eye when a stray kindling stick catapulted off an axe at the woodpile in the side lot of the weather-grayed farmhouse. The other, a city dweller, had his leg bowed permanently by a stray bullet that passed through his bunkhouse wall in the railroad camp where he worked in earlier days.

Each December school day ended with a chorus of "Hark the herald angels shout; a few more days and we'll be out." Then, free at last, we three boy cousins headed to the farm. We don't recall decorated trees and wrapped presents there, but we remember table-bending meals and pie safes full of between-meal pies and cakes and cold biscuits for finger-sticking and filling with sorghum. That was before TVA gave us lights, and so we three piled early into one of the two feather beds in the living room where our grandparents and the fire were. We huddled onionskin tight against each other with the oldest in the choice outside spot nearest the fire. In the flickering firelight, our grandfather's glass eye stared at us from its heavy water tumbler at one end of the mantel, and in a twin glass at the other end, our grandmother's dentures smiled down upon us; a snuff can divided them.

Then, Christmas still days away, we boarded the L&N for Memphis. We went to and from Memphis on the L&N, because we owned no car and because we got free passes since our dad worked for the railroad. Several Christmases the trains were so crowded with furloughed servicemen that we had to sit on their duffel bags in the aisles, except when one, obviously homesick for his own little brother, would ask one of us to sit on his lap. They lavished hoarded Hershey bars on us.

In Memphis, we three boy cousins slept on pallets we rolled up to clear a day-time lounge for our endless games of Battle and Crazy-8's, in full view of a grandmother who thought cards sinful. We played around the grandfather's easy chair, hiding marbles in his red tobacco can from which he rolled cigarettes, also on grandmother's unapproved list. He would limp out to get the newspaper and, with us at his feet, use it as his text in teaching us how to cuss without profanity as he explained how wronged his world was by FDR and Boss Crump. Looking up at him from our floor seats, he looked like Lionel Barrymore.

So we took our grandfathers with their wounds and ways and wrapped them in feather mattresses and *Press-Scimitar* sheets and tied them in our memories to Christmas tree cuttings and fruitcake slicings and passed through the Depression without ever knowing there had been one.

We needed no electric trains, for we had our L&N. Now, on my desk, runs an N-gauge model train; it has an L&N engine. Among my best memories are wartime Christmases and railroads.

Dad was working double shifts for the railroad during the war. Sometimes he manned the ticket office at Camp Tyson, the barrage-balloon army camp seven miles out from town. The camp brought hundreds of families to our town, and people took them in. We lived in a two-bedroom house—four of us—but we rented one of the bedrooms out to the Beans. For Christmas that year, when no one was getting metal toys because of the war, somehow the Beans came up with metal army trucks painted olive green, with cannons mounted on the backs that fired wooden shells. We were the envy of the neighborhood.

One Christmas my dad woke us in the middle of the night and took us to the depot. An unscheduled passenger train was switching engines, and it was packed with servicemen unlike any we had seen before. They wore gray uniforms instead of khaki ones. They were German prisoners of war, destined for one of the several southern prison farms. Perhaps they were part of Rommel's North African tank corps that he left behind to surrender. Word had spread throughout our little town, and a crowd had gathered, filling the lot beside the old depot.

The cars were brightly lit, and all the soldiers were singing, but in a strange language. We watched and listened, pondering how like our own uniformed uncles and neighbors they were in age and appearance. Somehow on that Christmas-week night in World War II at the L&N depot, hate we had nurtured every day, collecting tin foil and scrap metal and buying war stamps and war bonds and doing without tires and gasoline and sugar for the war effort, seemed out of place.

Just before the train pulled out, the aisle lights dimmed and the laughter on the train ebbed, and the POW's sang: "Stille Nacht, Heilige Nacht." And our watchful crowd joined in: "Silent Night, Holy Night."

And the L&N train pulled out and into our memories, revived and revisited by a snowy December afternoon and a little model train chugging around a desk.

December 16, 1985, and December 17, 2000

RELIGIONS OF THE SECULAR

A group of retirees who get together on Wednesdays invited me to lecture on southern religion. They had in mind Presbyterianism and Episcopalianism and were somewhat flabbergasted when I started the session by asking what particular religious denomination they had in mind: football or Elvis? Both football and Elvis have major religious bodies formed around them. Their followers number in the hundreds of thousands. Indeed, since numbers count for a great deal in religious denominations, they are the South's most successful religions. As with the more traditional religious faiths, football and Elvis have:

- rituals (pregame prayers, the national anthem, half-time ceremonies, and fanny pats for football / entrance screams, towel tossing, and pelvis grinding for Elvis)
- relics (trophy cases for football / pink Cadillacs and gold records for Elvis; autographs for both)
- symbols (Saints, Angels, or Padres for football / a guitar with sequin sideburns for Elvis)

- martyrs (the Gipper and Ronald Reagan for football / Priscilla for Elvis)
- prophets (Bear Bryant, Vince Lombardi, and Knute Rockne for football / Colonel Parker for Elvis)
- false prophets (Tampa Bay and Northwestern for football / imitators and not-so-look-a-likes for Elvis)
- deacons (cheerleaders and majorettes for football / bodyguards and groupies for Elvis)
- sacred places (stadia and end zones for football / Vegas stages and Graceland for Elvis)
- scriptures (sports pages, Sports Illustrated, regulations books, and statistics for football / entertainment gossip magazines, recordings, video biographies, and movies for Elvis)
- epiphanies (bowl games for football / an appearance on the Ed Sullivan Show for Elvis)
- tragedies (flunked drug tests and missed field goals for fooball/ flunked drug tests and the army draft for Elvis)
- miracles (completed field goals as the clock runs out for fooball / sightings in Indiana Burger Kings for Elvis)
- hymns ("Down the Field" and "Bulldog, Bulldog, Bow-Wow-Wow" for football / "Heartbreak Hotel" and "Love Me Tender" for Elvis)
- evangelists (press agents for both)
- communion meals (beer and hot dogs for football / pizza and country-fried steak for Elvis)
- offertory collection plates and their treasurers (television revenue and gate receipts for football / record sales and Graceland tickets for Elvis)
- televised services (ESPN any night or day, other channels Saturdays, Sundays, and Mondays only, for football / reruns and film festivals for Elvis)
- and, most especially, congregations of die-hard disciples and pilgrim zealots (the fans of both) and their low-blow skeptics and detractors (sportswriters for football / drama critics for Elvis).

There are no atheists in foxholes—or in Super Bowl stands, or in Graceland lines. If religion is, as Alfred North Whitehead said, whatever we hold to be most ultimate, or is, as Paul Tillich said, the Ground of Being, then football and Elvis faithful are fundamentalists in the heavenly city and doormen to the Houses of Lords. People are hungry for something into which they can place their atrophied faith, for something to which they can make unreserved commitments, something that doesn't threaten them with damnations they feel too much of everyday, something that promises them leisure and hope, symbols and ornate trappings. The momentary deluge of patriotism that saved the American flag industry is evidence of souls in search of a revival, but we can't invade a country every weekend. Football and Elvis sects meet a consistent consumer demand more regularly and at lower costs. Who remembers Sgt. York's or Audie Murphy's serial numbers or the titles of Billy Graham's sermons? Who doesn't know the numbers of their favorite quarterbacks or the lyrics of Elvis's biggest hits?

Facetious as it may sound, it is nevertheless a fact that football and following Elvis are forms of pop religion. That fact casts no aspersions upon the players or Elvis, nor upon the fans of either or of both. The breadth of their followings and depth of their faiths can also be found in bullfighting in Spain and in soccer in Italy.

But the fact of those faiths does cast a very bright spotlight on the real nature of our world. We blind ourselves badly when we fail to admit how seriously we take our passions. To acknowledge them openly is to confess to a search for meaning in modernity and to a need for faith in an age of facts.

November 11, 1991

SATAN

When I was fresh out of college, "Brother" Irion (we called all ministers "Brother" in those days), minister of First Methodist Church in my hometown, invited me to substitute for him at Sunday evening service.

I had studied a bit of history in college and had been struck by how many awful things had been done over the centuries by Christians claiming to be "fighting Satan." Slaughters of countrysides of people in eastern Europe, the Inquisition, the Salem witch trials, and episodes of the Crusades were all part of a long history of "defeating the Devil" that gave Christianity a bad name. Showing so much attention to Satan, it seemed to me, had detracted from the central figure of Christianity, Jesus of Nazareth, and had elevated the Evil One to too exalted a status in the church.

Satan is not mentioned often in the Bible at all: outside of the snake in the Garden, the tempters appearing to Job, and the temptations of Jesus, Satan is a very minor biblical character. But Christians later inflated Satan to a standing almost equal to God and saw history as a perpetual war between Good and Evil, God and the Devil. I wanted to show, in this modern age of science and facts, that Satan is just a figment of the imagination and, at most, a literary symbol used to explain the presence of evil in the world.

Looking back later, I realized what I was really trying to do, with a lot of references to books and quotes from scholars, was to show off my recent college education to hometown folks.

A sermon conceived in pride and youthful zeal isn't likely to get very far, and that one certainly didn't. About five minutes into this sermon demythologizing Satan, the sky outside grew enormously dark. The wind could be heard rising, and then hard rain pelted the stained-glass windows of the church. But I preached on.

Then suddenly, a bolt of lightning turned the world outside light blue for a second, followed by an indescribably loud clap of thunder. The lights in the sanctuary went out. But I preached on.

My good friend, Mac Luckey, was presiding at the service, and he was resourceful enough to light the candles of a candelabrum on the altar and to hold it beside me so that I could see my notes. I preached on.

All had grown calm and silent and dark outside. Then, abruptly, a mighty roar of wind could be heard. The wind pushed open the heavy front doors of the church, filled the vestibule, threw open the swinging doors into the darkened sanctuary, rushed down the center aisle . . .

And blew out the candles.

At this point, the weather finally had gotten my attention. I quickly announced that it was obvious that I needed to reconsider my views on the nonexistence of Satan and that perhaps we should all rapidly sing one verse of "Shall We Gather at the River" and get on home.

That autobiographical footnote has come to mind several times in recent months. During the rejoicing over the death of totalitarianism in the USSR, I have hesitated to celebrate either loudly or dogmatically because I know that strong winds can rise suddenly on calm nights. Strong-man rule can seem the answer to disoriented people unaccustomed to new abundances of personal liberty amid shortages of food and work.

The same restraint nagged me during the national euphoria over the success of allied troops and American weaponry in Iraq. History shows that frequent and sudden sandstorms are natural to that region, and that Operation Desert Storm may not be the last word in Iraq.

And here on the home front, this story reminds me that all of the separated thousand Points of Light, each bright and wonderful in its own way, held up for public praise recently, really show us that we are in a darkness and wind of economic hard times and governmental deficits, suffering people and blighted hopes. The Points of Light help us keep on preaching, but sooner or later we are going to have to adjourn to reconsider our views on the black hole in which they flicker.

November 25, 1991

PENTECOSTAL EXODUS

Every once in a while something in the newspapers other than the comics is good for a laugh. Folks around here have been relishing a wire-service story about twenty naked Spanish-speaking Pentecostals who showed up in Louisiana all crammed in a Pontiac in response to an order from God for them to leave behind their money, identification, and clothes and to head for Florida for the end of the world. To the astute analysts who gather each morning at the local doughnut shop, the story sounds suspicious.

In the first place, if the entire world is going to end, why leave home at all? This has the earmarks of one of those commercials for Disney World that we see right after some championship athletic event. For another thing, even though space was at a premium, how did they plan to get all the way to Florida without even a credit card or a road map or a package of Oreos? That's taking one's faith that "God will provide" pretty seriously.

The United Pentecostal Church was suspicious enough that it had a spokesman caution us not to be taken in by these twenty naked strangers. They are not, the spokesman assures us, United Pentecostal members. Well, maybe not. But you can't come much closer to being united than being naked with nineteen other people in a Pontiac.

Back in the old small-town days before Political Correctness dictionaries, it was accepted practice for Main Street mainstream Christians to nickname some vigorous Pentecostals from cinderblock churches across the tracks "Holy Rollers" because of their characteristic charismatic contortions and shouting in tongues. It was a class-conscious lack of class to label people that way, but it happened nonetheless. The image of twenty Pentecostals twisted into a car and shouting in Spanish may cause an untimely revival of the Holy Roller stereotype.

The local consensus is that these weren't Spanish-speaking Pentecostals at all, but opinions vary about who they really are. One theory holds that they are destitute David Duke supporters from Louisiana left stranded in North Carolina when the Duke presidential campaign suddenly ended last year. A more plausible theory is that they are illegal Mexican migrant workers who were trying to get to jobs in the peach and citrus groves in Georgia and Florida and who needed an alibi for not having green cards.

The most likely theory is that they were college students. College students for years have been seeing how many people they can cram into phone booths or VW Beetles. Back in the early '70s, college students also invented "streaking," racing naked around campuses. And ever since Henry Ford invented rumble seats, college students have been getting naked in the backseats of cars. On top of that, ever since the movie *Where the Boys Are* popularized the practice, about a million college students a year head for Florida.

All the evidence is that these twenty naked Pentecostals may actually be college students who stayed on in Florida after spring break last year, long enough to learn some Spanish from Cuban exiles there, and are inventing this story to cover their absenteeism (but not their bodies). Likely, their parents or professors have never missed them, and they probably were just getting an early start on Mardi Gras in Louisiana. Their story could have been a cover to convince a vigilant state trooper than they had a legitimate reason for being naked and packed so closely in their car. It could also have been a way to get some sympathy funding once their money ran out in Florida.

Fads being what they are on college campuses, we can fully expect a rash, in both the figurative and the literal sense, of stories this fall about college fraternities going for new Guinness records for packing naked people in a Pontiac; it would have been easier in the good old days of twelve-cylinder Packards.

Personally, since the news stories omit the ages of the twenty pilgrims, I am willing to give the "Ghost Riders" the benefit of the doubt and to take them at their word, that they were heading to Florida for the end of the world. There's nothing unusual about that. In fact, a few million others, including some of my relatives, are already there, nearly naked, determined to live out their "final days" waiting in condominium contentment for the end to come and just as willing to divest themselves of their life's savings in service to that faith.

What are another twenty senior citizens, more or less?

September 27, 1993

A WHITE CHRISTMAS

The most popular song of all time is reputedly Bing Crosby's "White Christmas." Crosby sang it thousands of time, but we usually associate it with two of his films: *Holiday Inn* (which co-starred Fred Astaire), and the similar *White Christmas* (which co-starred Danny Kaye). More pervasive than the movie versions, however, were the recordings. Even today, half a century later, hardly a drugstore or a truck stop in America this December doesn't have some version of Crosby's "White Christmas." It was especially popular during World War II. Even southern troops who had grown up with nothing more white for Christmas than cotton fields were ironically "dreaming of a white Christmas, just like the ones I used to know."

The irony was compounded by the fact that America's armed forces were still racially segregated in that war. In its beginning years, enlisted blacks served as stewards and cooks and in supply services. A black cook received the Navy Cross for shooting down five Japanese planes at Pearl Harbor. Officers were white. Only as the war went on did federal regulations begin to change. Black soldiers moved into the frontlines, black officers rose in the ranks, some troop integration was achieved, and in Tuskegee, Alabama, a distinguished cadre of combat pilots was trained and rendered sterling service in Europe. Blacks enlisted and served all out of proportion to their numbers in the population. Their motives were threefold: patriotism, employment, and aspiration. They loved their country, they had suffered more than any race or class in the Depression that the war ended, and they had high hopes that service to the nation would elevate their stations and fates.

For them, if there was any racial connotation at all to "dreaming of a white Christmas," it was dreaming of earning through military service access to places and privileges reserved for whites: an end to separate jobs, schools, housing, incomes, transportation, and entertainment. Changes were slower in coming than they hoped. No cheering crowds welcomed them back with ticker-tape parades. Few changes were made immediately in the Jim Crow laws and practices of the past. But when Korea and then Vietnam came along, blacks enlisted again, this time forming the very heart of the combat troops. Hope endured for moving off of society's old second-class doorsill onward and upward into first class.

But it took so much time that hope was chaffing. Raw places festered until they fostered the infectious civil rights movement of the 1960s. Civil rights legislation introduced and championed by Lyndon Johnson in 1964 and 1965 had all the appearances of curing the nation. In the buoyant atmosphere of major changes in biracial attitudes and practices, America seemed on the brink of fulfilling its cherished dreams of liberty and equality for all her people and of being a lighthouse of democracy to the world.

But enthusiasm for progress ebbed almost as fast as it arose. Separatism returned, welcomed back by whites who had favored it all along and embraced now by blacks who had wearied of the burden of history and of white paternalism. Gains in judicial, education, election, and economic processes and systems were offset by declines in biracial cooperation, biracial civility, and biracial aspirations. Simply said, we haven't learned how to love one another. Worst than that, we have forgotten why we wanted to.

Christmas may be the best time to pause and recall our best ideals. We wanted more closeness between blacks and whites for two reasons. First of all, we wanted it because we needed it. Given a choice between getting along together and of warring and competing with each other separately, we chose to try to get together; our mutual survival demanded it of us. But, second, we wanted an end to divisions between us because it was the right thing to do. It resonated with the spiritual principles that most all of our religions, regardless of denomination or sect, made paramount: the parenthood of God, the family of mankind, and the moral standards for serving God by loving and being stewards for each other. The Grace of God that is Christmas is that God gave us the gift of each other.

In our simmering racial separatism, we seem determined to make a curse of that gift. There is no North Pole as frigid as the continuing polarity between blacks and whites. We need very much to dream together again. The "visions of sugarplums" we conjure up this Christmas Eve need to be expectancies of getting better things from inside ourselves for each other. We need to be dreaming of a not-all-white Christmas but a Technicolored world. Wouldn't that be something angels could really proclaim? And we need to do more than dream. We need to awaken and to assemble true affection and respect across color lines to hang by the chimneys of our souls. The directions for assembling are hard to read, aren't they?

December 19, 1994

SNAKE HANDLING

Before I got a car in my senior year of college, I rode the L&N trains and Greyhound buses a lot. Once, in the late 1950s, I was seated by a fellow from the mountains of Kentucky, homeward bound from working somewhere in Ohio or Louisville. Unlike most mountain folk, this man was talkative. I learned a great deal about mountain culture from him. Most of what he taught me has been confirmed since then by books and visits to the mountains. However, one thing made my fellow sojourner especially memorable.

He was a snake handler on his way to mountain services.

Once over the shock of him telling me that, I begin peeking around to see what baggage he had stowed under our seat or in the overhead rack. As it turned out, chatting with him was one of the most educational experiences I ever had. The man was civil, patient, rational, talkative, and—as near as I could tell—unaccompanied by any snakes. And although I didn't rush out to my hometown snake farm to start my own congregation, I did come away with far more understanding and appreciation for snake-handling religion than I ever would have had otherwise.

That memory has come back as I have read a couple of new books. One from Alabama, at the lower tip of Appalachia, is Dennis Covington's *Salvation on Sand Mountain* (Addison-Wesley). The other is David L. Kimbrough's *Taking Up Serpents: Snake Handlers of Eastern Kentucky* (University of North Carolina Press).

Kimbrough investigated snake-handling religion as an academic exercise, working on his graduate history degree at Indiana University. He followed the Saylor family and George Hensley, famous around Harlan, Kentucky. Covington was a Birmingham-based stringer for the *New York Times,* drawn to exploring the religion after covering a trial in which a minister got ninety-nine years for trying to kill his wife with church snakes.

Both men became personally involved in the religion they were studying. Covington actually handled snakes and even took up preaching until he had second thoughts about the risks he ran and about the church's stand on women in the pulpit. Kimbrough was better able to retain his objectivity, although he had an obvious fascination with the practitioners and a high degree of tolerance for what, to mainstream Protestantism, has to appear as unorthodox religion.

Although not mountain holiness folk, both Covington and Kimbrough had grandparents who were, thus easing their acceptance as reporters by the congregations. Both point out that snake handling (and strychnine swallowing and fire handling) are religious phenomena of this century, started when mountain people were forced down off the mountains for economic reasons to work in the valleys and towns. Faced with the tempestuous temptations of urban and industrial life, they resorted to extremes of faith to protect them from the evil spirits roaming around them.

The clash of two cultures within the personal lives of mobile people is a theme all of us can appreciate. The contrasts between isolated and protected rural or mountain lifestyles and the hustle and complexity of factory and city life are widespread and obvious. Change has been an epidemic in this century now ending, and it brings with it mixed blessings: improved living conditions sometimes, but stresses on values and families as well. A society on the move, as America has been, comes to more crossroads than a fixed society where change is measured in centuries rather than seconds.

We resort to all sorts of ways for living precariously at the crossroads. Sometimes we adapt rapidly. Other times, we build fences around sacred certainties. The raging battles we have had over flying some flags and burning others is but one example of how we get caught at the crossroads and sometimes take up metaphorical serpents to hold on to something we fear we will lose. The list of other examples can be as long and big as a boa: medical care, abortion, school prayer, single-sex education, political correctness, and deficit spending are just the first page in a catalog of changes so thick it makes the Sears catalog look thin.

Changes abound in our times, and we are trying hard to find some grace abounding in them. Televised congressional hearings and afternoon and late-night talk shows bear remarkable similarities to snake-handling services to which our mountain kinfolk retreated in trying to come to grips with change and evil in the world.

All of us engage in some form or another of taking up serpents; highly emotional wrestling with faith and change is a sign of our times. We differ from each other mostly over choices of what changes most threaten us and over what methods are most appropriate for handling them.

September 17, 1995

MISTLETOE

Oak-worshiping Druids of France and England believed mistletoe increased fertility and, because it doesn't fall easily, cured epilepsy. Appearing from nowhere, it was believed to have been created by lightning striking its host tree. Hanging it over doors or hearths would prevent fires often caused by lightning striking homes. Since lightning was thought to be demonic, mistletoe also warded off bad spirits and bad luck. Because it remains green in winter when the host tree seems dead, Druids thought it was the true life force of the tree. In modern centuries, it was thought that mistletoe had to be shot down (not chopped) and caught before touching the ground.

In 1950 I was fourteen, already shaving twice a week, and hopping cars for the Triangle Cafe. Once the predawn hunters had finished their breakfasts, traffic in our little west Tennessee town was usually slack on the Friday after Thanksgiving, so that morning my boss, C. C. Chambers (a town fixture known as "Crawdad"), loaded me and a gun into his 1930 Model A Ford, a shiny beauty with a beige body, dark brown fenders, red spoke wheels, and a wooden box trunk where its rumble seat once was, and drove us out to the old Caldwell farm out in the county.

A mowed field separated the old family farmhouse from the stockyard, and we traipsed down it until we came to its far fence. There, straddling the fence line, towered a huge oak, not as big as those around Mobile or Charleston, but big enough to make an impression. This solitary giant oak stood out for its size and also for being the only tree for a hundred yards around, except for some cedars we had passed at the upper edge of the field, and also, unlike the grove of naked hardwoods silhouetted against the sky beyond the cattle pen and behind its barn, for being fully green.

Our mission that gray November morning was to shoot enough mistletoe to fill the car trunk and then to peddle it door to door back in town that afternoon. The idea of our mistletoe adorning most of the doorframes of the town overwhelmed my imagination.

It was almost like a religious calling. I was the Chosen One, handpicked out of the dozen carhops Crawdad employed to follow my leader. Just as Moses in Egypt had tapped some worthy person to go house to house telling the Hebrews to put lamb's blood on their doors, and just as Samuel had anointed Saul, so here was I, an awkward adolescent high school freshman, elected to harvest good luck and to spread it throughout our entire town of 6,204 citizens. Besides that, selling it at five dollars a bunch, even after halving with Crawdad, I could be the richest kid in E. W. Grove High.

Crawdad's rifle was an old bolt-action model with its magazine missing, good only for single shots. He took a box of Remington .22 hollow-point longs from his coat pocket and slid a shell into the chamber, pulled down the bolt handle, and set the safety while he explained that the hollow-point would make the bullet flatten once the stem of a mistletoe clump was struck, and that we had to shoot at a slight angle away from the house and also not straight up so the bullets would miss it and us.

We shot well, wasting only a couple of shells. (My years of Red Ryder BB-gun experience finally paid off.) Within an hour we were out of bullets and trunk space and headed for town with forty-eight good-sized bunches of the white-berried Christmas talisman. We thought it would sell fast and leave us enough daylight hours for a restocking trip.

When dark fell, we had sold only one sprig of the stuff. By the time I had bought a Nehi and Moon Pie for lunch, and paid Crawdad for my half of the gas and shells, I came out in the hole.

But Crawdad explained it pretty well on Christmas Eve. We were down on our knees at the midnight party in his little house and he was showing me how to pump the pedals of the upright organ with my hands so that his wife could play carols. He had picked me to pump because I was the worst singer. There was a lot of mistletoe hanging around, and I made some cynical crack about how he came by so much of it. I think I suggested we had erred by trying to sell it to widows and wives well beyond kissing age.

"Christmas isn't about parasites or money," he answered, while I tried to prime the organ's bellows. "It's about extraordinary moments in the middle of ordinary times. The trip was worth taking."

Maybe he saw that his philosophy was too deep for me because, after a pause, he added: "When you're old enough, you'll remember the smells of the barnyard and the clean shots."

And so I do.

Extra-Ordinary!

November 11, 1996

THE CANE RIDGE REVIVAL OF 1801

Woodstock Festival, some half a million people at Bethel, New York, in 1969, astounded the nation.

Observers of American history were not astonished much at all. In August 1801 at a frontier revival at Cane Ridge, in rural Bourbon County, Kentucky, a crowd estimated at thirty thousand to forty thousand people gathered for a week. Sometimes three or four preachers spoke simultaneously.

Cane Ridge and Woodstock share similarities. Both were held outdoors in rural locations. Both lacked adequate housing, food, medical, security, parking, and restroom facilities. Both events were marked by secondary reports of liquor, free sex, and emotional outbursts. Both events had founding sponsors who saw their events move out of their control and become taken over by masses of participants. Both events made a lasting impact on American history. Both events attracted record crowds. Proportionate to the population and means of transportation of their respective times, the religious revival of 1801 actually outdid in attendance the rock festival 168 years later. Both events were attended mostly by young adults. Both events attracted hordes of people seeking to find themselves or something spiritual.

Memory of Woodstock is still relatively fresh; films and books recorded, interpreted, and passed it on. Cane Ridge had no photographers, or video cameras, and few newspapers, to analyze and report it. Its record was in changed lives and new church buildings.

Barton W. Stone, a young Presbyterian minister in Bourbon County, Kentucky, with North Carolina and Virginia roots, had been wrestling with his church's doctrine of the Elect, shifting toward believing in possible universal salvation in a worldwide church not subdivided into denominations or separated by creeds.

Stone began his ministry in Tennessee, serving in the western portion of the central Tennessee presbytery, and then moved to Kentucky where he served three small churches before spending a year in South Carolina raising money for Transylvania College in Lexington, chartered by the Presbyterians in 1780. In 1797 he accepted a call to be minister of the combined Concord and Cane Ridge churches in Bourbon County, about fifteen miles out from Paris, Kentucky, the county seat. The Cane Ridge Church was built in 1797, only five years after Kentucky (Virginia's western county) gained statehood and only a few years after Daniel Boone and his colleagues and rivals opened up Kentucky in the late 1770s. The nearest large city, Lexington, was born in 1780. Western Kentucky was still Indian-held. Kentucky was truly still a frontier.

Hearing of massive revivals down in south-central Kentucky in Logan County, Kentucky, on the Tennessee border, Stone went there to witness for himself the 1800 revivals begun in June by Presbyterian James McGready (whom Stone had met at Hampden-Sidney College when Stone was a student there). Fellow Presbyterian William McGee, with whom Stone served in Tennessee, was there, aiding the effort, as was McGee's Methodist minister brother, John McGee.

Thousands of people attended one or more of these first revivals. The Logan County Revivals of 1800–1801 were the first camp meetings in America and the first massive outpouring in what historians often call the Second Great Awakening, which set a pattern of popular enthusiasm, mass meetings, protracted revivals, lay leadership, and frontier settlement for the whole western portion of the nation throughout the nineteenth century. Before the Revolutionary War, America was confined to the east of the Appalachian Mountains. Afterward, the nation moved westward rapidly, and religion followed and tamed the wild frontier.

When Stone returned to Cane Ridge in the spring of 1801, he preached about what he had seen and heard. In August 1801, crowds began to gather. By foot, horse, and wagon they came, from Ohio and the Old Northwest Territory, from Illinois, from Indiana, from Kentucky, and from Tennessee. They stayed a week, until food in the area gave out. When they left, they took with them an epidemic resolve to transform their personal lives and to bring laws, institutions, and meaning to their communities. They left an indelible mark on American history and American religion, called the Cane Ridge Revival.

Some among them, Stone included, left the Presbyterians to start a non-denominational Christian movement. Others were attracted later into becoming Shakers, Methodists, and Baptists. Some returned to Presbyterianism. Churches sprang up everywhere in Cane Ridge's wake.

No one present, nor those who came afterward, remained unchanged.

February 23, 1998

BAPTISM

Kris Neely is going around the world in eight months by boats. He will sail or paddle or ferry the Caribbean, the Amazon, the Cape of Good Hope, the Zambesi, the Nile, the Jordan, the Mediterranean, the Ganges, the Yangtze, the Pacific, and the Bering. His purpose is to study the spiritual, economic, historical, and sociological relationships between people and water. Heretofore a landlubber, Kris spent his last days before setting sail reflecting on water in his own life, citing examples of his father cooling him off in a shower when he had a temper tantrum and later of his baptism by immersion. Hearing his plans raised my own submerged memories of spiritual water.

After I graduated from college and had gone to work, I wanted badly to go on to graduate school, but there was no money. I applied frequently for scholarships, but without success.

Finally, the Danforth Foundation agreed to consider me, and I was to be interviewed by the foundation's president himself, Dr. Kenneth I. Brown.

The interview day came, and I met Dr. Brown in a hotel suite in downtown Lexington, Kentucky. It was a pleasant half-hour conversation, but at the end Dr. Brown showed me a book he had written, *And Be Baptized.* He explained that studying varying forms of baptism had become a great interest to him, and his book described most of the forms baptism took.

But he noted that a large Christian church in Lexington was said to have a unique form of immersion that he wanted to examine while he was in town, and he asked if I could meet him there that afternoon and be the "candidate for baptism" as the minister demonstrated his method to Dr. Brown.

That February day had turned out to be the coldest day of the year. The temperature was at zero, the windchill factor was below zero, and the streets were covered with ice. Somehow I slid back to work and then back downtown to play my part in the baptismal demonstration. I stripped to my underwear and donned a black robe with fishing weights sewn in the hem to keep it from floating and met the minister, similarly attired, at the steps leading down into the baptismal pool. Dr. Brown sat out in the sanctuary, watching through a window framing the pool.

As luck would have it, the cold weather had blown out the hot water heater, and the pool was filled with icy water. The minister and I decided to tough it out, and sucking in our breaths we descended into the pool. He stood upright in the center and seated me on a weighted metal stool. Then, holding my nose and mouth, he dunked me.

Not just once, however. Dr. Brown came up to the window and leaned in, asking us to repeat it so that he could see better. We did. Then he came around to the steps and asked us to do it again. We did. Then he asked us to wait a minute, and he left. When he returned, he had undressed and donned a robe, too, and descended into the pool with us. Then he watched from three angles while the minister dunked me three more times.

Then he said I might as well learn how the American Baptists, his denomination, baptized, and he had me stand, and he dunked me. By then I had been baptized seven times but was beginning to feel close to being not saved at all. The question was whether I would drown then or die of pneumonia later.

Then Dr. Brown, knowing that I was going to go to seminary, said I should learn how to do a baptism. We switched roles, and he became the candidate and I the baptizer. I clasped his back with one hand and put my other hand over his mouth while pinching his nose and leaned him backwards. At that point I dropped him.

To make matters worse, this sixty-five-year-old was wearing a hearing aid. As he disappeared beneath the icy water, the hearing aid made a loud sizzling noise.

My only thought was "There goes my scholarship."

The story ends happily. Dr. Brown sputtered to the surface, had me dunk him at least three different ways, and then ran out of the pool to catch a plane. He threw his wet underwear into my dressing room cubicle and shouted to me to dry it and mail it to him. Without his hearing aid, he didn't hear my good-bye.

A couple of months later I had a six-year graduate fellowship to Yale University, plus instructions to call him KIB instead of Dr. Brown.

But I wonder to this day what KIB's secretary in St. Louis thought when she opened that envelope and pulled out a pair of men's shorts.

November 5, 2000

TENTING

Driving across Georgia and then across Tennessee in June, I was astonished to find huge fireworks tents at almost every cloverleaf. Part of my astonishment was realizing that there are thousands of people "out there" with money to burn. Fireworks are not inexpensive, but apparently people don't mind seeing their money go up in smoke.

But the other part of my astonishment was the number of tents. We don't see many tents around the South. Air-conditioning has made them obsolete, and the carnivals, circuses, and revivals we attended fifty years ago have moved indoors, into convention centers and churches, to stay cool.

The fireworks tents of 2001 remind me of revival, carnival, and watermelon tents of 1950. On my first long vacation trip, just before entering high school, we drove, four adults and two boys in a two-door Ford, across Tennessee and into North Carolina and Virginia mountains. Strategically spaced along the two-lane roads (interstate four-lanes were not yet created) were watermelon tents. Ice-cold watermelon slices were served atop plywood sheets laid across wooden horses. You could get a bottle Coke for a nickel and a slice of watermelon for a dime.

Each summer, a carnival would come to town. Big vacant lots, either out Rison Street or down past the hitch yard on East Washington Street, would be covered with sawdust and dozens of tents, offering games and shows. And each summer, there would be at least one tent revival, usually on a lot at the "Y" made by three roads converging at the western city limits, a site that would be replaced by a carburetor-plant parking lot once prosperity and diversified economies came along.

One of the penalties of memory as one ages is that one also begins recalling foolish things one did that were later regretted. Although our crimes were not of the scale that makes hunts for guilty Nazis continue even today, they do weigh heavy. Maybe confessing now will put us at peace and purge our consciences.

One summer, probably around 1955, my two best friends and I, home from college for the summer, went to Youth Night at the summer revival out at the "Y." At the end of the service, the itinerant preacher, whose fascination with eternal fires was appropriate for the summer temperature under that tent, called for the young people present to come forward and mount the wooden stage while the choir and congregation sang. Soon there was a steady line as the best young souls of the county filed solemnly forward and climbed up on the stage and faced the beaming faces of parents, grandparents, and deacons. Gradually, the line diminished, but the choir sang on, with the minister exhorting at the end of each verse: "One more verse," he would say. "There are some young souls hesitating, and we and the Lord are waiting for them."

We Three Musketeers kept looking around, and it seemed to us all the young people were on stage. Verse followed verse, exhortation followed exhortation, and suddenly we noticed that all the young people on the stage in front of us were staring at us, and that all the adults to our left were turned at staring at us, too. Reality struck: they thought we were young people! Didn't they know that we were sophisticated, nonemotional, rational nineteen-year-old college students?

We were in a pickle of a dilemma. We would not capitulate to the emotions and heat, but it was evident that they were going to wait us out. Fortunately, the minister made a mistake. After five stanzas solely for the benefit of us three reluctant sinners, the minister asked for another verse, but this time with "every head bowed, and every eye shut." It was a chance to come forward without being watched and to hide ourselves in the throng on stage. So, as the closed-eye stanza was sung, the three of us, simultaneously, silently, and spontaneously, rose from our plank pews and walked.

But not forward. We walked out under the tent flap to our right. The choir sang on as we escaped.

And then, compounding our backsliding from proffered grace, we drove across town to the old fairgrounds—to a carnival. Having sinned once that night, we went for a record. We went into "the girlie show," quite a different tent from the one we left at the Y.

We saw things there that taught us rapidly why tent revivals were necessary. Guilt-ridden, with every eye fixed on the show, we again slid out the side of a tent.

August 5, 2001

SEPTEMBER 11

My weekly ramblings usually are about southern things, the peculiarities of southern people and places past and present: passenger trains, preachers, poetry, pigeons, pitchforks, pork and pig pullings, poverty, pot pies, persimmons, paw paws, and possums.

A month after the horrors of September 11, it's time to get back to such uniquely southern topics. But grieving won't let me; every time I lift my fingers to write, they freeze. And yet, despite the fact that the atrocities occurred in New York City, Pennsylvania, and Washington, something seems very southern about them.

I remember laboring through endless pages of *War and Peace,* enthralled by descriptions of wrecked aristocracies and snow-covered Russian battlefields, only to decide it was a story I had heard before. Napoleon's retreat from Moscow was not nearly as real to me as Lee's retreat from Petersburg or Johnston's retreat from Chattanooga. Buildings burning in Russia were less real than those burned in Atlanta

Anyone with knowledge of southern history and symbols knows the South understands how to live with tragedy.

I grew up, as did most southerners, hearing grandparents and old maid aunts tell of great-uncles who died at Fort Pillow, Chickamauga, and Franklin (and one killed by a falling tree while home on furlough). I grew up playing in the trenches of Fort Donelson, where a best friend's father once found a pistol, and I grew up visiting the Shiloh battlefield and cemetery. I grew up on a hilltop named for Bedford Forrest, on which minié balls and cannon shot still surfaced. I grew up amid family farms with no farmhands to till them and no income for taxes.

I grew up in a region where cemeteries of fallen Civil War soldiers were still decorated annually with flags and flowers and where every courthouse had a granite statue of a Confederate soldier bearing arms. I grew up in a South in which descendants of slaves and of former slaveholders were trying to invent new patterns of interdependence.

The Civil War left deep scars on southern people and places, but the real scars came after the war in the realization of loss. There were two hundred thousand widows of soldiers around, and three hundred thousand veterans (most of them handicapped physically or psychologically), and four hundred thousand fatherless children, and miles of ransacked homesteads with no cows or crops or even a mule, and towns with no jobs. The eagle was the nation's symbol, but surely the buzzard was the South's.

I was born and spent my early years in the Depression, which seemed to trouble southerners less than the rest of the nation because the South had been in a depression for sixty years by the time the "Great" one of the 1930s rolled in. I grew up in a post–Civil War South in which unemployment was higher than anywhere in the nation, disease and poor health were more widespread than anywhere in the nation, education was poorer and ignorance more common than anywhere in the nation, the economy was less diversified and helpful than anywhere in the nation, and railroads and roads were less developed than anywhere in the nation. I grew up in a South in which many men and women were working hard to "forget and forgive" their invaders from the North, while many others were determined to keep on hating.

A desolate and destitute region had every reason to lament the fortunes of war and depression. But desolation and destitution did not make for despair. The South may have lacked in everything else, but it did have people, good people who somehow learned to shoulder tragedy for a century or more, despite poverty and penury and prejudices and prostration. Dignity and pride saw them through decades of depression and despair. The best southern people, as William Faulkner saw, "not only endured, but prevailed." The South rose (not "rose again," however, for it had always been a region of hard times).

Southern people have experience with tragedy that the rest of the nation lacks. Stricken fellow citizens can endure, and they can prevail. The South wants New York, Pennsylvania, and D.C. to know that.

October 7, 2001

SARVISBERRY TREES

A haunting photo from September 11 is of an Episcopalian graveyard in New York, its ancient gravestones draped in loose papers from the fallen World Trade Center buildings.

Near the rubble of the tragedy stands little St. Paul's Chapel, a mission church of nearby Trinity Church. The priest in charge of St. Paul's is Lyndon Harris, a member of Wofford College's Class of 1983. A few months before September 11 he was doing things like hosting meetings on downtown homelessness or lecturing on the literary words of Susan Hovatch. After September 11, his little mission church fed some two thousand people a day for months on end.

That poignant black-and-white photo of the littered cemetery—supposedly where Alexander Hamilton is buried bearing Aaron Burr's bullet and near the financial district he loved so well—comes more frequently to our mind than does the immense awe of watching the giant buildings telescope into themselves.

The little cemetery especially rose to mind as a Kentucky friend described last week her cancellation of a trip simply because she wanted to watch the leaves of a backyard "sarvisberry" tree take on their fall colors.

"Sarvis" is a pronunciation common in Appalachia, western Carolina, and middle Tennessee for "service." The sarvisberry, or serviceberry, tree, a tree of many names, is also called the Juneberry tree (because its red and purple berries ripen in June), the josh pear tree (according to Thoreau, "josh" is a form of "juicy"), the Indian pear, the chuckley pear, the shadbush (because its berries fall into mountain creeks and attract shad), and saskatoon (a Cree word, *mis-ask-quah-toomina,* shortened by white settlers). Once ripened the berries ferment, and one place calls the tree the chequers tree, because a brewery by that name used the berries to make beer when sugar was unavailable. The French Canadians called the tree *petites poires,* or *amélanchier.*

Indians and mountain folks claim medicinal properties for the tree, good for nausea and headache, and the berries are rich in Vitamin C, manganese, calcium, and potassium. Birds and fish get tipsy from its berries. The berries are also edible straight from the vine or picked, and Thoreau found them "agreeable" but not as pleasing as huckleberries or blueberries. Some serviceberry trees grow as high as twenty feet, but others often are satisfied with being shrubs.

With five-leafed white blossoms blooming in early spring across the northern states and lower Canada and on mountainsides of lower states, the serviceberry tree is mistaken for white dogwood. In the fall, its leaves take on vibrant browns and golds. The serviceberry is a spectacular spectator's tree because of its white spring blossoms, its early summer red and purple berries attracting birds seen no other time of the year, and its autumn hues of glory.

What links this tree in our minds with the small strewn cemetery of New York is its most common name: serviceberry.

One legend has it that it got that name from blooming always at Easter, announcing Easter services. Another legend holds that its berries were used to make communion wine for church services in the hills. Another mountain legend has it that its blooms coincide with the coming of circuit-rider preachers at winter's end and the resuming of church services. Yet another legend has it that its blooming is a signal that it is time for graveyard cleanings.

Indians, especially Blackfoot and Cree tribes, considered the serviceberry tree sacred, and people lucky enough to have ornamental varieties in their yards or wild ones within sight would probably agree.

A tree of hope and healing, and hinting of higher powers and purposes, sarvisberry blossoms this coming spring will remind some of us of the loose desk papers that fell upon St. Paul's Chapel and Trinity Church last September, and remind us that healing and hope lie just ahead in the cycles of God's creation and grace.

November 4, 2001

"SOUTHERN SEEN"
SUBSCRIBING NEWSPAPERS

ALABAMA

Auburn	*Auburn Bulletin/Eagle*
Auburn	*Davis Publications*
Bay Minette	*The Baldwin Times/Weekend*
Butler	*The Choctaw Advocate*
Enterprise	*Enterprise Ledger*
Lanett	*The Valley Times–News*
Red Bay	*The Red Bay News*
Troy	*The Troy Messenger*

GEORGIA

Carrollton	*Daily Times–Georgian*
Cartersville	*The Daily Tribune News*
Clayton	*The Clayton Tribune*
Columbus	*The Columbus Enquirer*
Columbus	*The Ledger*
Conyers	*Rockdale Dispatch*
Cordele	*Dispatch*
Elberton	*Star Beacon*
Fitzgerald	*The Herald-Leader*
Gainesville	*The Times*
Reidsville	*The Tattnall Journal*
Vidalia	*The Advance*

KENTUCKY

Bardstown	*The Kentucky Standard*
Berea	*The Berea Citizen*
Danville	*The Danville Examiner*
Fulton	*The Fulton Daily Leader*
Greensburg	*Record-Herald*
Hazard	*Hazard Herald-Voice*
Hyden	*Leslie County News*
Jackson	*The Jackson Times*
rvine	*Citizen Voice & Times*
Lexington	*Lexington Herald-Leader*
London	*The Sentinel-Echo*
Middlesboro	*The Daily News*
Murray	*The Murray Ledger and Times*
Richmond	*The Richmond Register*
Shepherdsville	*Pioneer News*
Versailles	*The Woodford Sun*

MISSISSIPPI

Brookhaven	*Brookhaven Daily Leader*
Cleveland	*The Boliver Commercial*
Columbia	*Columbian Progress*
Greenwood	*Greenwood Commonwealth*
Gulfport	*The Star Journal*
Holly Springs	*The South Reporter*
Natchez	*Natchez Democrat*

NORTH CAROLINA

Ahoskie	*The News-Herald*
Burnsville	*The Yancey Journal*
Clinton	*The Sampson Independent*
Eden	*Eden Daily Times*
Franklin	*The Franklin Press*
Goldsboro	*The Goldsboro News Argus*
Kannapolis	*The Daily Independent*
Laurinburg	*The Laurinburg Exchange*
Lincolnton	*Lincoln Times-News*
Manteo	*The Coastland Times*
Mooresville	*Mooresville Tribune*

Mt. Airy	*The Mount Airy News*
Morganton	*The News Herald*
North Wilkesboro	*The Journal-Patriot*
Pineville	*The Pineville Pioneer*
Research Triangle Pk	*The Leader Newsmagazine*
Rocky Mount	*Evening Telegram*
Shelby	*Shelby Daily Star*
Southern Pines	*Southern Pines Pilot*
Taylorsville	*The Taylorsville Times*
Thomasville	*The Morning Times*
Troy	*Montgomery Herald*
Wallace	*The Wallace Enterprise*
Washington	*Washington Daily News*
Washington	*West Craven Highlights*

SOUTH CAROLINA

Bennettsville	*Marlboro Herald-Advocate*
Camden	*Chronicle-Independent*
Charleston	*The Evening Post*
Chester	*News and Reporter*
Clemson	*Clemson Messenger*
Darlington	*The News and Press*
Easley	*The Easley Press*
Gaffney	*The Gaffney Ledger*
Georgetown	*Georgetown Times News*
Greenwood	*The Index-Journal*
Greer	*The Greer Citizen*
Kingstree	*The News*
Lancaster	*The Lancaster News*
Lancaster	*Tri-County Publishing Co.*
Laurens	*Laurens County Advertiser*
Marion	*Marion Star & Mullins Enterprise*
Moncks Corner	*The Berkeley Democrat*
Newberry	*The Newberry Observer*
Orangeburg	*The Times and Democrat*
Seneca	*The Journal-Tribune*
Southern Pines	*The Pilot*
Spartanburg	*Herald-Journal*
Williamston	*The Journal, Inc.*
Woodruff	*The Woodruff News*

TENNESSEE

Blountville	*Sullivan County News*
Bolivar	*Bolivar Bulletin-Times*
Brownsville	*States-Graphic*
Camden	*The Camden Chronicle*
Carthage	*The Carthage Courier*
Cleveland	*The Cleveland Daily Banner*
Columbia	*The Daily Herald*
Covington	*The Covington Leader*
Crossville	*Crossville Chronicle*
Dyersburg	*State Gazette*
Franklin	*The Review-Appeal*
Huntingdon	*Carroll County News*
Jackson	*The Jackson Sun*
Kingston	*Roane County News*
Knoxville	*The Farragut Press Enterprise*
Luttrell	*News Leader*
Maryville	*Maryville-Alcoa Daily Times*
Maynardville	*The Union News Leader*
Murfreesboro	*Daily News Journal*
Paris	*Post-Intelligencer*
Parsons	*The News Leader*
Pulaski	*Citizen-Press*
Pulaski	*Giles Free Press*
Savannah	*The Courier*
Smyrna	*Rutherford Courier*
Union City	*Daily Messenger*
Waverly	*News-Democrat*

VIRGINIA

Ashland	*Hanover Herald-Progress*
Big Stone Gap	*The Post*
Blackstone	*Courier-Record*
Bristol	*Sullivan County News*
Clarksville	*The News-Progress*
Danville	*Danville Register*
Fincastle	*The Fincastle Herald &*
	Botetourt News
Franklin	*The Tidewater News*

Hopewell	*The Hopewell News*
Manassas	*Journal Messenger*
Marion	*Smyth County News*
Pearisburg	*Virginian Leader*
Petersburg	*The Progress-Index*
Richlands	*Richlands News-Press*
Richlands	*Tazewell County Free Press*
Staunton	*The Daily News Leader*
Tappahannock	*Rappahannock Times*
Tazewell	*Clinch Valley News*
Warrenton	*The Fauquier Democrat*
Williamsburg	*The Virginia Gazette*

Southern Seen was designed and typeset on a Macintosh computer system using QuarkXPress software. The body text is set in 11/14 Adobe Garamond and display type is set in Trajan. This book was manufactured by Thomson-Shore, Inc.